SUGAR² RUNE

Sugar Sugar Rune

1

MOYOCO ANNO

TRANSLATED BY YAYOI IHNE

ADAPTED BY NUNZIO DEFILIPPIS & CHRISTINA WEIR

LETTERED BY FOLTZ DESIGN

DEL REY

BALLANTINE BOOKS · NEW YORK

Sugar Sugar Rune 1 is a work of fiction. Names, characters, places, and incidents are the products of the author's imagination or are used fictitiously. Any resemblance to actual events, locales, or persons, living or dead, is entirely coincidental.

2005 Del Rey Trade Paperback Edition

Published in the United States by Del Rey Books, an imprint of The Random House Publishing Group, a division of Random House, Inc., New York.

DEL REY is a registered trademark and the Del Rey colophon is a trademark of Random House, Inc.

First published in Japan in 2004 by Kodansha Ltd., Tokyo.

Library of Congress Control Number: 2005930869

ISBN 0-345-48629-3

Printed in the United States of America

www.delreymanga.com

3 4 5 6 7 8 9

Text design by Foltz Design

Original cover design by Akiko Omo

CONTENTS

HONORIFICS EXPLAINED

Throughout the Del Rey Manga books, you will find Japanese honorifics left intact in the translations. For those not familiar with how the Japanese use honorifics, and, more important, how they differ from American honorifics, we present this brief overview.

Politeness has always been a critical facet of Japanese culture. Ever since the feudal era, when Japan was a highly stratified society, use of honorifics–which can be defined as polite speech that indicates relationship or status–has played an essential role in the Japanese language. When addressing someone in Japanese, an honorific usually takes the form of a suffix attached to one's name (e.g., "Asuna-san"), as a title at the end of one's name, or in place of the name itself (e.g., "Negi-sensei" or simply "Sensei!").

Honorifics can be expressions of respect or endearment. In the context of manga and anime, honorifics give insight into the nature of the relationship between characters. Many translations into English leave out these important honorifics, and therefore distort the feel of the original Japanese. Because Japanese honorifics contain nuances that English honorifics lack, it is our policy at Del Rey not to translate them. Here, instead, is a guide to some of the honorifics you may encounter in Del Rey Manga.

-SAN: This is the most common honorific and is equivalent to Mr., Miss, Ms., Mrs., etc. It is the all-purpose honorific and can be used in any situation where politeness is required.

-SAMA: This is one level higher than -san. It is used to confer great respect.

-DONO: This comes from the word tono, which means lord. It is an even higher level than -sama and confers utmost respect.

-KUN: This suffix is used at the end of boys' names to express familiarity or endearment. It is also somtimes used by men among friends, or when addressing someone younger or of lower station.

-CHAN: This is used to express endearment, mostly toward girls. It is also used for little boys, pets, and between lovers. It gives a sense of childish cuteness.

BOZU: This is an informal way to refer to a boy, similar to the English terms "kid" or "squirt."

**SEMPAI/
SENPAI:** This title suggests that the addressee is one's senior in a group or organization. It is most often used in a school setting, where underclassmen refer to their upperclassmen as sempai. It can also be used in the workplace, such as when a newer employee addresses an employee who has seniority in the company.

KOHAI: This is the opposite of -sempai, and is used toward underclassmen in school or newcomers in the workplace. It connotes that the addressee is of a lower station.

SENSEI: Literally meaning "one who has come before," this title is used for teachers, doctors, or masters of any profession or art.

-[BLANK]: This is usually forgotten on these lists, but it's perhaps the most significant difference between Japanese and English. The lack of honorific means that the speaker has permission to address the person in a very intimate way. Usually, only family, spouses, or very close friends have this kind of license. Known as yobisute, it can be gratifying when someone who has earned the intimacy starts to call one by one's name without an honorific. But when that intimacy hasn't been earned, it can also be insulting.

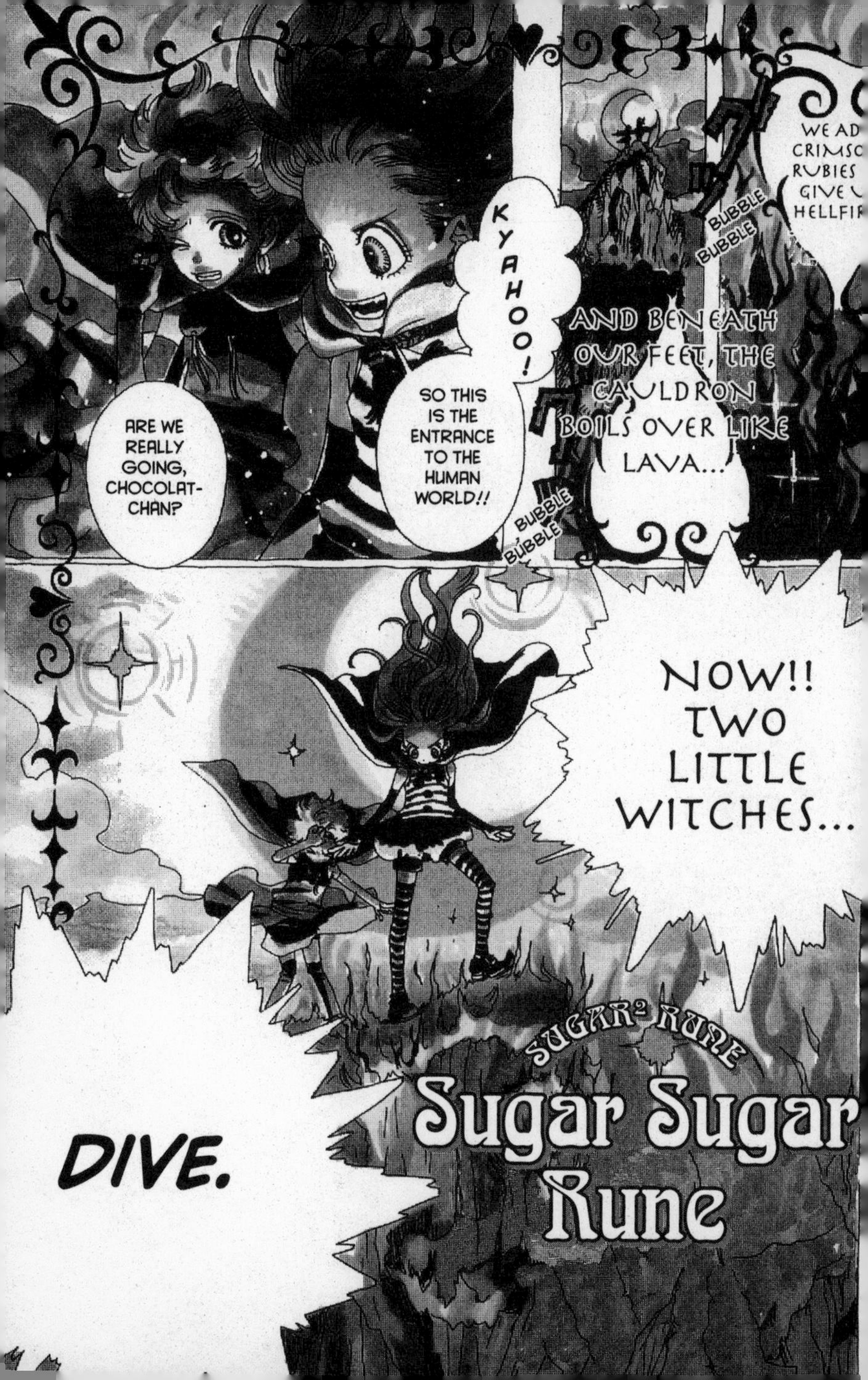
BUBBLE BUBBLE
AND BENEATH OUR FEET, THE CAULDRON BOILS OVER LIKE LAVA...
BUBBLE BUBBLE
KYAHOO!
SO THIS IS THE ENTRANCE TO THE HUMAN WORLD!!
ARE WE REALLY GOING, CHOCOLAT-CHAN?
NOW!! TWO LITTLE WITCHES...
SUGAR² RUNE
Sugar Sugar Rune
DIVE.

RUNE 1

Chocolat, Hearts, and the Shooting Star

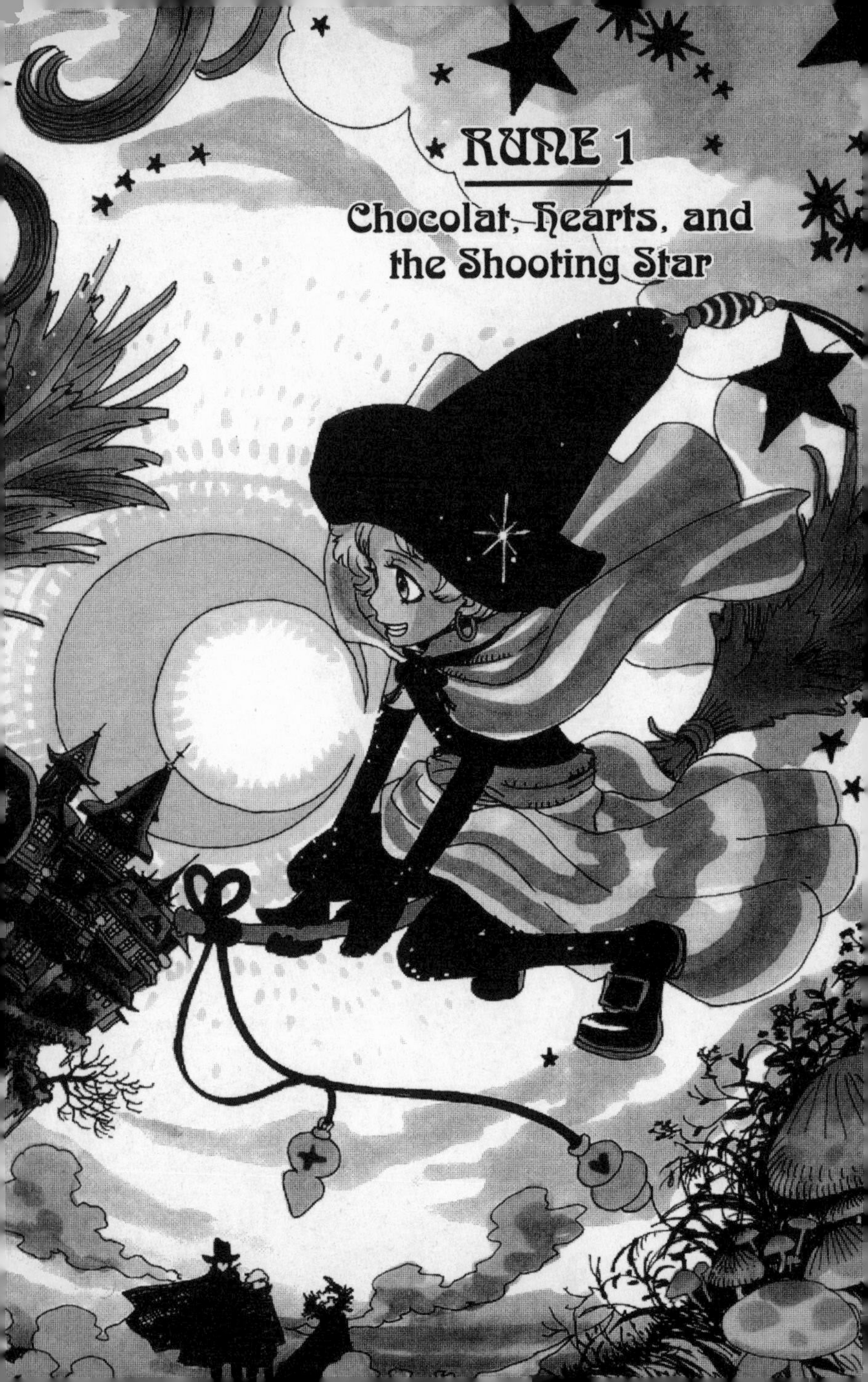

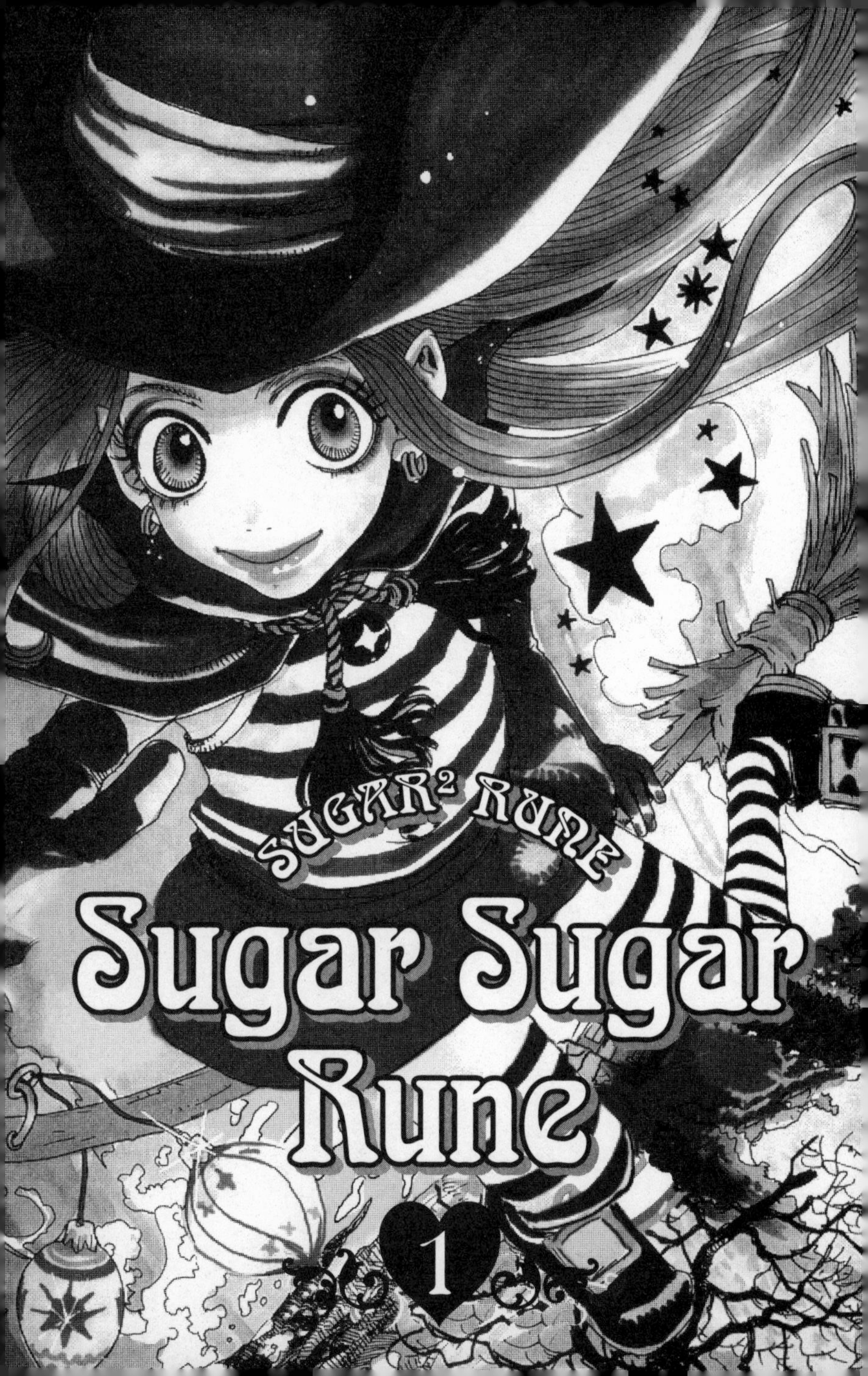
SUGAR² RUNE
Sugar Sugar Rune
1

CONTENTS

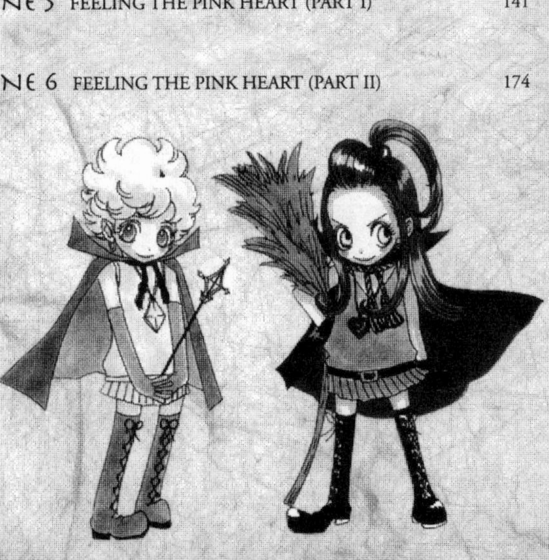

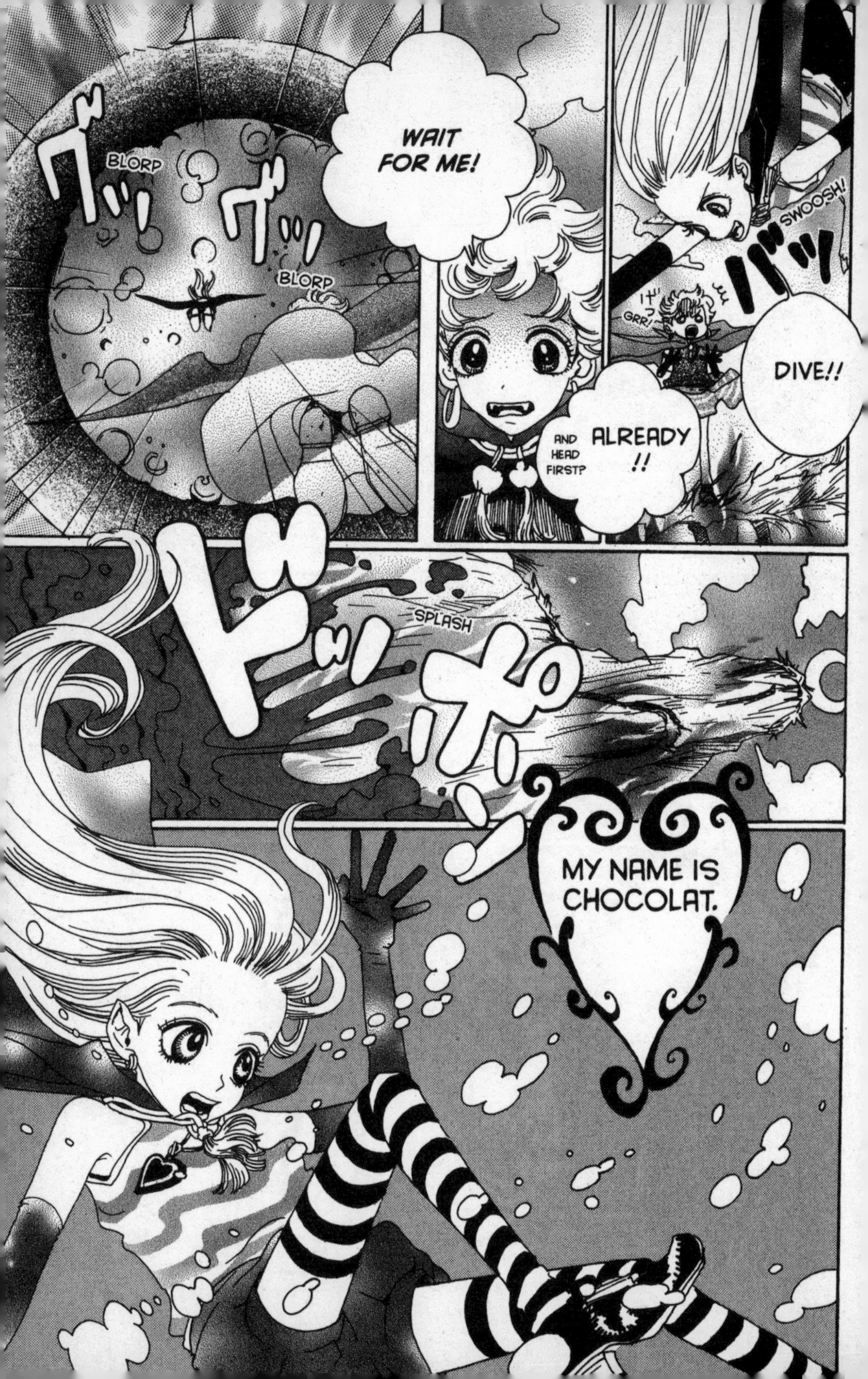
SWOOSH!
GRR!
DIVE!!
ALREADY!!
AND HEAD FIRST?
WAIT FOR ME!
BLORP
BLORP
SPLASH
MY NAME IS CHOCOLAT.

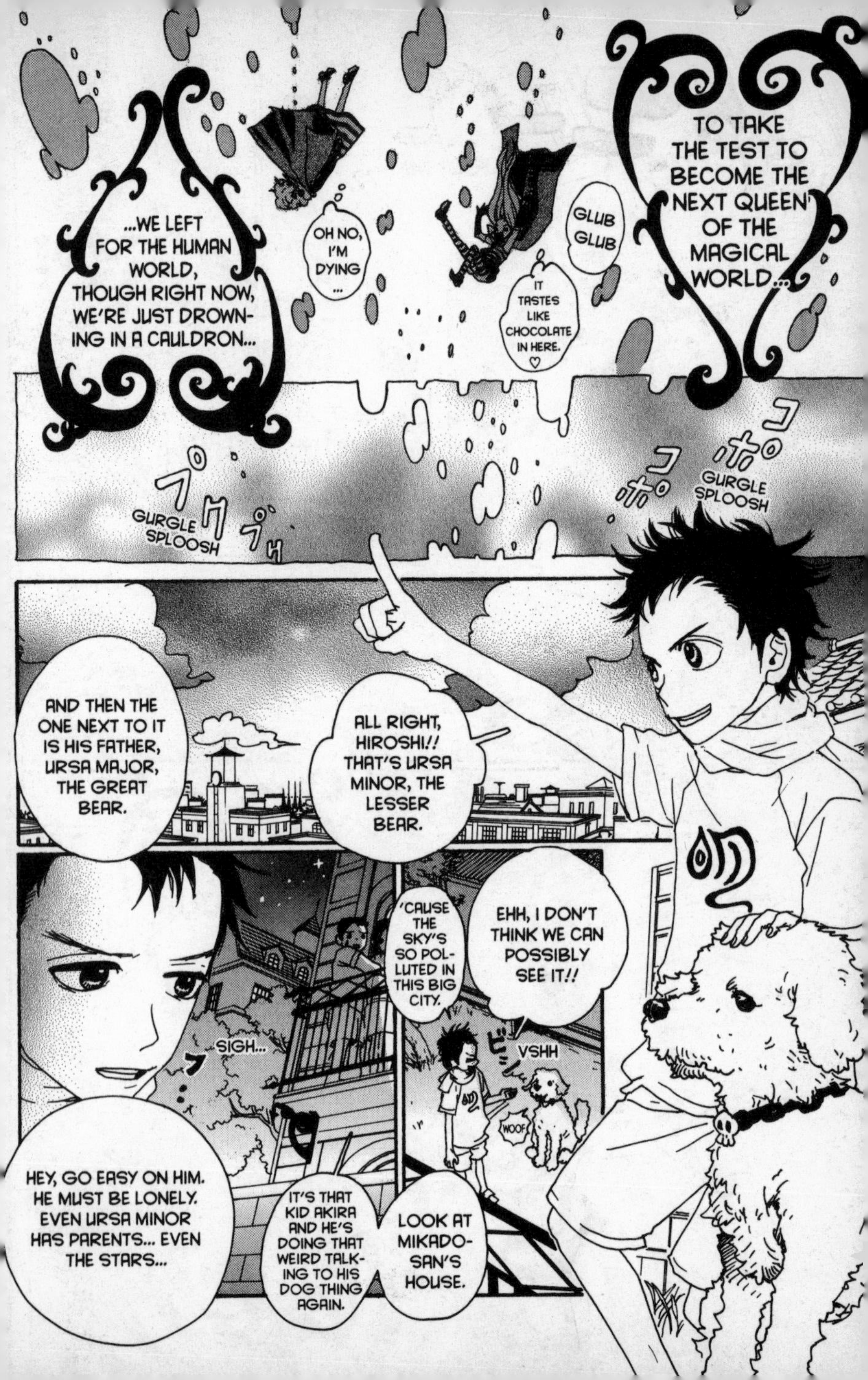
TO TAKE THE TEST TO BECOME THE NEXT QUEEN OF THE MAGICAL WORLD...
GLUB GLUB
IT TASTES LIKE CHOCOLATE IN HERE. ♡
OH NO, I'M DYING ...
...WE LEFT FOR THE HUMAN WORLD, THOUGH RIGHT NOW, WE'RE JUST DROWNING IN A CAULDRON...
GURGLE SPLOOSH
GURGLE SPLOOSH
ALL RIGHT, HIROSHI!! THAT'S URSA MINOR, THE LESSER BEAR.
AND THEN THE ONE NEXT TO IT IS HIS FATHER, URSA MAJOR, THE GREAT BEAR.
EHH, I DON'T THINK WE CAN POSSIBLY SEE IT!!
'CAUSE THE SKY'S SO POLLUTED IN THIS BIG CITY.
VSHH
WOOF
SIGH...
LOOK AT MIKADO-SAN'S HOUSE.
IT'S THAT KID AKIRA AND HE'S DOING THAT WEIRD TALKING TO HIS DOG THING AGAIN.
HEY, GO EASY ON HIM. HE MUST BE LONELY. EVEN URSA MINOR HAS PARENTS... EVEN THE STARS...

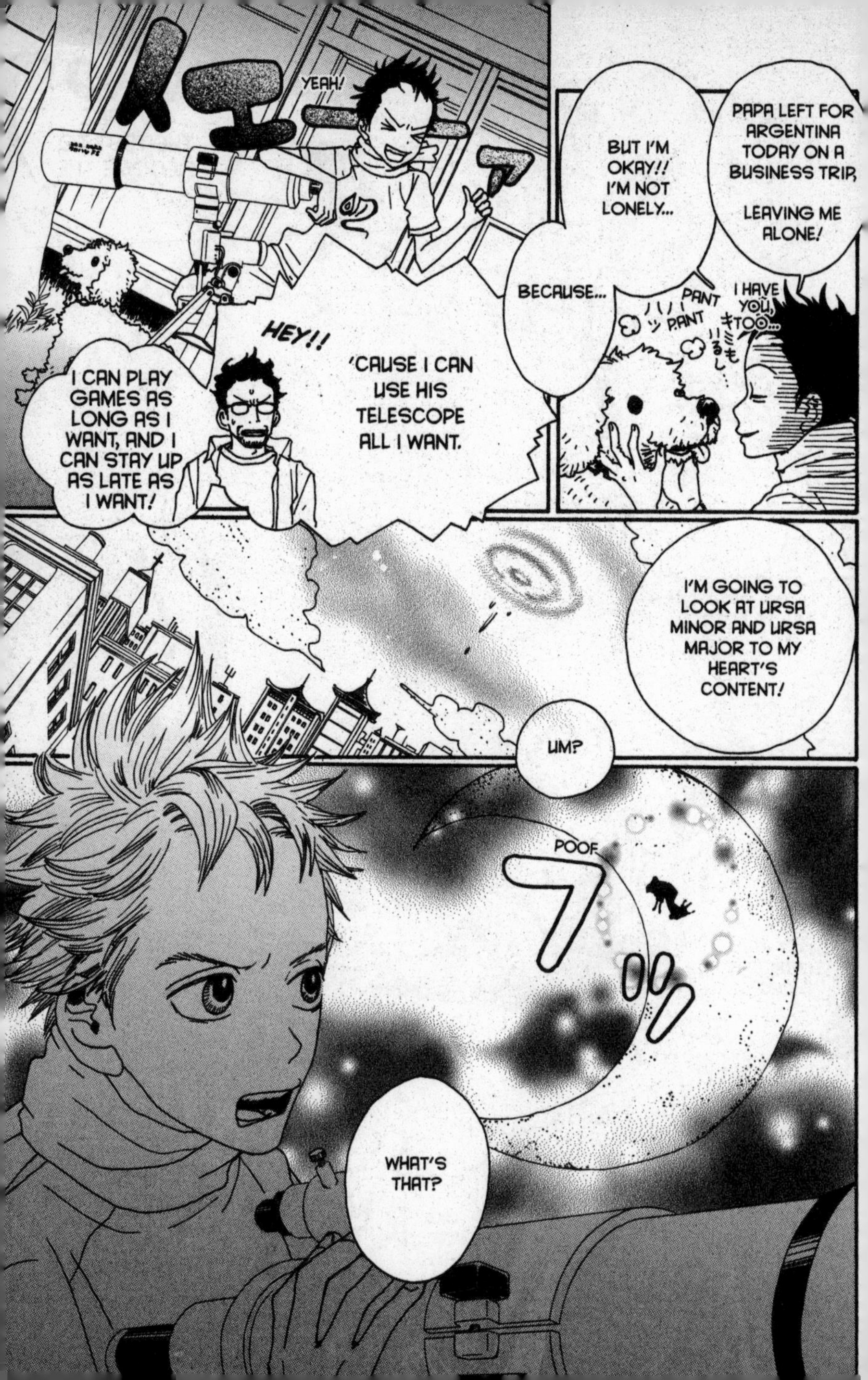
PAPA LEFT FOR ARGENTINA TODAY ON A BUSINESS TRIP,
LEAVING ME ALONE!
BUT I'M OKAY!! I'M NOT LONELY...
BECAUSE...
PANT PANT
I HAVE YOU, TOO...
'CAUSE I CAN USE HIS TELESCOPE ALL I WANT.
YEAH!
HEY!!
I CAN PLAY GAMES AS LONG AS I WANT, AND I CAN STAY UP AS LATE AS I WANT!
I'M GOING TO LOOK AT URSA MINOR AND URSA MAJOR TO MY HEART'S CONTENT!
UM?
POOF
WHAT'S THAT?

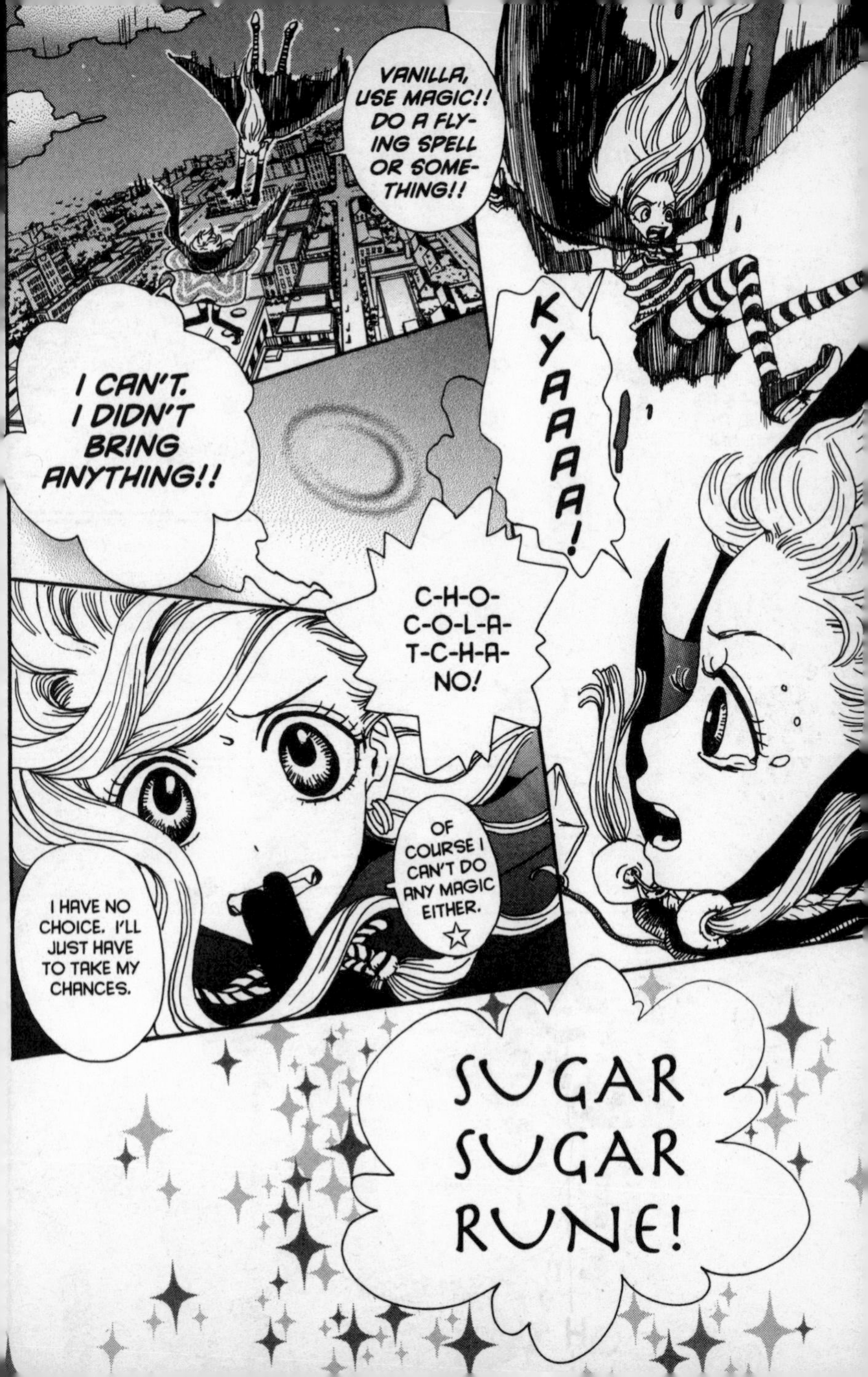

VANILLA, USE MAGIC!! DO A FLY-ING SPELL OR SOME-THING!!
I CAN'T. I DIDN'T BRING ANYTHING!!
KYAAAAA!
C-H-O-C-O-L-A-T-C-H-A-NO!
OF COURSE I CAN'T DO ANY MAGIC EITHER. ☆
I HAVE NO CHOICE. I'LL JUST HAVE TO TAKE MY CHANCES.
SUGAR SUGAR RUNE!

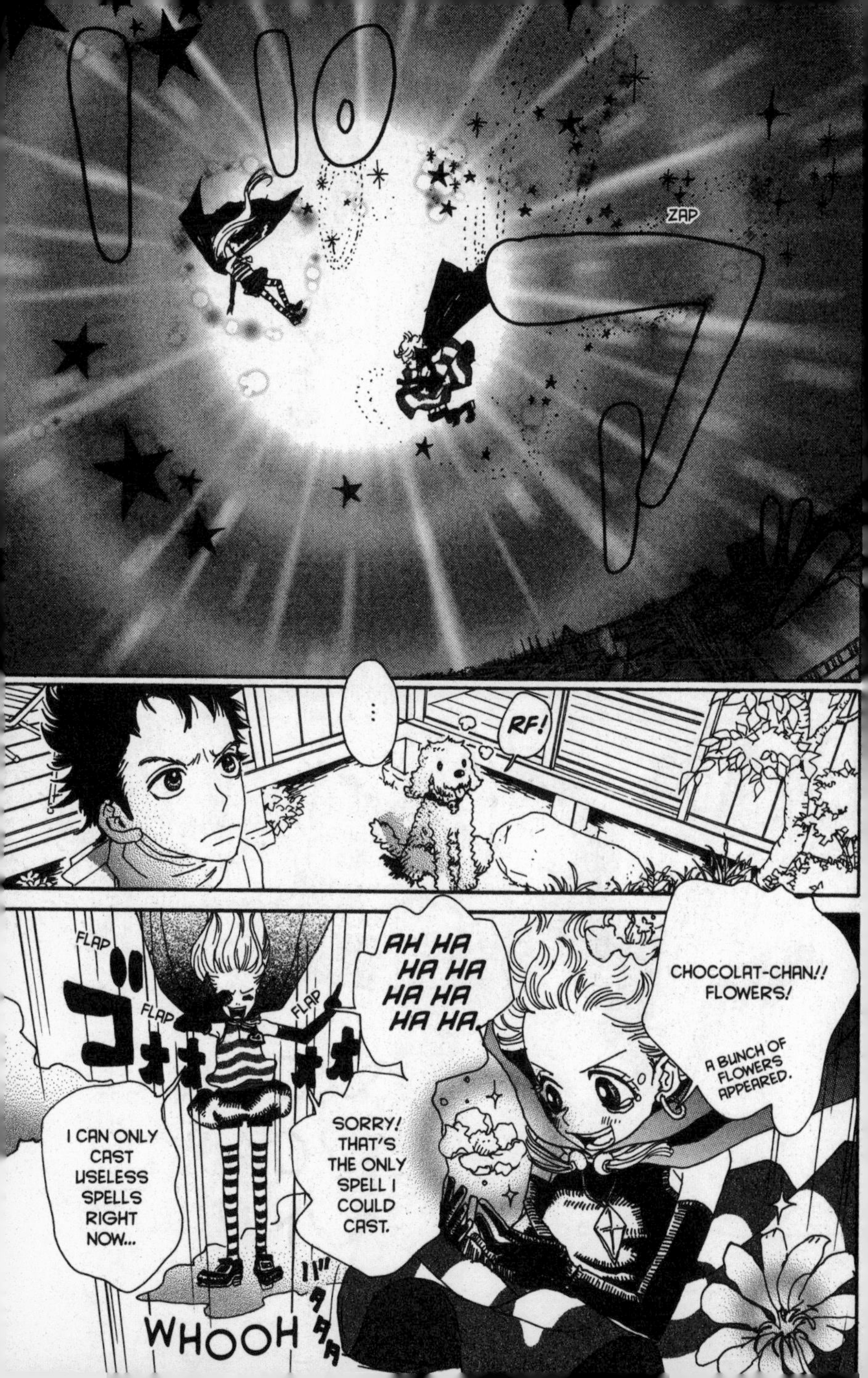
ZAP
RF!
...
CHOCOLAT-CHAN!! FLOWERS!
A BUNCH OF FLOWERS APPEARED.
AH HA HA HA HA HA HA HA.
SORRY! THAT'S THE ONLY SPELL I COULD CAST.
FLAP
FLAP
FLAP
I CAN ONLY CAST USELESS SPELLS RIGHT NOW...
WHOOH

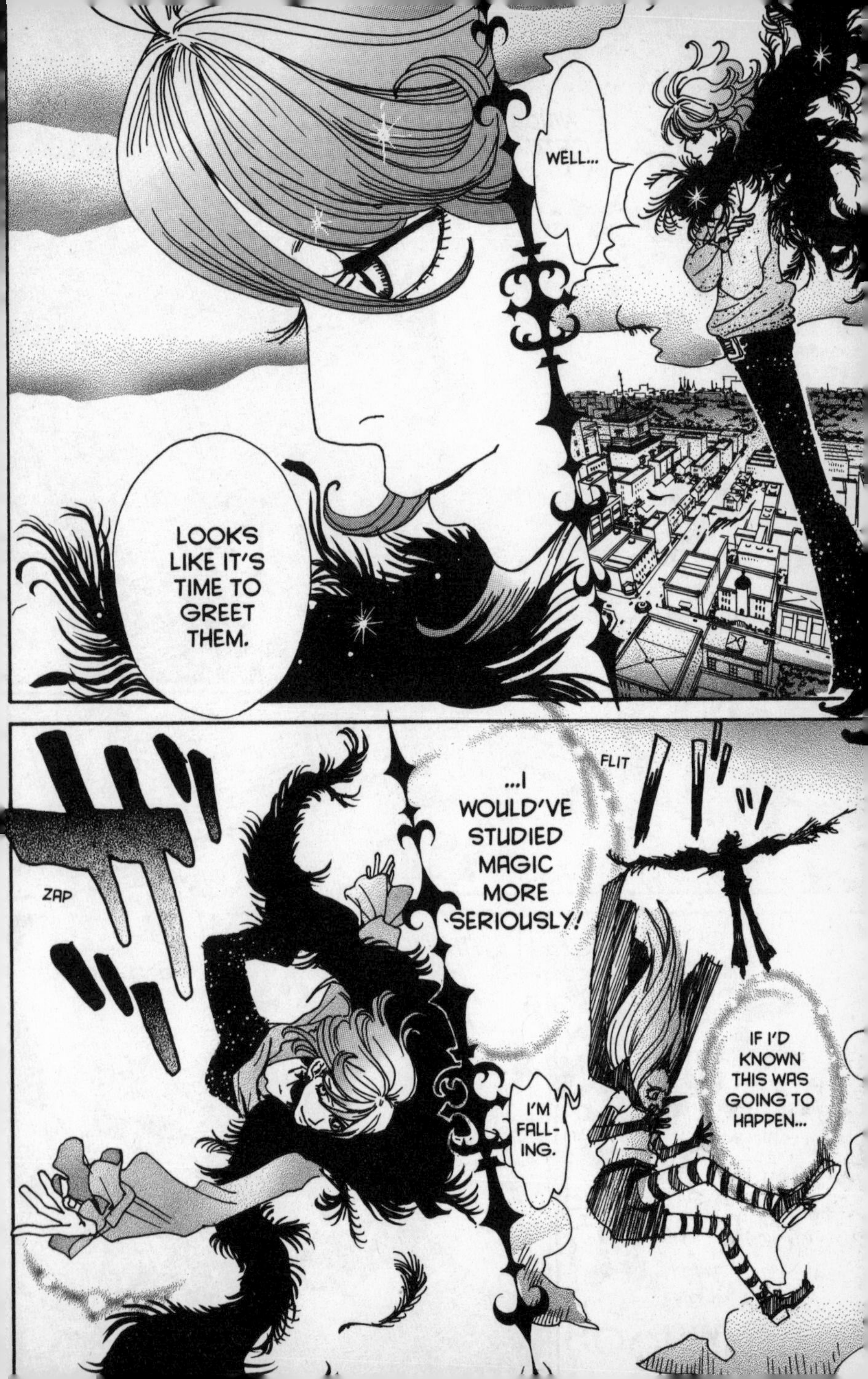
WELL...
LOOKS LIKE IT'S TIME TO GREET THEM.
FLIT
IF I'D KNOWN THIS WAS GOING TO HAPPEN...
...I WOULD'VE STUDIED MAGIC MORE SERIOUSLY!
I'M FALL-ING.
ZAP

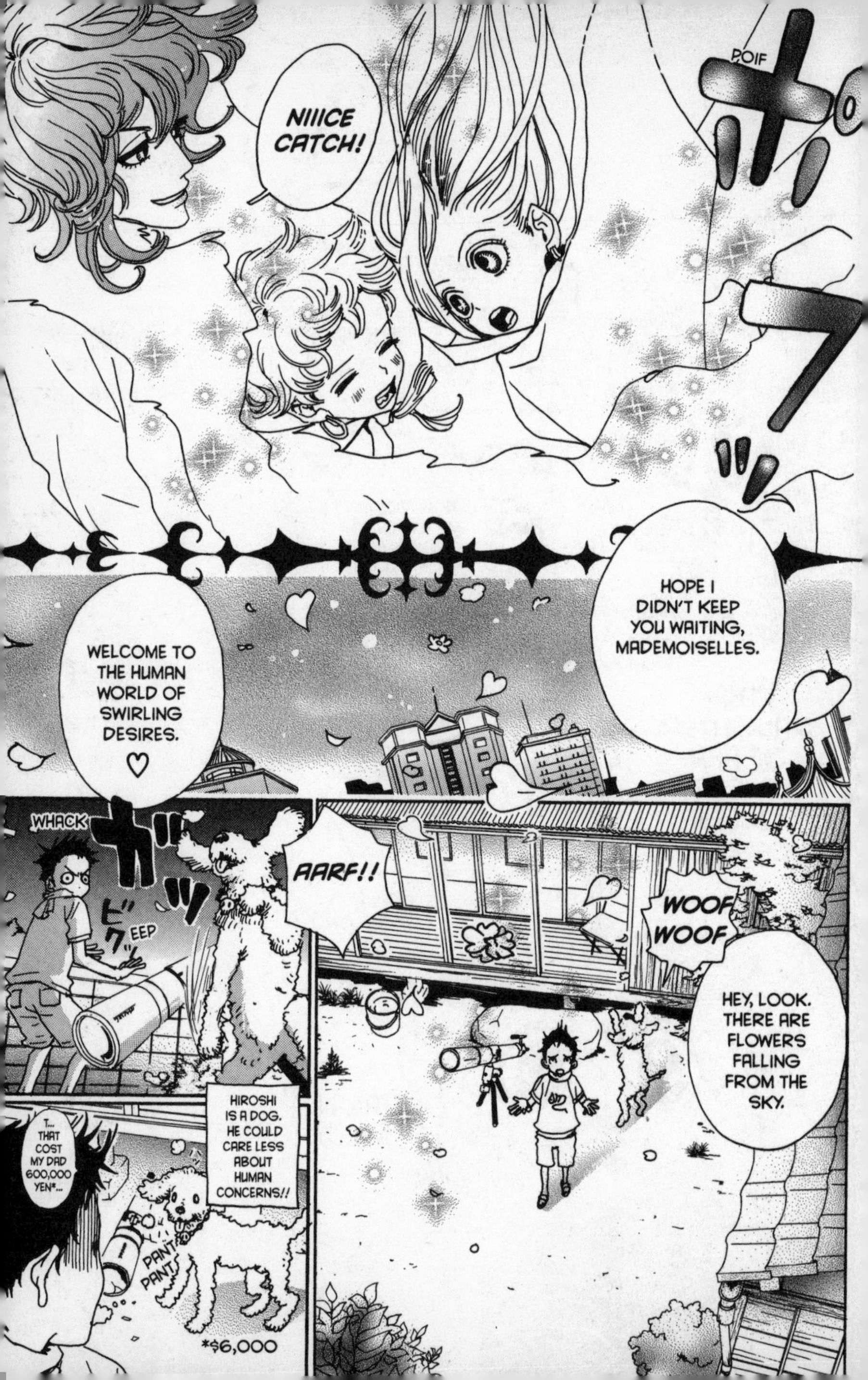
POIF
NIIICE CATCH!
HOPE I DIDN'T KEEP YOU WAITING, MADEMOISELLES.
WELCOME TO THE HUMAN WORLD OF SWIRLING DESIRES. ♡
WOOF WOOF
HEY, LOOK. THERE ARE FLOWERS FALLING FROM THE SKY.
AARF!!
WHACK
EEP
HIROSHI IS A DOG. HE COULD CARE LESS ABOUT HUMAN CONCERNS!!
T... THAT COST MY DAD 600,000 YEN*...
PANT PANT
*$6,000

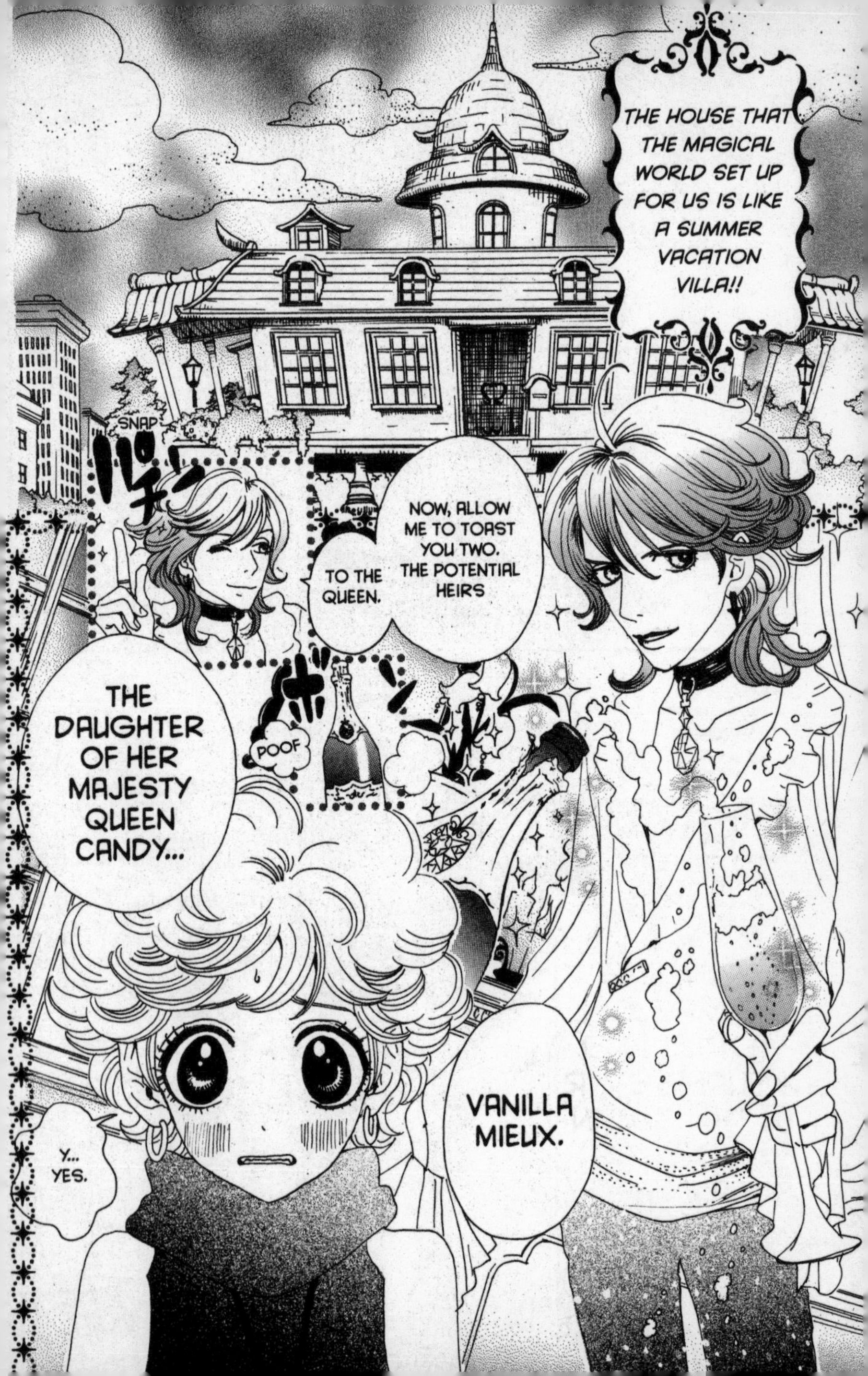
THE HOUSE THAT THE MAGICAL WORLD SET UP FOR US IS LIKE A SUMMER VACATION VILLA!!
NOW, ALLOW ME TO TOAST YOU TWO. THE POTENTIAL HEIRS
TO THE QUEEN.
SNAP
POOF
THE DAUGHTER OF HER MAJESTY QUEEN CANDY...
VANILLA MIEUX.
Y... YES.

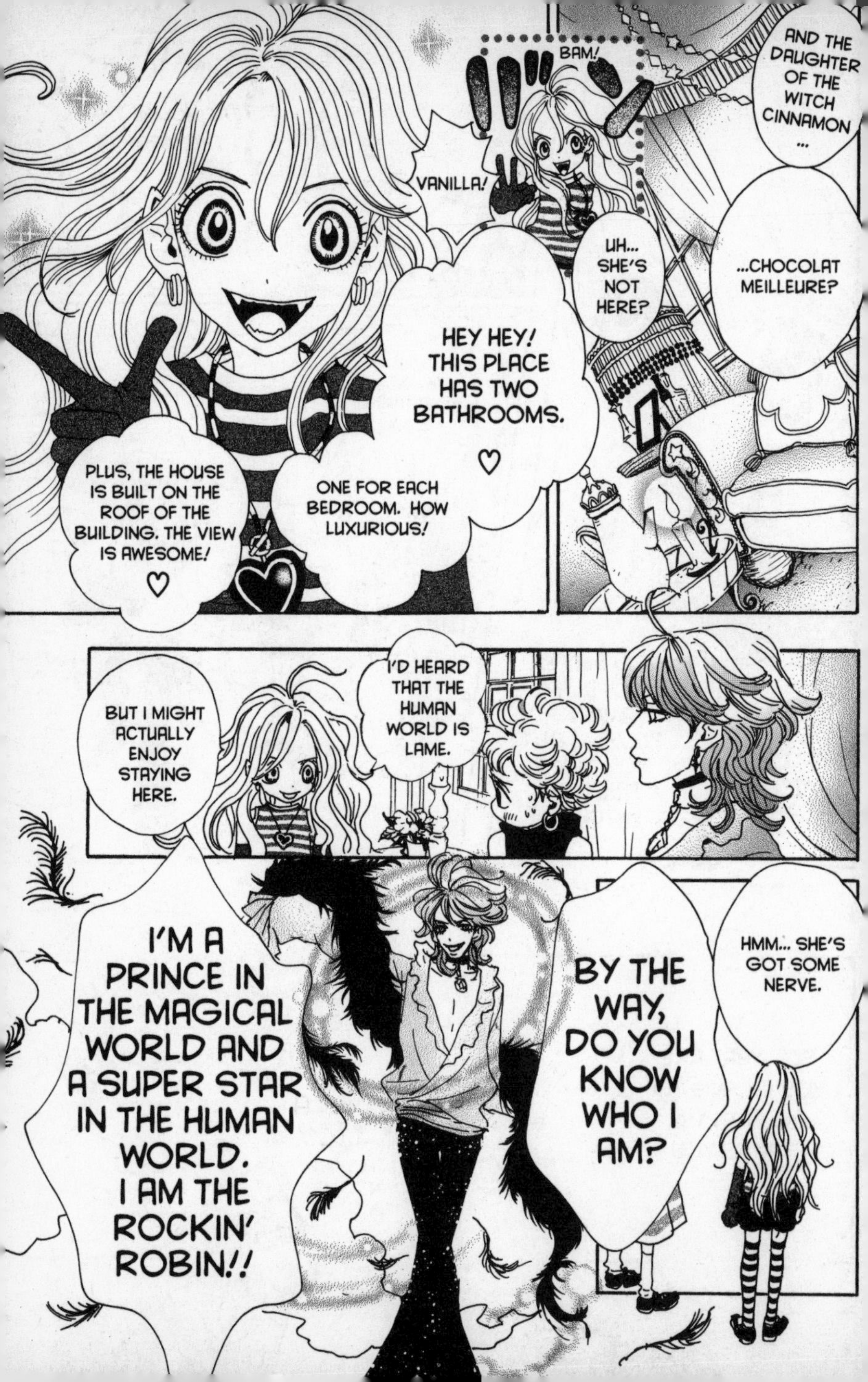
AND THE DAUGHTER OF THE WITCH CINNAMON ...
...CHOCOLAT MEILLEURE?
BAM!
VANILLA!
UH... SHE'S NOT HERE?
HEY HEY! THIS PLACE HAS TWO BATHROOMS. ♡
ONE FOR EACH BEDROOM. HOW LUXURIOUS!
PLUS, THE HOUSE IS BUILT ON THE ROOF OF THE BUILDING. THE VIEW IS AWESOME! ♡
I'D HEARD THAT THE HUMAN WORLD IS LAME.
BUT I MIGHT ACTUALLY ENJOY STAYING HERE.
HMM... SHE'S GOT SOME NERVE.
BY THE WAY, DO YOU KNOW WHO I AM?
I'M A PRINCE IN THE MAGICAL WORLD AND A SUPER STAR IN THE HUMAN WORLD. I AM THE ROCKIN' ROBIN!!

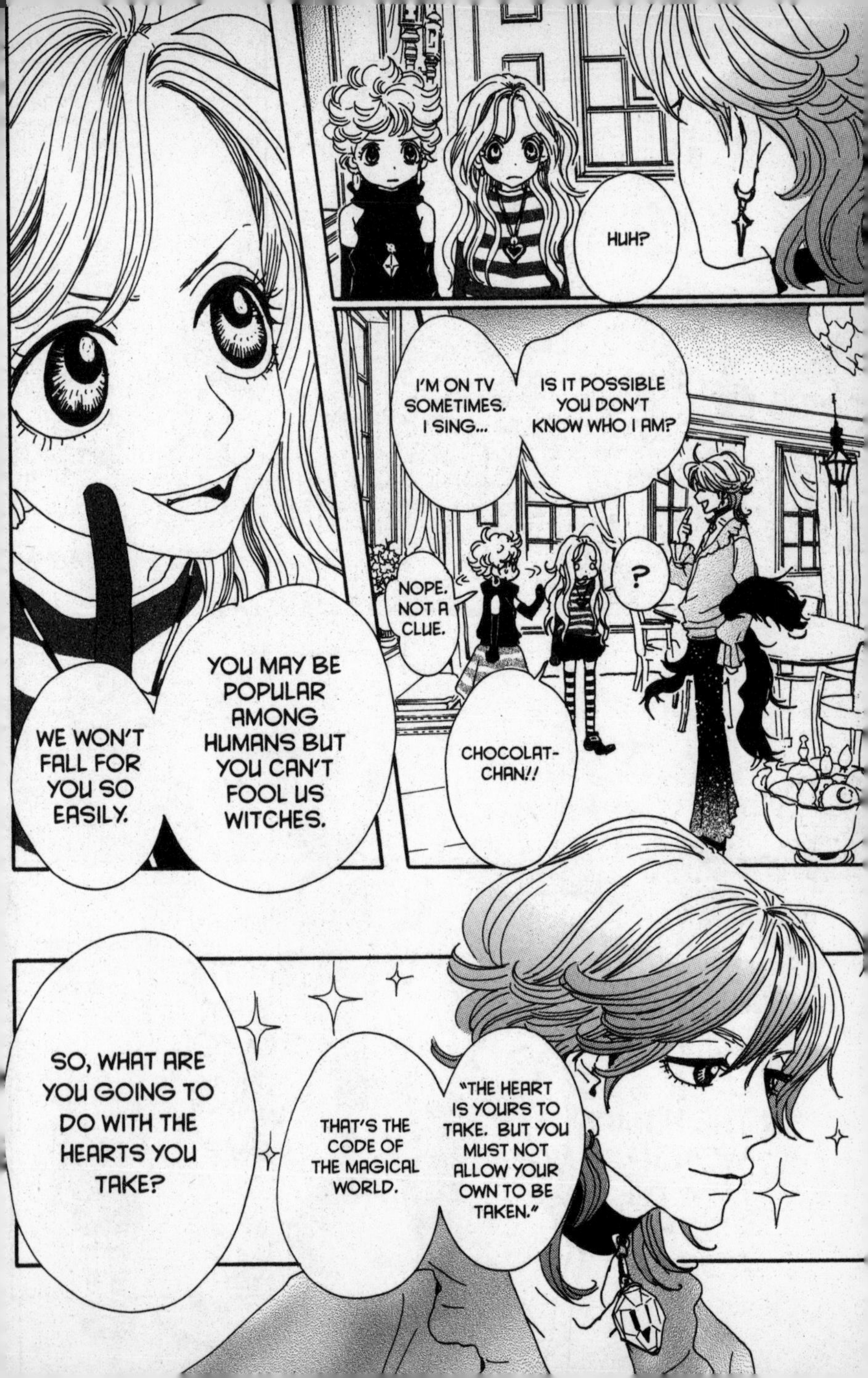
HUH?
IS IT POSSIBLE YOU DON'T KNOW WHO I AM?
I'M ON TV SOMETIMES. I SING...
?
NOPE. NOT A CLUE.
CHOCOLAT-CHAN!!
YOU MAY BE POPULAR AMONG HUMANS BUT YOU CAN'T FOOL US WITCHES.
WE WON'T FALL FOR YOU SO EASILY.
"THE HEART IS YOURS TO TAKE. BUT YOU MUST NOT ALLOW YOUR OWN TO BE TAKEN."
THAT'S THE CODE OF THE MAGICAL WORLD.
SO, WHAT ARE YOU GOING TO DO WITH THE HEARTS YOU TAKE?

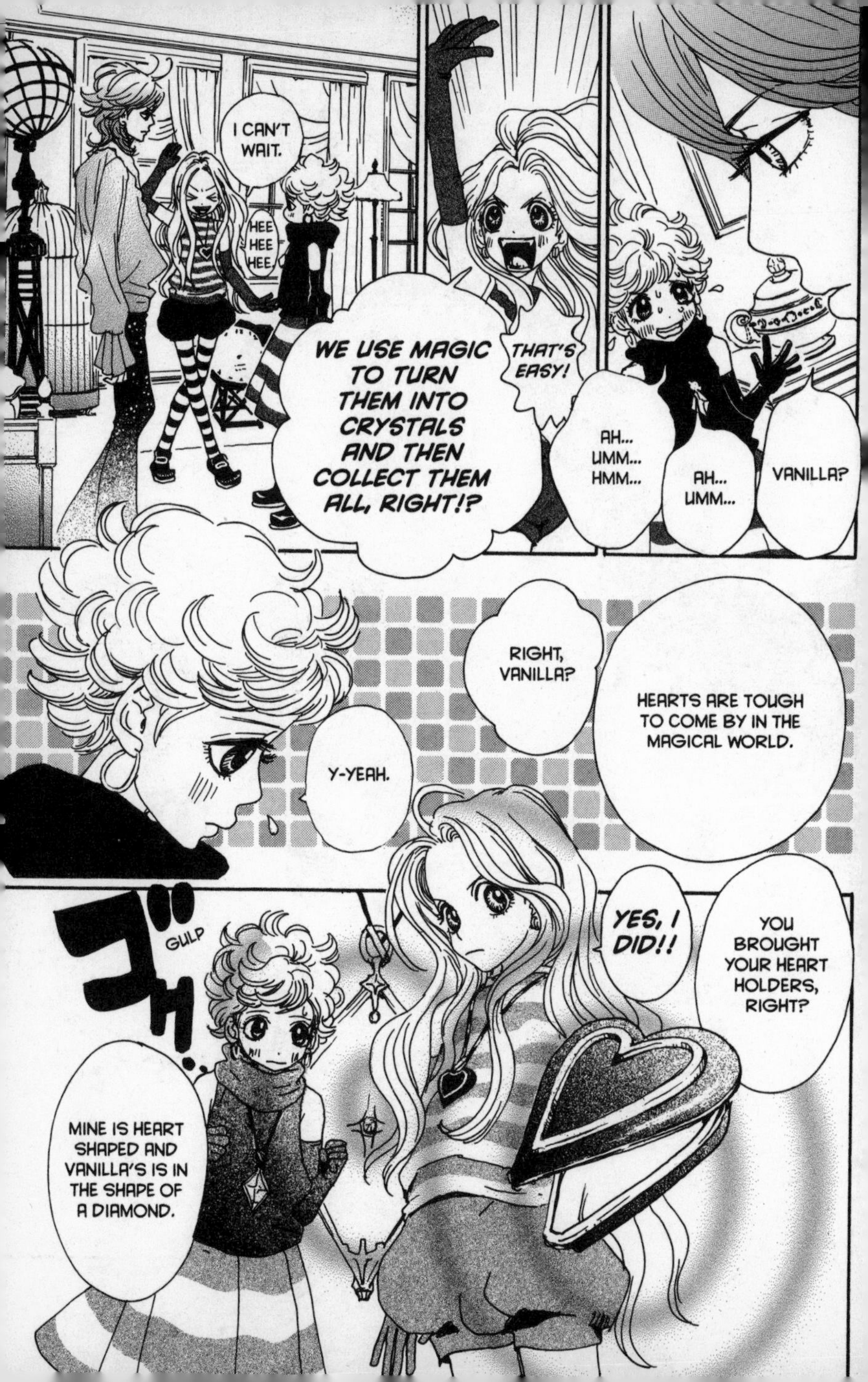
VANILLA?
AH... UMM...
AH... UMM... HMM...
THAT'S EASY!
WE USE MAGIC TO TURN THEM INTO CRYSTALS AND THEN COLLECT THEM ALL, RIGHT!?
I CAN'T WAIT.
HEE HEE HEE.
HEARTS ARE TOUGH TO COME BY IN THE MAGICAL WORLD.
RIGHT, VANILLA?
Y-YEAH.
YOU BROUGHT YOUR HEART HOLDERS, RIGHT?
YES, I DID!!
GULP
MINE IS HEART SHAPED AND VANILLA'S IS IN THE SHAPE OF A DIAMOND.

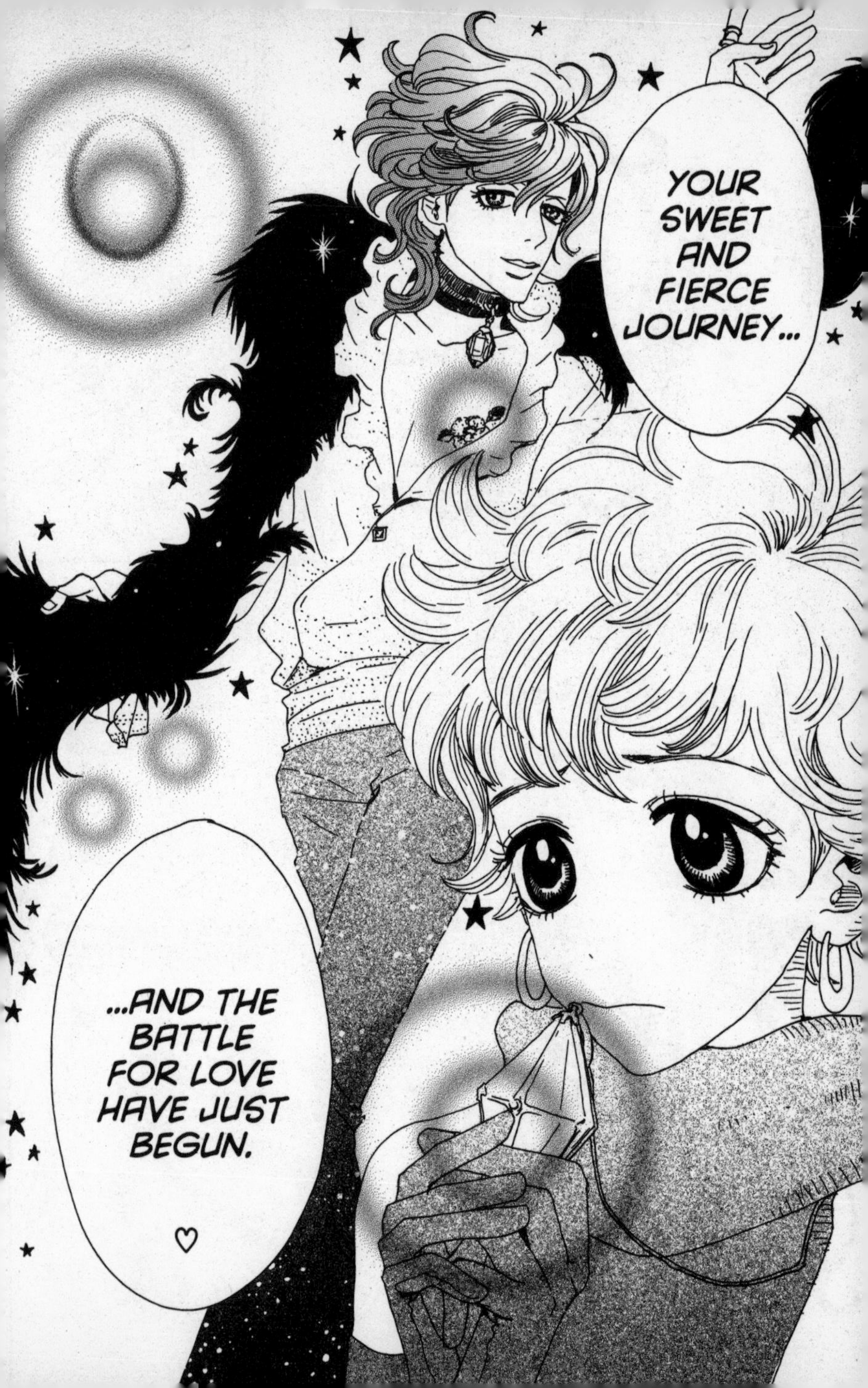
YOUR SWEET AND FIERCE JOURNEY...
...AND THE BATTLE FOR LOVE HAVE JUST BEGUN. ♡

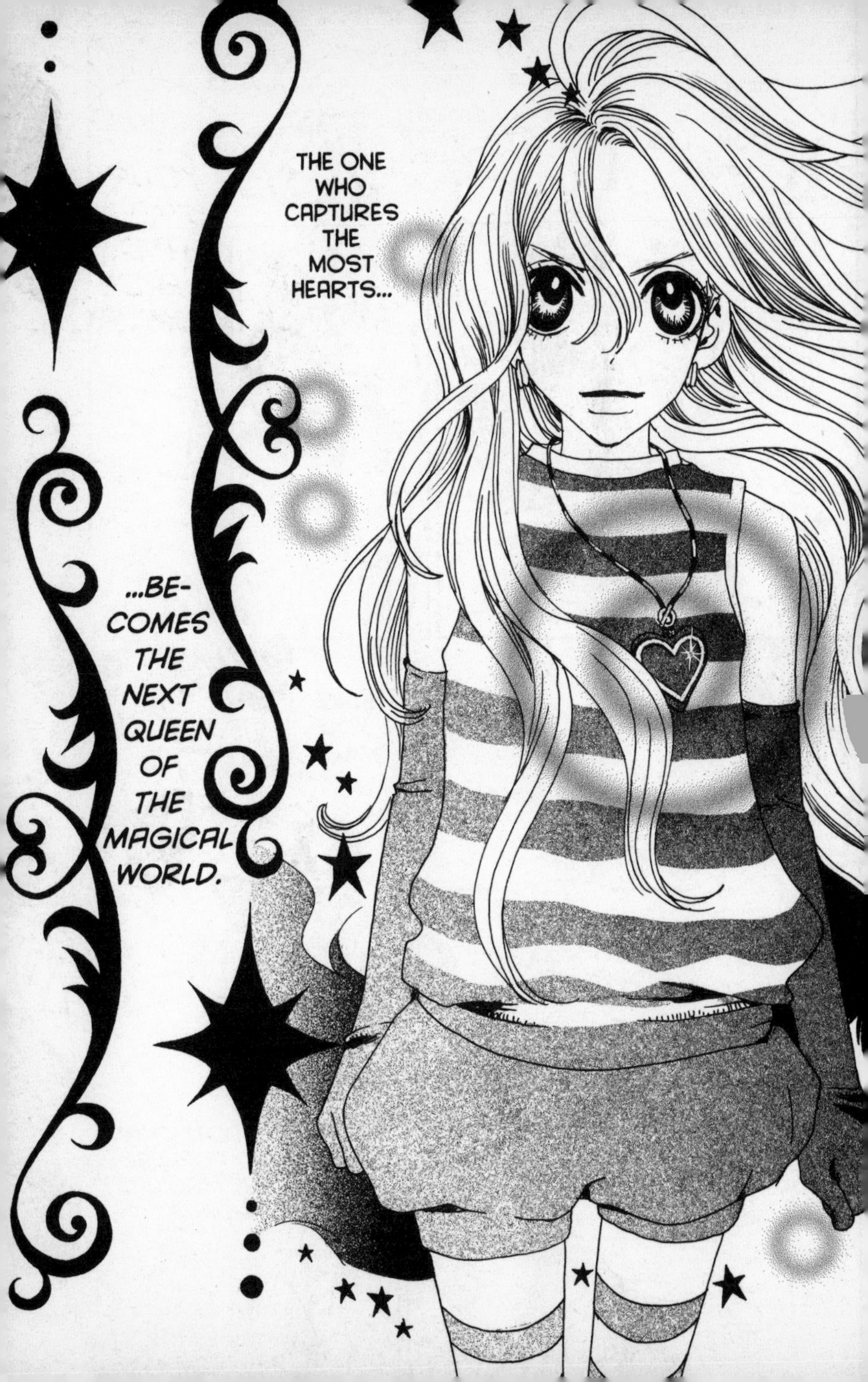
THE ONE WHO CAPTURES THE MOST HEARTS...
...BE-COMES THE NEXT QUEEN OF THE MAGICAL WORLD.

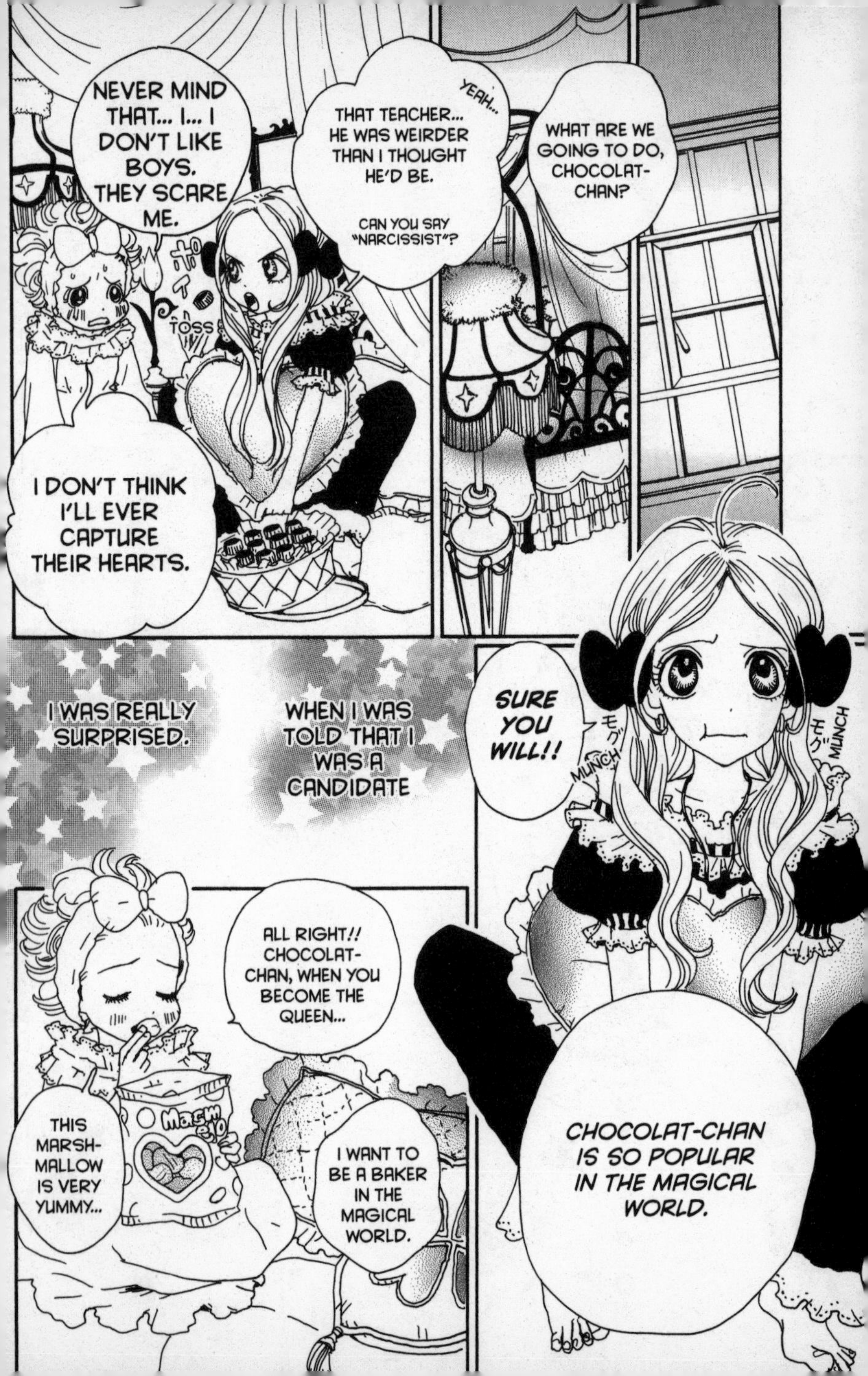
WHAT ARE WE GOING TO DO, CHOCOLAT-CHAN?
YEAH...
THAT TEACHER... HE WAS WEIRDER THAN I THOUGHT HE'D BE.
CAN YOU SAY "NARCISSIST"?
NEVER MIND THAT... I... I DON'T LIKE BOYS. THEY SCARE ME.
ポイ
TOSS
I DON'T THINK I'LL EVER CAPTURE THEIR HEARTS.
モグ
MUNCH
SURE YOU WILL!!
モグ
MUNCH
CHOCOLAT-CHAN IS SO POPULAR IN THE MAGICAL WORLD.
WHEN I WAS TOLD THAT I WAS A CANDIDATE
I WAS REALLY SURPRISED.
ALL RIGHT!! CHOCOLAT-CHAN, WHEN YOU BECOME THE QUEEN...
I WANT TO BE A BAKER IN THE MAGICAL WORLD.
THIS MARSH-MALLOW IS VERY YUMMY...

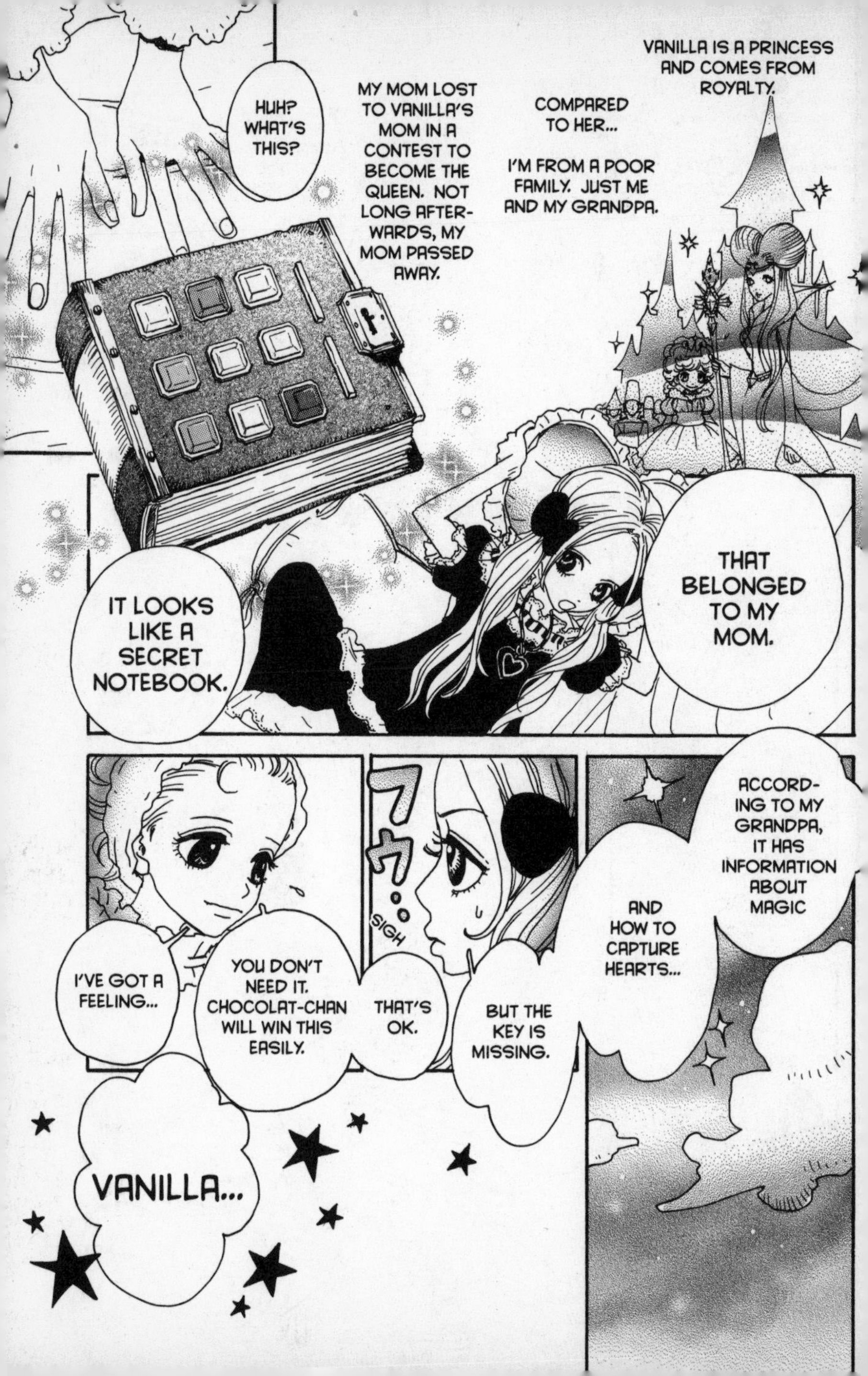
VANILLA IS A PRINCESS AND COMES FROM ROYALTY.
COMPARED TO HER...
I'M FROM A POOR FAMILY. JUST ME AND MY GRANDPA.
MY MOM LOST TO VANILLA'S MOM IN A CONTEST TO BECOME THE QUEEN. NOT LONG AFTER-WARDS, MY MOM PASSED AWAY.
HUH? WHAT'S THIS?
THAT BELONGED TO MY MOM.
IT LOOKS LIKE A SECRET NOTEBOOK.
ACCORD-ING TO MY GRANDPA, IT HAS INFORMATION ABOUT MAGIC
AND HOW TO CAPTURE HEARTS...
BUT THE KEY IS MISSING.
フウ…
SIGH
THAT'S OK.
YOU DON'T NEED IT. CHOCOLAT-CHAN WILL WIN THIS EASILY.
I'VE GOT A FEELING...
VANILLA...

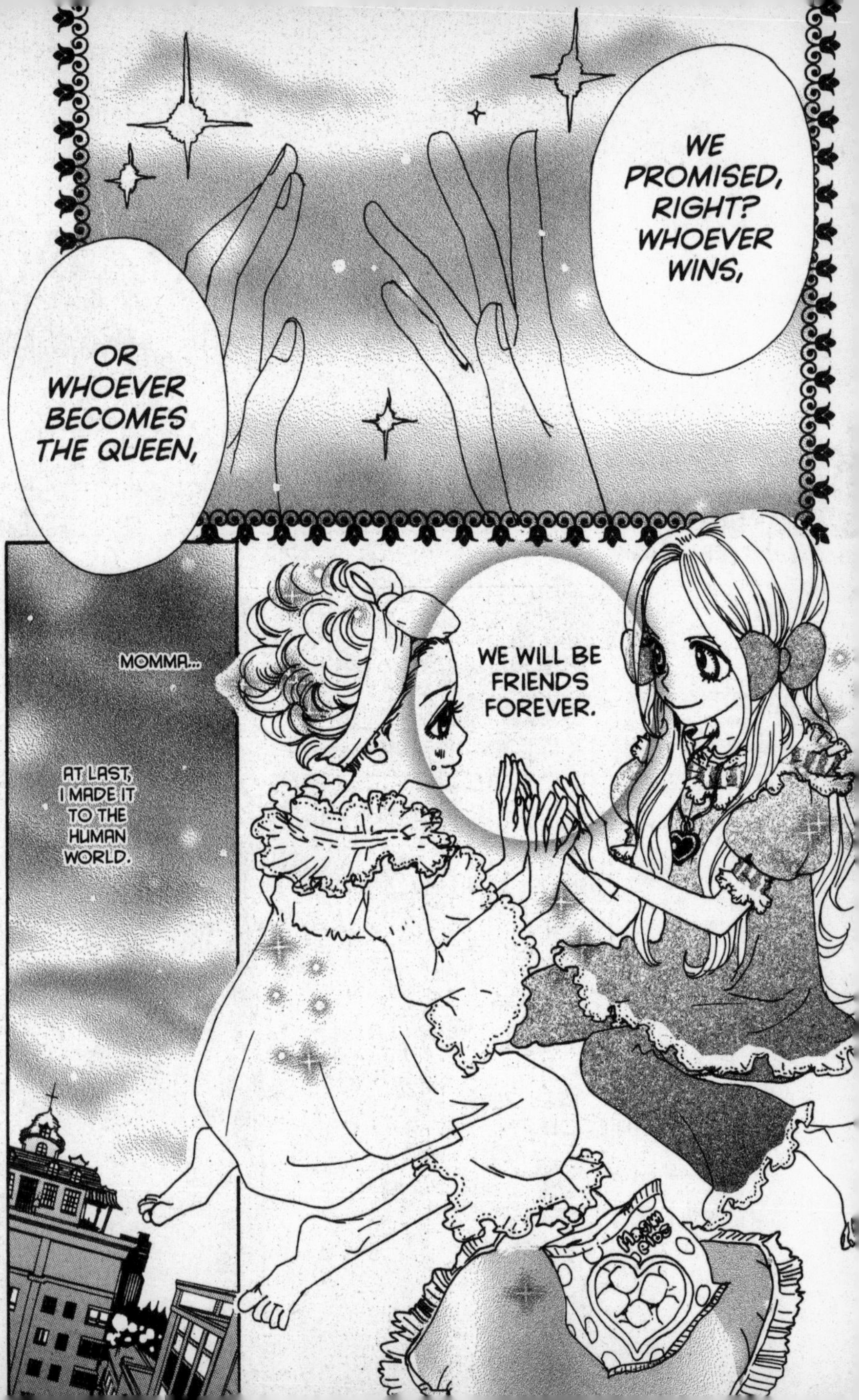
WE PROMISED, RIGHT? WHOEVER WINS,
OR WHOEVER BECOMES THE QUEEN,
WE WILL BE FRIENDS FOREVER.
MOMMA...
AT LAST, I MADE IT TO THE HUMAN WORLD.

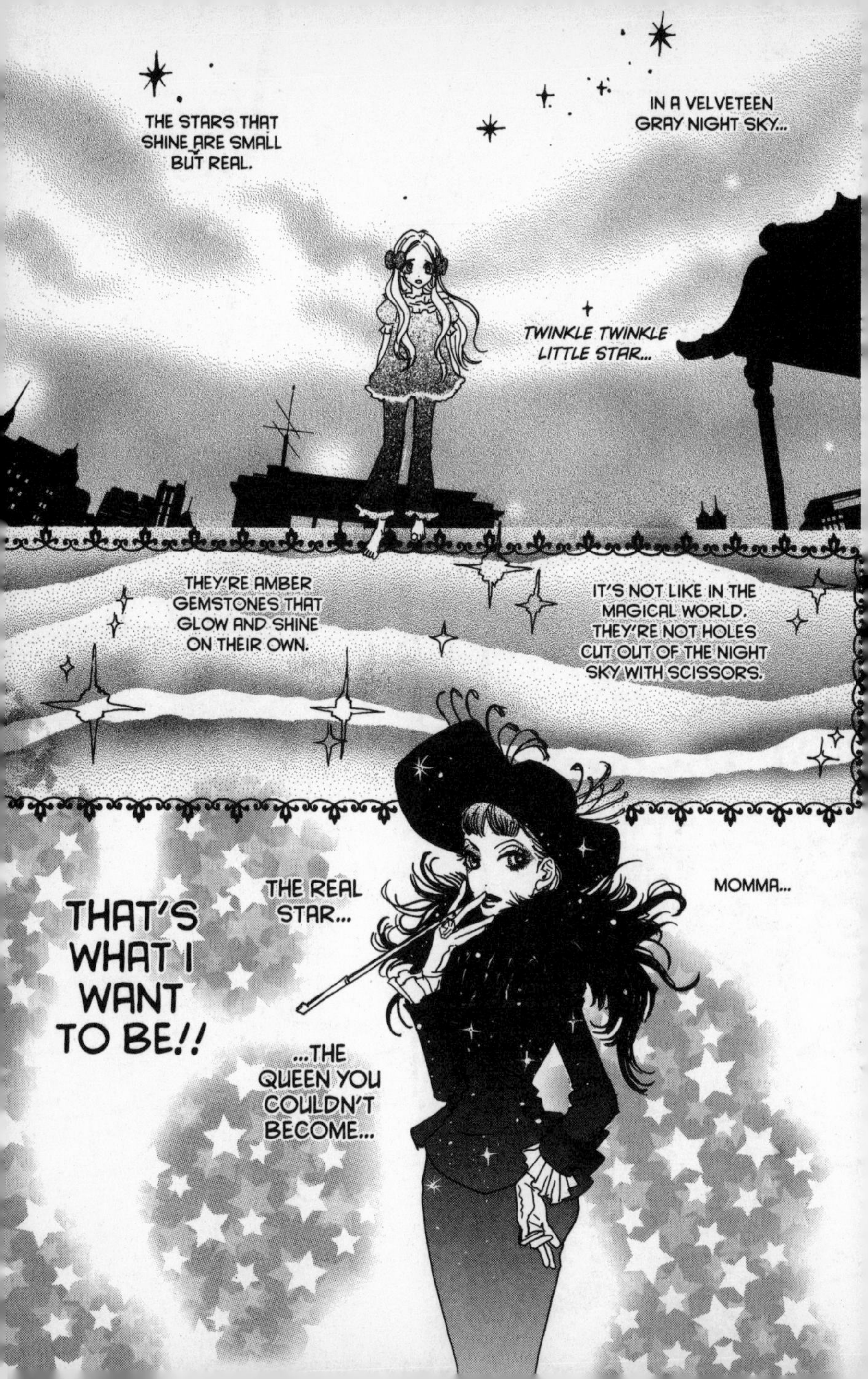
IN A VELVETEEN GRAY NIGHT SKY...
THE STARS THAT SHINE ARE SMALL BUT REAL.
TWINKLE TWINKLE LITTLE STAR...
IT'S NOT LIKE IN THE MAGICAL WORLD. THEY'RE NOT HOLES CUT OUT OF THE NIGHT SKY WITH SCISSORS.
THEY'RE AMBER GEMSTONES THAT GLOW AND SHINE ON THEIR OWN.
MOMMA...
THE REAL STAR...
...THE QUEEN YOU COULDN'T BECOME...
THAT'S WHAT I WANT TO BE!!

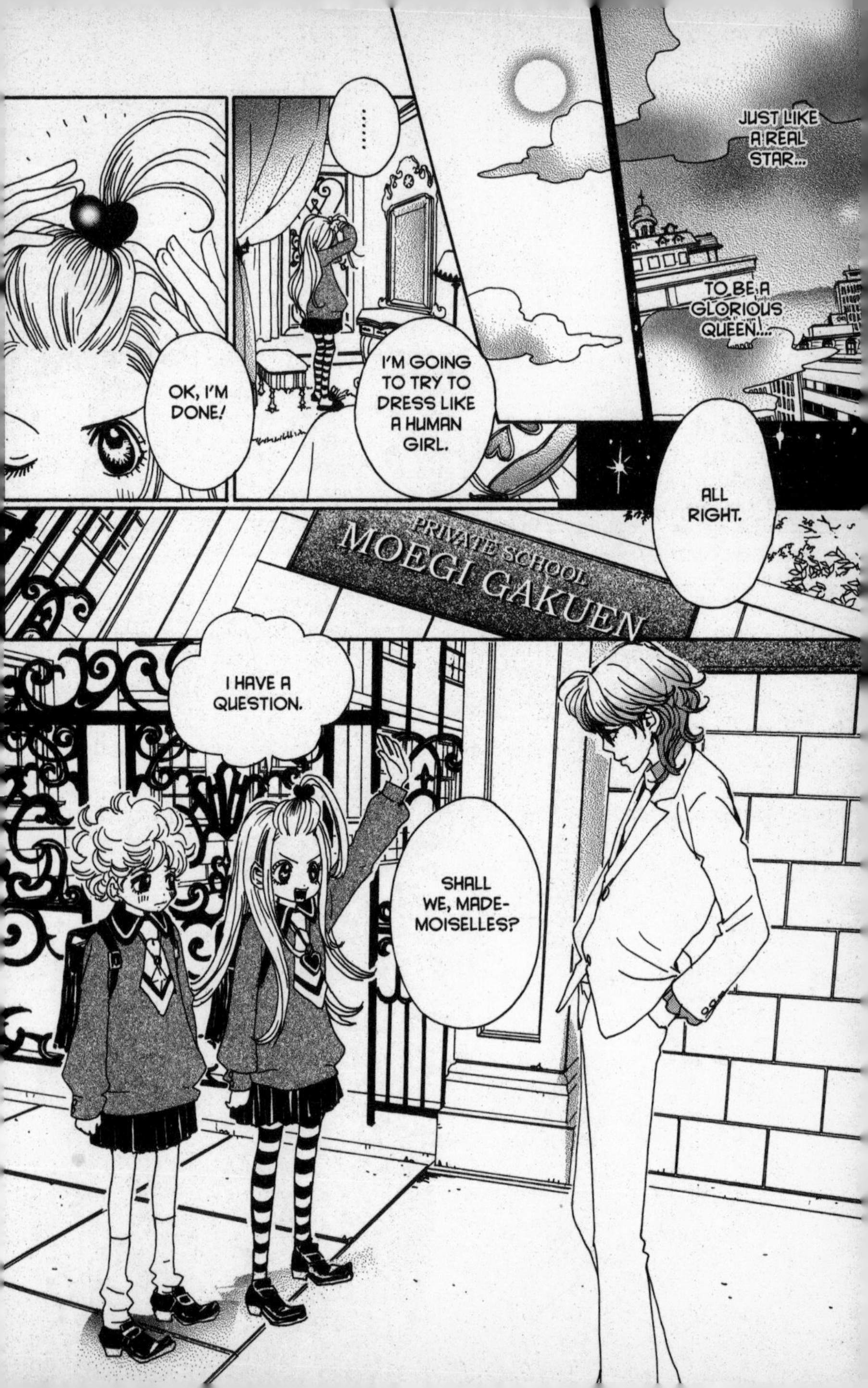

JUST LIKE A REAL STAR...
TO BE A GLORIOUS QUEEN...
......
I'M GOING TO TRY TO DRESS LIKE A HUMAN GIRL.
OK, I'M DONE!
ALL RIGHT.
PRIVATE SCHOOL MOEGI GAKUEN
SHALL WE, MADE-MOISELLES?
I HAVE A QUESTION.

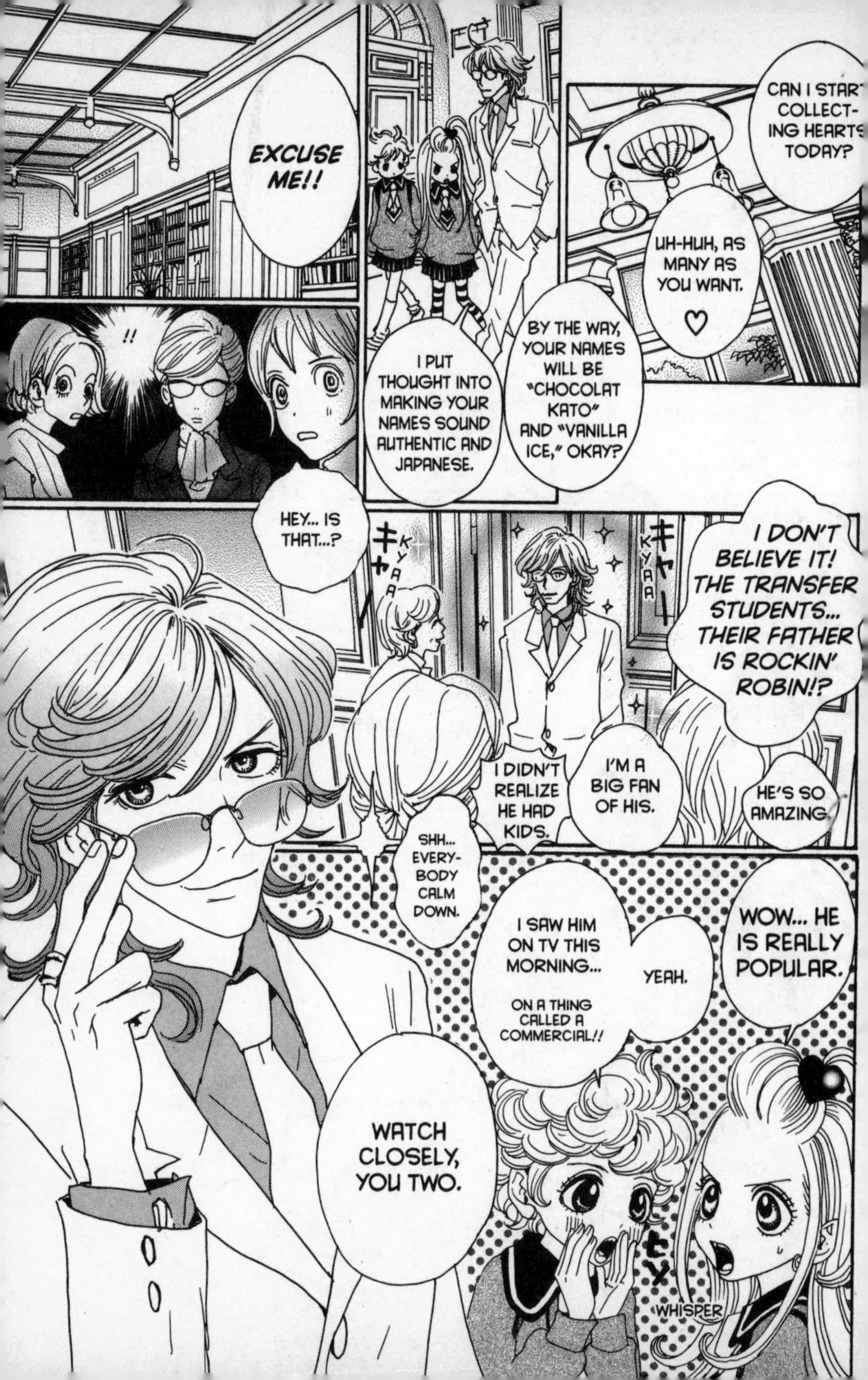

CAN I START COLLECTING HEARTS TODAY?
UH-HUH, AS MANY AS YOU WANT. ♡
BY THE WAY, YOUR NAMES WILL BE "CHOCOLAT KATO" AND "VANILLA ICE," OKAY?
I PUT THOUGHT INTO MAKING YOUR NAMES SOUND AUTHENTIC AND JAPANESE.
EXCUSE ME!!
!!
HEY... IS THAT...?
キャー KYAA
キャー KYAA
I DON'T BELIEVE IT! THE TRANSFER STUDENTS... THEIR FATHER IS ROCKIN' ROBIN!?
HE'S SO AMAZING.
I'M A BIG FAN OF HIS.
I DIDN'T REALIZE HE HAD KIDS.
WOW... HE IS REALLY POPULAR.
YEAH.
I SAW HIM ON TV THIS MORNING...
ON A THING CALLED A COMMERCIAL!!
WHISPER
SHH... EVERYBODY CALM DOWN.
WATCH CLOSELY, YOU TWO.

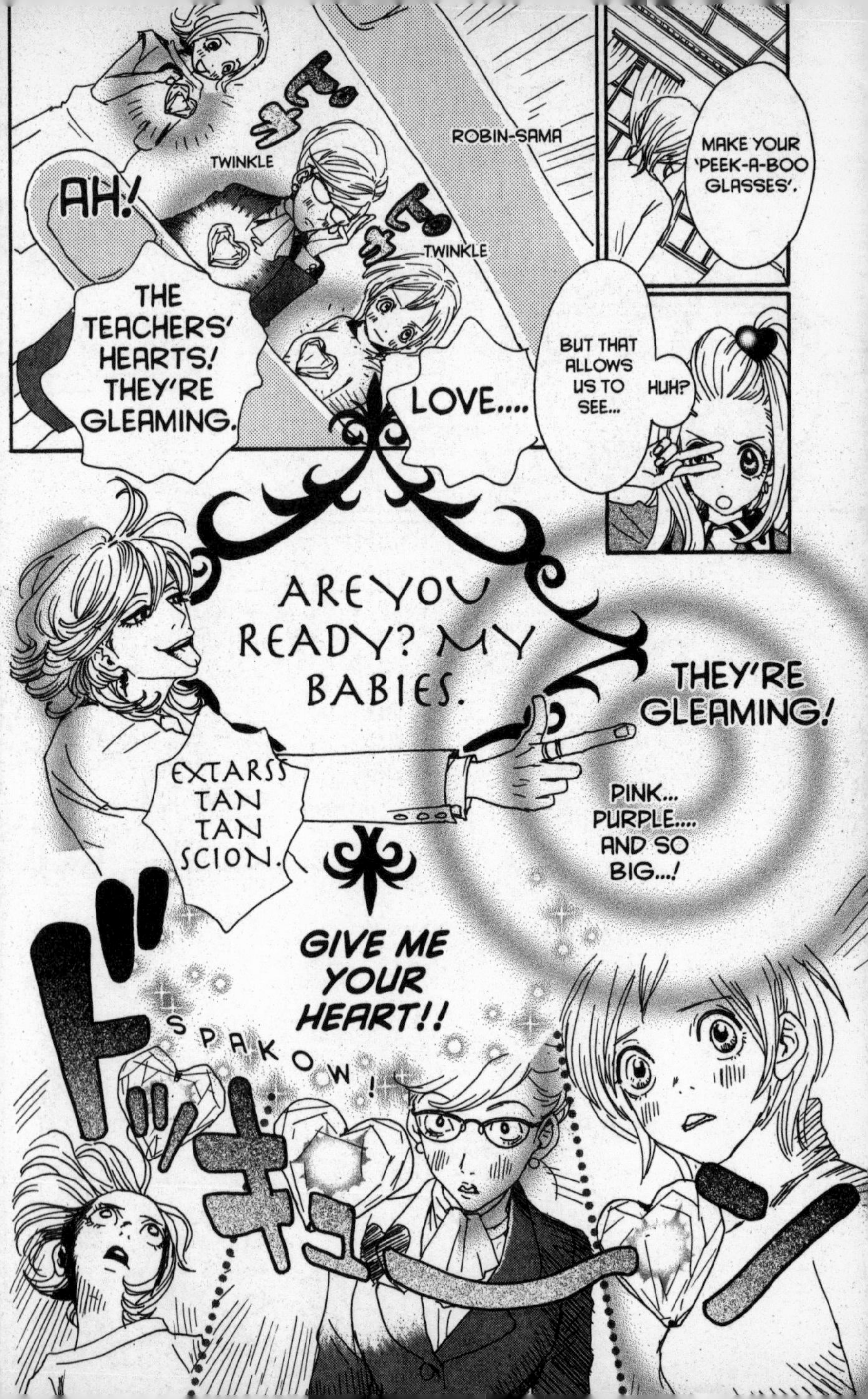
MAKE YOUR 'PEEK-A-BOO GLASSES'.
HUH?
BUT THAT ALLOWS US TO SEE...
ROBIN-SAMA
TWINKLE
AH!
TWINKLE
THE TEACHERS' HEARTS! THEY'RE GLEAMING.
LOVE....
ARE YOU READY? MY BABIES.
THEY'RE GLEAMING!
PINK... PURPLE.... AND SO BIG...!
EXTARSS TAN TAN SCION.
GIVE ME YOUR HEART!!
SPAKOW!

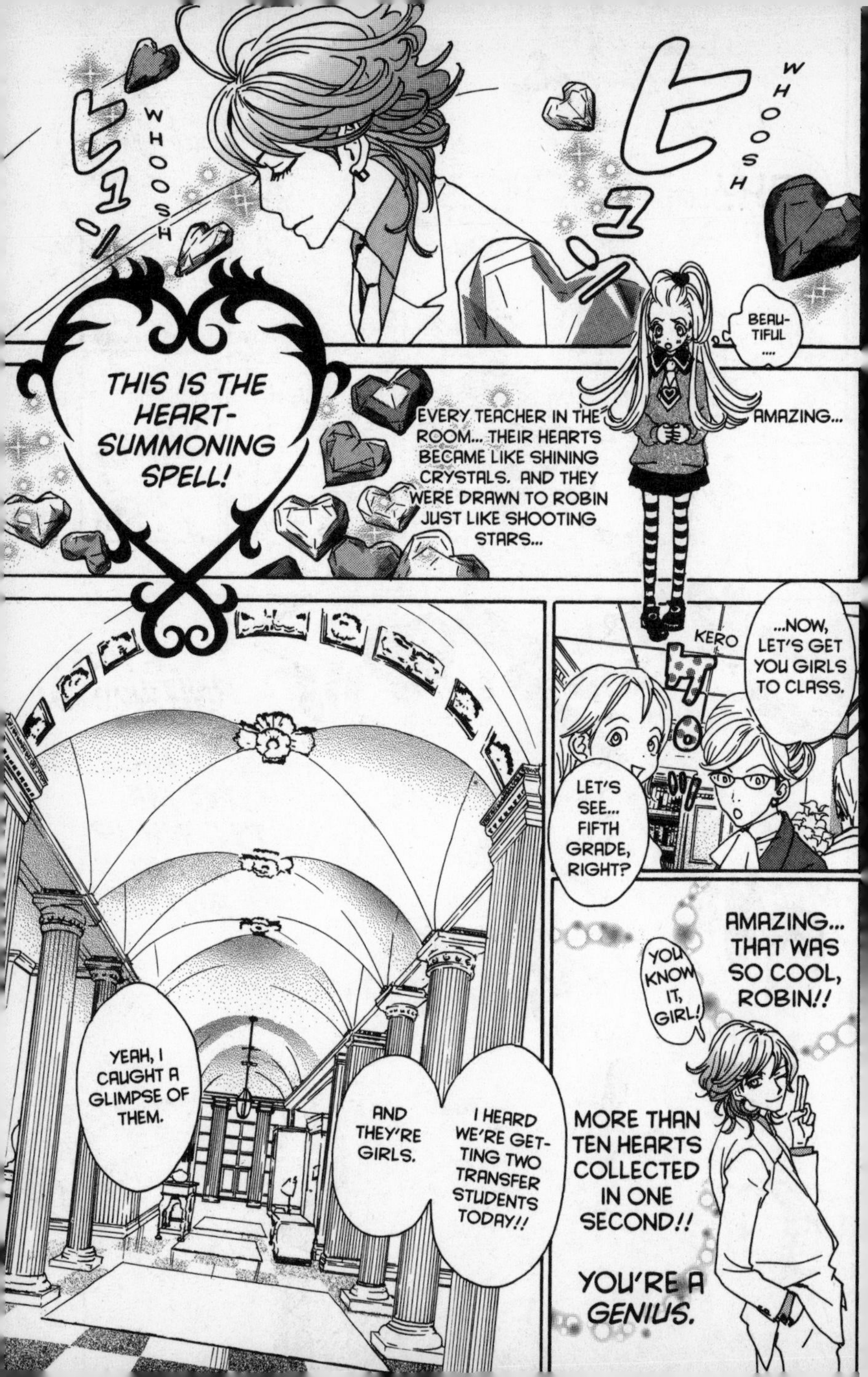
WHOOSH
WHOOSH
BEAU-TIFUL ....
AMAZING...
EVERY TEACHER IN THE ROOM... THEIR HEARTS BECAME LIKE SHINING CRYSTALS. AND THEY WERE DRAWN TO ROBIN JUST LIKE SHOOTING STARS...
THIS IS THE HEART-SUMMONING SPELL!
...NOW, LET'S GET YOU GIRLS TO CLASS.
KERO
LET'S SEE... FIFTH GRADE, RIGHT?
AMAZING... THAT WAS SO COOL, ROBIN!!
YOU KNOW IT, GIRL!
MORE THAN TEN HEARTS COLLECTED IN ONE SECOND!!
YOU'RE A GENIUS.
I HEARD WE'RE GET-TING TWO TRANSFER STUDENTS TODAY!!
AND THEY'RE GIRLS.
YEAH, I CAUGHT A GLIMPSE OF THEM.

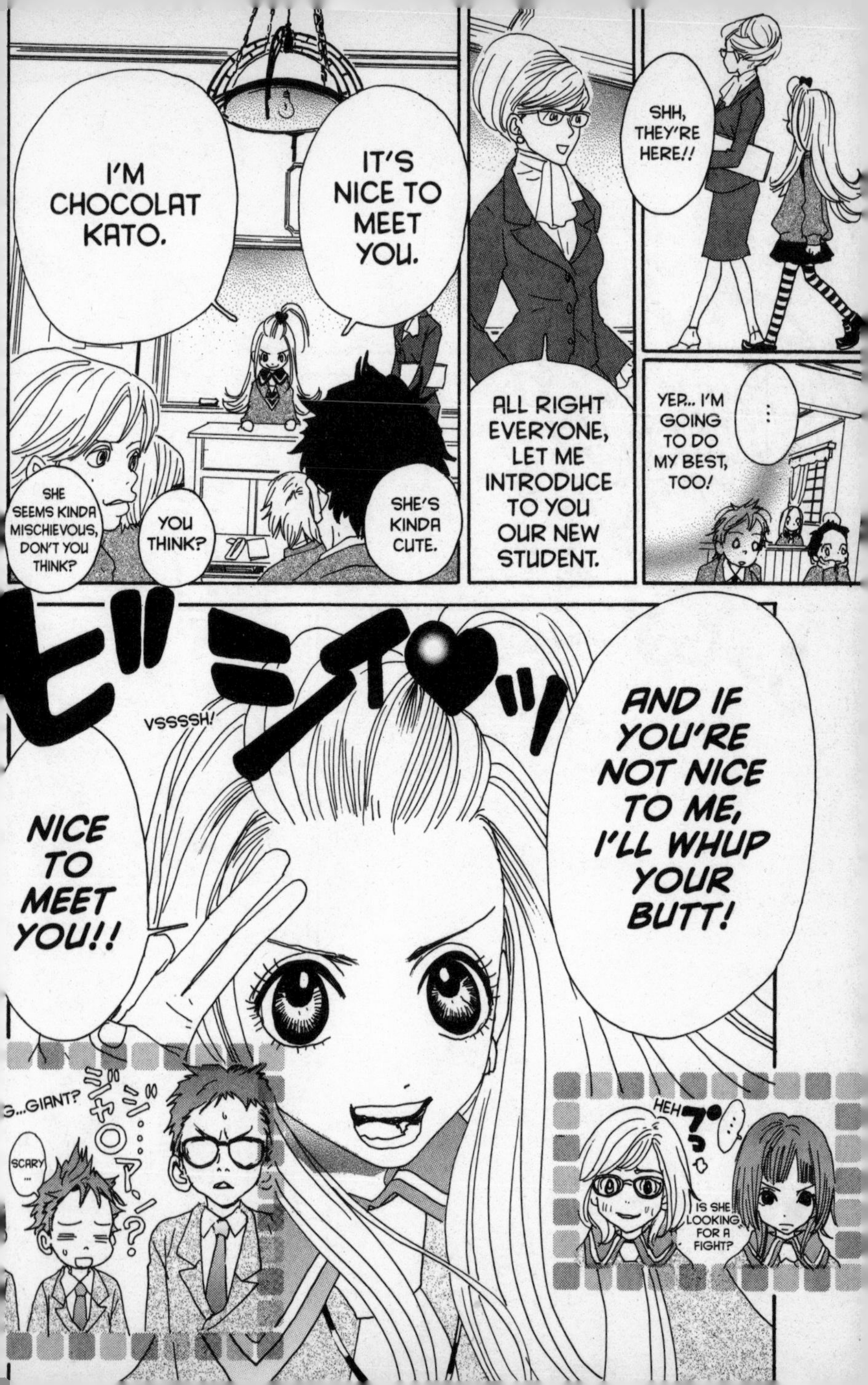
SHH, THEY'RE HERE!!
...
YEP... I'M GOING TO DO MY BEST, TOO!
ALL RIGHT EVERYONE, LET ME INTRODUCE TO YOU OUR NEW STUDENT.
IT'S NICE TO MEET YOU.
I'M CHOCOLAT KATO.
SHE'S KINDA CUTE.
YOU THINK?
SHE SEEMS KINDA MISCHIEVOUS, DON'T YOU THINK?
ビシィッ
VSSSSH!
AND IF YOU'RE NOT NICE TO ME, I'LL WHUP YOUR BUTT!
NICE TO MEET YOU!!
HEH
...
IS SHE LOOKING FOR A FIGHT?
G...GIANT?
SCARY ...

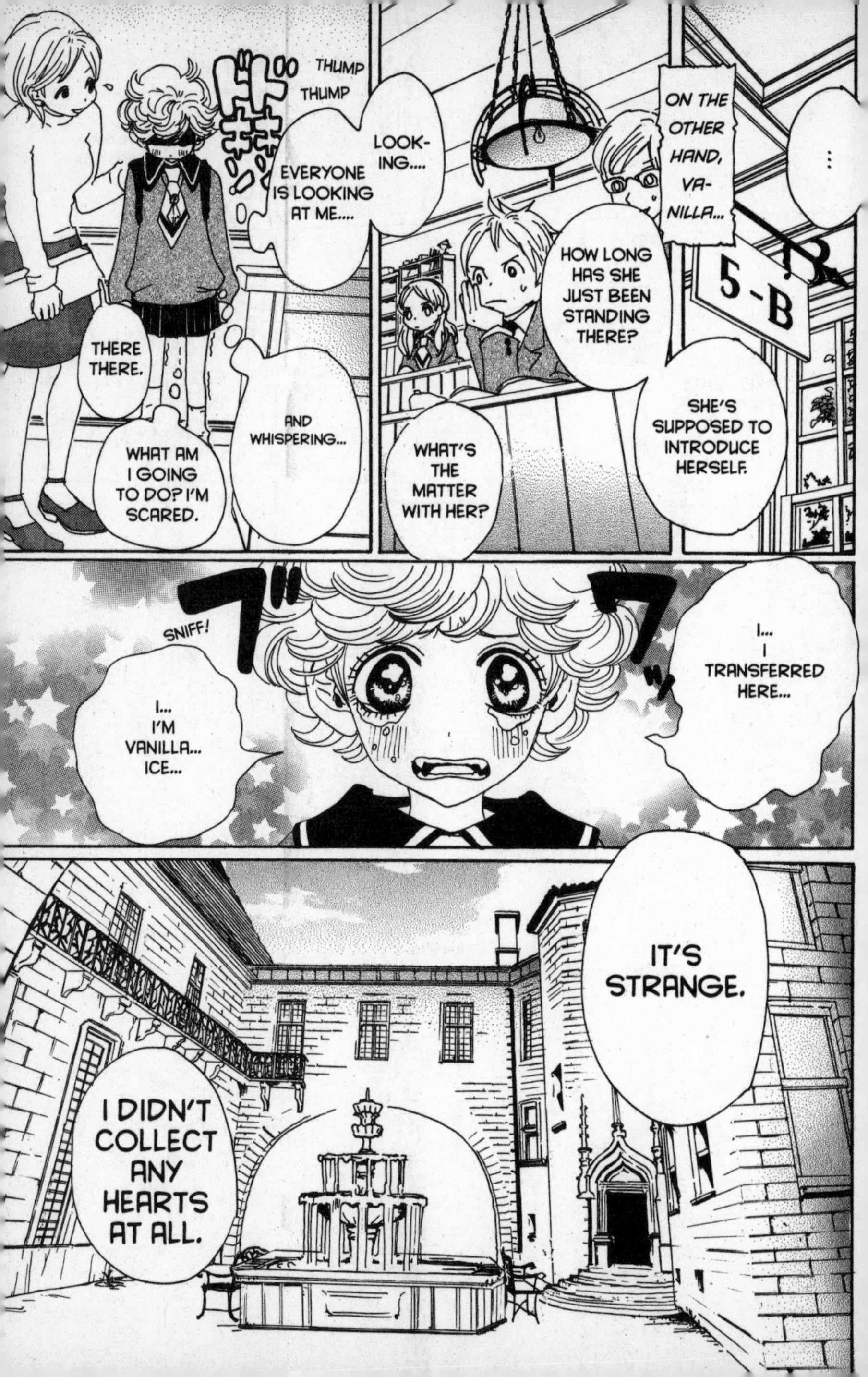
...
ON THE OTHER HAND, VANILLA...
HOW LONG HAS SHE JUST BEEN STANDING THERE?
SHE'S SUPPOSED TO INTRODUCE HERSELF.
WHAT'S THE MATTER WITH HER?
THUMP THUMP
LOOKING....
EVERYONE IS LOOKING AT ME....
AND WHISPERING...
THERE THERE.
WHAT AM I GOING TO DO? I'M SCARED.
I... I TRANSFERRED HERE...
SNIFF!
I... I'M VANILLA... ICE...
IT'S STRANGE.
I DIDN'T COLLECT ANY HEARTS AT ALL.

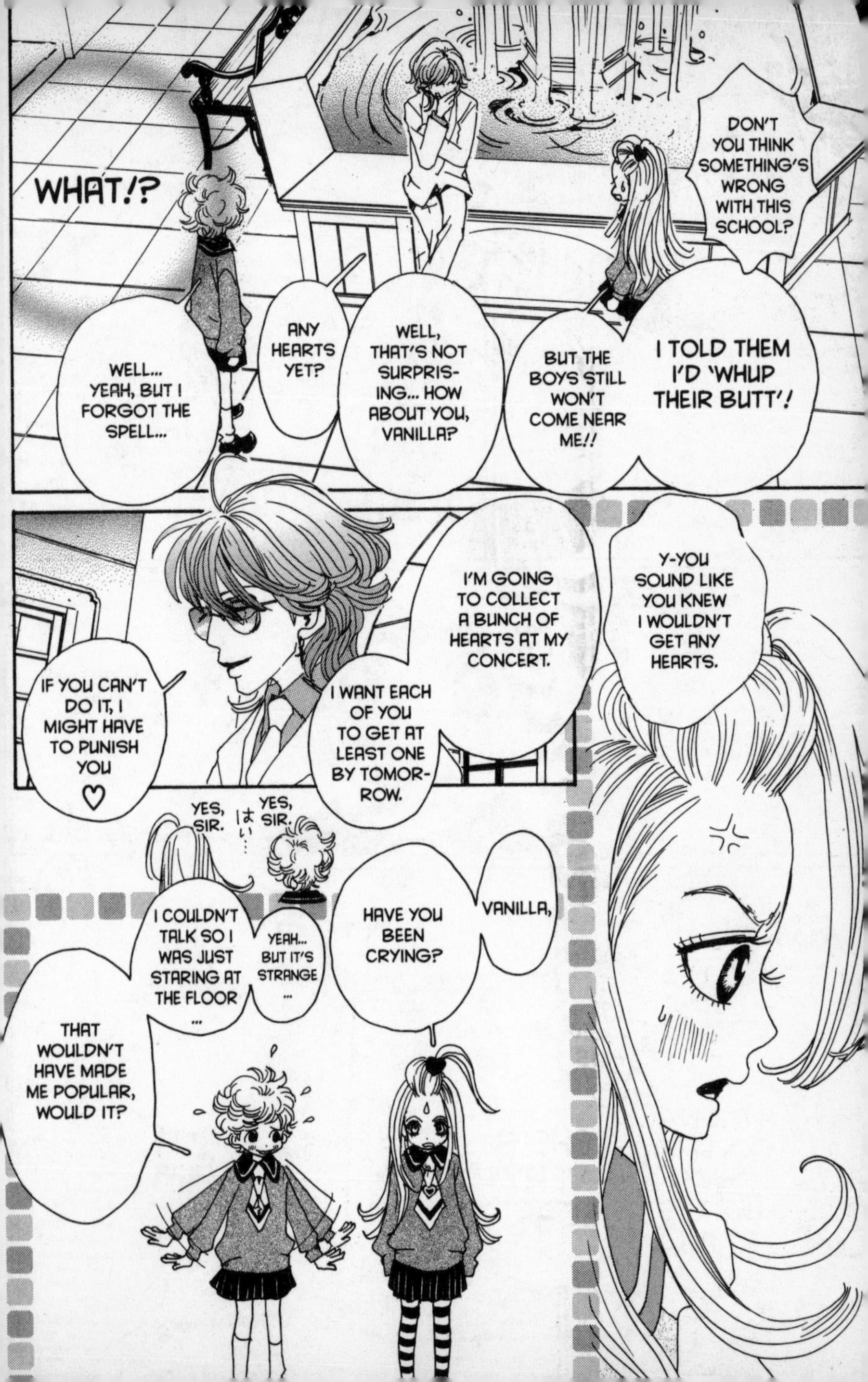
DON'T YOU THINK SOMETHING'S WRONG WITH THIS SCHOOL?
WHAT!?
I TOLD THEM I'D 'WHUP THEIR BUTT'!
BUT THE BOYS STILL WON'T COME NEAR ME!!
WELL, THAT'S NOT SURPRIS-ING... HOW ABOUT YOU, VANILLA?
ANY HEARTS YET?
WELL... YEAH, BUT I FORGOT THE SPELL...
Y-YOU SOUND LIKE YOU KNEW I WOULDN'T GET ANY HEARTS.
I'M GOING TO COLLECT A BUNCH OF HEARTS AT MY CONCERT.
I WANT EACH OF YOU TO GET AT LEAST ONE BY TOMOR-ROW.
IF YOU CAN'T DO IT, I MIGHT HAVE TO PUNISH YOU ♡
YES, SIR.
はい…
YES, SIR.
VANILLA,
HAVE YOU BEEN CRYING?
YEAH... BUT IT'S STRANGE...
I COULDN'T TALK SO I WAS JUST STARING AT THE FLOOR...
THAT WOULDN'T HAVE MADE ME POPULAR, WOULD IT?

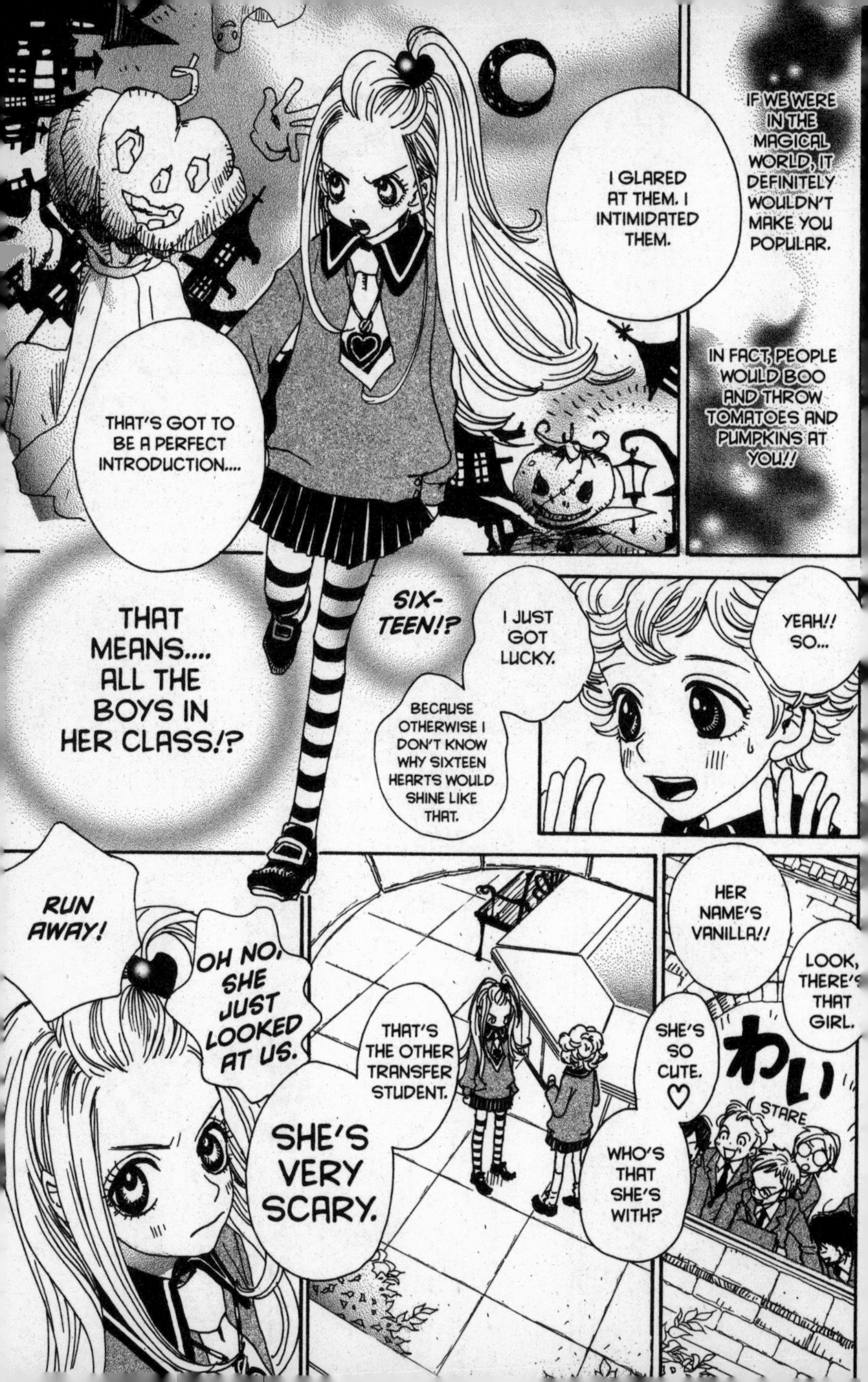
IF WE WERE IN THE MAGICAL WORLD, IT DEFINITELY WOULDN'T MAKE YOU POPULAR.
IN FACT, PEOPLE WOULD BOO AND THROW TOMATOES AND PUMPKINS AT YOU!!
I GLARED AT THEM. I INTIMIDATED THEM.
THAT'S GOT TO BE A PERFECT INTRODUCTION....
YEAH!! SO...
I JUST GOT LUCKY.
BECAUSE OTHERWISE I DON'T KNOW WHY SIXTEEN HEARTS WOULD SHINE LIKE THAT.
SIX-TEEN!?
THAT MEANS.... ALL THE BOYS IN HER CLASS!?
LOOK, THERE'S THAT GIRL.
HER NAME'S VANILLA!!
わい
STARE
SHE'S SO CUTE. ♡
WHO'S THAT SHE'S WITH?
THAT'S THE OTHER TRANSFER STUDENT.
SHE'S VERY SCARY.
OH NO, SHE JUST LOOKED AT US.
RUN AWAY!

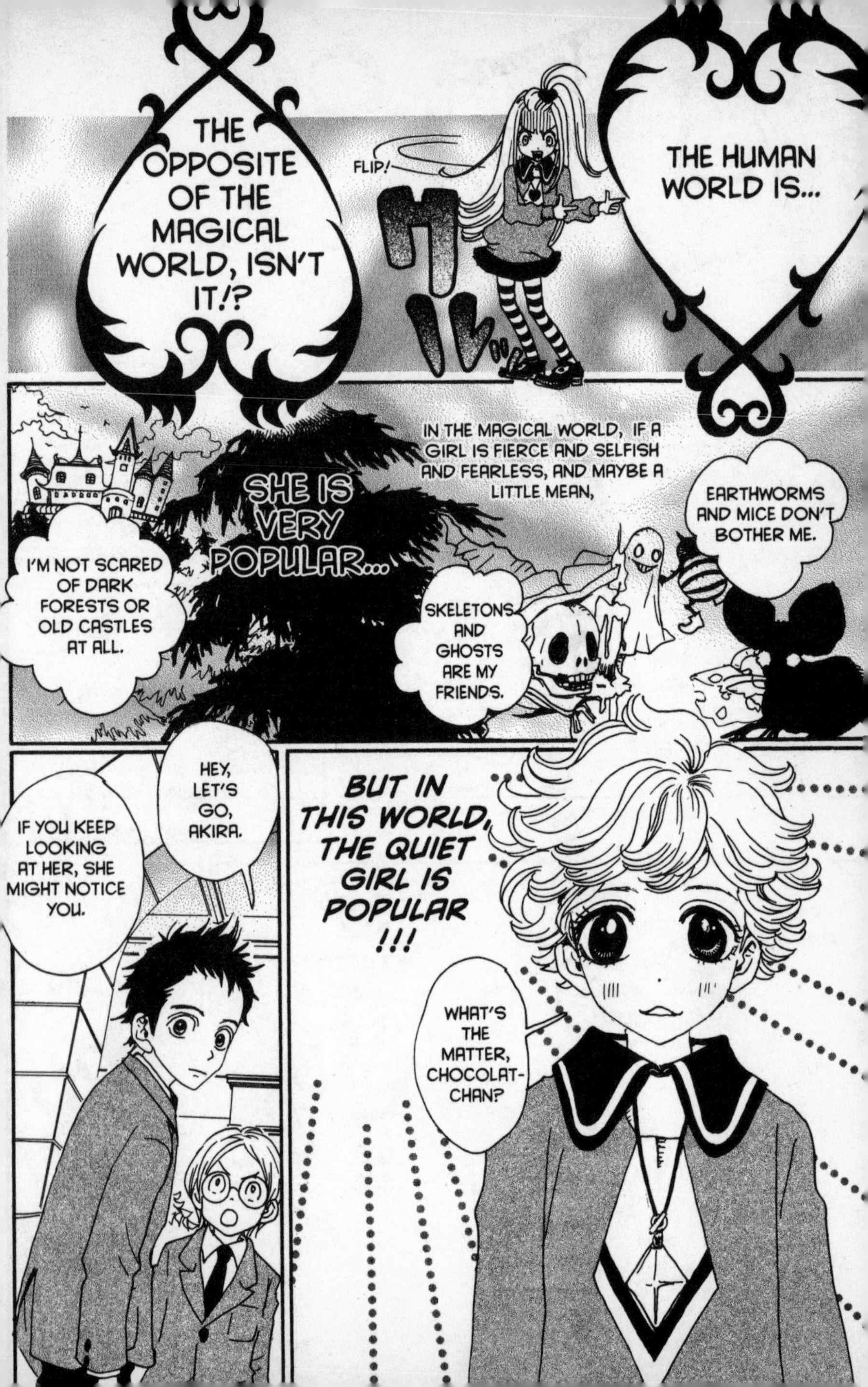
THE HUMAN WORLD IS...
FLIP!
THE OPPOSITE OF THE MAGICAL WORLD, ISN'T IT!?
IN THE MAGICAL WORLD, IF A GIRL IS FIERCE AND SELFISH AND FEARLESS, AND MAYBE A LITTLE MEAN,
EARTHWORMS AND MICE DON'T BOTHER ME.
SKELETONS AND GHOSTS ARE MY FRIENDS.
SHE IS VERY POPULAR...
I'M NOT SCARED OF DARK FORESTS OR OLD CASTLES AT ALL.
BUT IN THIS WORLD, THE QUIET GIRL IS POPULAR!!!
WHAT'S THE MATTER, CHOCOLAT-CHAN?
HEY, LET'S GO, AKIRA.
IF YOU KEEP LOOKING AT HER, SHE MIGHT NOTICE YOU.

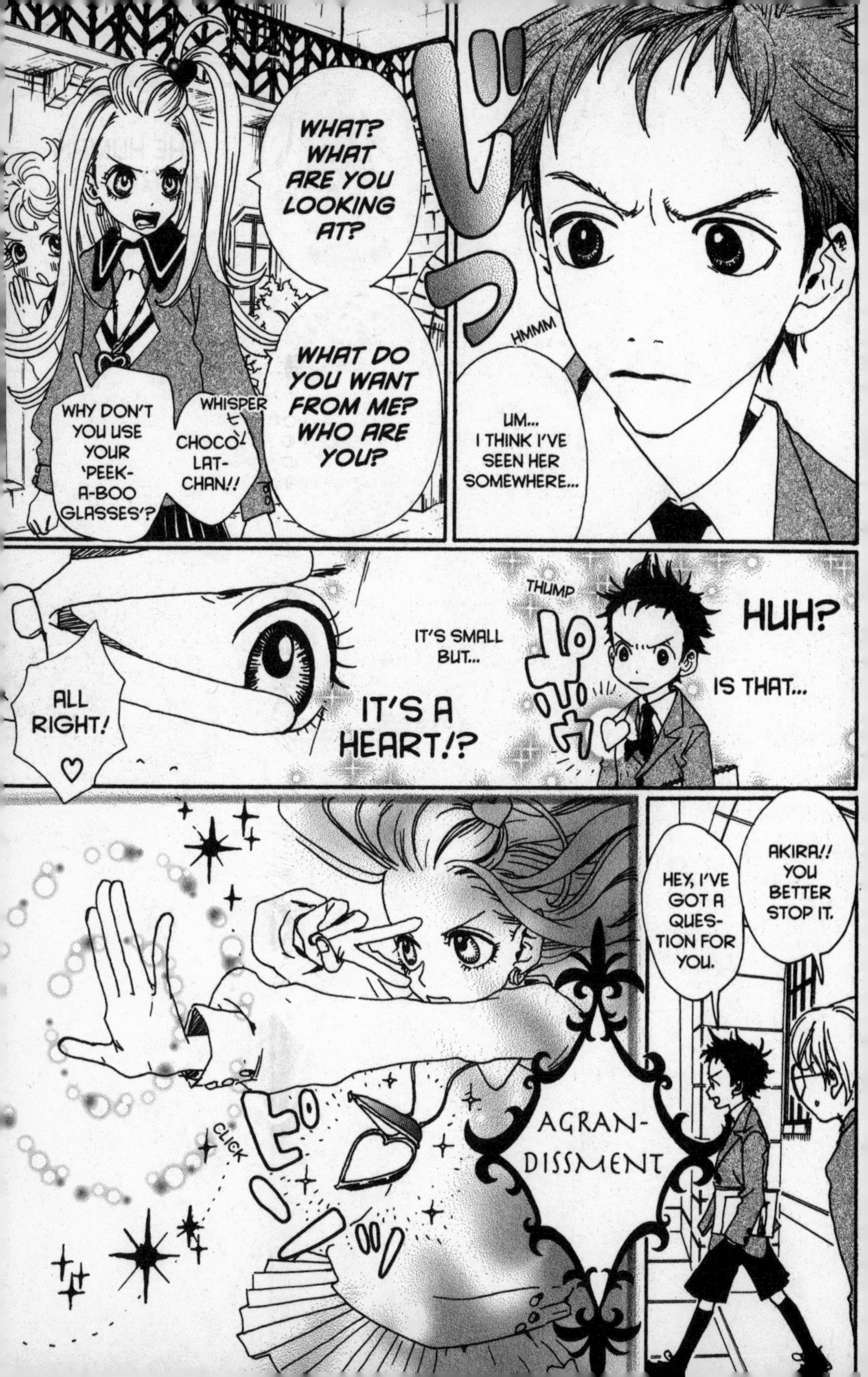
HMMM
UM... I THINK I'VE SEEN HER SOMEWHERE...
WHAT? WHAT ARE YOU LOOKING AT?
WHAT DO YOU WANT FROM ME? WHO ARE YOU?
WHISPER
CHOCO LAT-CHAN!!
WHY DON'T YOU USE YOUR 'PEEK-A-BOO GLASSES'?
HUH?
THUMP
IS THAT...
IT'S SMALL BUT...
IT'S A HEART!?
ALL RIGHT! ♡
AKIRA!! YOU BETTER STOP IT.
HEY, I'VE GOT A QUES-TION FOR YOU.
CLICK
AGRAN-DISSMENT

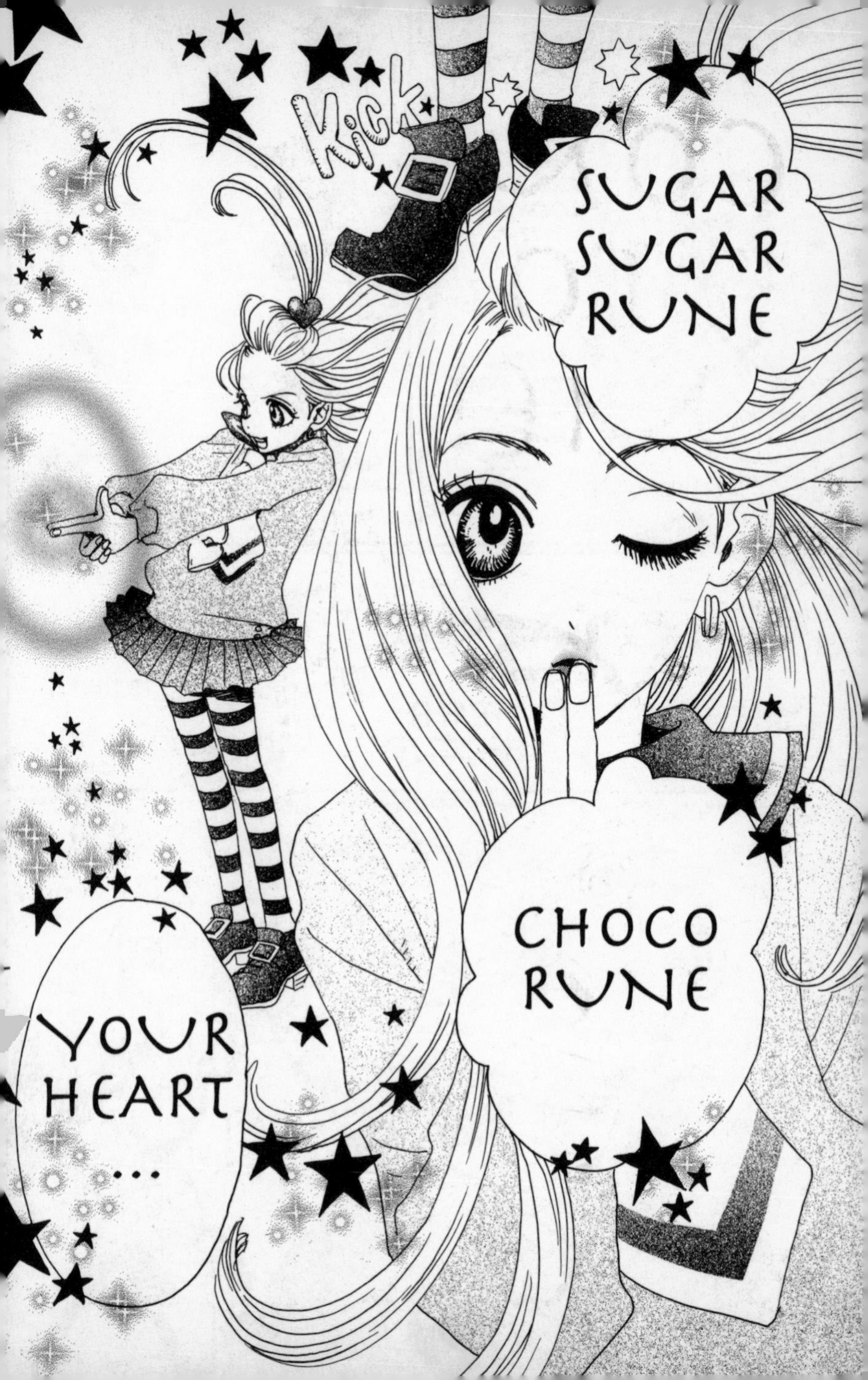
SUGAR SUGAR RUNE
KICK
CHOCO RUNE
YOUR HEART ...

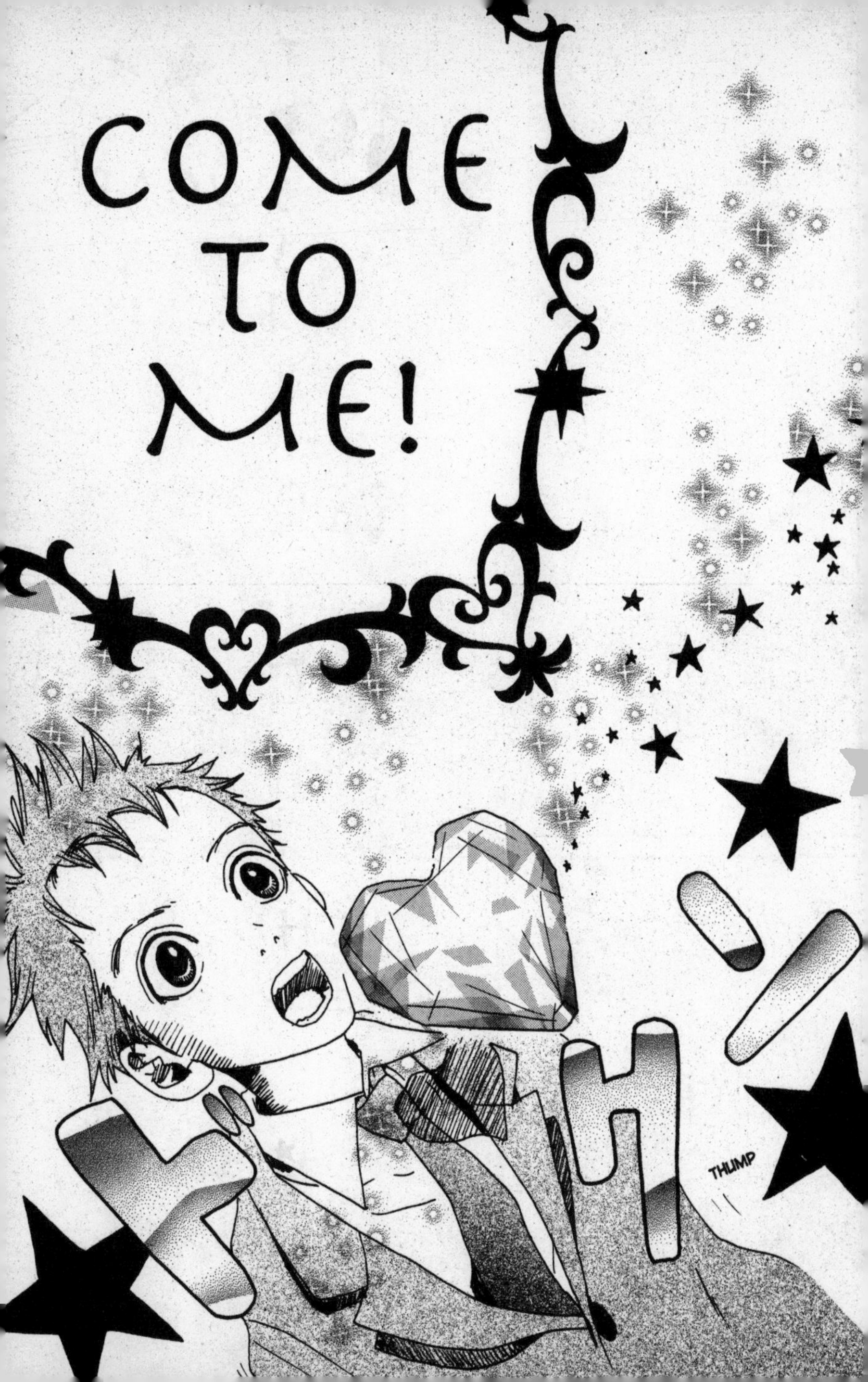
COME TO ME!
THUMP

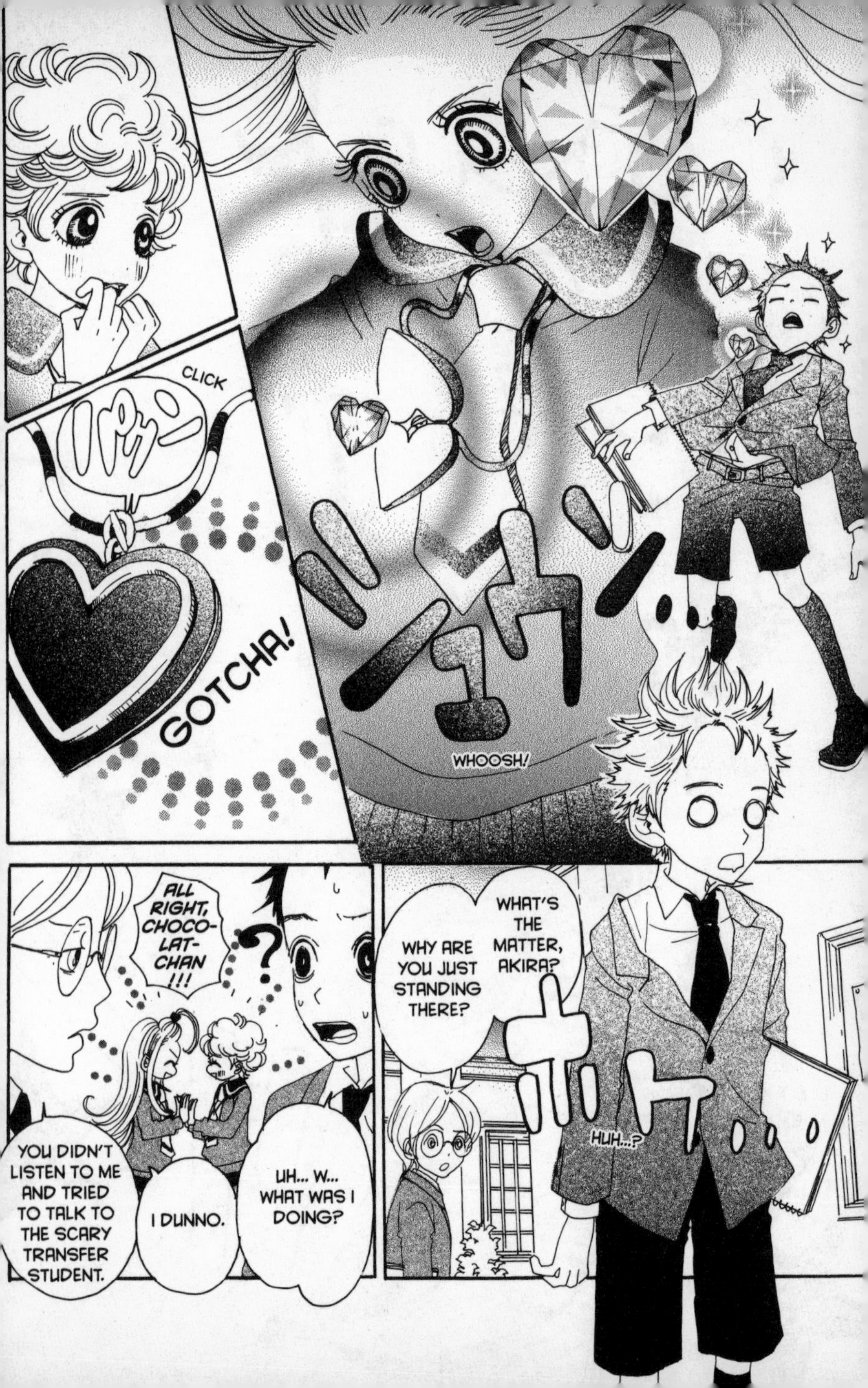
WHOOSH!
CLICK
GOTCHA!
WHAT'S THE MATTER, AKIRA?
WHY ARE YOU JUST STANDING THERE?
HUH...?
ALL RIGHT, CHOCOLAT-CHAN!!!
UH... W... WHAT WAS I DOING?
I DUNNO.
YOU DIDN'T LISTEN TO ME AND TRIED TO TALK TO THE SCARY TRANSFER STUDENT.

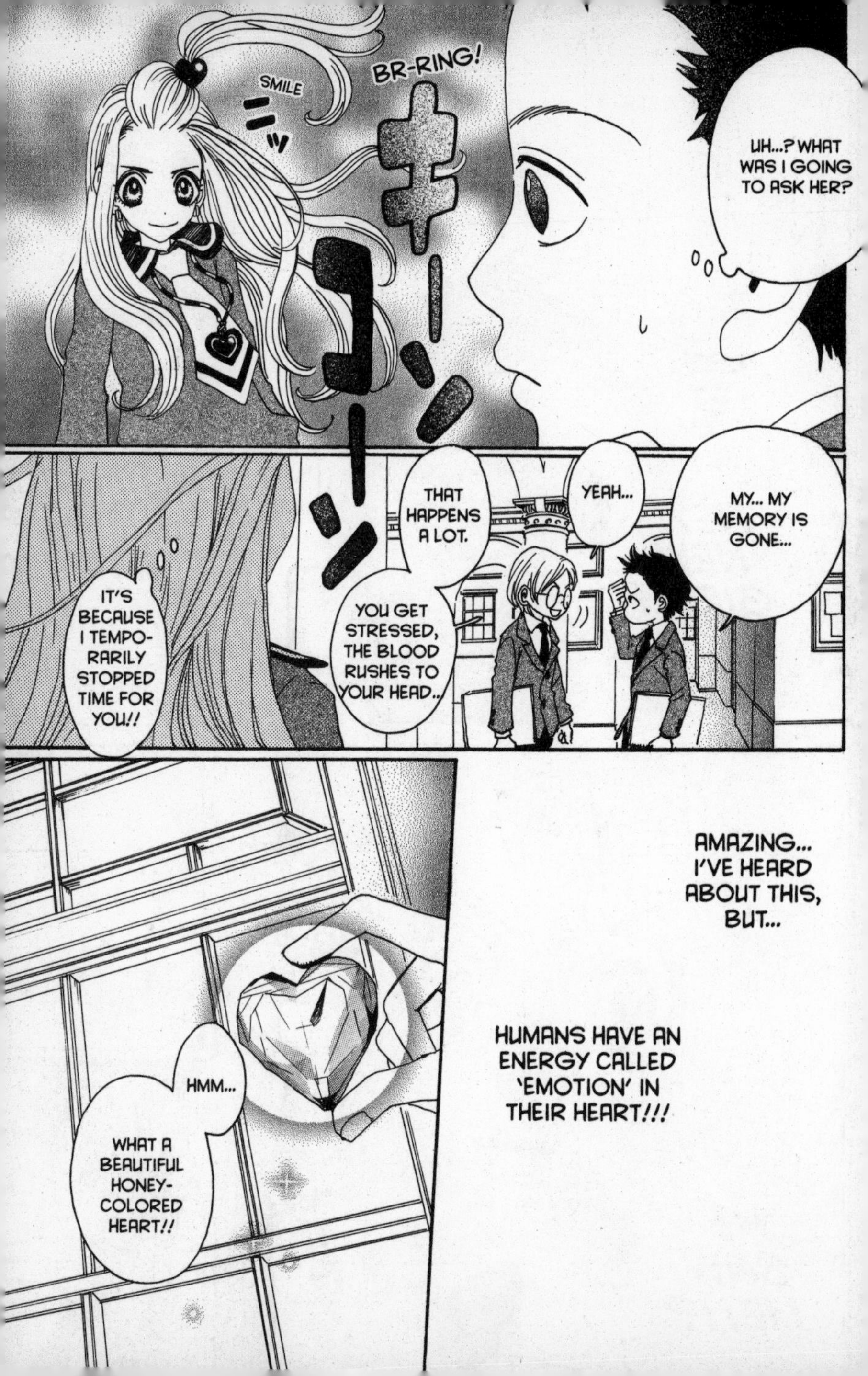
UH...? WHAT WAS I GOING TO ASK HER?
BR-RING!
SMILE
MY... MY MEMORY IS GONE...
YEAH...
THAT HAPPENS A LOT.
YOU GET STRESSED, THE BLOOD RUSHES TO YOUR HEAD..
IT'S BECAUSE I TEMPO-RARILY STOPPED TIME FOR YOU!!
AMAZING... I'VE HEARD ABOUT THIS, BUT...
HUMANS HAVE AN ENERGY CALLED 'EMOTION' IN THEIR HEART!!!
HMM...
WHAT A BEAUTIFUL HONEY-COLORED HEART!!

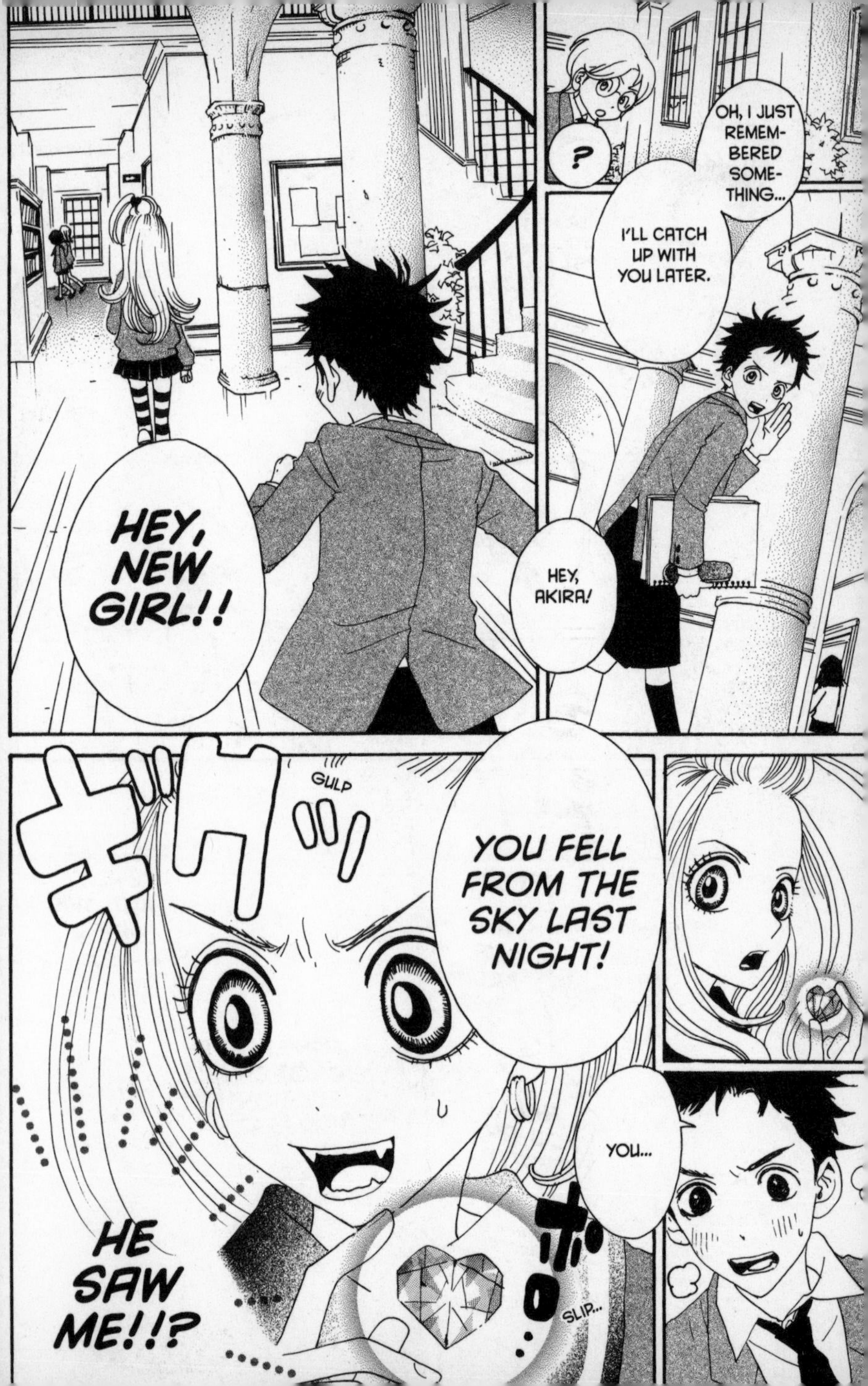
OH, I JUST REMEMBERED SOMETHING...
?
I'LL CATCH UP WITH YOU LATER.
HEY, AKIRA!
HEY, NEW GIRL!!
YOU...
YOU FELL FROM THE SKY LAST NIGHT!
GULP
HE SAW ME!!?
SLIP...

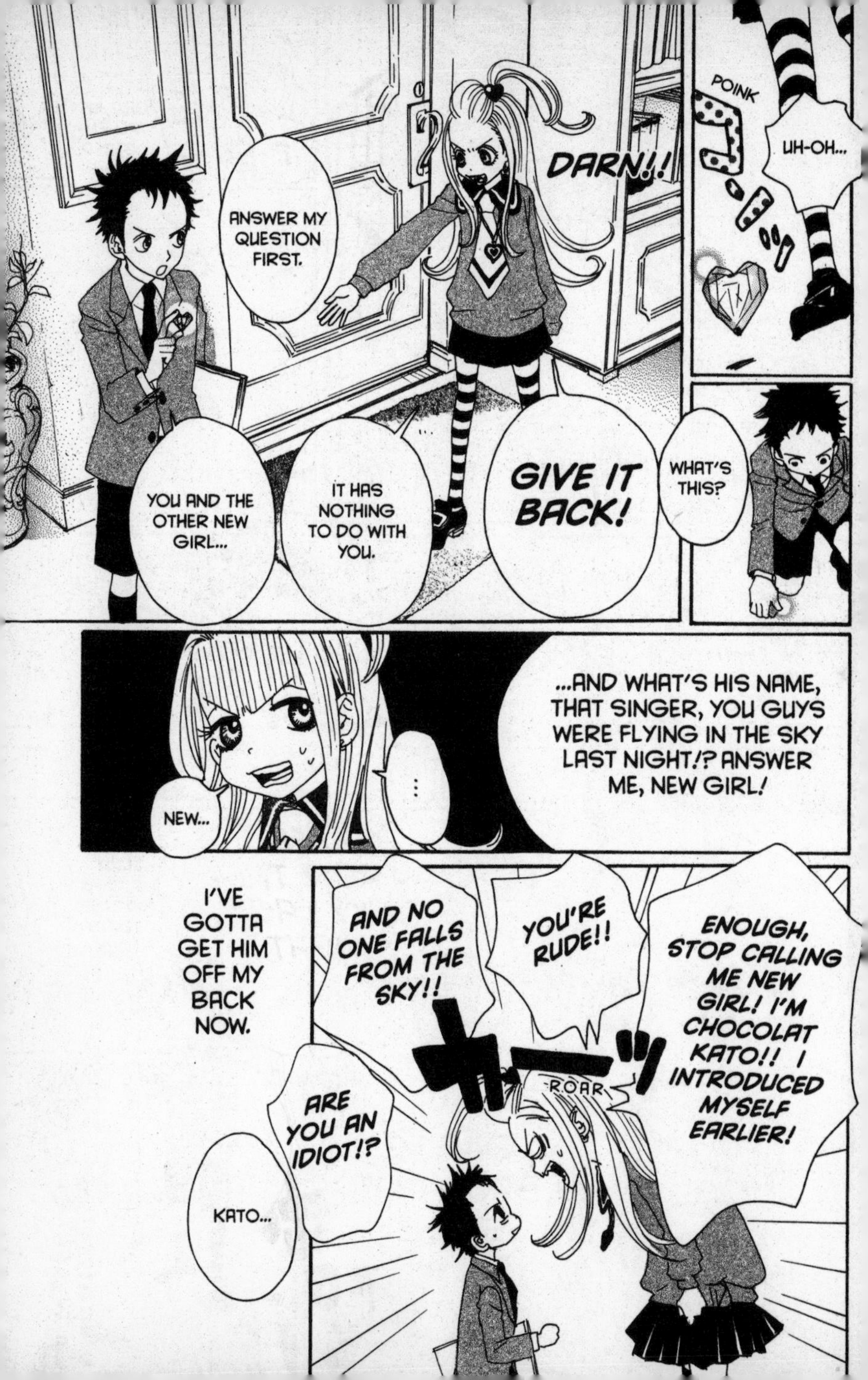
POINK
UH-OH...
WHAT'S THIS?
DARN!!
ANSWER MY QUESTION FIRST.
GIVE IT BACK!
...
IT HAS NOTHING TO DO WITH YOU.
YOU AND THE OTHER NEW GIRL...
...AND WHAT'S HIS NAME, THAT SINGER, YOU GUYS WERE FLYING IN THE SKY LAST NIGHT!? ANSWER ME, NEW GIRL!
...
NEW...
ENOUGH, STOP CALLING ME NEW GIRL! I'M CHOCOLAT KATO!! I INTRODUCED MYSELF EARLIER!
YOU'RE RUDE!!
AND NO ONE FALLS FROM THE SKY!!
ROAR
I'VE GOTTA GET HIM OFF MY BACK NOW.
ARE YOU AN IDIOT!?
KATO...

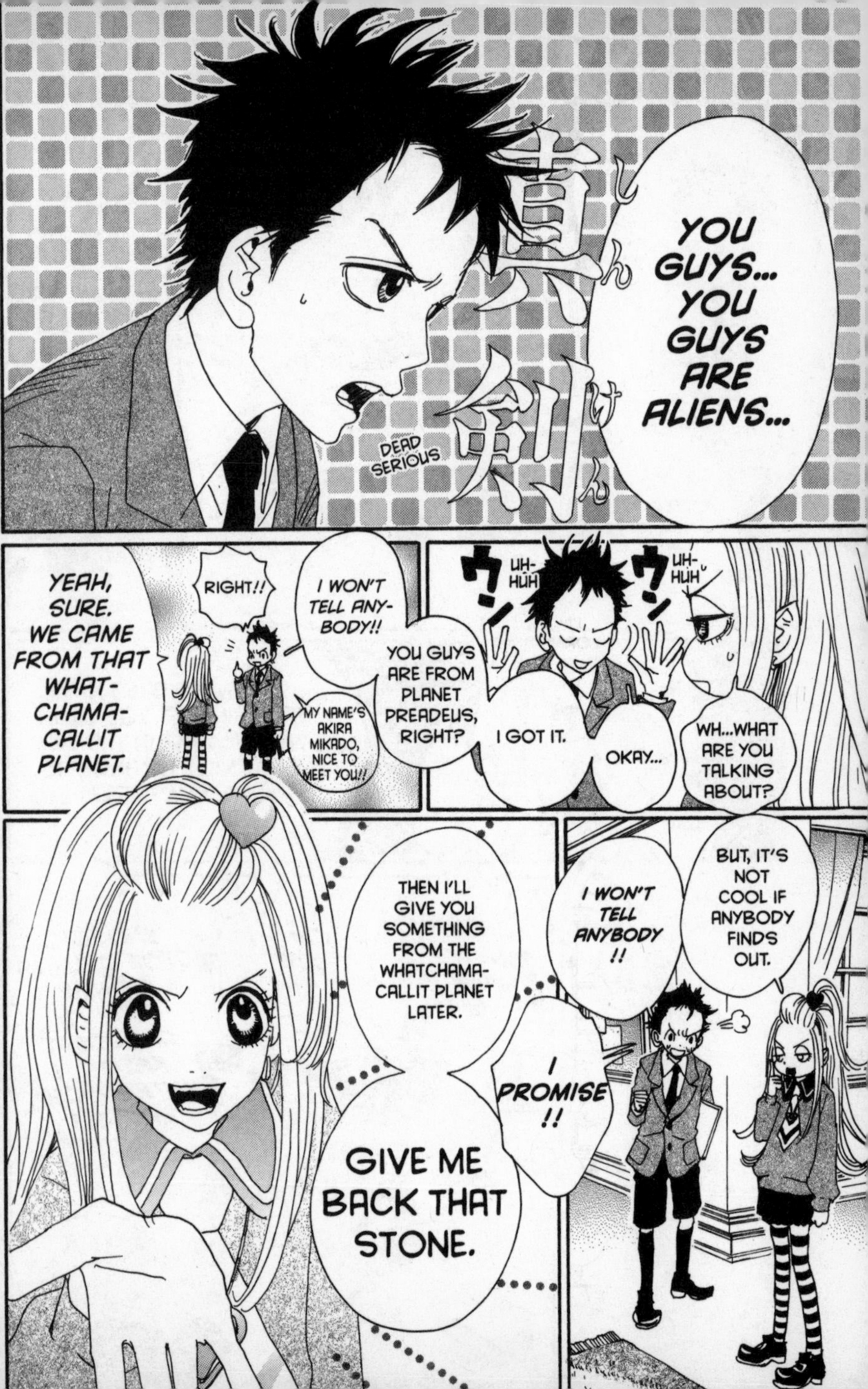

真剣
DEAD SERIOUS
YOU GUYS... YOU GUYS ARE ALIENS...
ウン
UH-HUH
ウン
UH-HUH
WH...WHAT ARE YOU TALKING ABOUT?
OKAY...
I GOT IT.
YOU GUYS ARE FROM PLANET PREADEUS, RIGHT?
I WON'T TELL ANY-BODY!!
RIGHT!!
YEAH, SURE. WE CAME FROM THAT WHAT-CHAMA-CALLIT PLANET.
MY NAME'S AKIRA MIKADO, NICE TO MEET YOU!!
BUT, IT'S NOT COOL IF ANYBODY FINDS OUT.
I WON'T TELL ANYBODY !!
I PROMISE !!
THEN I'LL GIVE YOU SOMETHING FROM THE WHATCHAMA-CALLIT PLANET LATER.
GIVE ME BACK THAT STONE.

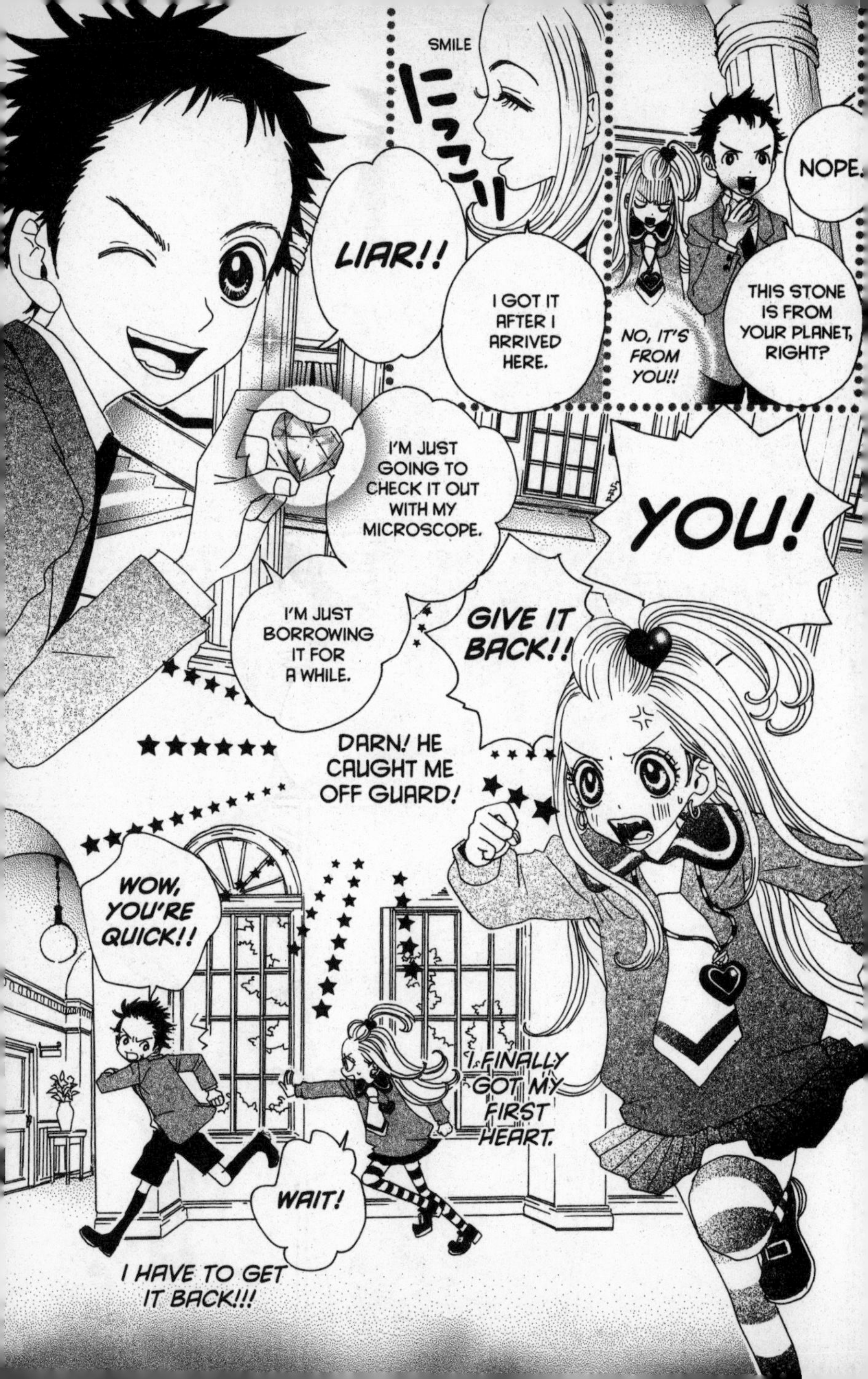
NOPE.
THIS STONE IS FROM YOUR PLANET, RIGHT?
NO, IT'S FROM YOU!!
SMILE
I GOT IT AFTER I ARRIVED HERE.
LIAR!!
YOU!
I'M JUST GOING TO CHECK IT OUT WITH MY MICROSCOPE.
GIVE IT BACK!!
I'M JUST BORROWING IT FOR A WHILE.
DARN! HE CAUGHT ME OFF GUARD!
I FINALLY GOT MY FIRST HEART.
WOW, YOU'RE QUICK!!
WAIT!
I HAVE TO GET IT BACK!!!

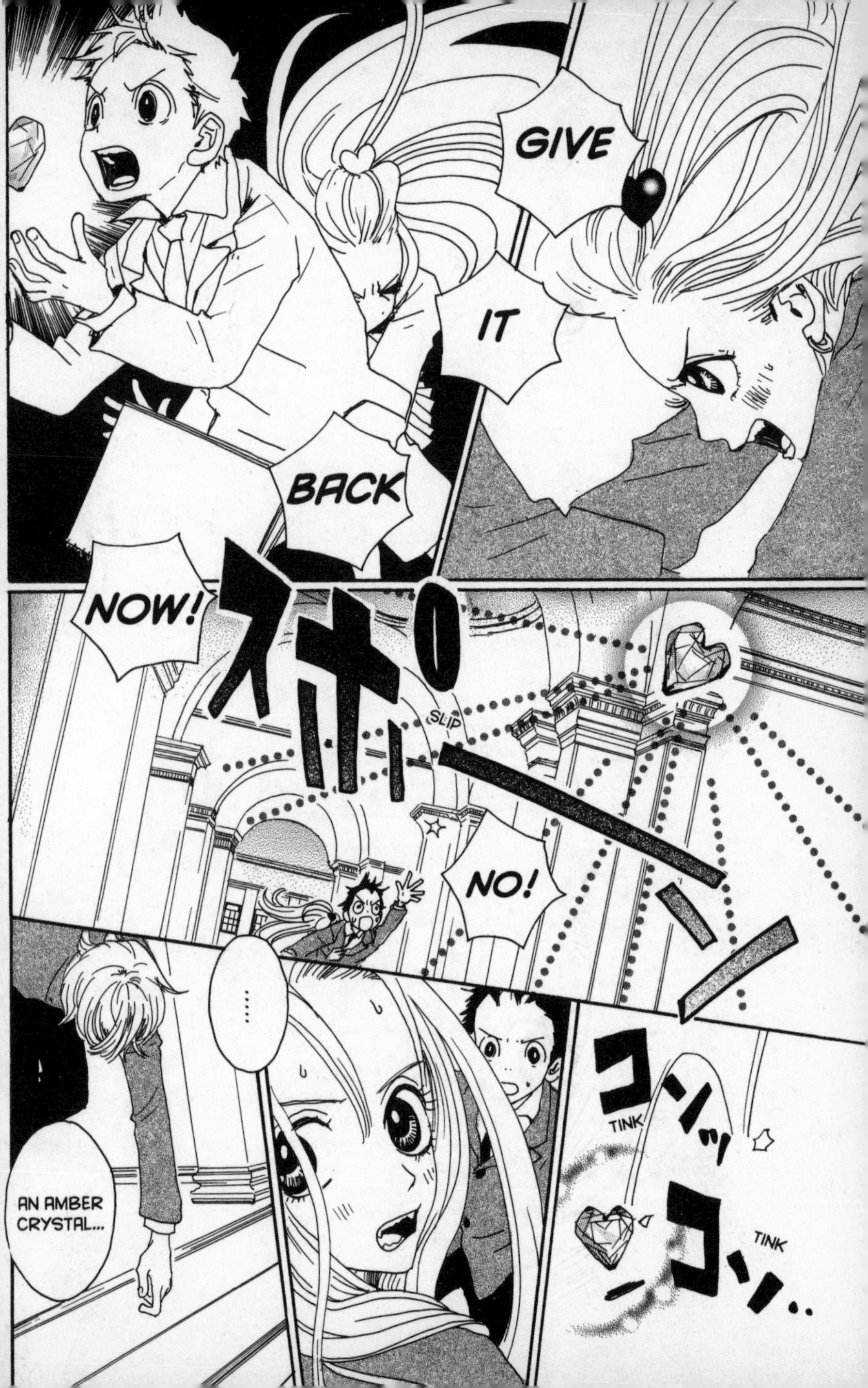
GIVE
IT
BACK
NOW!
SLIP
NO!
TINK
TINK
......
AN AMBER CRYSTAL...

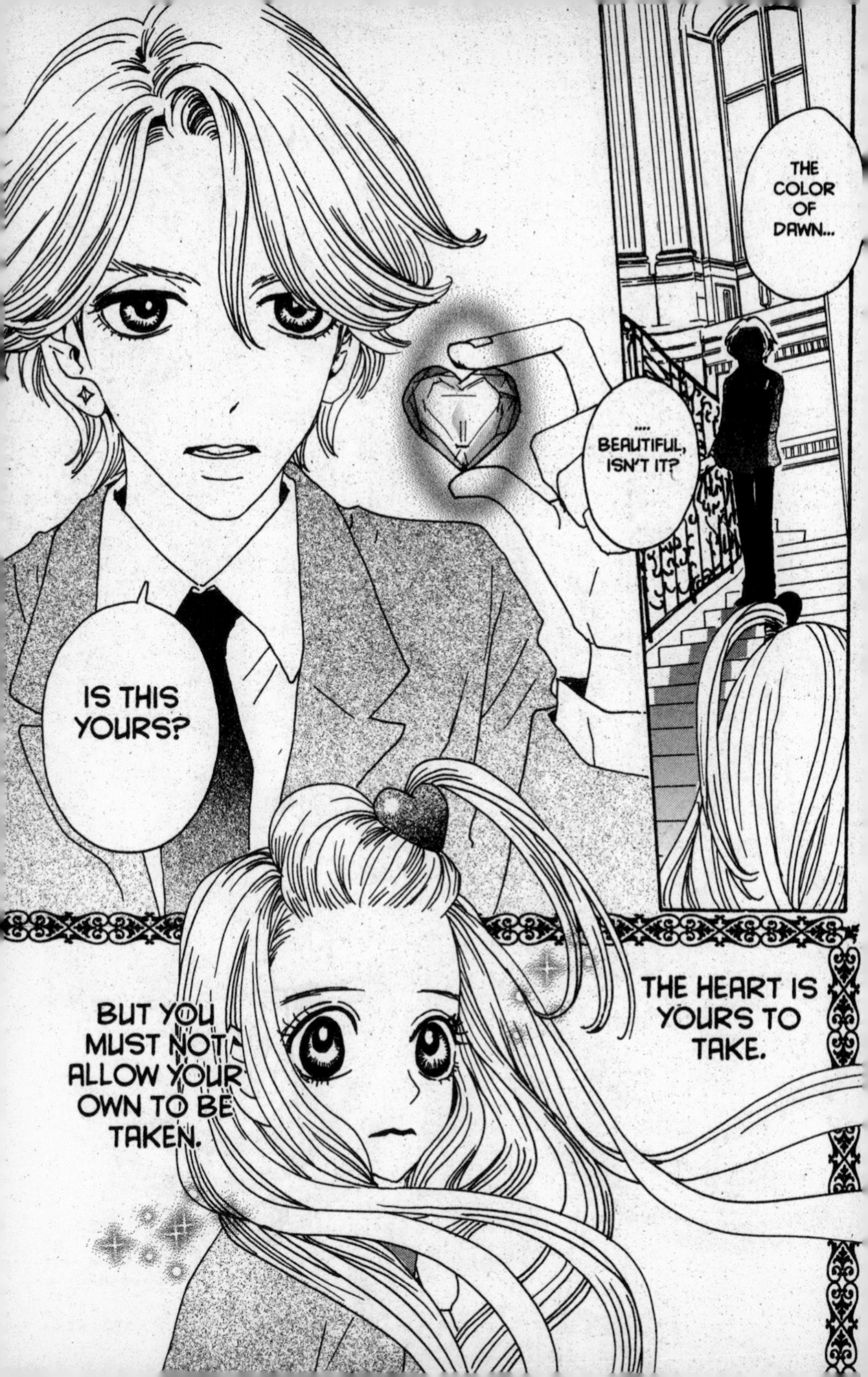
THE COLOR OF DAWN...
.... BEAUTIFUL, ISN'T IT?
IS THIS YOURS?
THE HEART IS YOURS TO TAKE.
BUT YOU MUST NOT ALLOW YOUR OWN TO BE TAKEN.

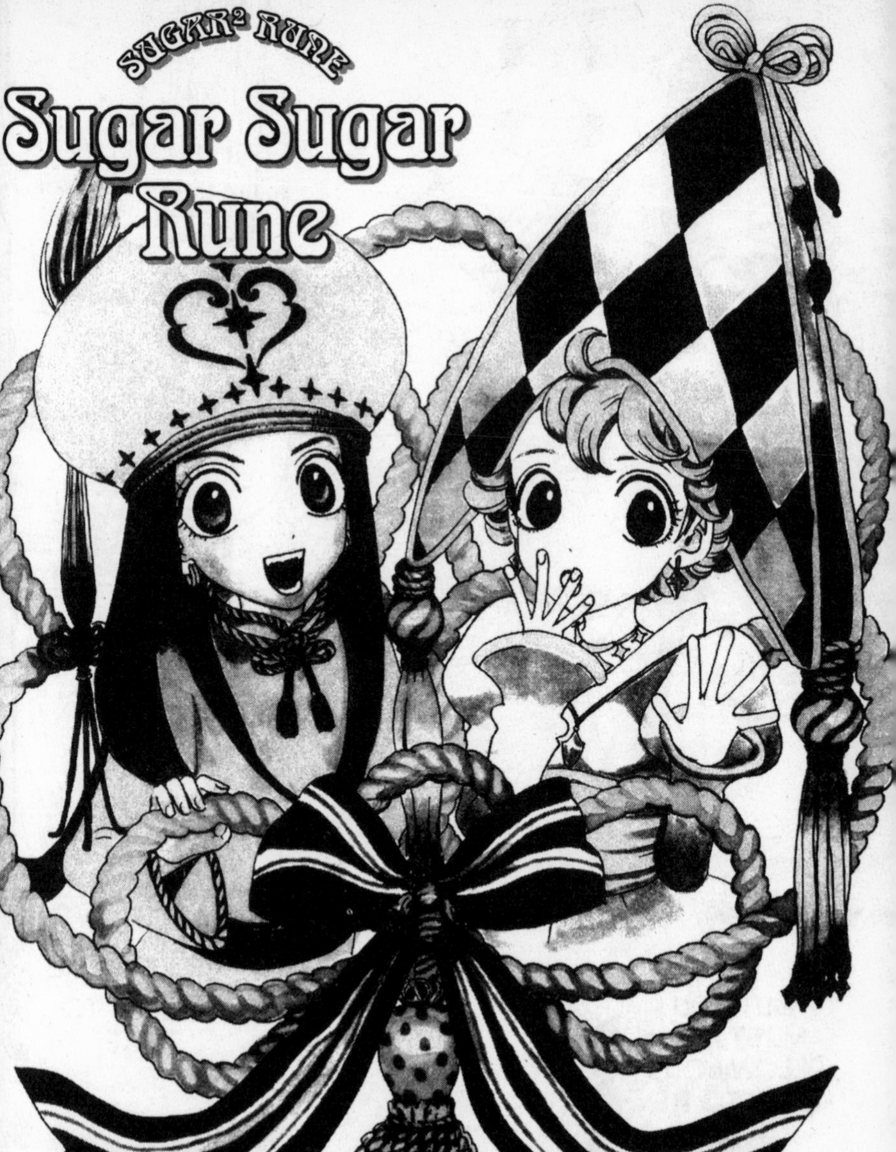
SUGAR² RUNE
Sugar Sugar Rune

RUNE 2
Heart of Chocolat, Heart of Vanilla

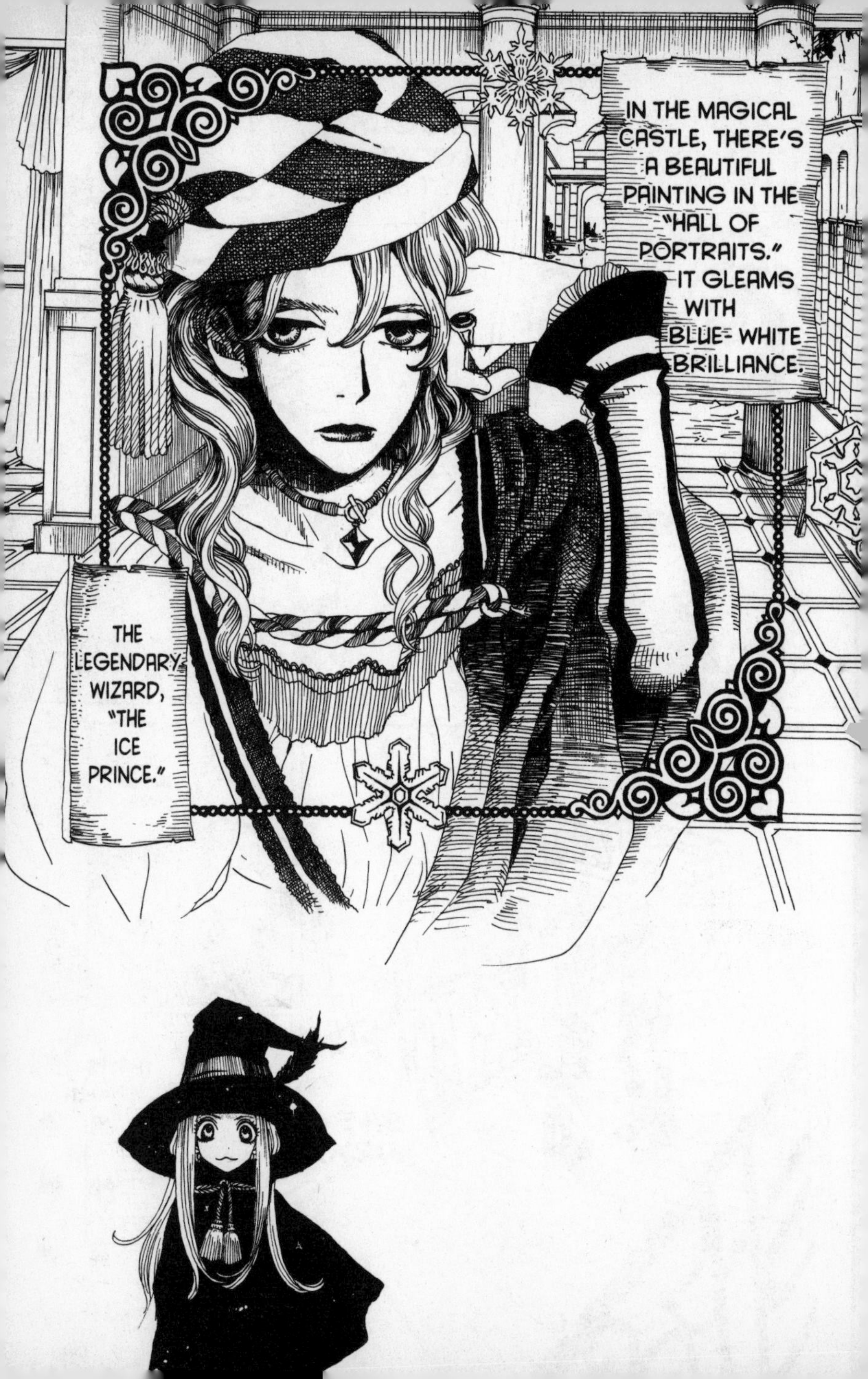
IN THE MAGICAL CASTLE, THERE'S A BEAUTIFUL PAINTING IN THE "HALL OF PORTRAITS."
IT GLEAMS WITH BLUE-WHITE BRILLIANCE.
THE LEGENDARY WIZARD, "THE ICE PRINCE."

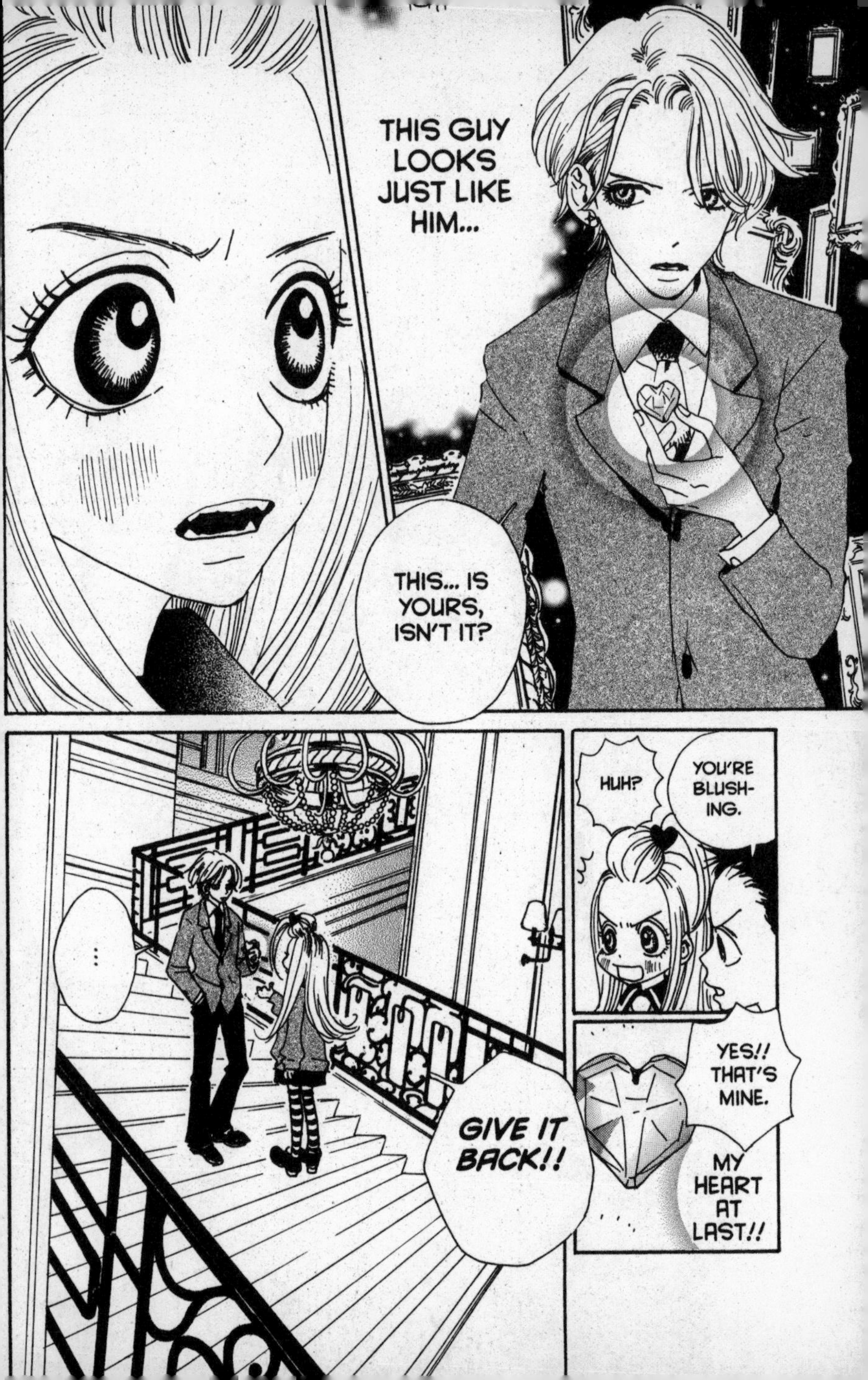
THIS GUY LOOKS JUST LIKE HIM...
THIS... IS YOURS, ISN'T IT?
YOU'RE BLUSH-ING.
HUH?
YES!! THAT'S MINE.
MY HEART AT LAST!!
GIVE IT BACK!!
...

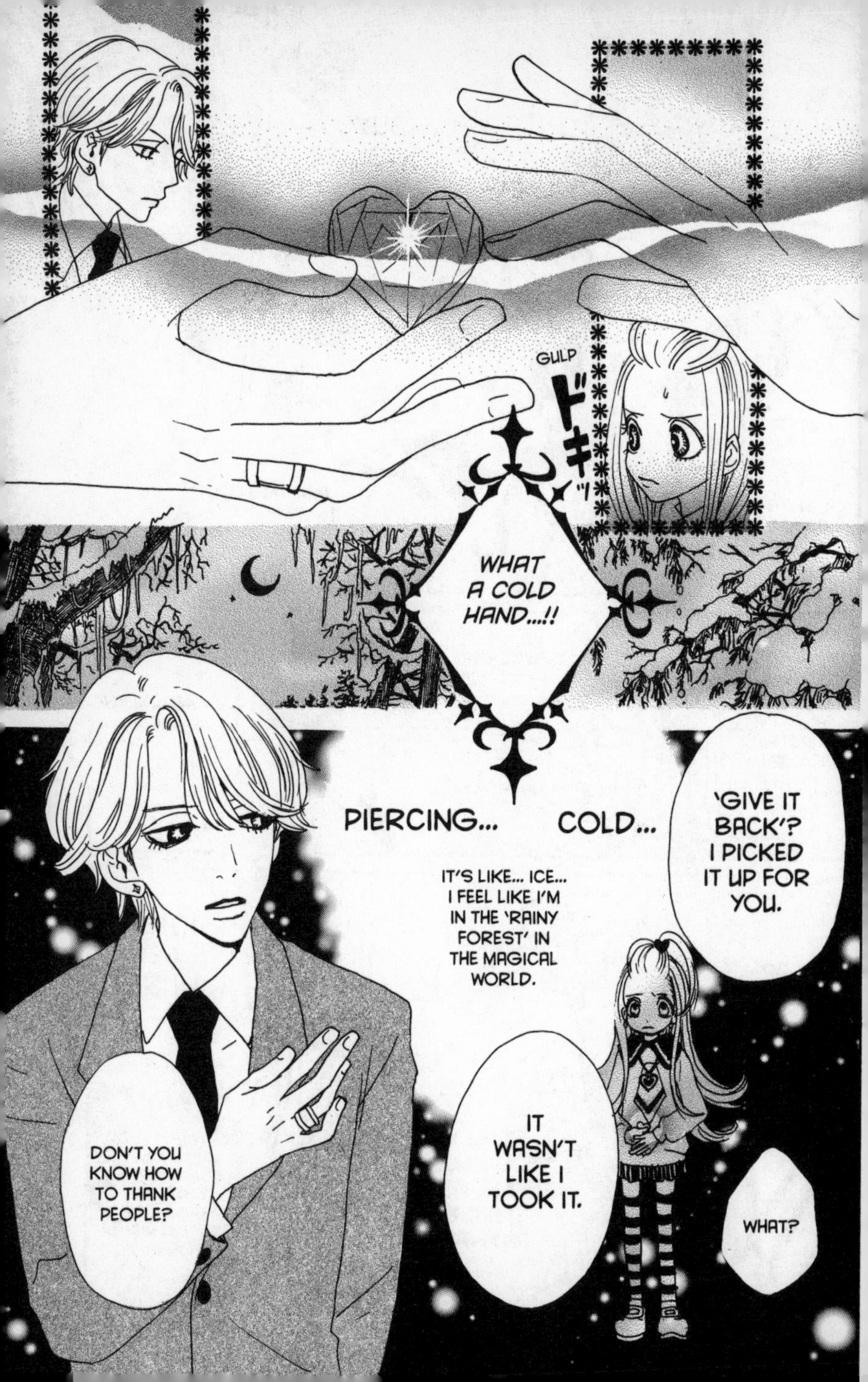
GULP
ドキッ
WHAT A COLD HAND...!!
PIERCING... COLD...
'GIVE IT BACK'? I PICKED IT UP FOR YOU.
IT'S LIKE... ICE... I FEEL LIKE I'M IN THE 'RAINY FOREST' IN THE MAGICAL WORLD.
WHAT?
IT WASN'T LIKE I TOOK IT.
DON'T YOU KNOW HOW TO THANK PEOPLE?

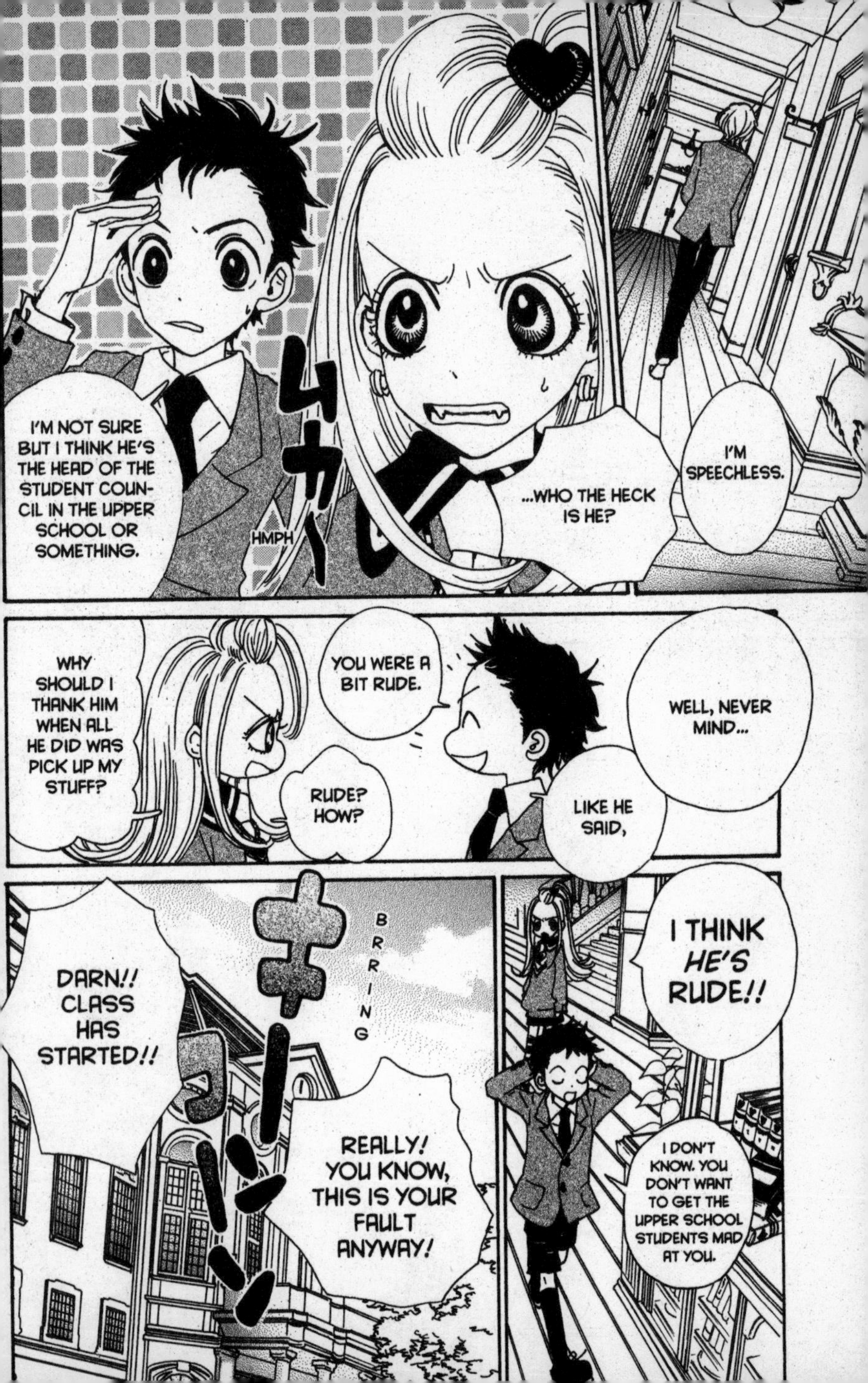
I'M SPEECHLESS.
...WHO THE HECK IS HE?
HMPH
I'M NOT SURE BUT I THINK HE'S THE HEAD OF THE STUDENT COUNCIL IN THE UPPER SCHOOL OR SOMETHING.
WELL, NEVER MIND...
LIKE HE SAID,
YOU WERE A BIT RUDE.
RUDE? HOW?
WHY SHOULD I THANK HIM WHEN ALL HE DID WAS PICK UP MY STUFF?
I THINK *HE'S* RUDE!!
I DON'T KNOW. YOU DON'T WANT TO GET THE UPPER SCHOOL STUDENTS MAD AT YOU.
BRRING
DARN!! CLASS HAS STARTED!!
REALLY! YOU KNOW, THIS IS YOUR FAULT ANYWAY!

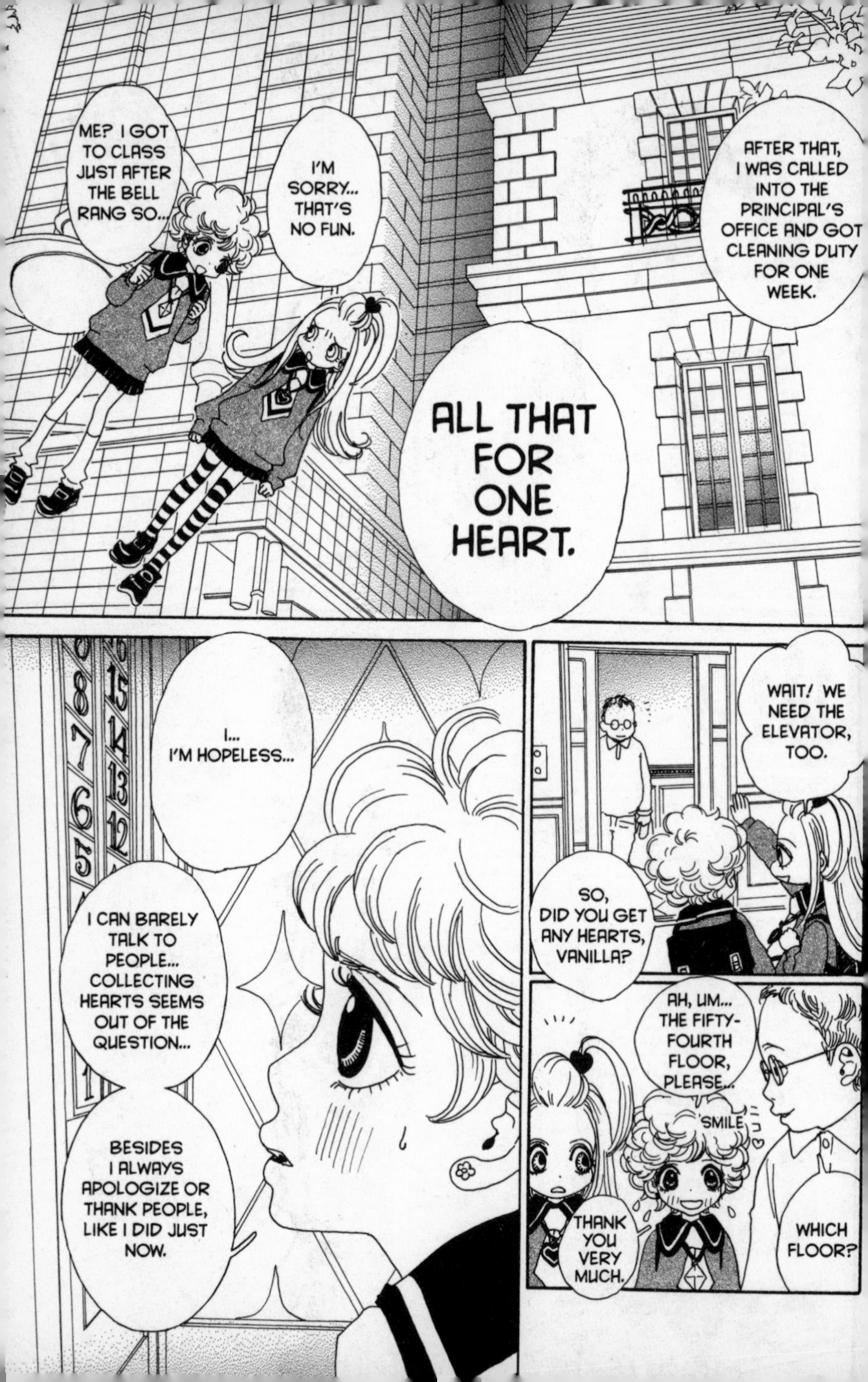
AFTER THAT, I WAS CALLED INTO THE PRINCIPAL'S OFFICE AND GOT CLEANING DUTY FOR ONE WEEK.
ALL THAT FOR ONE HEART.
I'M SORRY... THAT'S NO FUN.
ME? I GOT TO CLASS JUST AFTER THE BELL RANG SO...
WAIT! WE NEED THE ELEVATOR, TOO.
SO, DID YOU GET ANY HEARTS, VANILLA?
AH, UM... THE FIFTY-FOURTH FLOOR, PLEASE...
SMILE
WHICH FLOOR?
THANK YOU VERY MUCH.
I... I'M HOPELESS...
I CAN BARELY TALK TO PEOPLE... COLLECTING HEARTS SEEMS OUT OF THE QUESTION...
BESIDES I ALWAYS APOLOGIZE OR THANK PEOPLE, LIKE I DID JUST NOW.

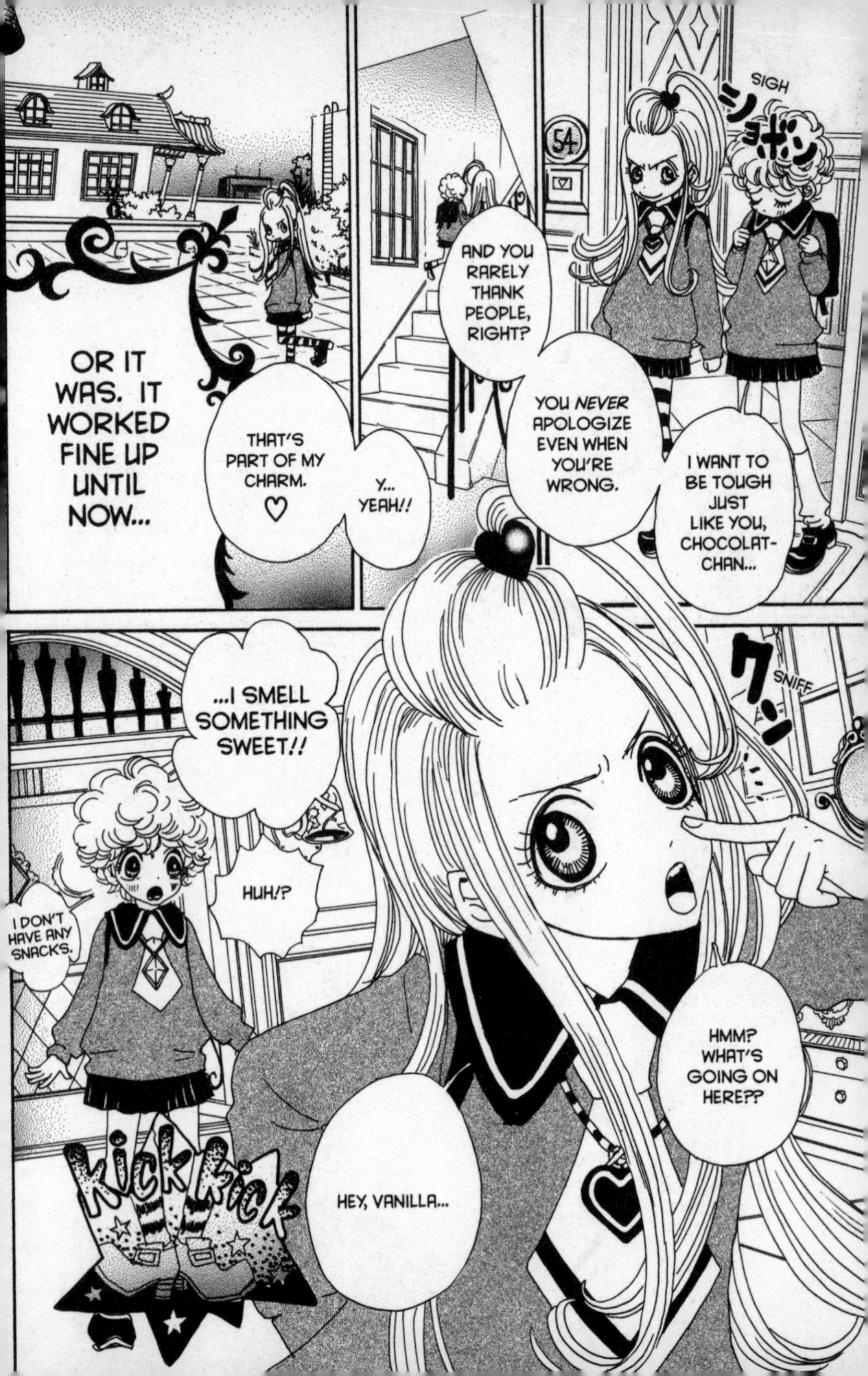
SIGH
ショボン
I WANT TO BE TOUGH JUST LIKE YOU, CHOCOLAT-CHAN...
YOU NEVER APOLOGIZE EVEN WHEN YOU'RE WRONG.
AND YOU RARELY THANK PEOPLE, RIGHT?
Y... YEAH!!
THAT'S PART OF MY CHARM. ♡
OR IT WAS. IT WORKED FINE UP UNTIL NOW...
クン
SNIFF
...I SMELL SOMETHING SWEET!!
HUH!?
I DON'T HAVE ANY SNACKS.
HMM? WHAT'S GOING ON HERE??
HEY, VANILLA...
KICK KICK

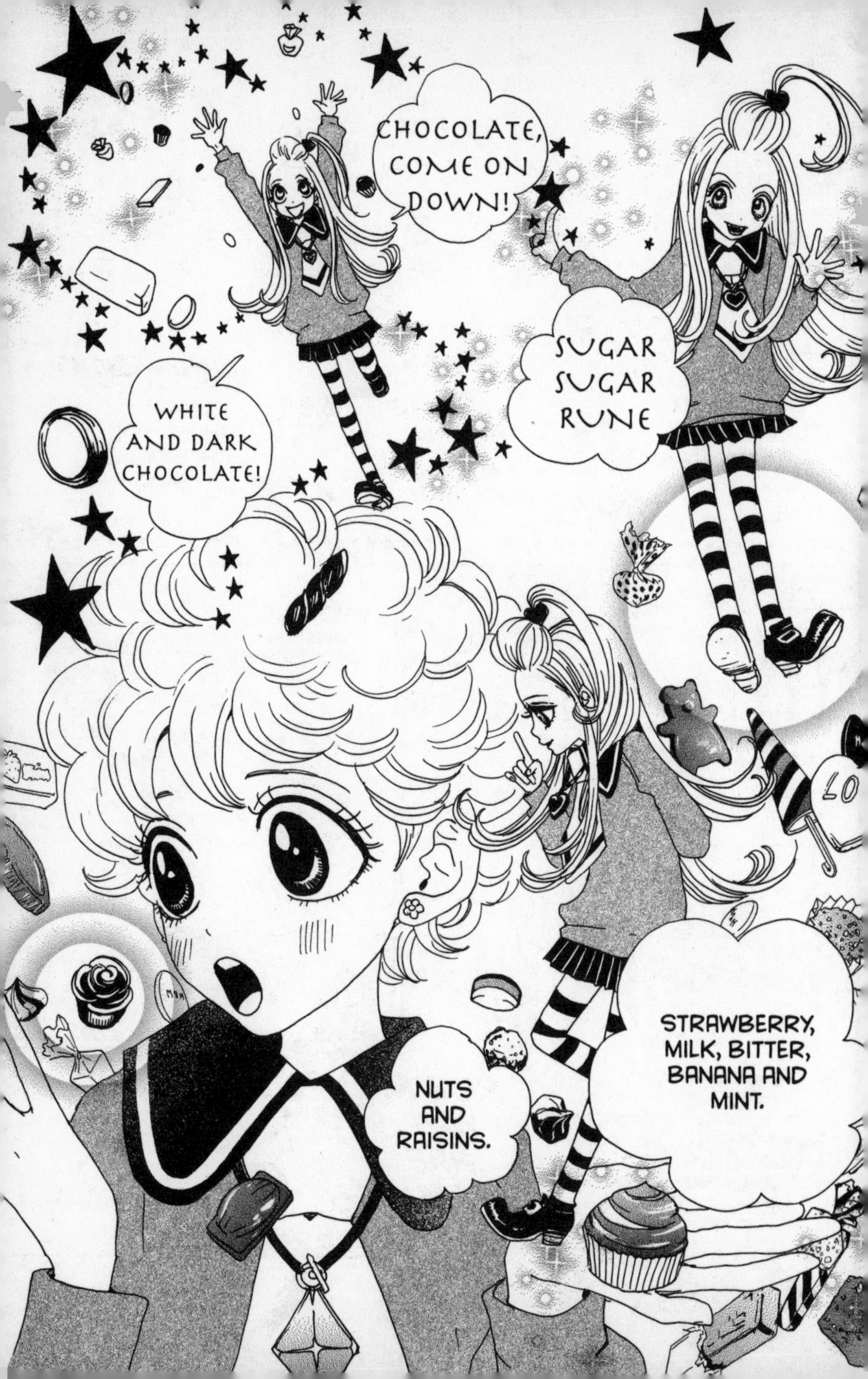
CHOCOLATE, COME ON DOWN!
SUGAR SUGAR RUNE
WHITE AND DARK CHOCOLATE!
STRAWBERRY, MILK, BITTER, BANANA AND MINT.
NUTS AND RAISINS.

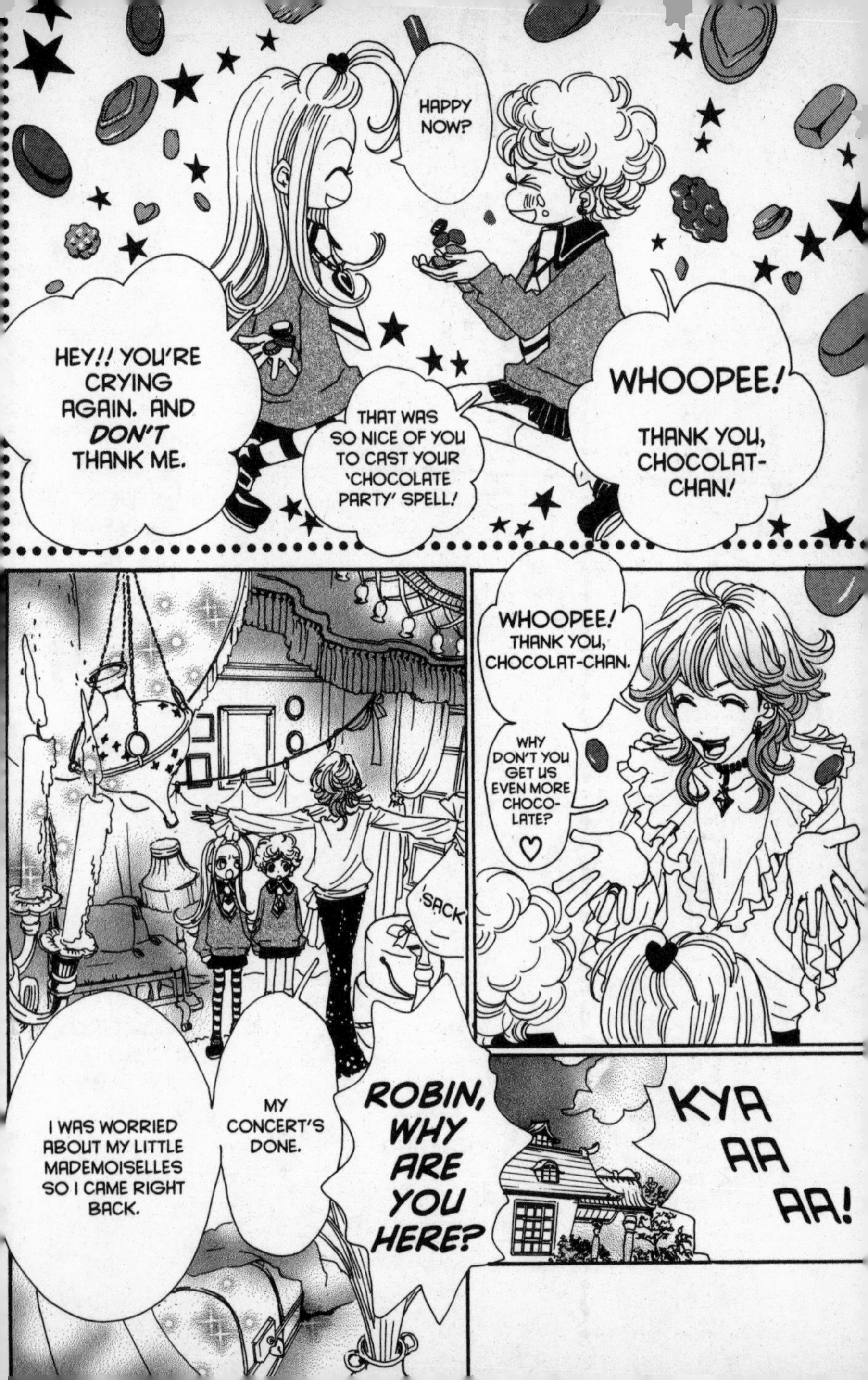
HAPPY NOW?
WHOOPEE! THANK YOU, CHOCOLAT-CHAN!
THAT WAS SO NICE OF YOU TO CAST YOUR 'CHOCOLATE PARTY' SPELL!
HEY!! YOU'RE CRYING AGAIN. AND DON'T THANK ME.
WHOOPEE! THANK YOU, CHOCOLAT-CHAN.
WHY DON'T YOU GET US EVEN MORE CHOCOLATE? ♡
KYAAAAAA!
ROBIN, WHY ARE YOU HERE?
SACK
MY CONCERT'S DONE.
I WAS WORRIED ABOUT MY LITTLE MADEMOISELLES SO I CAME RIGHT BACK.

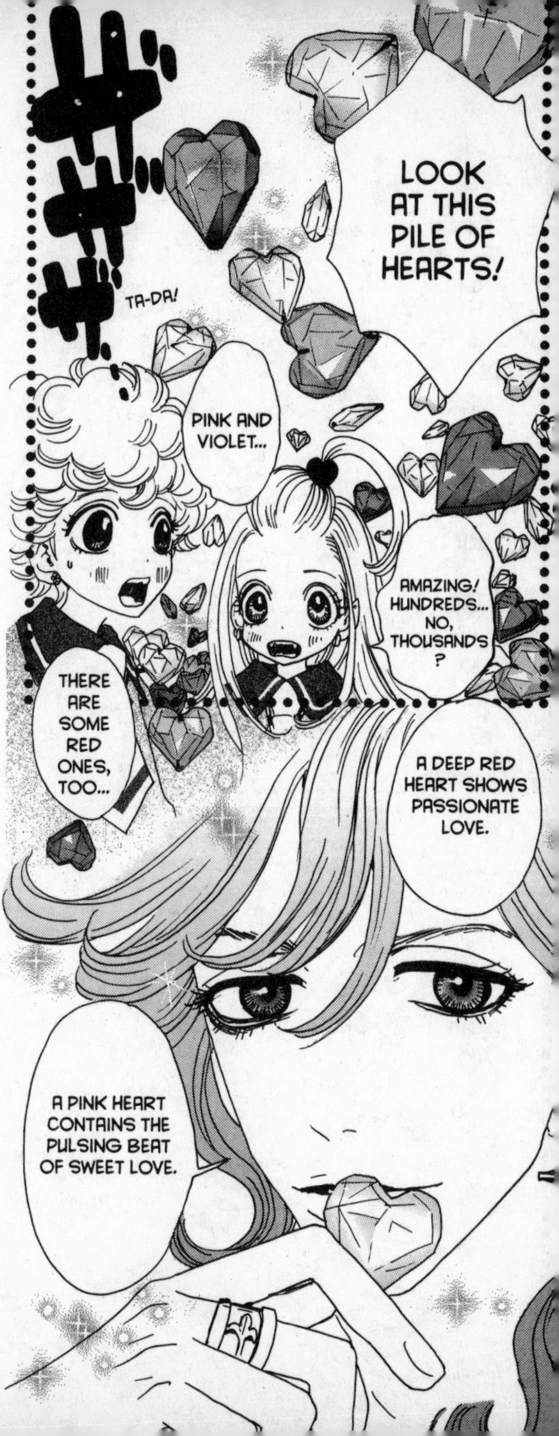
LOOK AT THIS PILE OF HEARTS!
TA-DA!
PINK AND VIOLET...
AMAZING! HUNDREDS... NO, THOUSANDS?
THERE ARE SOME RED ONES, TOO...
A DEEP RED HEART SHOWS PASSIONATE LOVE.
A PINK HEART CONTAINS THE PULSING BEAT OF SWEET LOVE.

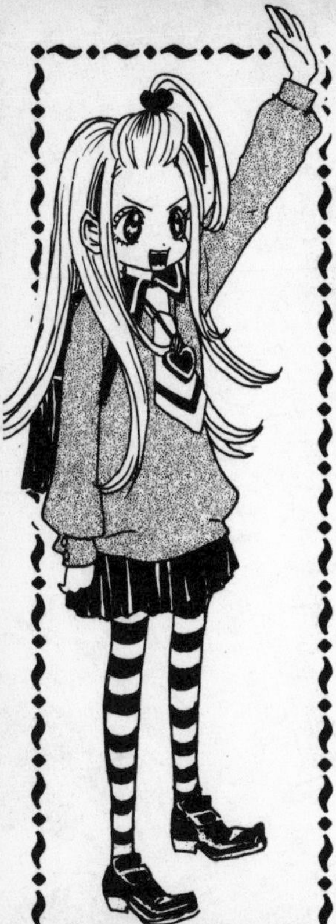

CHOCOLAT MEILLEURE (CHOCOLAT KATO)

HEIGHT: 153CM

AGE: 10 HUMAN YEARS OLD

HOBBY: COLLECTING FROGS, PRETENDING TO BE A SPIDER.

SPECIALTY: CAN DEFEAT A GIANT SPIDER BY HERSELF.

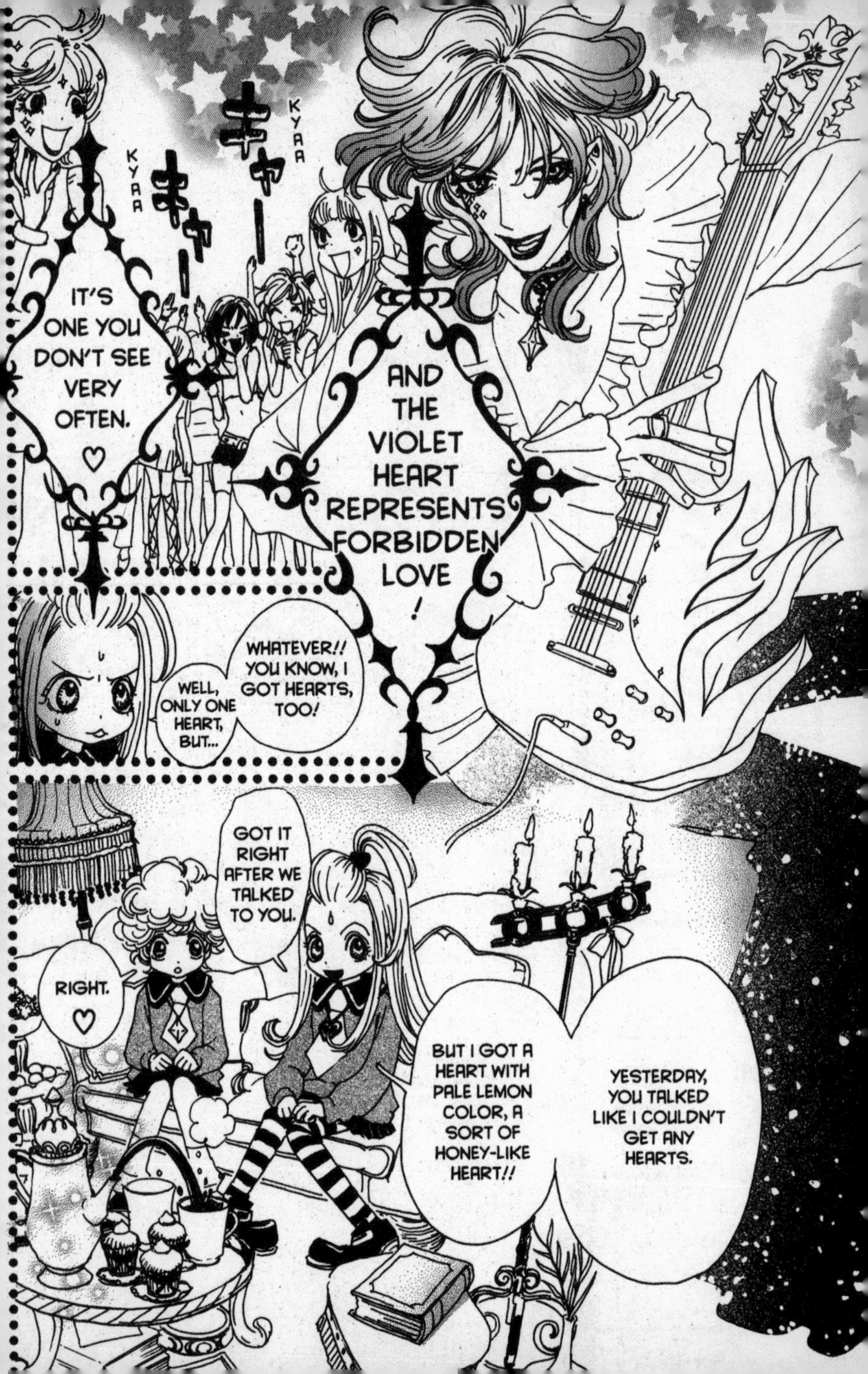
AND THE VIOLET HEART REPRESENTS FORBIDDEN LOVE!
キャー
KYAA
キャー
KYAA
IT'S ONE YOU DON'T SEE VERY OFTEN. ♡
WHATEVER!! YOU KNOW, I GOT HEARTS, TOO!
WELL, ONLY ONE HEART, BUT...
YESTERDAY, YOU TALKED LIKE I COULDN'T GET ANY HEARTS.
BUT I GOT A HEART WITH PALE LEMON COLOR, A SORT OF HONEY-LIKE HEART!!
GOT IT RIGHT AFTER WE TALKED TO YOU.
RIGHT. ♡

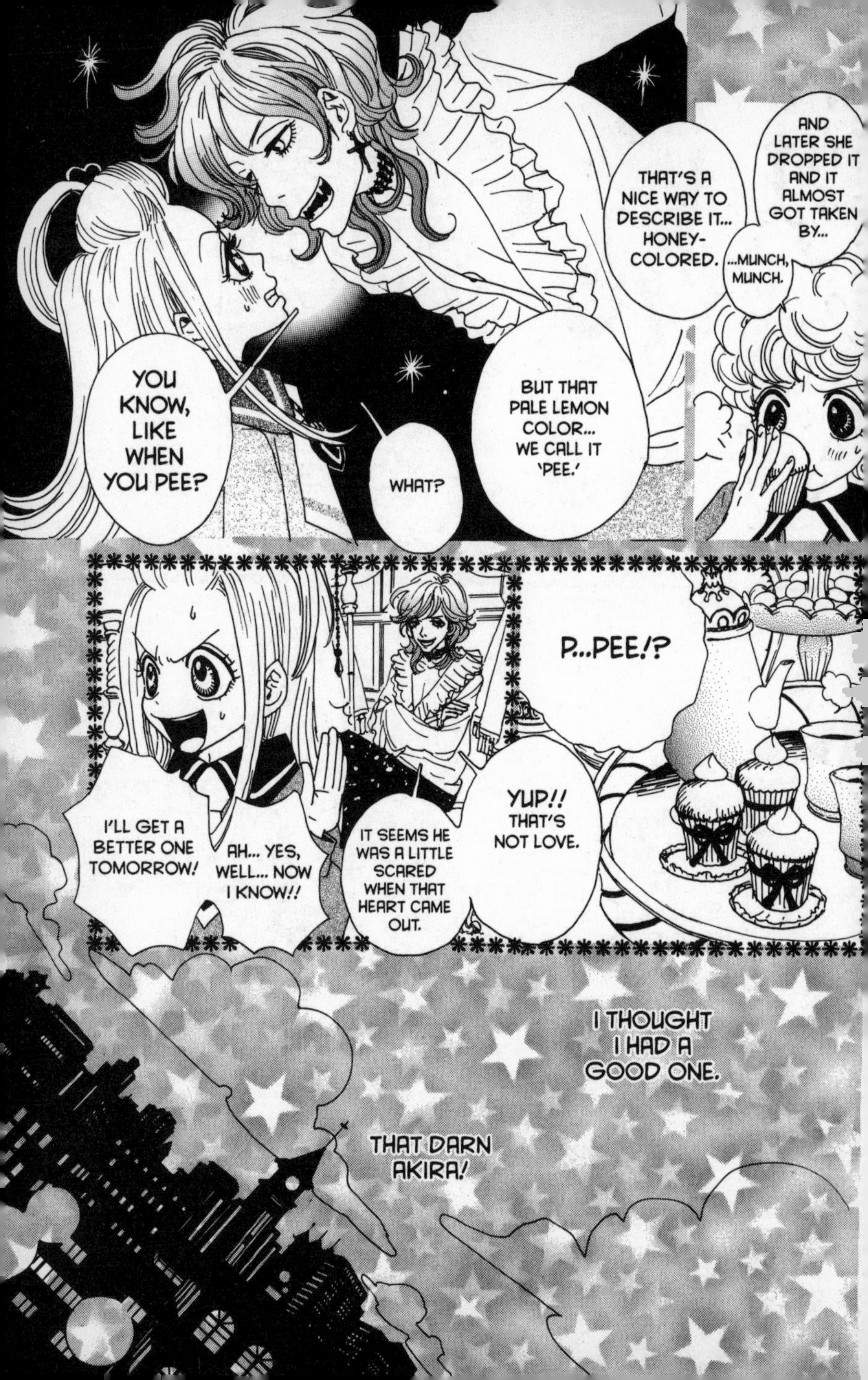
AND LATER SHE DROPPED IT AND IT ALMOST GOT TAKEN BY...
...MUNCH, MUNCH.
THAT'S A NICE WAY TO DESCRIBE IT... HONEY-COLORED.
BUT THAT PALE LEMON COLOR... WE CALL IT 'PEE.'
WHAT?
YOU KNOW, LIKE WHEN YOU PEE?
P...PEE!?
YUP!! THAT'S NOT LOVE.
IT SEEMS HE WAS A LITTLE SCARED WHEN THAT HEART CAME OUT.
AH... YES, WELL... NOW I KNOW!!
I'LL GET A BETTER ONE TOMORROW!
I THOUGHT I HAD A GOOD ONE.
THAT DARN AKIRA!

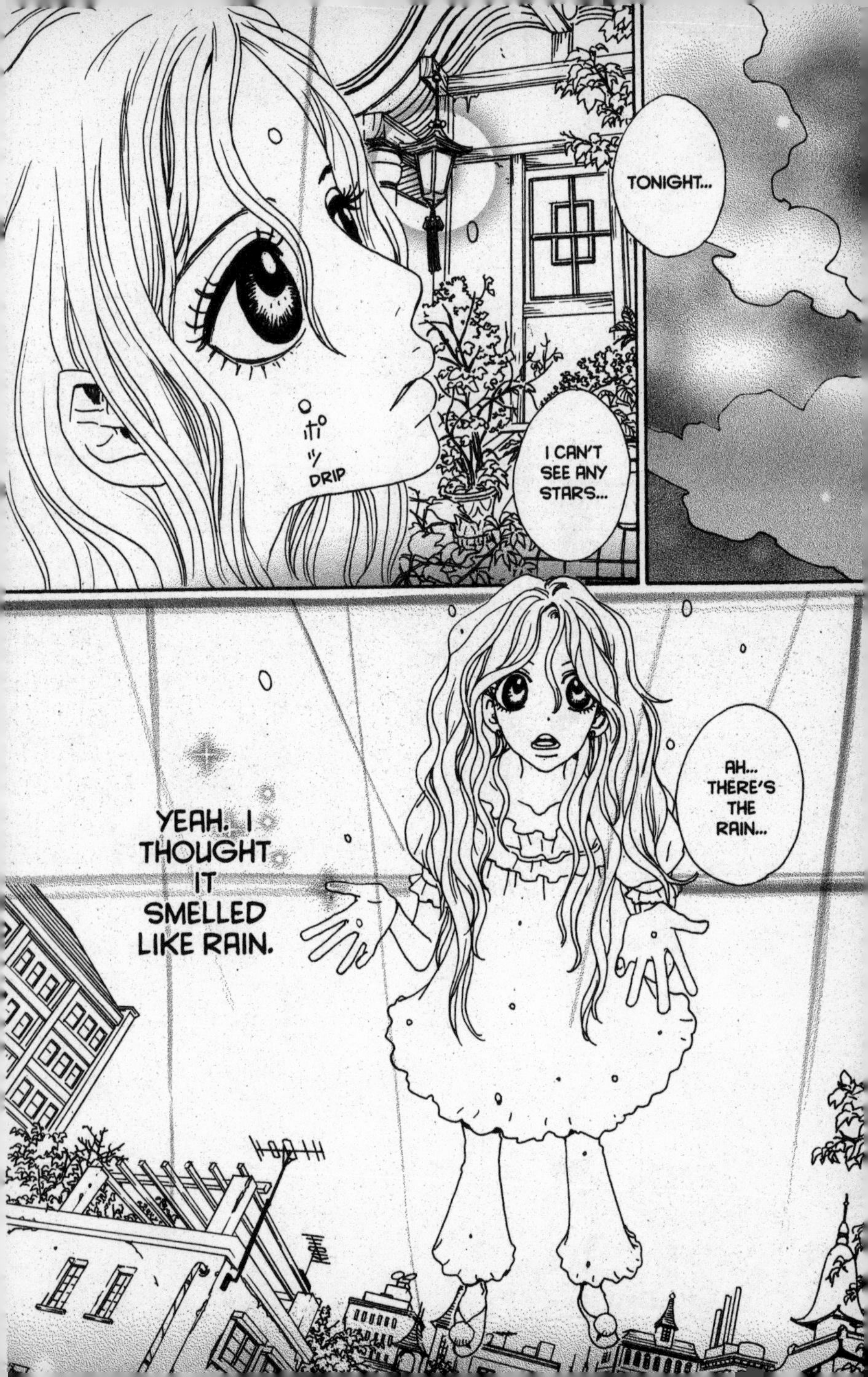
TONIGHT...
I CAN'T SEE ANY STARS...
DRIP
AH... THERE'S THE RAIN...
YEAH. I THOUGHT IT SMELLED LIKE RAIN.

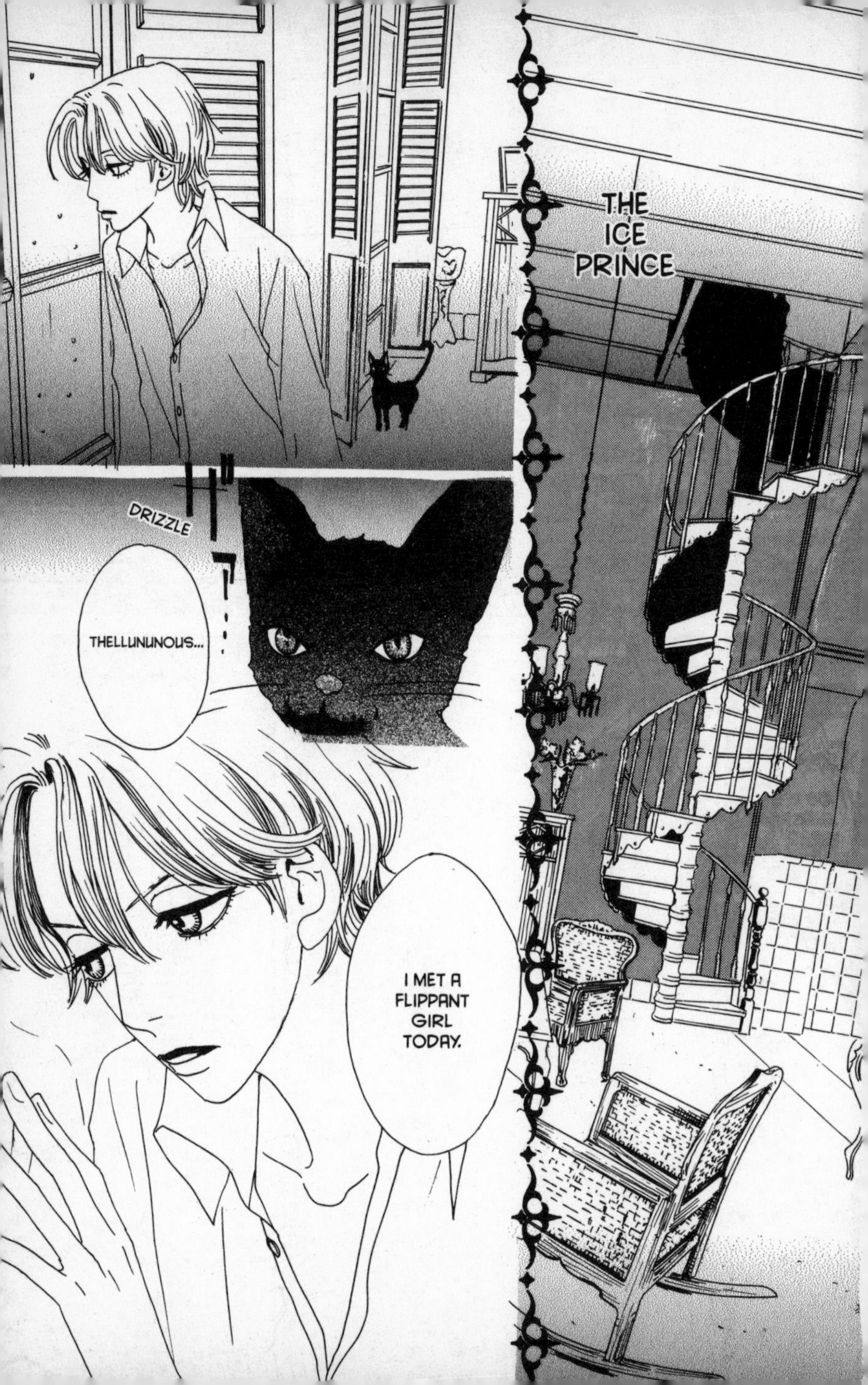
THE ICE PRINCE
DRIZZLE
ザァ…
THELLUNUNOUS...
I MET A FLIPPANT GIRL TODAY.

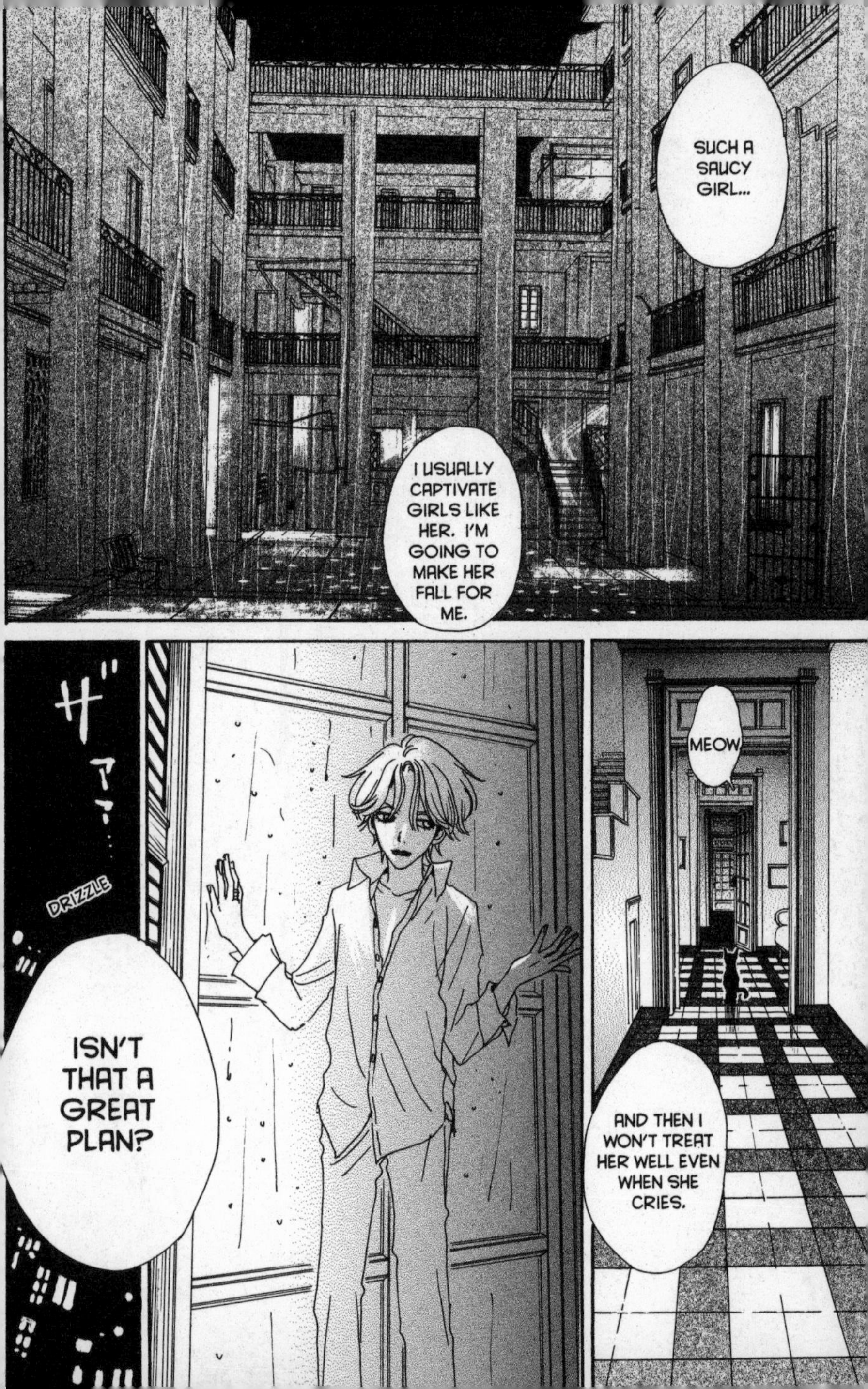
SUCH A SAUCY GIRL...
I USUALLY CAPTIVATE GIRLS LIKE HER. I'M GOING TO MAKE HER FALL FOR ME.
MEOW
AND THEN I WON'T TREAT HER WELL EVEN WHEN SHE CRIES.
DRIZZLE
ISN'T THAT A GREAT PLAN?

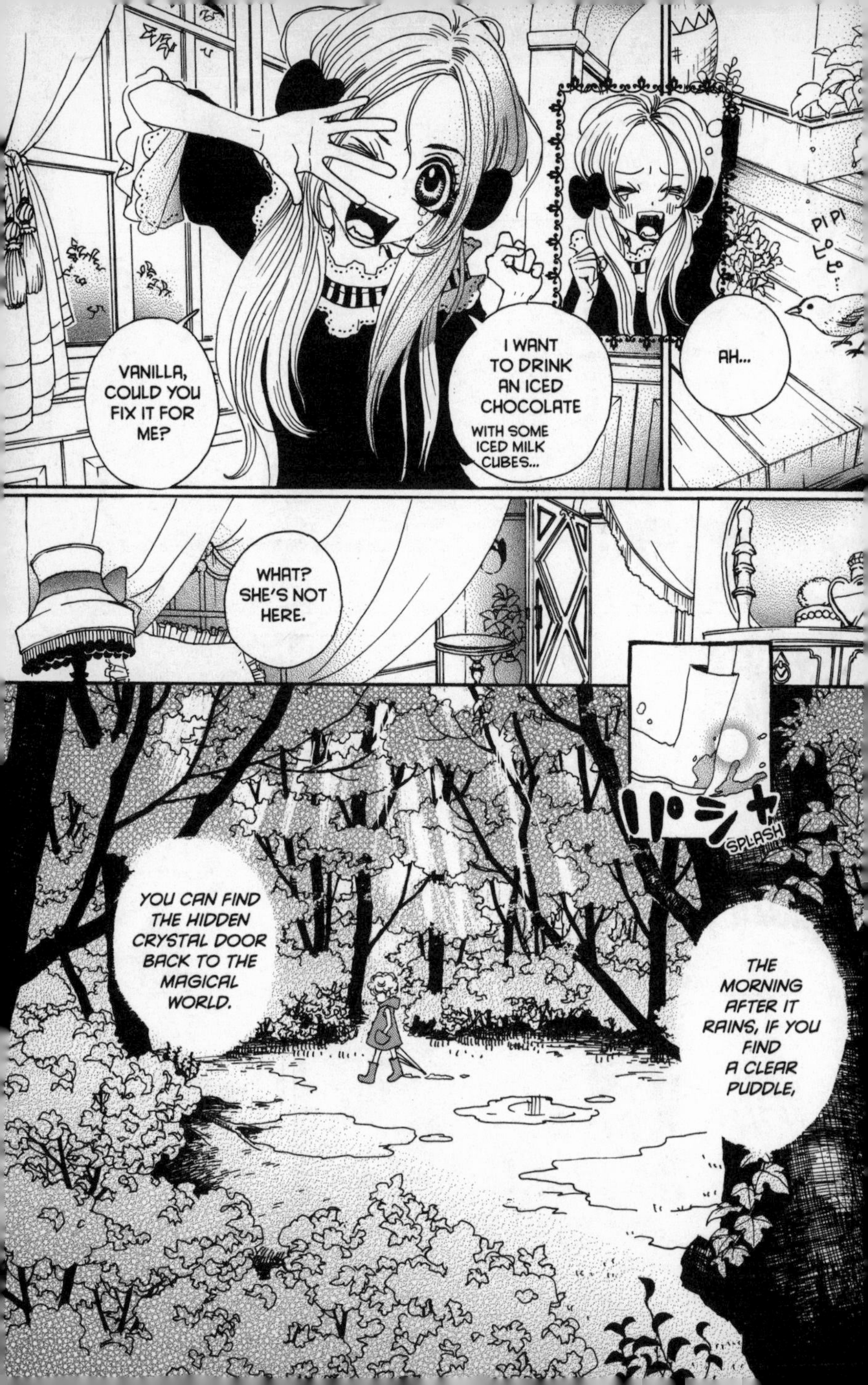
PI PI
ピピ…
AH...
I WANT TO DRINK AN ICED CHOCOLATE
WITH SOME ICED MILK CUBES...
VANILLA, COULD YOU FIX IT FOR ME?
WHAT? SHE'S NOT HERE.
パシャ
SPLASH
THE MORNING AFTER IT RAINS, IF YOU FIND A CLEAR PUDDLE,
YOU CAN FIND THE HIDDEN CRYSTAL DOOR BACK TO THE MAGICAL WORLD.

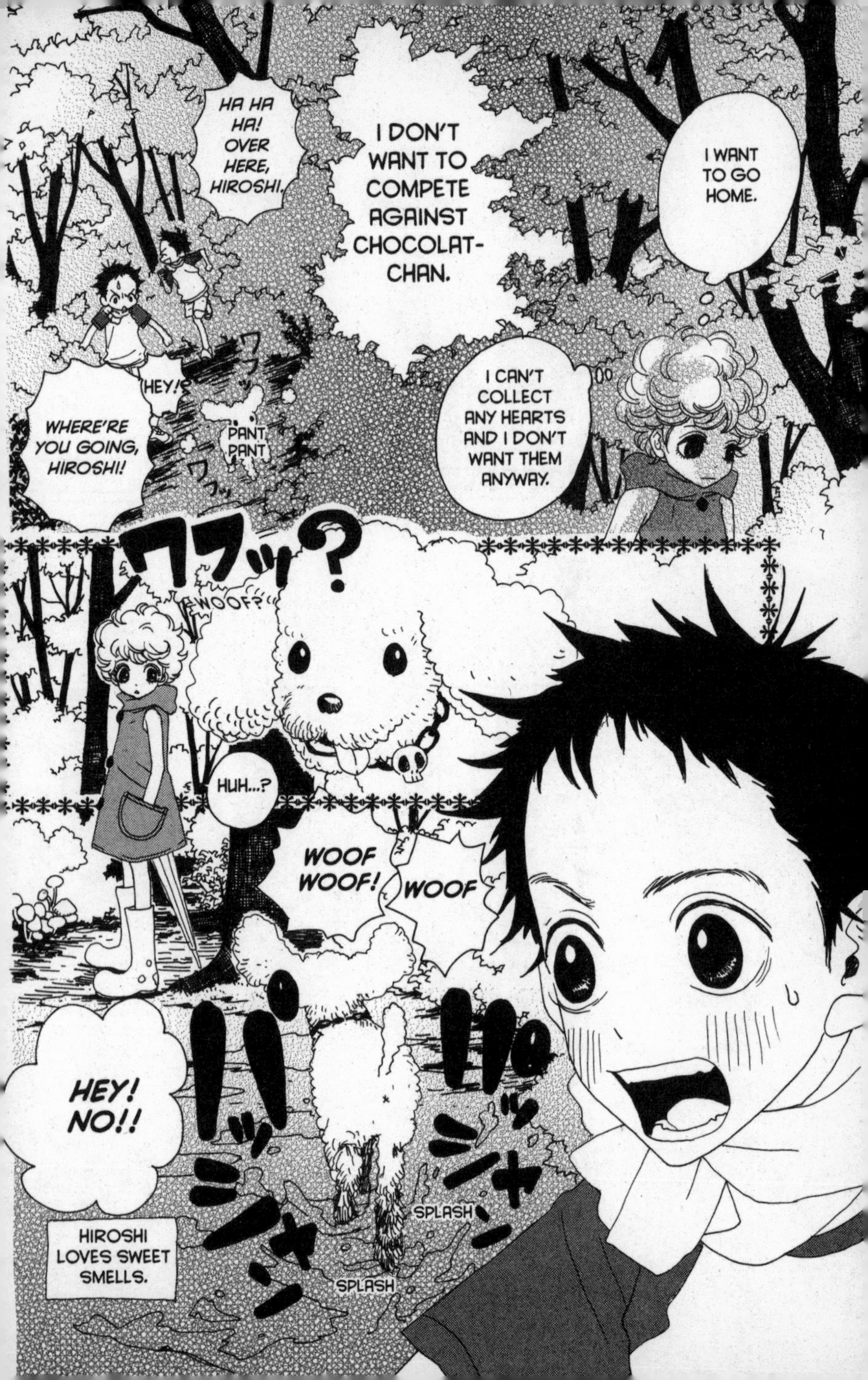
I WANT TO GO HOME.
I CAN'T COLLECT ANY HEARTS AND I DON'T WANT THEM ANYWAY.
I DON'T WANT TO COMPETE AGAINST CHOCOLAT-CHAN.
HA HA HA! OVER HERE, HIROSHI.
HEY!
PANT PANT
WHERE'RE YOU GOING, HIROSHI!
ワフッ?
WOOF?
HUH...?
WOOF WOOF!
WOOF
HEY! NO!!
SPLASH
SPLASH
HIROSHI LOVES SWEET SMELLS.

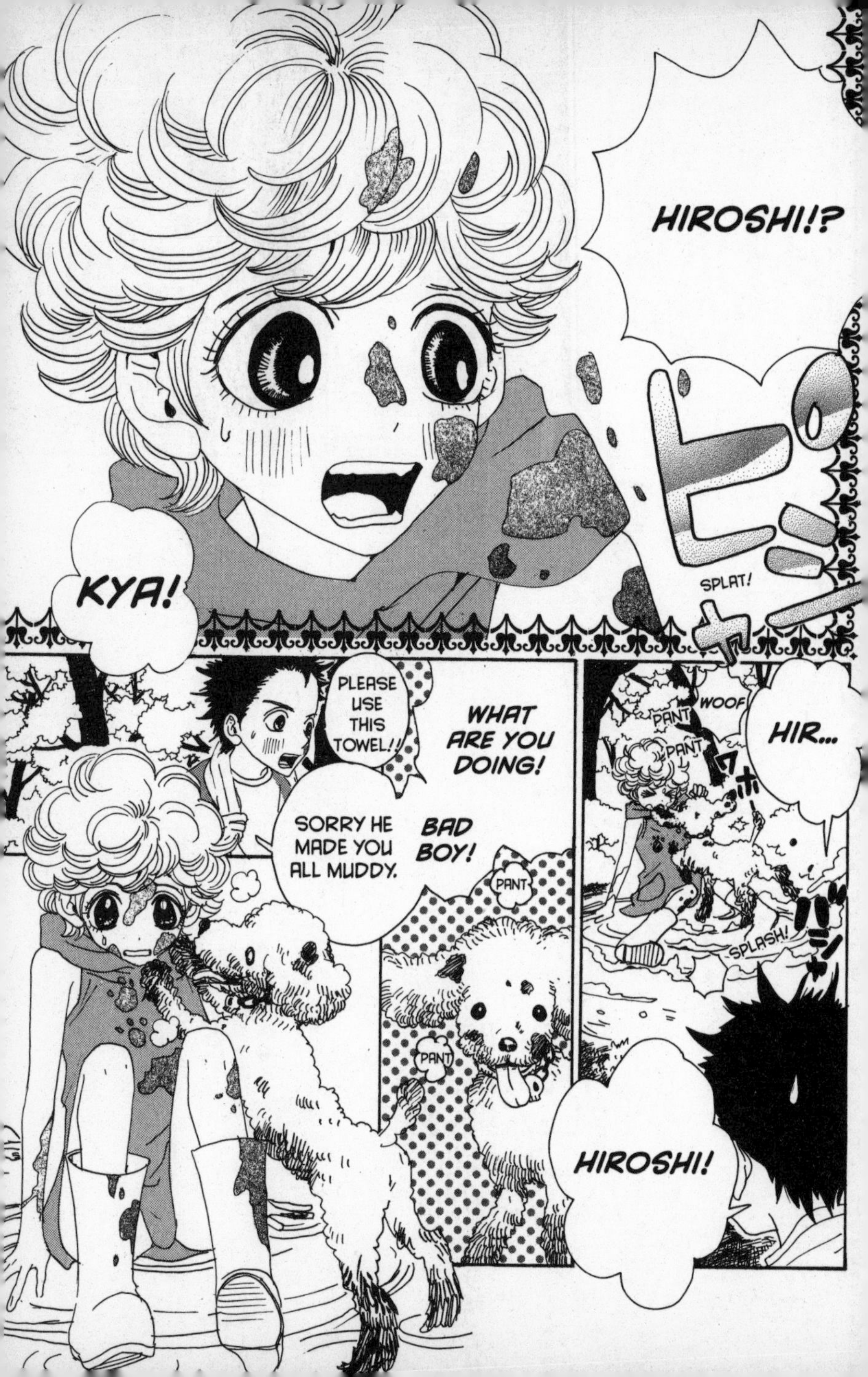
HIROSHI!?
SPLAT!
KYA!
HIR...
WOOF
PANT
PANT
SPLASH!
HIROSHI!
WHAT ARE YOU DOING!
BAD BOY!
PANT
PANT
PLEASE USE THIS TOWEL!!
SORRY HE MADE YOU ALL MUDDY.

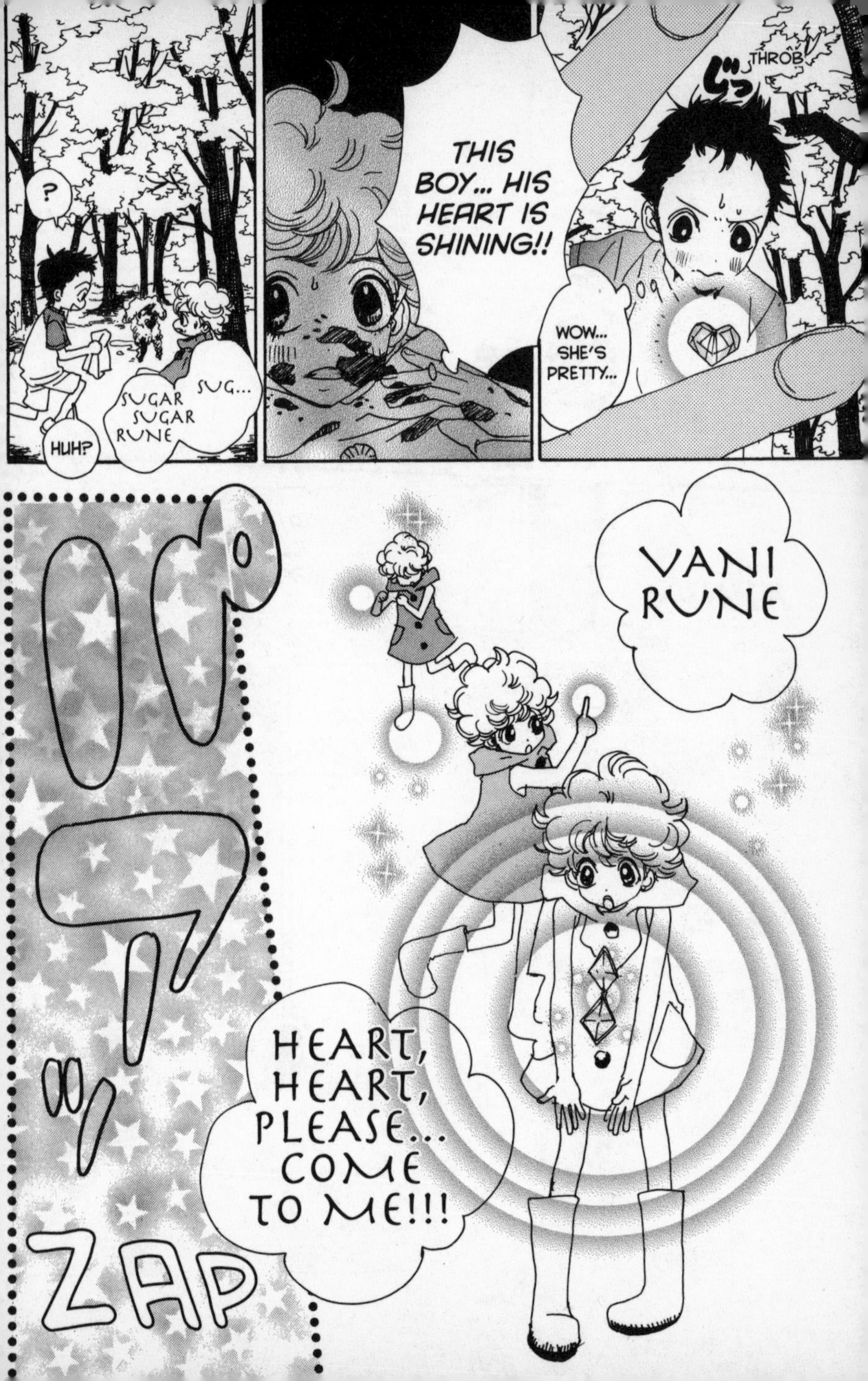
THROB
WOW... SHE'S PRETTY...
THIS BOY... HIS HEART IS SHINING!!
?
SUG...
SUGAR SUGAR RUNE
HUH?
VANI RUNE
HEART, HEART, PLEASE... COME TO ME!!!
ZAP

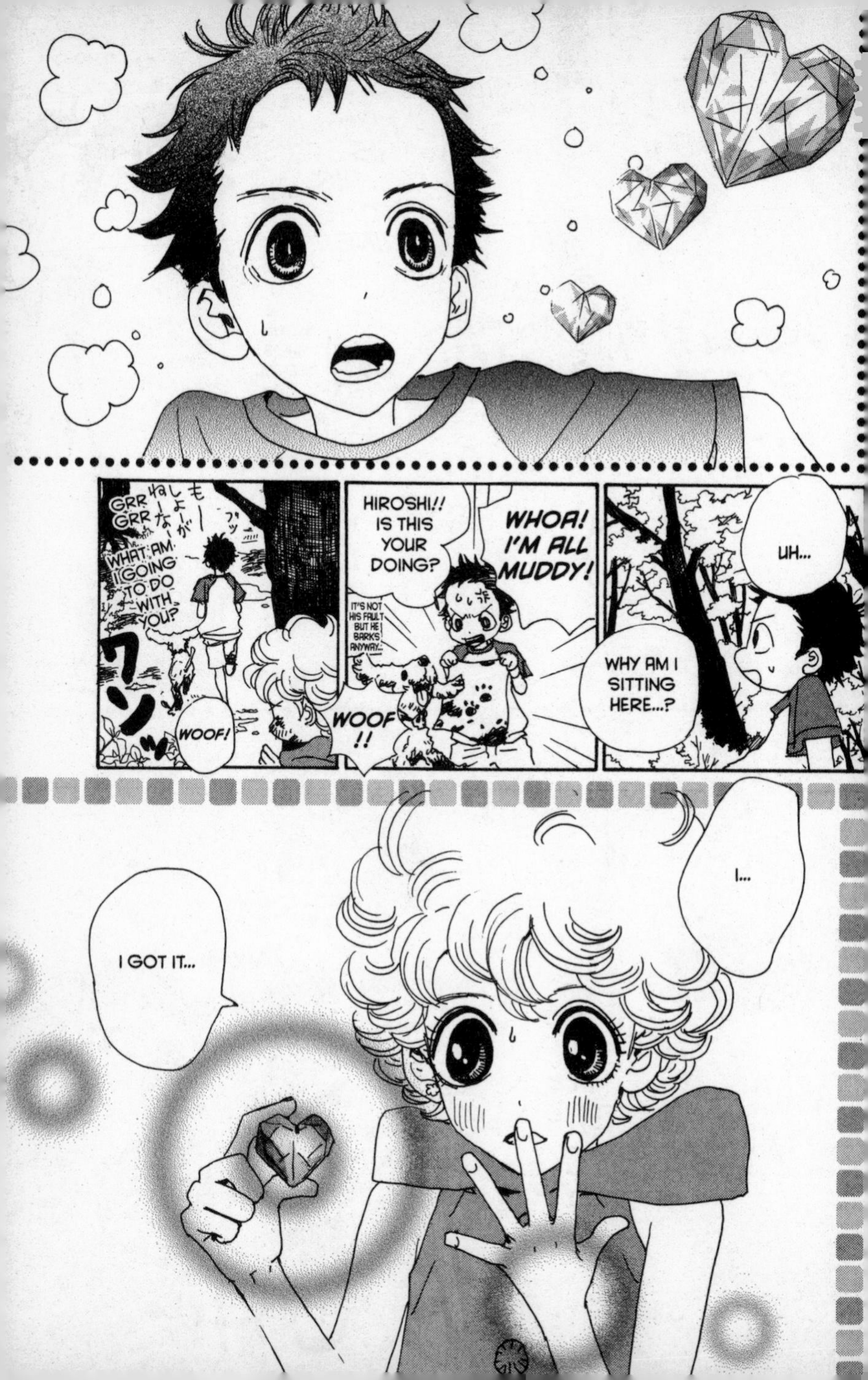
UH...
WHY AM I SITTING HERE...?
WHOA! I'M ALL MUDDY!
HIROSHI!! IS THIS YOUR DOING?
IT'S NOT HIS FAULT BUT HE BARKS ANYWAY...
WOOF!!
もーしょーがねーな
GRR GRR
WHAT AM I GOING TO DO WITH YOU?
ワン
WOOF!
I...
I GOT IT...

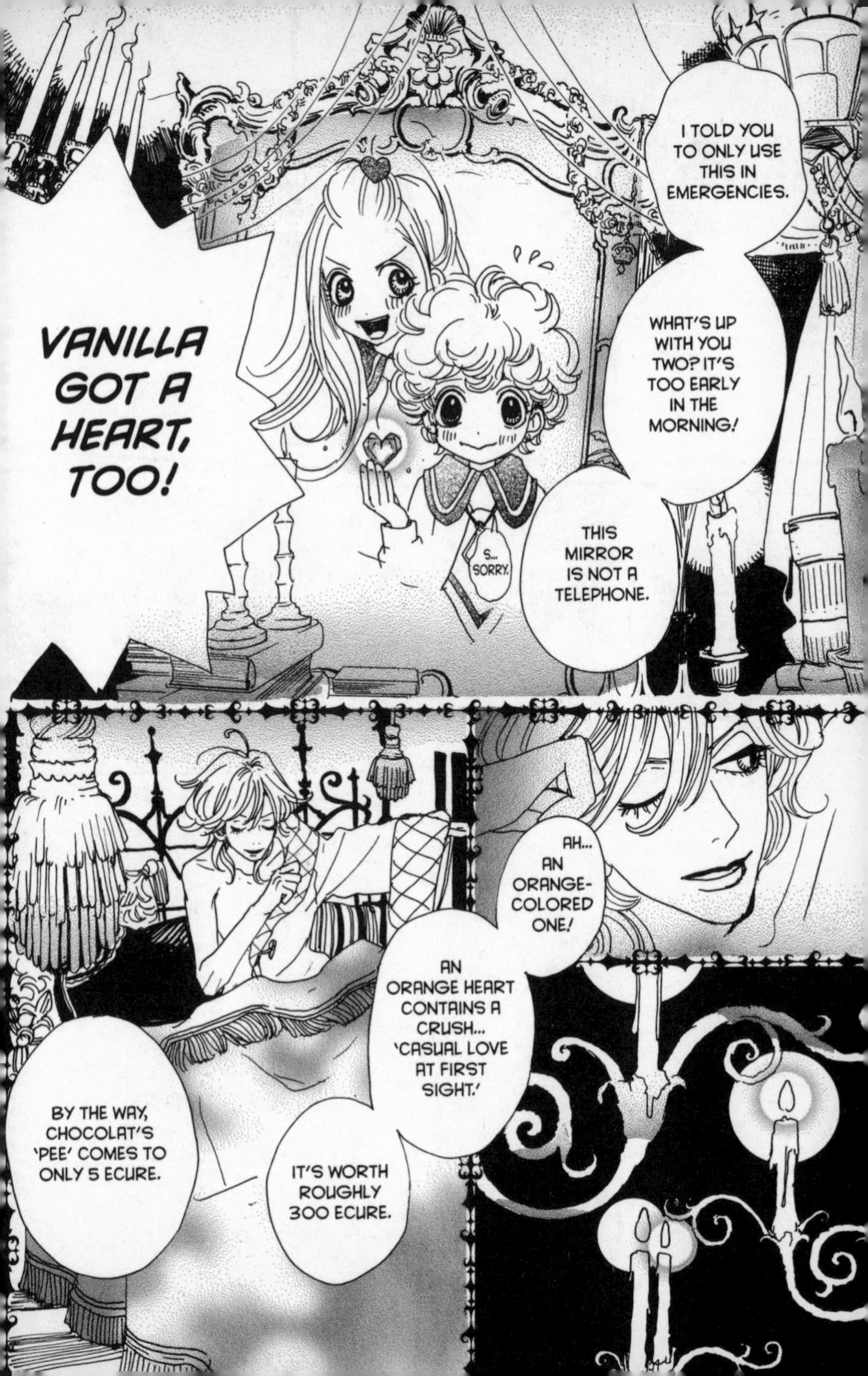

I TOLD YOU TO ONLY USE THIS IN EMERGENCIES.
WHAT'S UP WITH YOU TWO? IT'S TOO EARLY IN THE MORNING!
THIS MIRROR IS NOT A TELEPHONE.
S... SORRY.
VANILLA GOT A HEART, TOO!
AH... AN ORANGE-COLORED ONE!
AN ORANGE HEART CONTAINS A CRUSH... 'CASUAL LOVE AT FIRST SIGHT.'
IT'S WORTH ROUGHLY 300 ECURE.
BY THE WAY, CHOCOLAT'S 'PEE' COMES TO ONLY 5 ECURE.

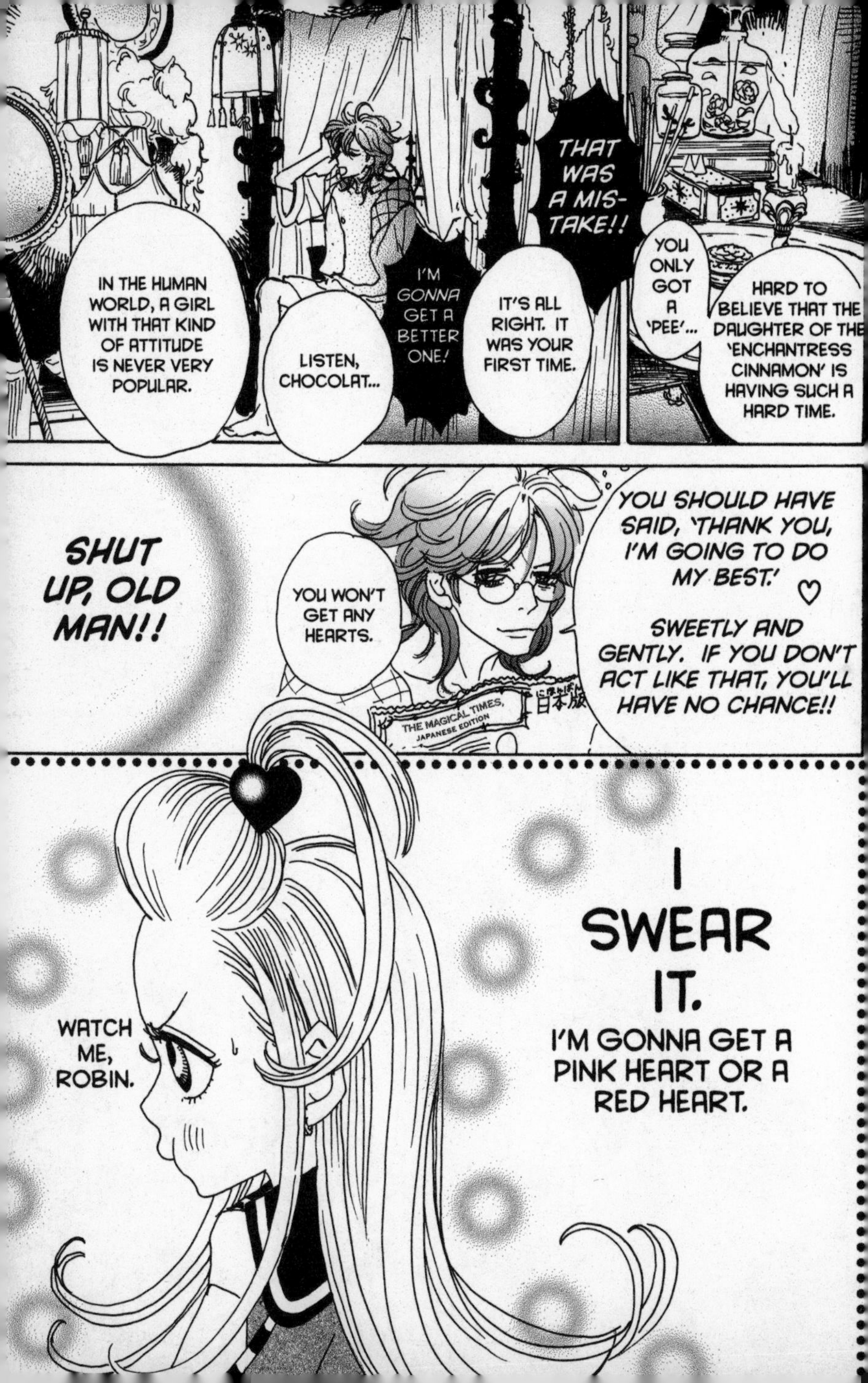
HARD TO BELIEVE THAT THE DAUGHTER OF THE 'ENCHANTRESS CINNAMON' IS HAVING SUCH A HARD TIME.
YOU ONLY GOT A 'PEE'...
THAT WAS A MIS-TAKE!!
IT'S ALL RIGHT. IT WAS YOUR FIRST TIME.
I'M GONNA GET A BETTER ONE!
LISTEN, CHOCOLAT...
IN THE HUMAN WORLD, A GIRL WITH THAT KIND OF ATTITUDE IS NEVER VERY POPULAR.
YOU SHOULD HAVE SAID, 'THANK YOU, I'M GOING TO DO MY BEST.' ♡
SWEETLY AND GENTLY. IF YOU DON'T ACT LIKE THAT, YOU'LL HAVE NO CHANCE!!
YOU WON'T GET ANY HEARTS.
THE MAGICAL TIMES, JAPANESE EDITION
日本版
SHUT UP, OLD MAN!!
I SWEAR IT.
I'M GONNA GET A PINK HEART OR A RED HEART.
WATCH ME, ROBIN.

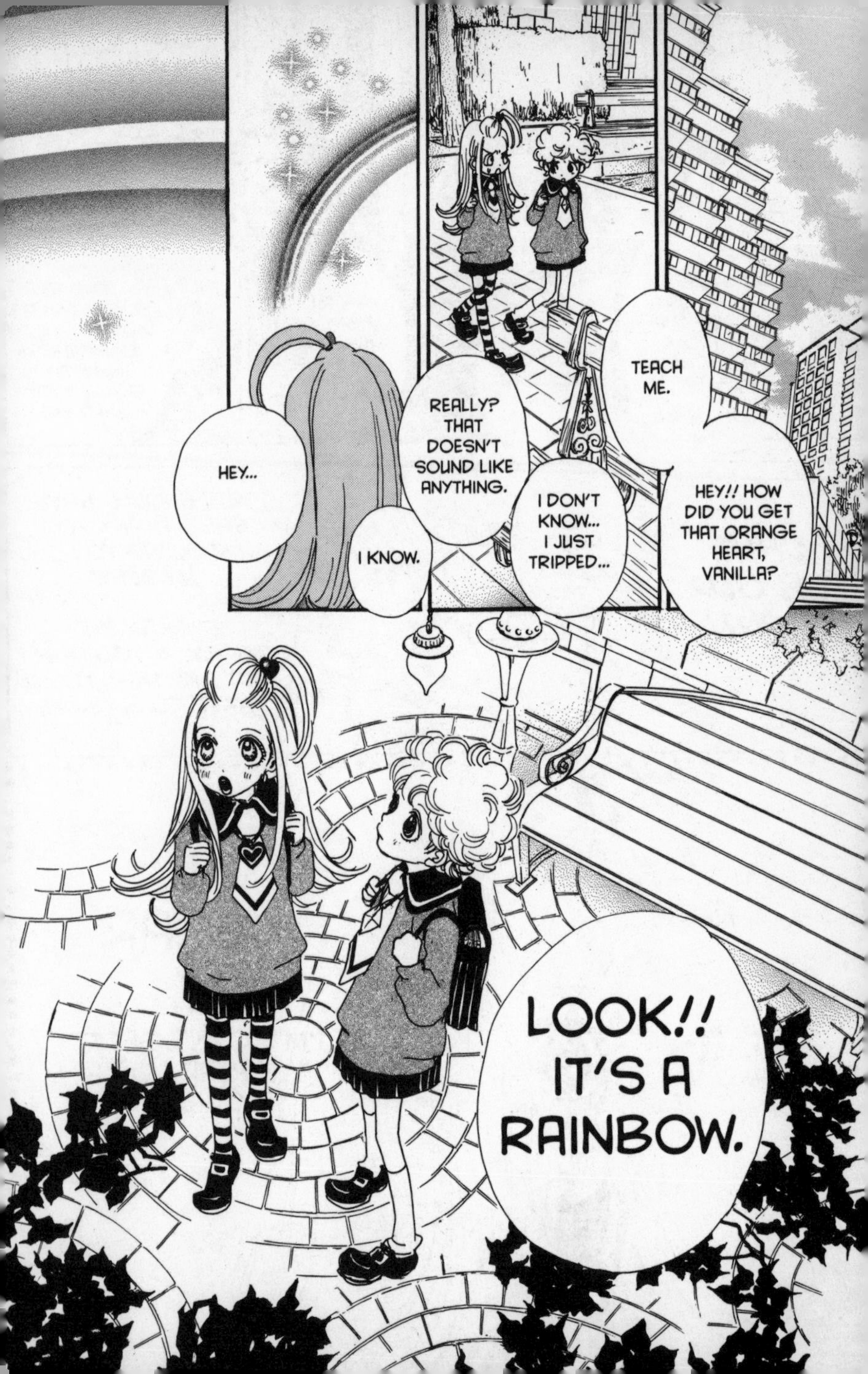
HEY!! HOW DID YOU GET THAT ORANGE HEART, VANILLA?
TEACH ME.
I DON'T KNOW... I JUST TRIPPED...
REALLY? THAT DOESN'T SOUND LIKE ANYTHING.
I KNOW.
HEY...
LOOK!! IT'S A RAINBOW.

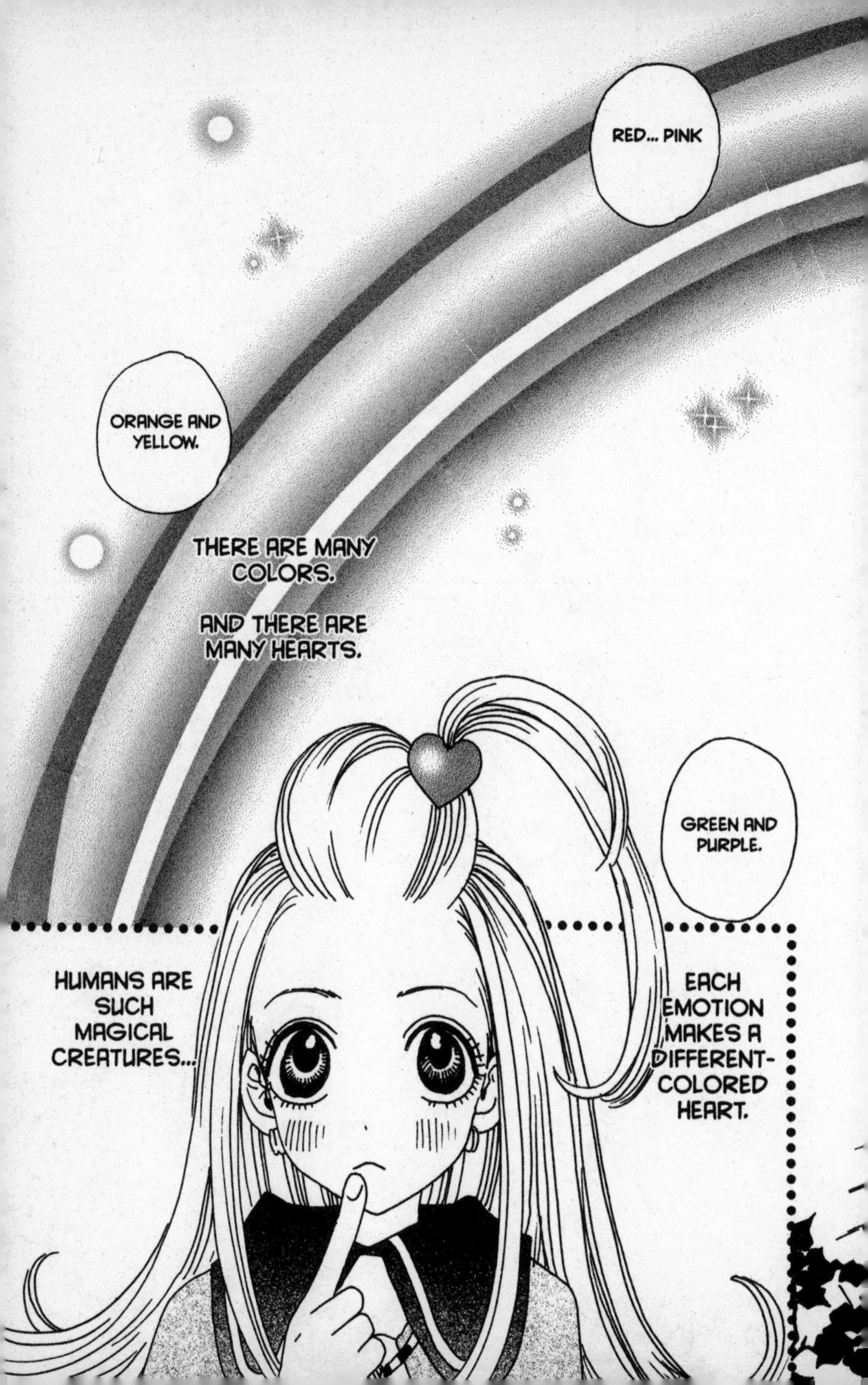
RED... PINK
ORANGE AND YELLOW.
THERE ARE MANY COLORS.
AND THERE ARE MANY HEARTS.
GREEN AND PURPLE.
EACH EMOTION MAKES A DIFFERENT-COLORED HEART.
HUMANS ARE SUCH MAGICAL CREATURES...

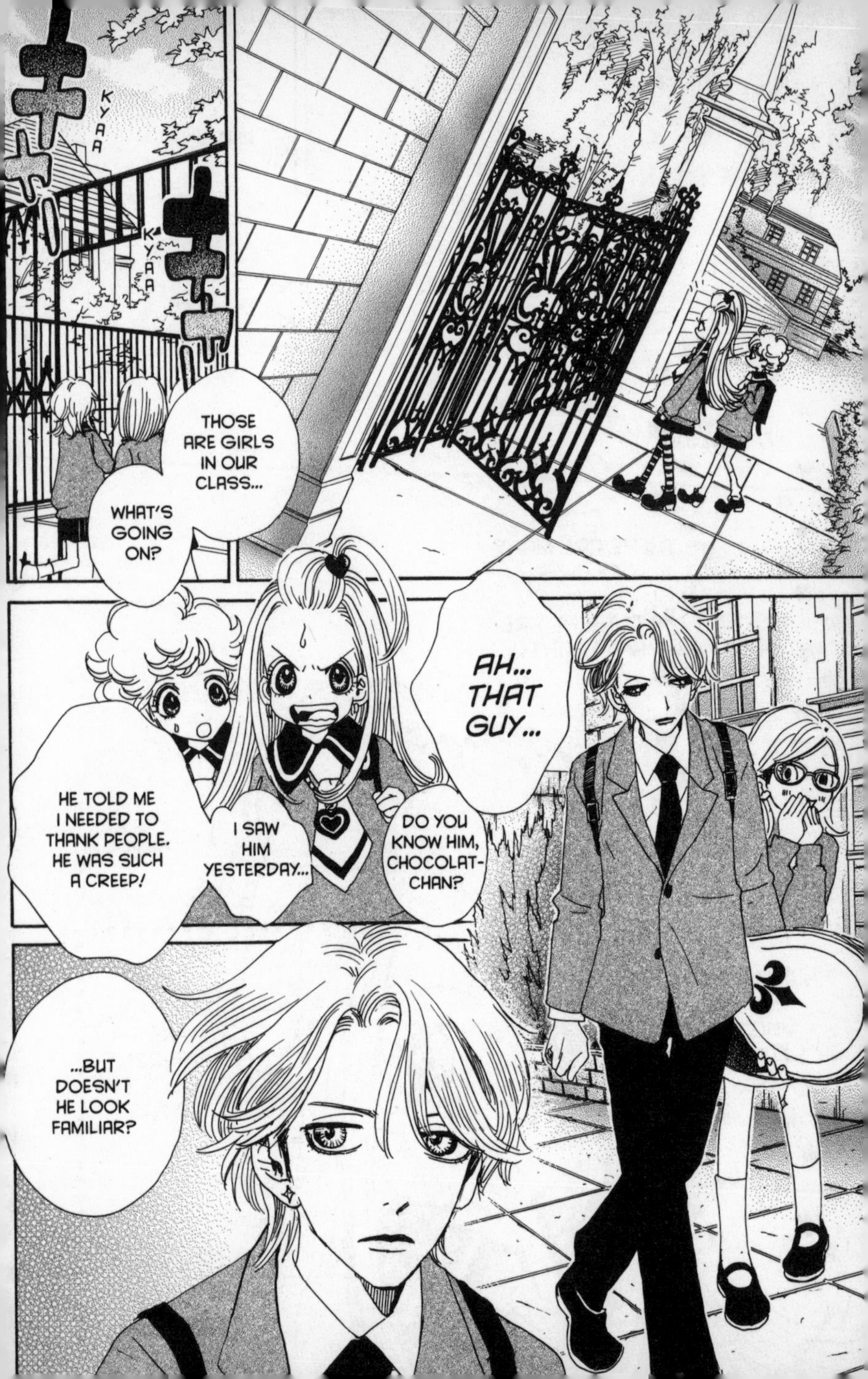
KYAA
KYAA
THOSE ARE GIRLS IN OUR CLASS...
WHAT'S GOING ON?
AH... THAT GUY...
DO YOU KNOW HIM, CHOCOLAT-CHAN?
I SAW HIM YESTERDAY...
HE TOLD ME I NEEDED TO THANK PEOPLE. HE WAS SUCH A CREEP!
...BUT DOESN'T HE LOOK FAMILIAR?

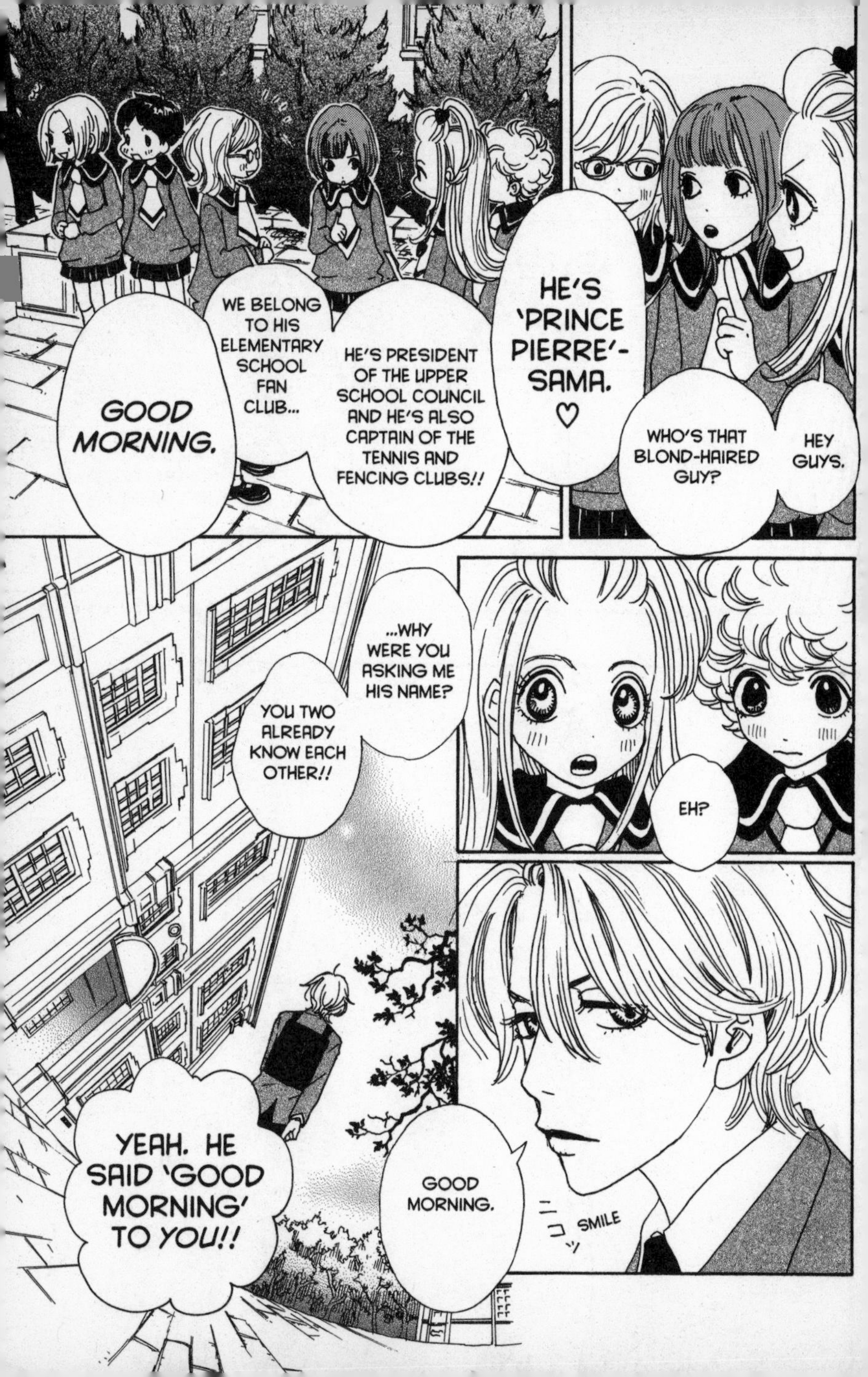
HEY GUYS.
WHO'S THAT BLOND-HAIRED GUY?
HE'S 'PRINCE PIERRE'-SAMA. ♡
HE'S PRESIDENT OF THE UPPER SCHOOL COUNCIL AND HE'S ALSO CAPTAIN OF THE TENNIS AND FENCING CLUBS!!
WE BELONG TO HIS ELEMENTARY SCHOOL FAN CLUB...
GOOD MORNING.
EH?
GOOD MORNING.
SMILE
...WHY WERE YOU ASKING ME HIS NAME?
YOU TWO ALREADY KNOW EACH OTHER!!
YEAH. HE SAID 'GOOD MORNING' TO YOU!!

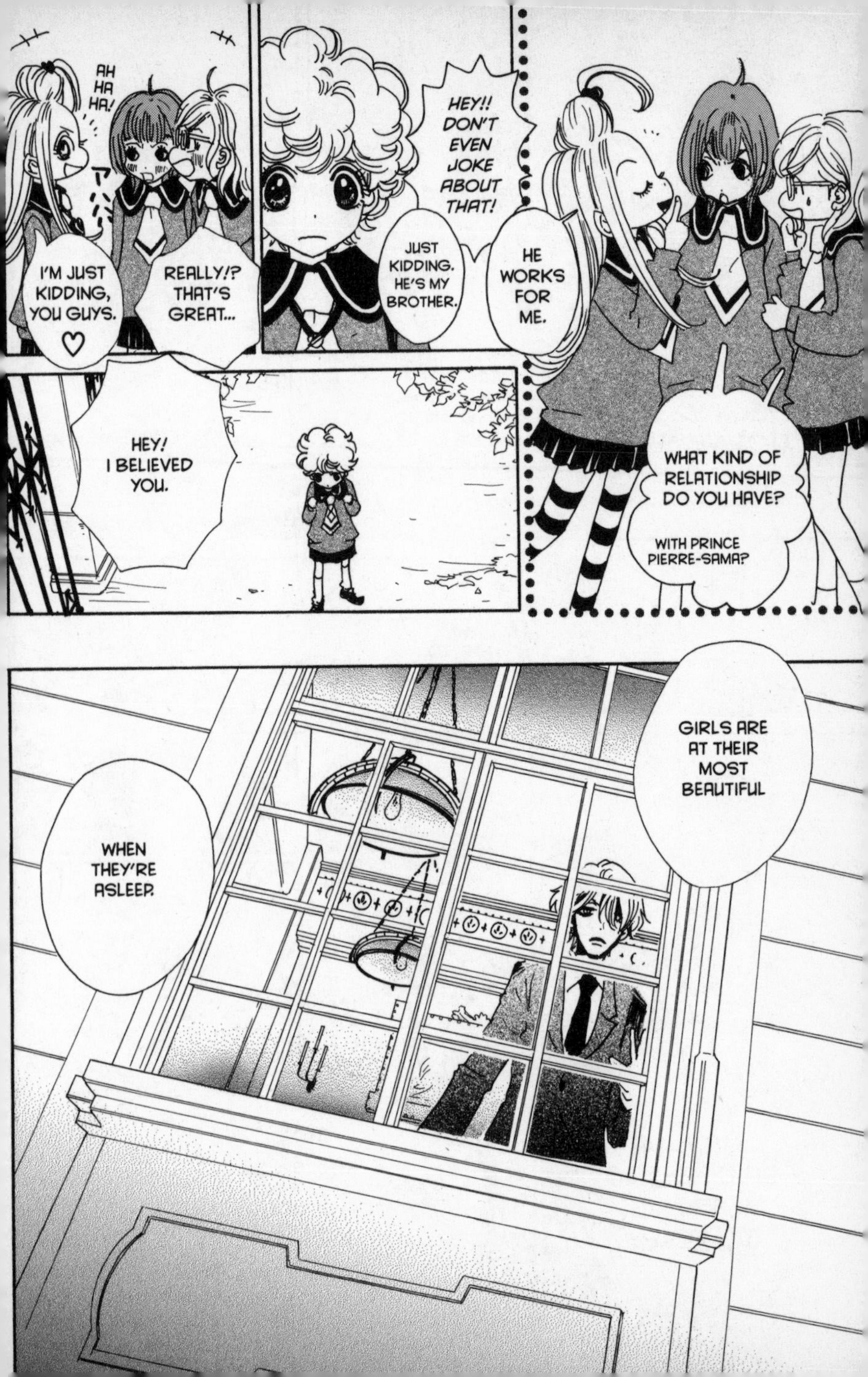
WHAT KIND OF RELATIONSHIP DO YOU HAVE?
WITH PRINCE PIERRE-SAMA?
HE WORKS FOR ME.
HEY!! DON'T EVEN JOKE ABOUT THAT!
JUST KIDDING. HE'S MY BROTHER.
REALLY!? THAT'S GREAT...
AH HA HA!
アハハ
I'M JUST KIDDING, YOU GUYS. ♡
HEY! I BELIEVED YOU.
GIRLS ARE AT THEIR MOST BEAUTIFUL
WHEN THEY'RE ASLEEP.

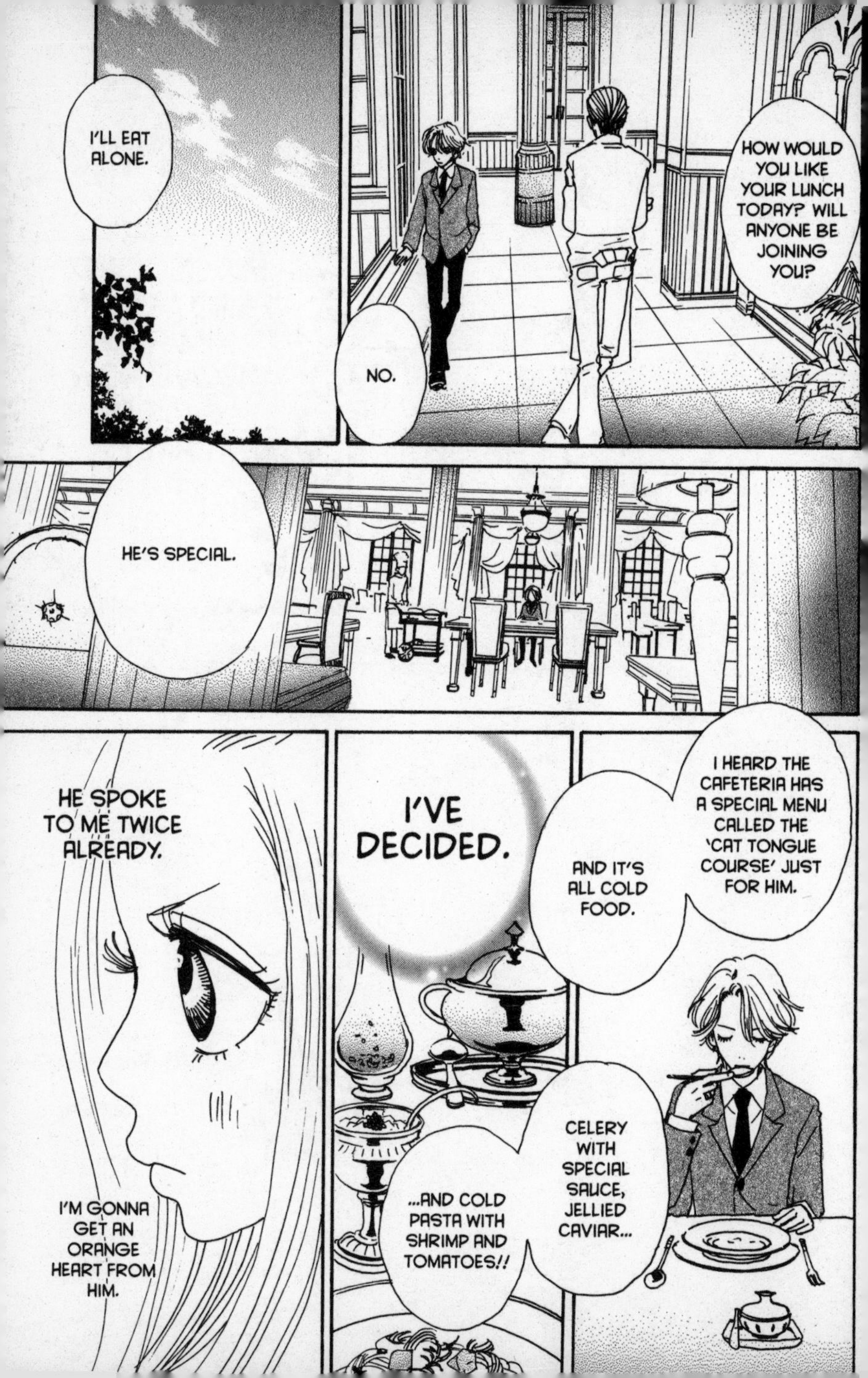

HOW WOULD YOU LIKE YOUR LUNCH TODAY? WILL ANYONE BE JOINING YOU?
NO.
I'LL EAT ALONE.
HE'S SPECIAL.
I HEARD THE CAFETERIA HAS A SPECIAL MENU CALLED THE 'CAT TONGUE COURSE' JUST FOR HIM.
AND IT'S ALL COLD FOOD.
CELERY WITH SPECIAL SAUCE, JELLIED CAVIAR...
...AND COLD PASTA WITH SHRIMP AND TOMATOES!!
I'VE DECIDED.
HE SPOKE TO ME TWICE ALREADY.
I'M GONNA GET AN ORANGE HEART FROM HIM.

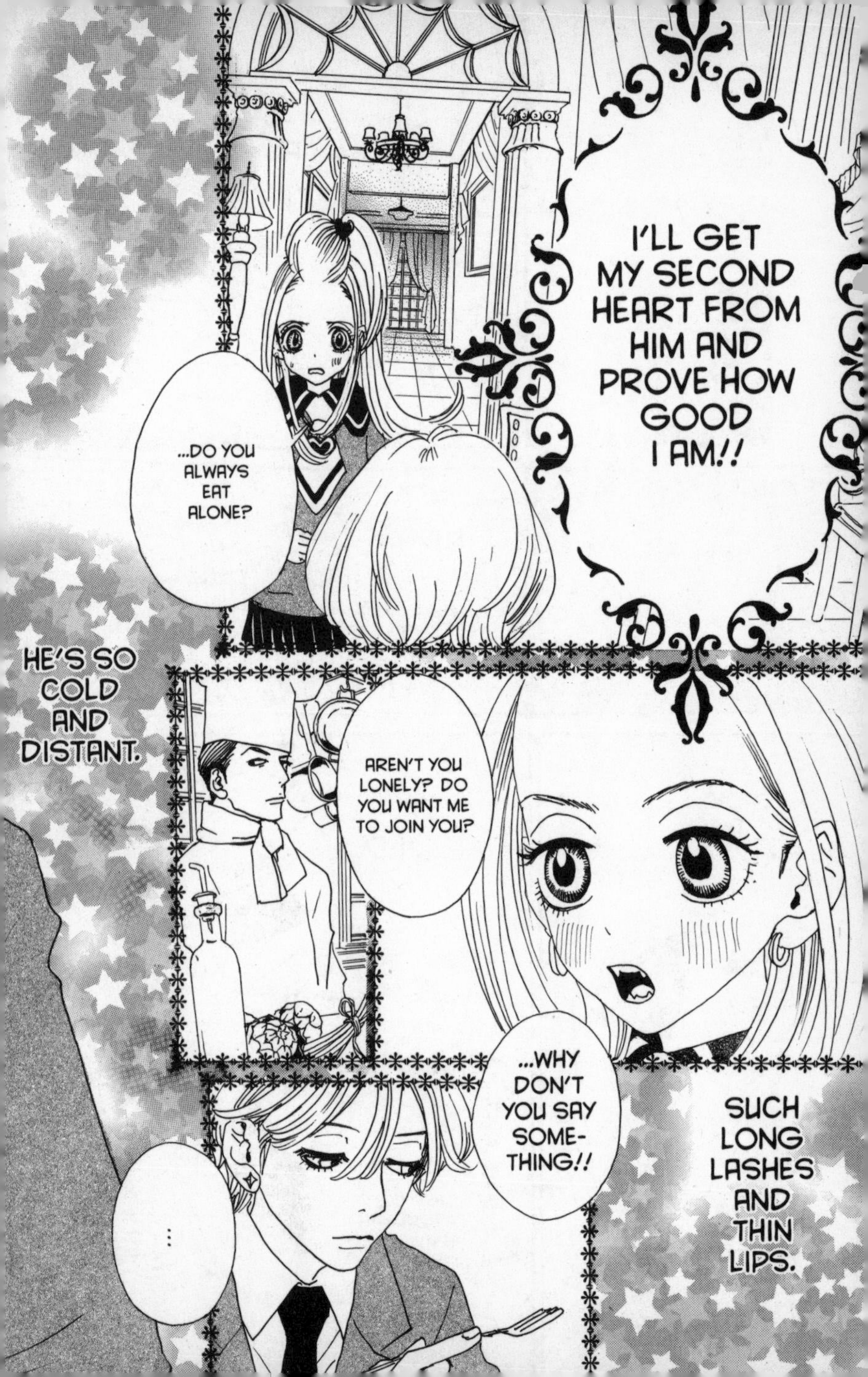
I'LL GET MY SECOND HEART FROM HIM AND PROVE HOW GOOD I AM!!
...DO YOU ALWAYS EAT ALONE?
AREN'T YOU LONELY? DO YOU WANT ME TO JOIN YOU?
HE'S SO COLD AND DISTANT.
SUCH LONG LASHES AND THIN LIPS.
...WHY DON'T YOU SAY SOME-THING!!
...

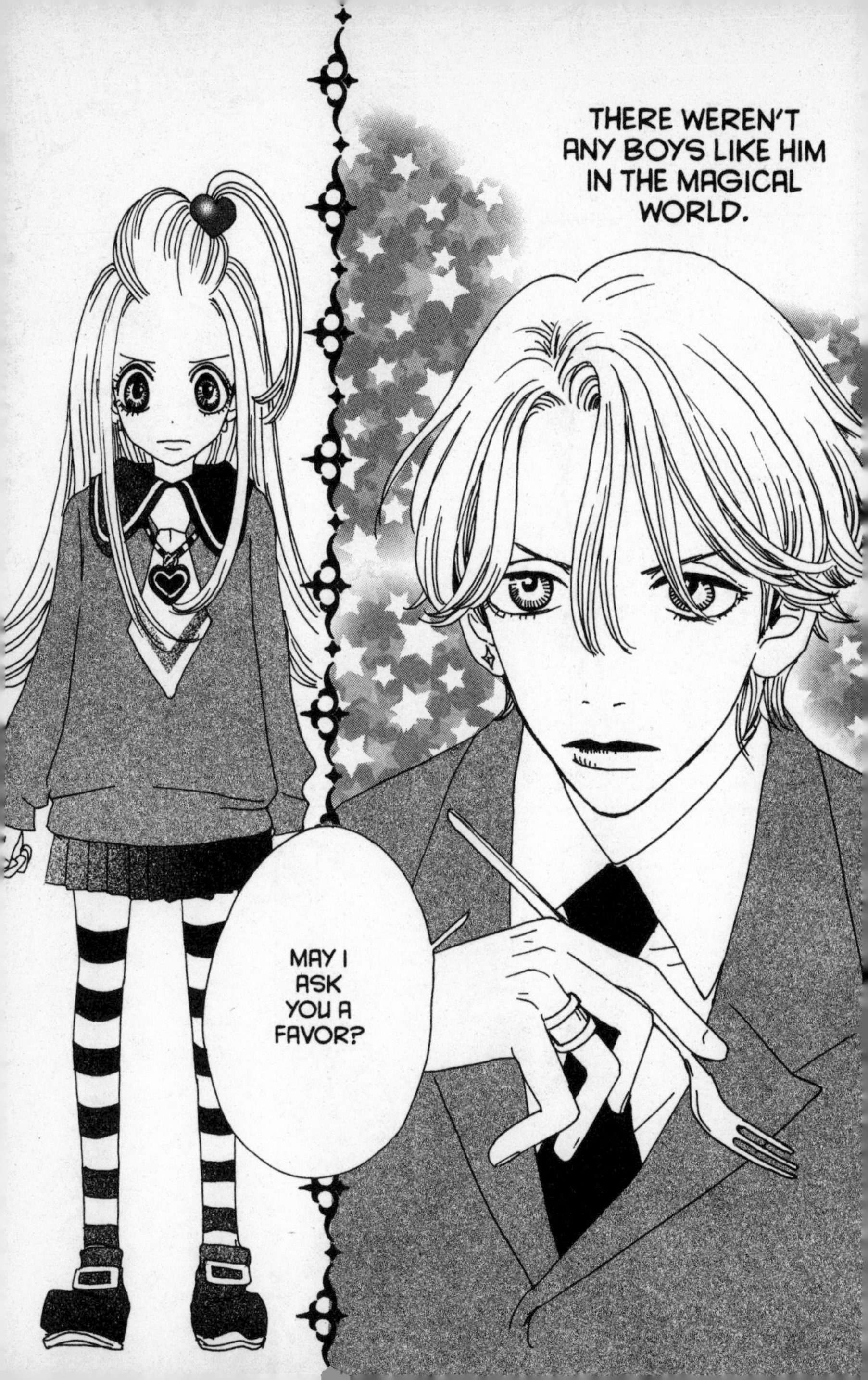
THERE WEREN'T ANY BOYS LIKE HIM IN THE MAGICAL WORLD.
MAY I ASK YOU A FAVOR?

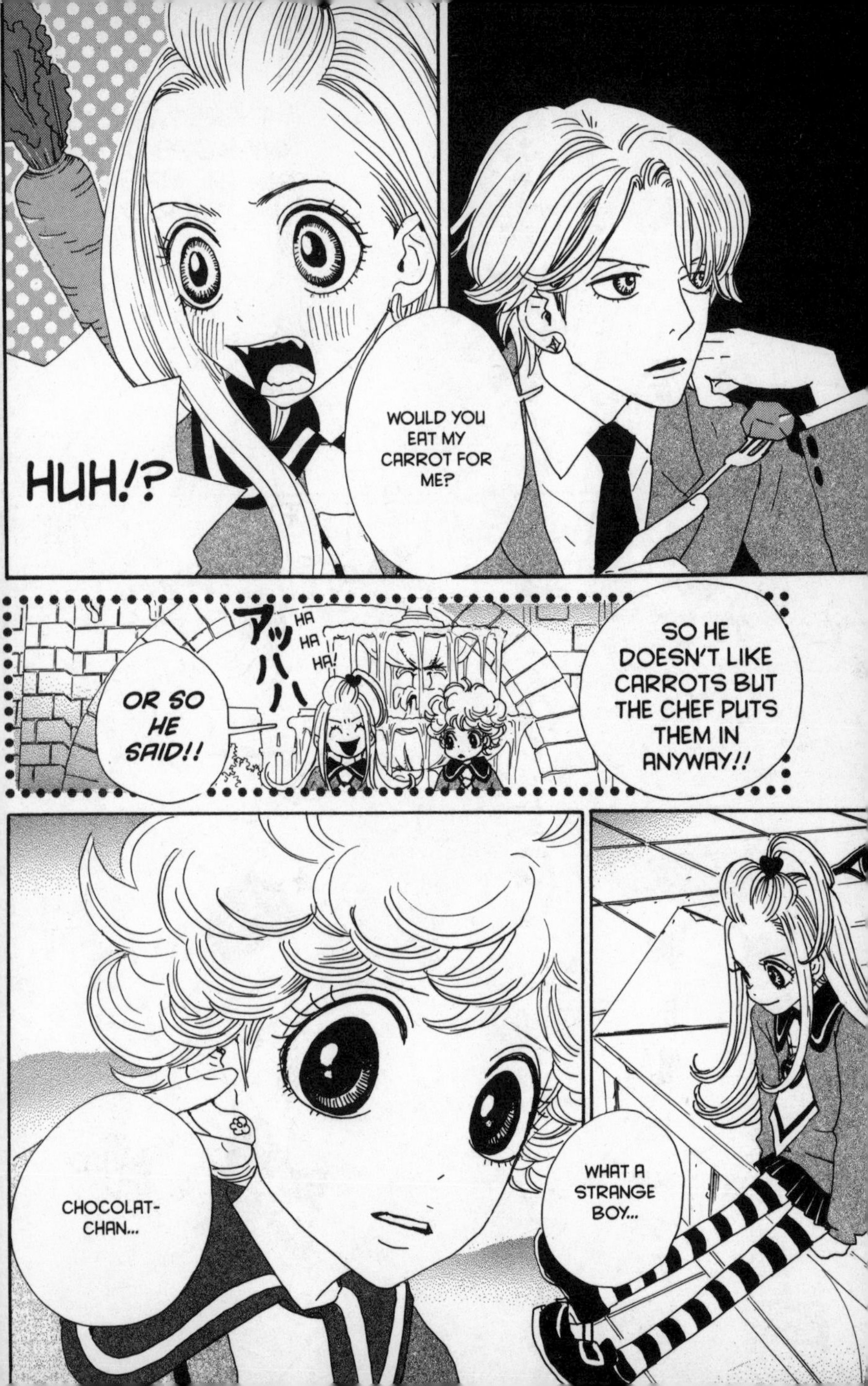
WOULD YOU EAT MY CARROT FOR ME?
HUH!?
SO HE DOESN'T LIKE CARROTS BUT THE CHEF PUTS THEM IN ANYWAY!!
アッハハ
HA HA HA!
OR SO HE SAID!!
WHAT A STRANGE BOY...
CHOCOLAT-CHAN...

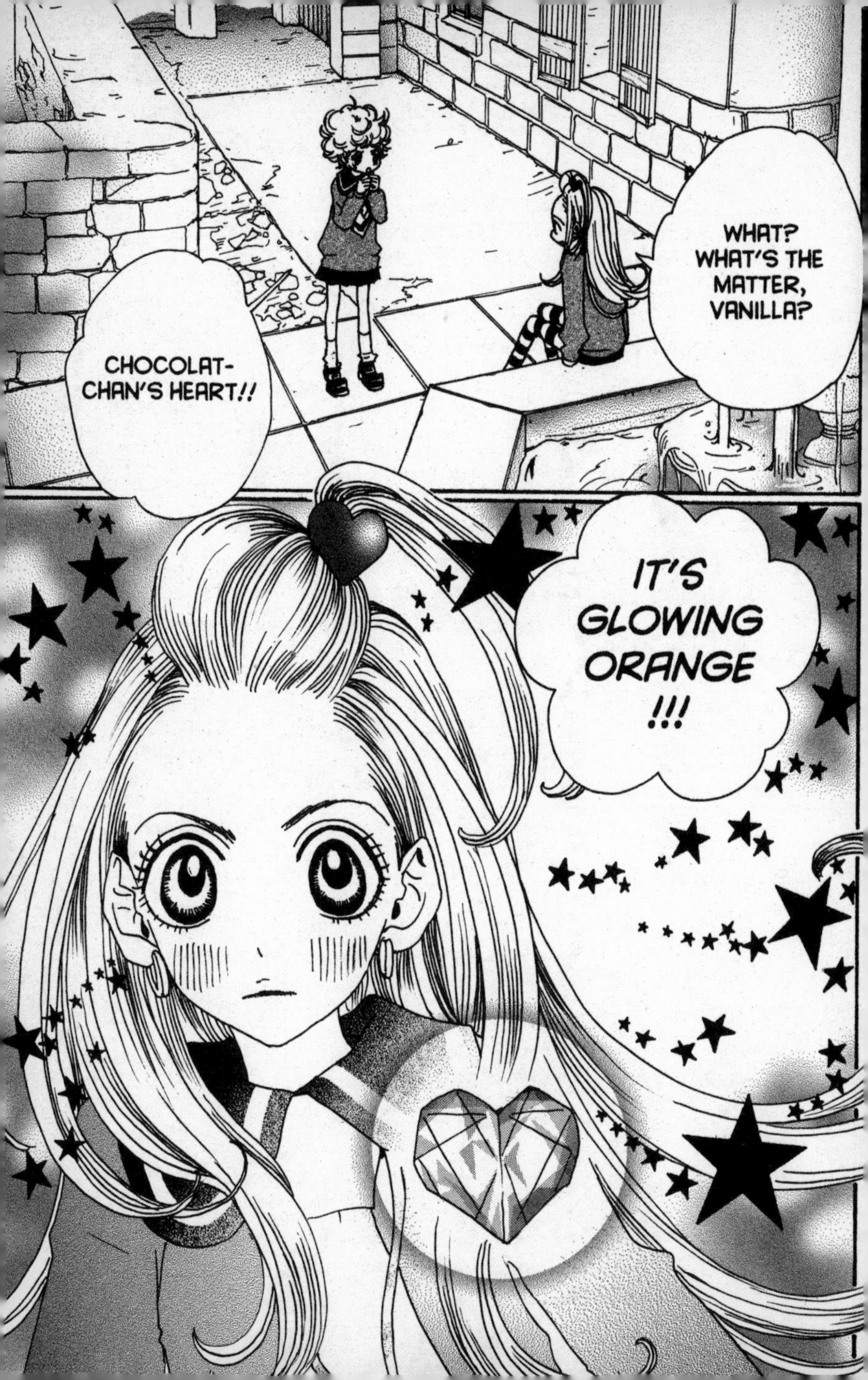
WHAT? WHAT'S THE MATTER, VANILLA?
CHOCOLAT-CHAN'S HEART!!
IT'S GLOWING ORANGE !!!

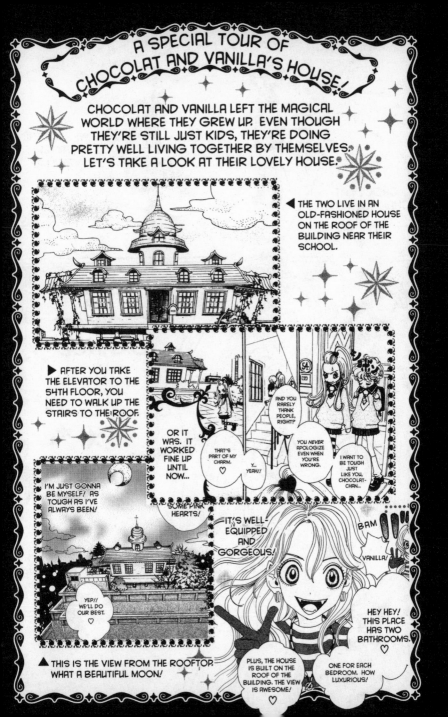

A SPECIAL TOUR OF CHOCOLAT AND VANILLA'S HOUSE!

CHOCOLAT AND VANILLA LEFT THE MAGICAL WORLD WHERE THEY GREW UP. EVEN THOUGH THEY'RE STILL JUST KIDS, THEY'RE DOING PRETTY WELL LIVING TOGETHER BY THEMSELVES. LET'S TAKE A LOOK AT THEIR LOVELY HOUSE.

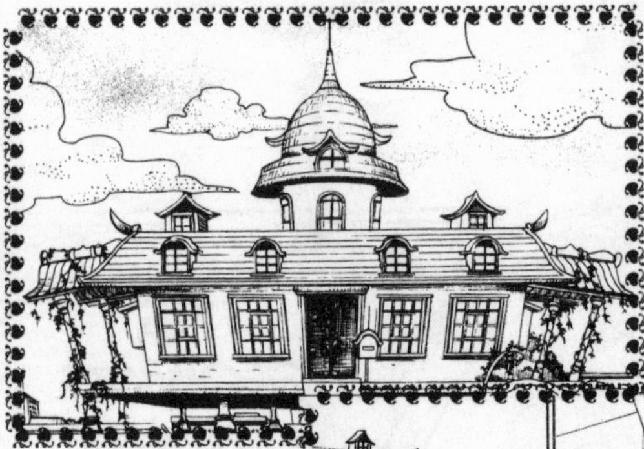

◀ THE TWO LIVE IN AN OLD-FASHIONED HOUSE ON THE ROOF OF THE BUILDING NEAR THEIR SCHOOL.

▶ AFTER YOU TAKE THE ELEVATOR TO THE 54TH FLOOR, YOU NEED TO WALK UP THE STAIRS TO THE ROOF.

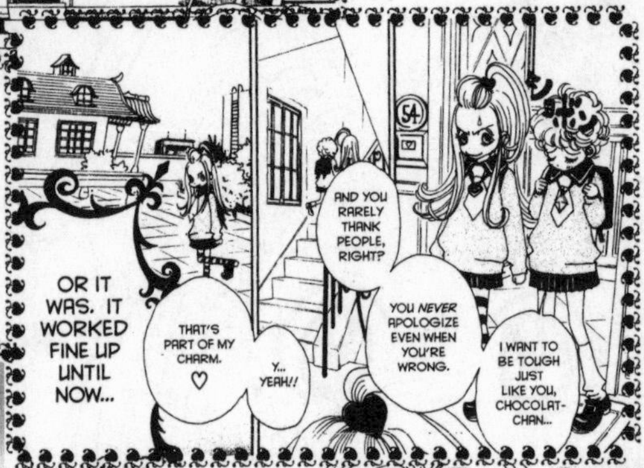
I WANT TO BE TOUGH JUST LIKE YOU, CHOCOLAT-CHAN...
YOU NEVER APOLOGIZE EVEN WHEN YOU'RE WRONG.
AND YOU RARELY THANK PEOPLE, RIGHT?
Y... YEAH!!
THAT'S PART OF MY CHARM. ♡
OR IT WAS. IT WORKED FINE UP UNTIL NOW...

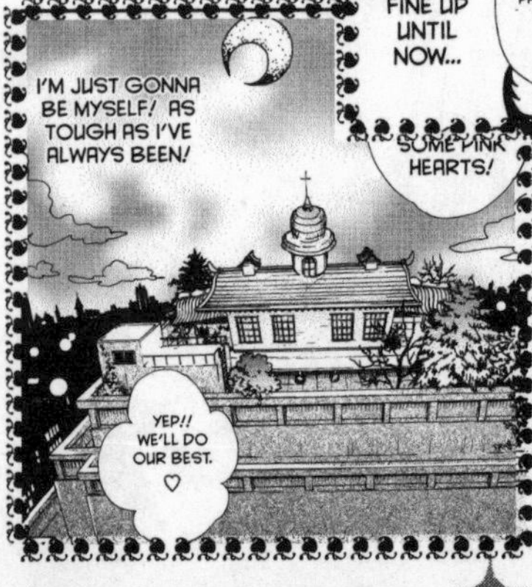
SOME PINK HEARTS!
I'M JUST GONNA BE MYSELF! AS TOUGH AS I'VE ALWAYS BEEN!
YEP!! WE'LL DO OUR BEST. ♡

▲ THIS IS THE VIEW FROM THE ROOFTOP. WHAT A BEAUTIFUL MOON!

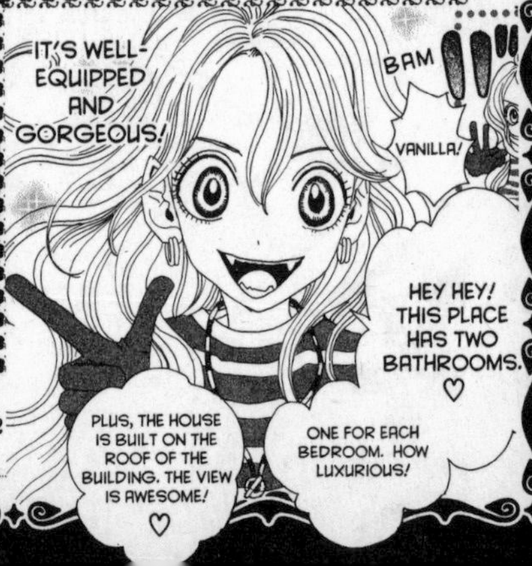
BAM
VANILLA!
IT'S WELL-EQUIPPED AND GORGEOUS!
HEY HEY! THIS PLACE HAS TWO BATHROOMS. ♡
ONE FOR EACH BEDROOM. HOW LUXURIOUS!
PLUS, THE HOUSE IS BUILT ON THE ROOF OF THE BUILDING. THE VIEW IS AWESOME! ♡

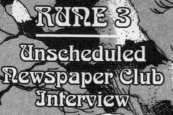

RUNE 3
Unscheduled
Newspaper Club
Interview

SUGAR² RUNE
Sugar Sugar
Rune

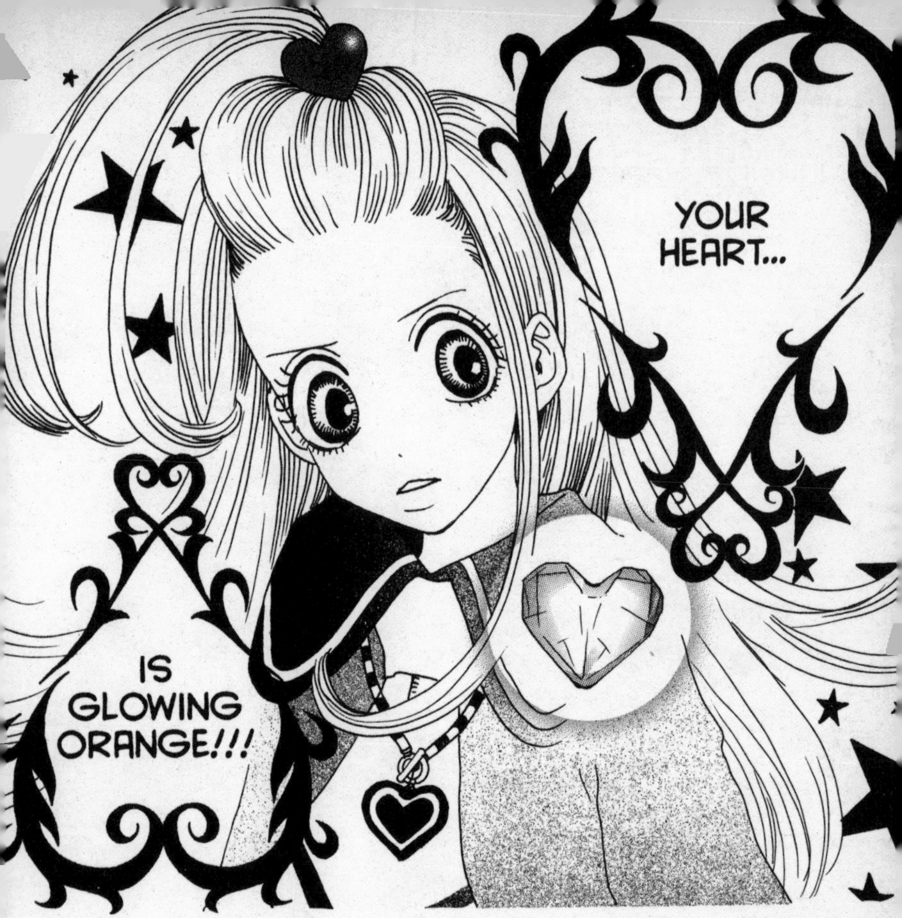
YOUR HEART...
IS GLOWING ORANGE!!!

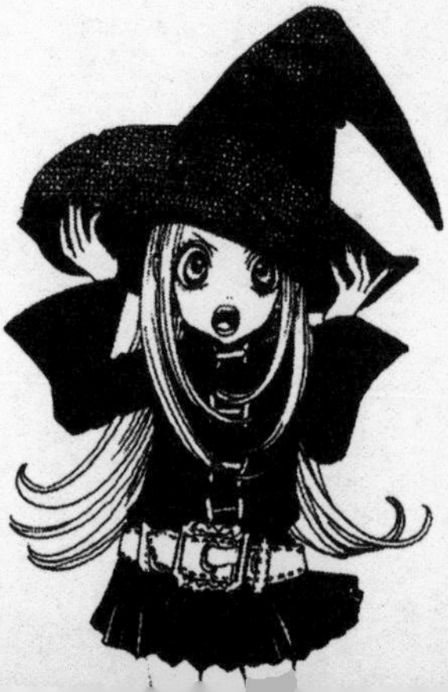

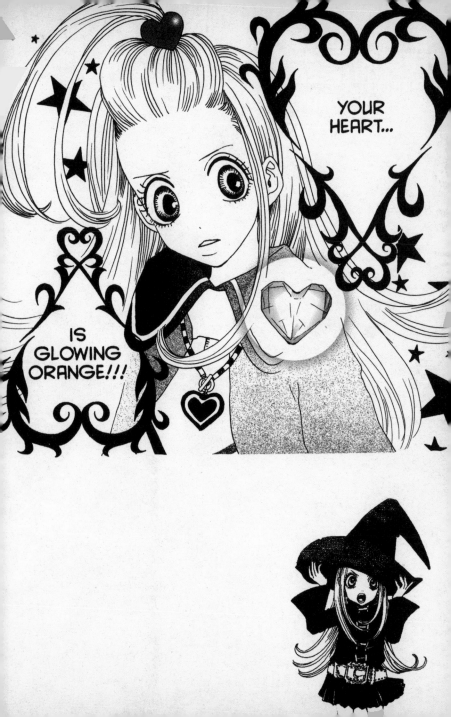

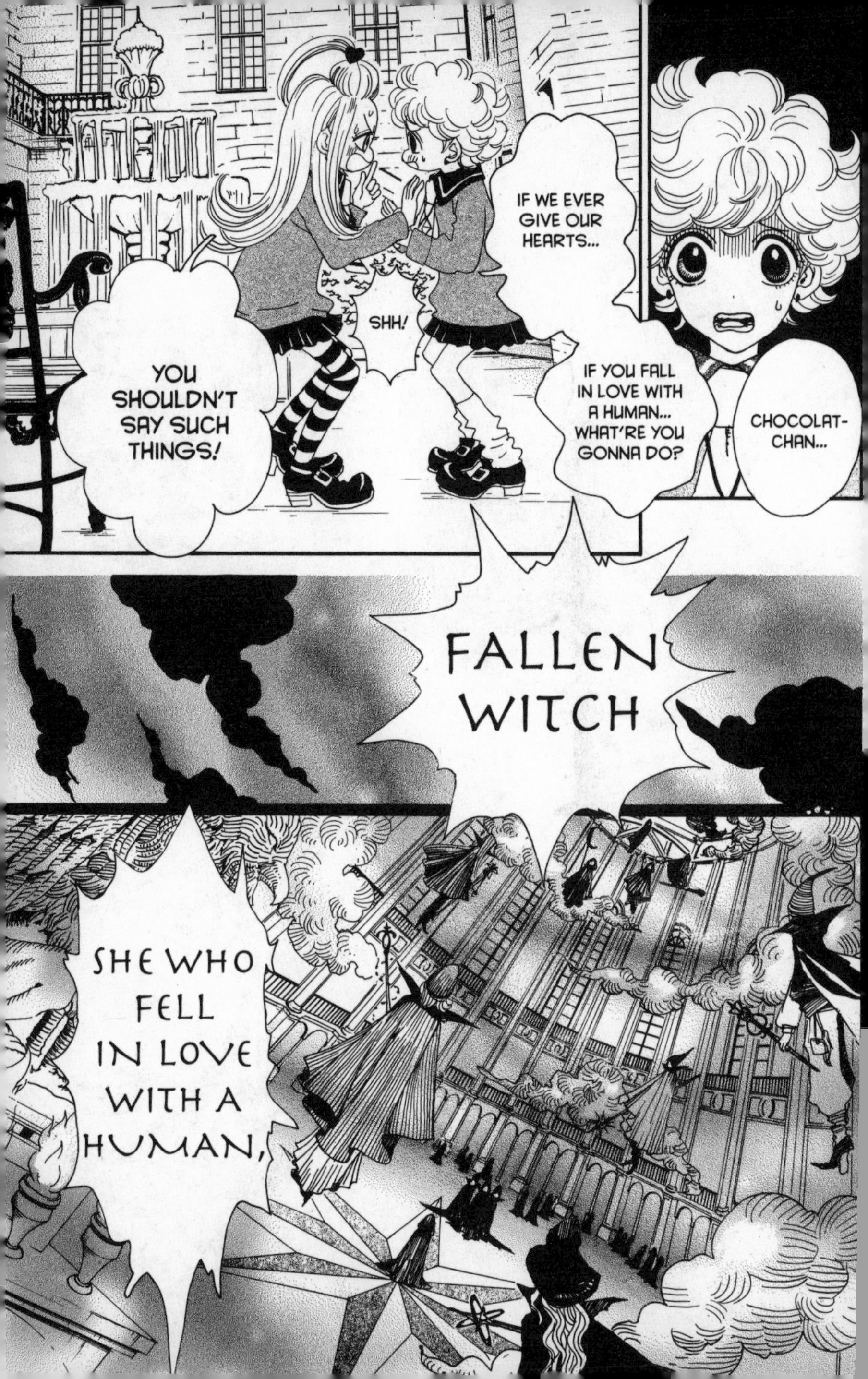

CHOCOLAT-CHAN...
IF WE EVER GIVE OUR HEARTS...
IF YOU FALL IN LOVE WITH A HUMAN... WHAT'RE YOU GONNA DO?
SHH!
YOU SHOULDN'T SAY SUCH THINGS!
FALLEN WITCH
SHE WHO FELL IN LOVE WITH A HUMAN,

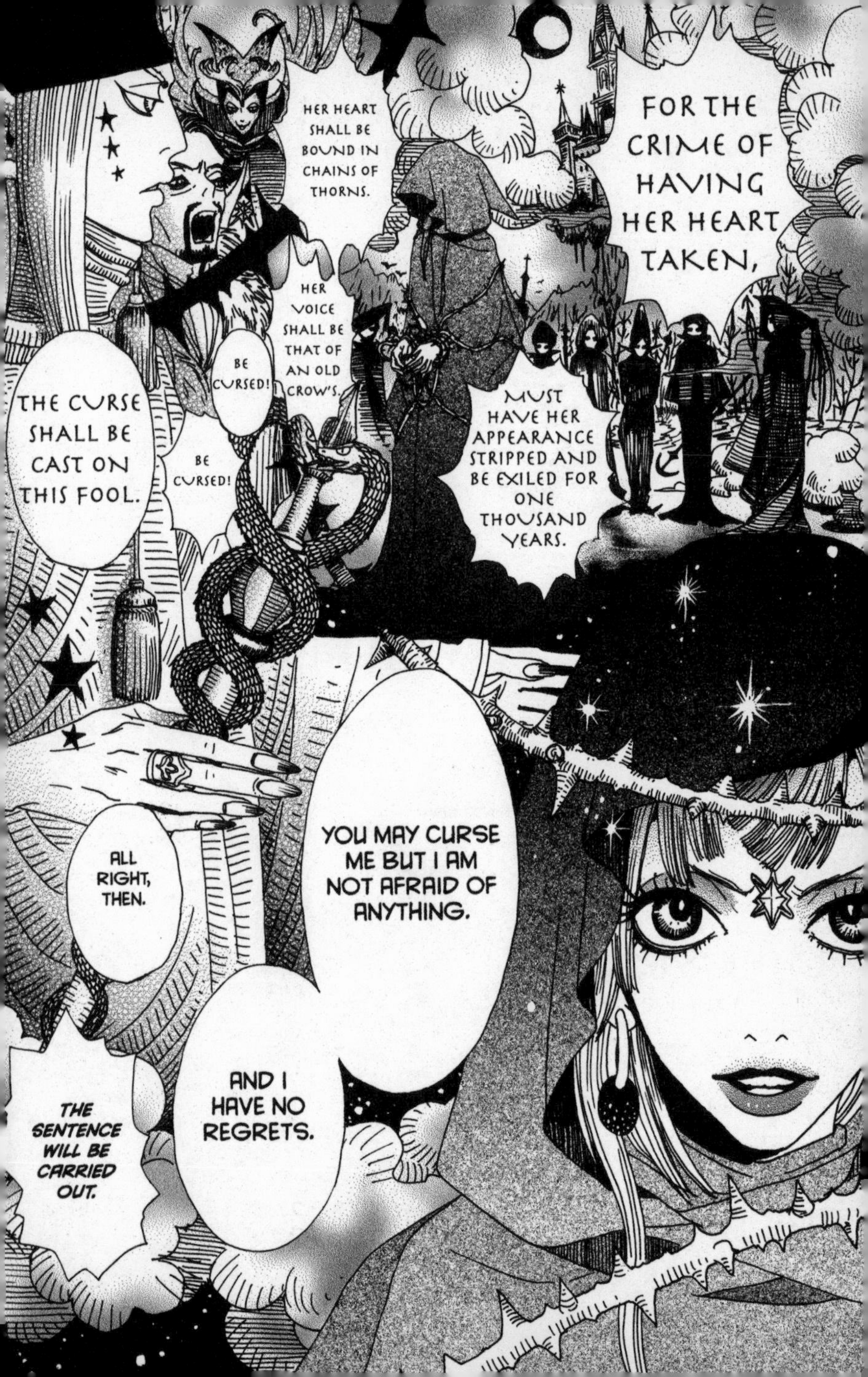
FOR THE CRIME OF HAVING HER HEART TAKEN,
MUST HAVE HER APPEARANCE STRIPPED AND BE EXILED FOR ONE THOUSAND YEARS.
HER HEART SHALL BE BOUND IN CHAINS OF THORNS.
HER VOICE SHALL BE THAT OF AN OLD CROW'S.
BE CURSED!
BE CURSED!
THE CURSE SHALL BE CAST ON THIS FOOL.
YOU MAY CURSE ME BUT I AM NOT AFRAID OF ANYTHING.
AND I HAVE NO REGRETS.
ALL RIGHT, THEN.
THE SENTENCE WILL BE CARRIED OUT.

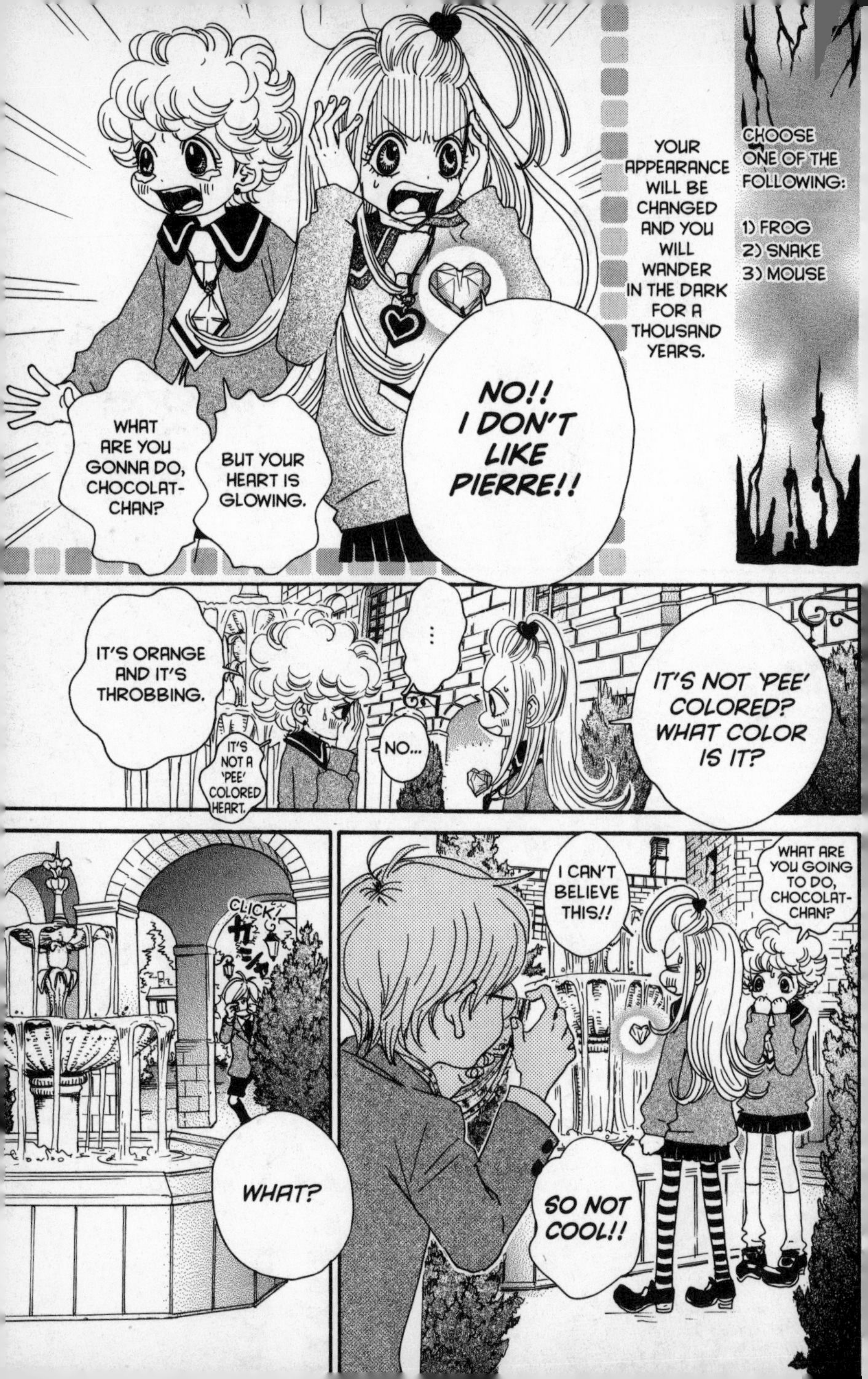
CHOOSE ONE OF THE FOLLOWING:
1) FROG
2) SNAKE
3) MOUSE
YOUR APPEARANCE WILL BE CHANGED AND YOU WILL WANDER IN THE DARK FOR A THOUSAND YEARS.
NO!! I DON'T LIKE PIERRE!!
BUT YOUR HEART IS GLOWING.
WHAT ARE YOU GONNA DO, CHOCOLAT-CHAN?
IT'S NOT 'PEE' COLORED? WHAT COLOR IS IT?
...
NO...
IT'S NOT A 'PEE' COLORED HEART.
IT'S ORANGE AND IT'S THROBBING.
WHAT ARE YOU GOING TO DO, CHOCOLAT-CHAN?
I CAN'T BELIEVE THIS!!
SO NOT COOL!!
CLICK!
WHAT?

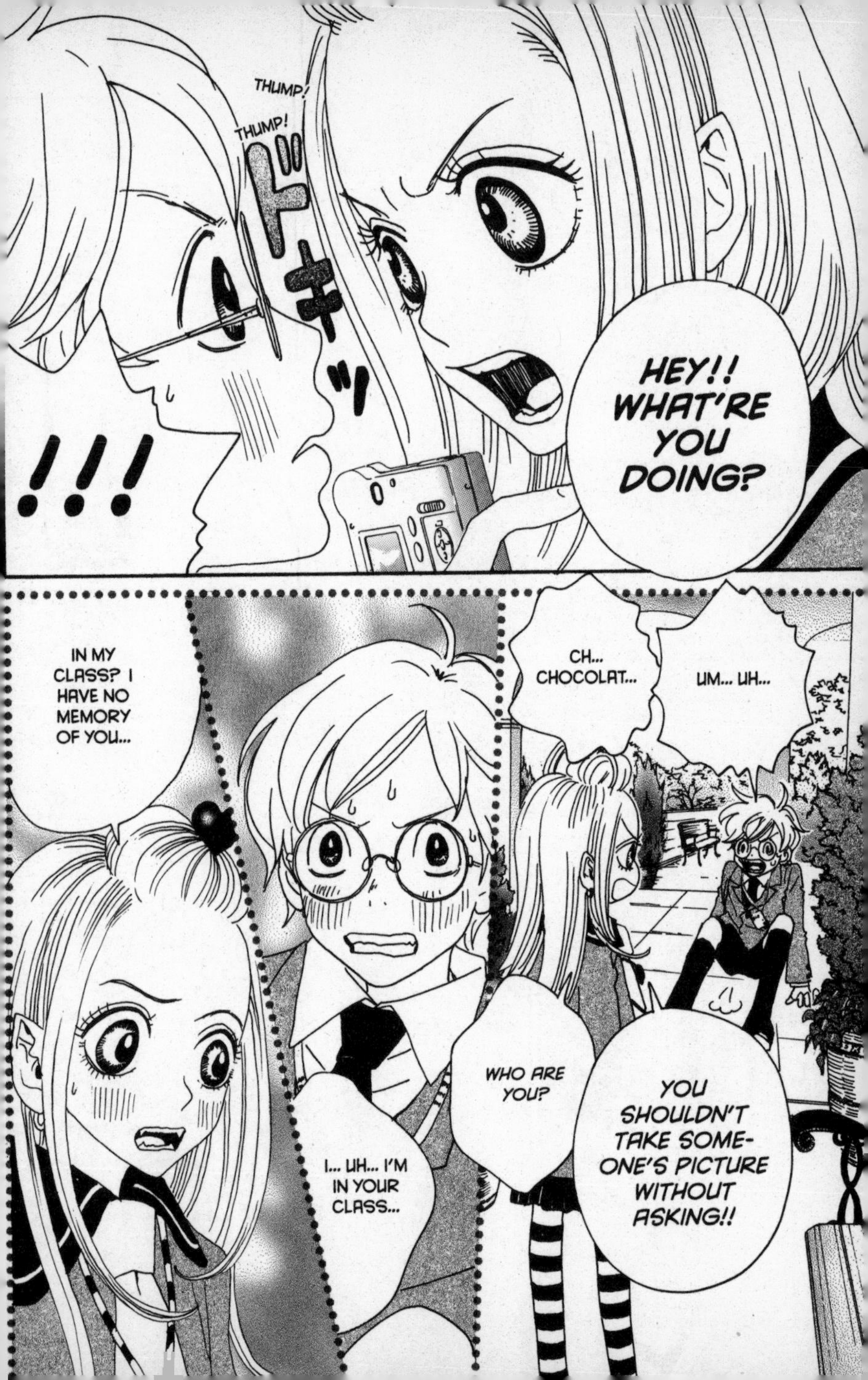
HEY!! WHAT'RE YOU DOING?
THUMP!
THUMP!
ドキッ
!!!
UM... UH...
CH... CHOCOLAT...
YOU SHOULDN'T TAKE SOME-ONE'S PICTURE WITHOUT ASKING!!
WHO ARE YOU?
I... UH... I'M IN YOUR CLASS...
IN MY CLASS? I HAVE NO MEMORY OF YOU...

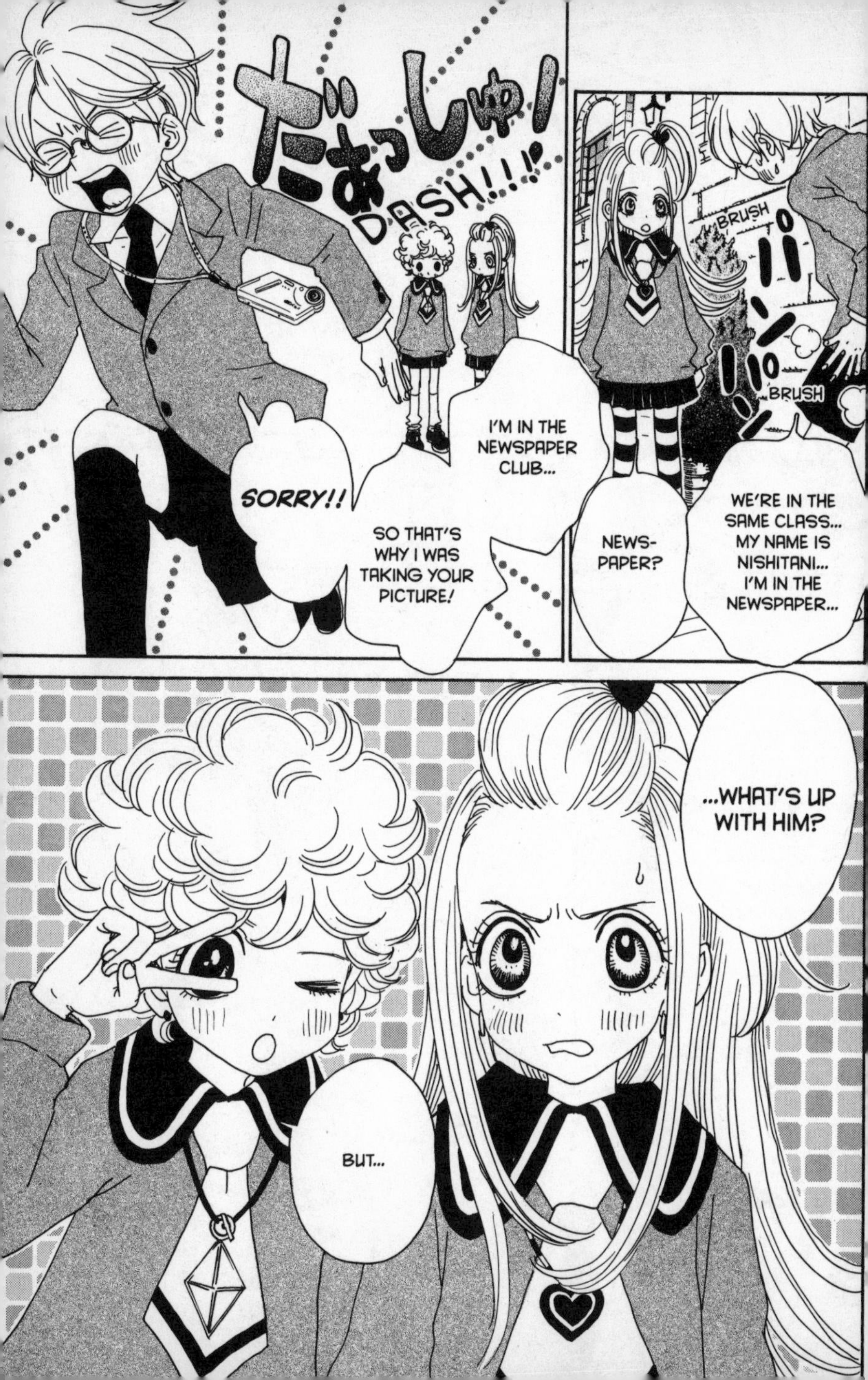
BRUSH
BRUSH
WE'RE IN THE SAME CLASS... MY NAME IS NISHITANI... I'M IN THE NEWSPAPER...
NEWS-PAPER?
だぁっしゅ!
DASH!!!!
I'M IN THE NEWSPAPER CLUB...
SO THAT'S WHY I WAS TAKING YOUR PICTURE!
SORRY!!
...WHAT'S UP WITH HIM?
BUT...

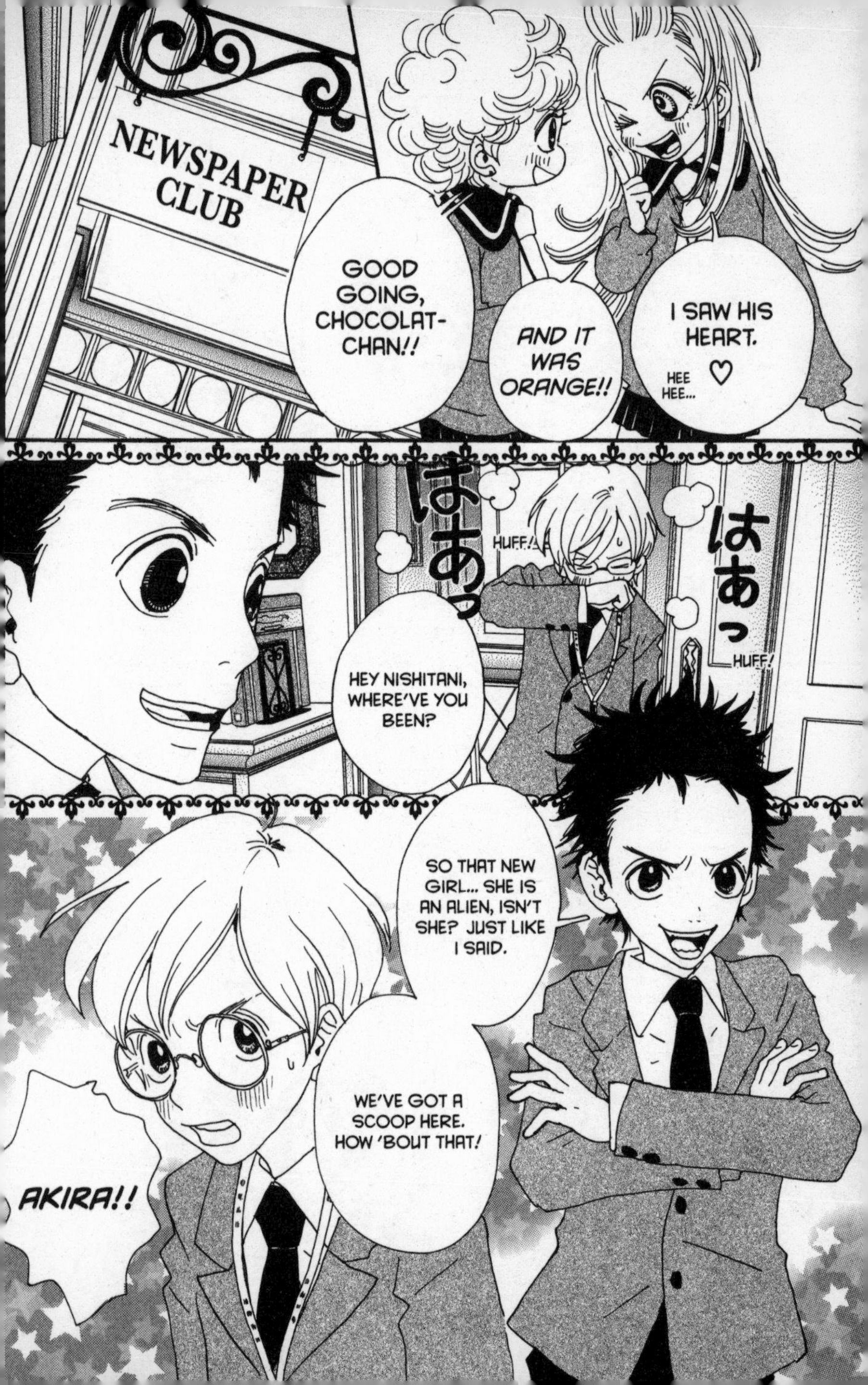
I SAW HIS HEART. ♡
HEE HEE...
AND IT WAS ORANGE!!
GOOD GOING, CHOCOLAT-CHAN!!
NEWSPAPER CLUB
はあっ
HUFF!
はあっ
HUFF!
HEY NISHITANI, WHERE'VE YOU BEEN?
SO THAT NEW GIRL... SHE IS AN ALIEN, ISN'T SHE? JUST LIKE I SAID.
WE'VE GOT A SCOOP HERE. HOW 'BOUT THAT!
AKIRA!!

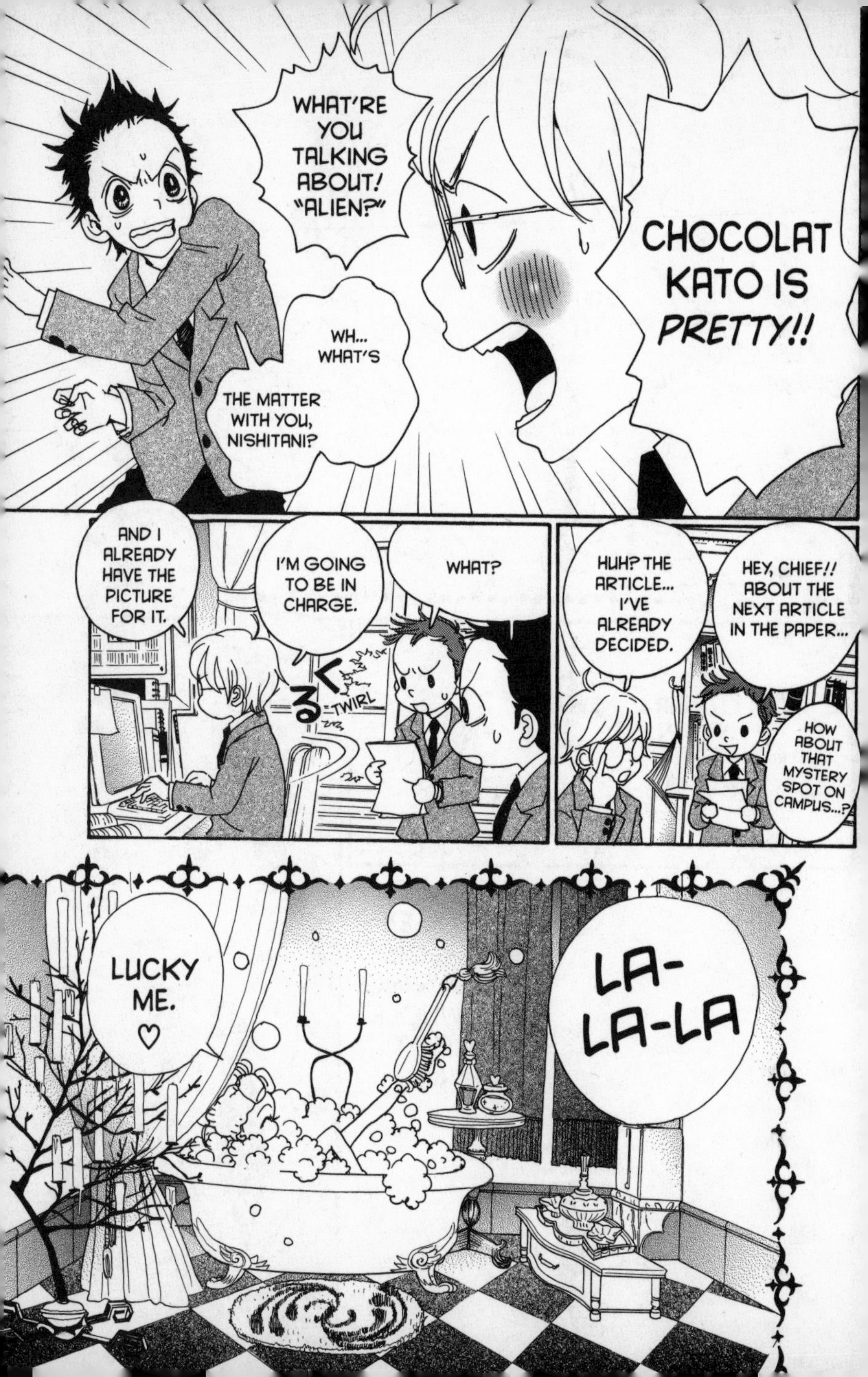
CHOCOLAT KATO IS PRETTY!!
WHAT'RE YOU TALKING ABOUT! "ALIEN?"
WH... WHAT'S THE MATTER WITH YOU, NISHITANI?
HEY, CHIEF!! ABOUT THE NEXT ARTICLE IN THE PAPER...
HOW ABOUT THAT MYSTERY SPOT ON CAMPUS...?
HUH? THE ARTICLE... I'VE ALREADY DECIDED.
WHAT?
I'M GOING TO BE IN CHARGE.
くる TWIRL
AND I ALREADY HAVE THE PICTURE FOR IT.
LA-LA-LA
LUCKY ME. ♡

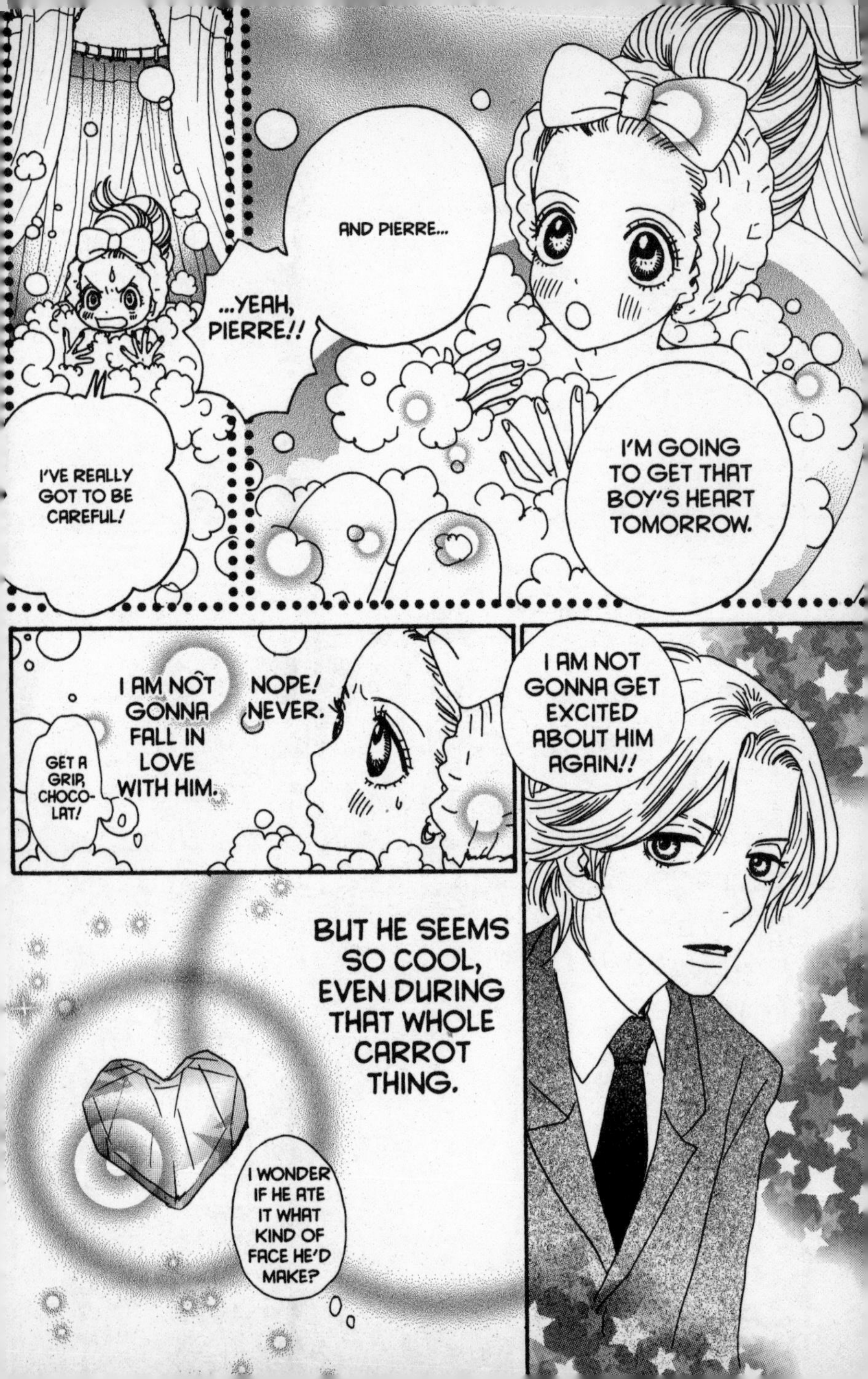
I'M GOING TO GET THAT BOY'S HEART TOMORROW.
AND PIERRE...
...YEAH, PIERRE!!
I'VE REALLY GOT TO BE CAREFUL!
I AM NOT GONNA GET EXCITED ABOUT HIM AGAIN!!
NOPE! NEVER.
I AM NOT GONNA FALL IN LOVE WITH HIM.
GET A GRIP, CHOCOLAT!
BUT HE SEEMS SO COOL, EVEN DURING THAT WHOLE CARROT THING.
I WONDER IF HE ATE IT WHAT KIND OF FACE HE'D MAKE?

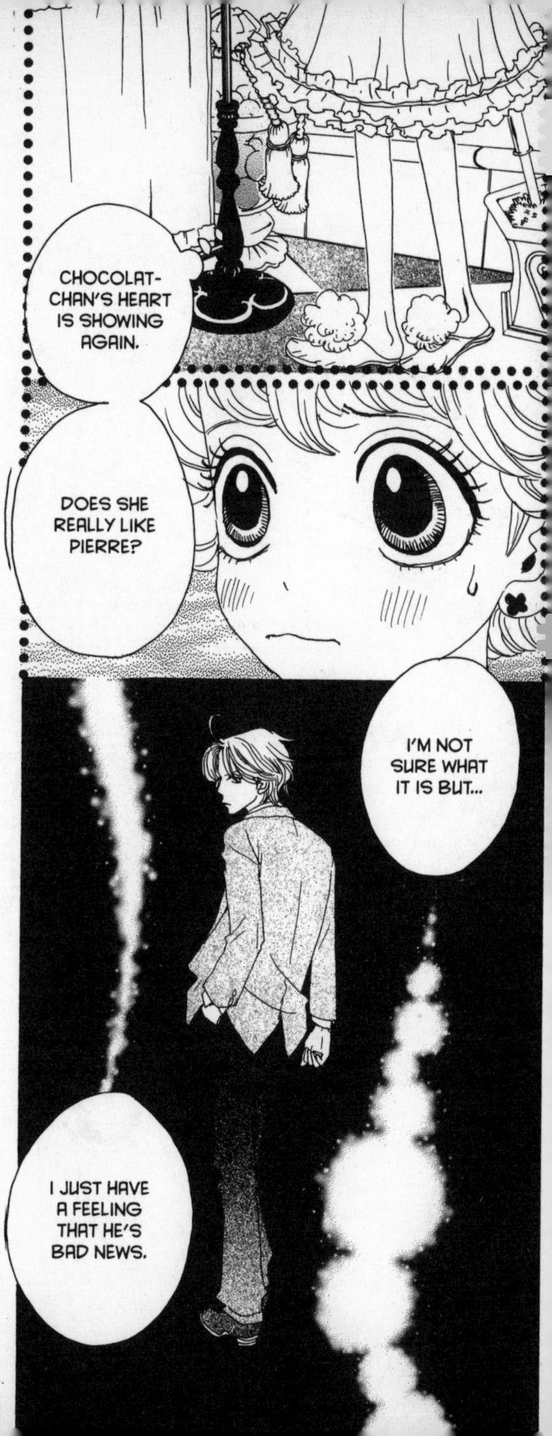
CHOCOLAT-CHAN'S HEART IS SHOWING AGAIN.
DOES SHE REALLY LIKE PIERRE?
I'M NOT SURE WHAT IT IS BUT...
I JUST HAVE A FEELING THAT HE'S BAD NEWS.

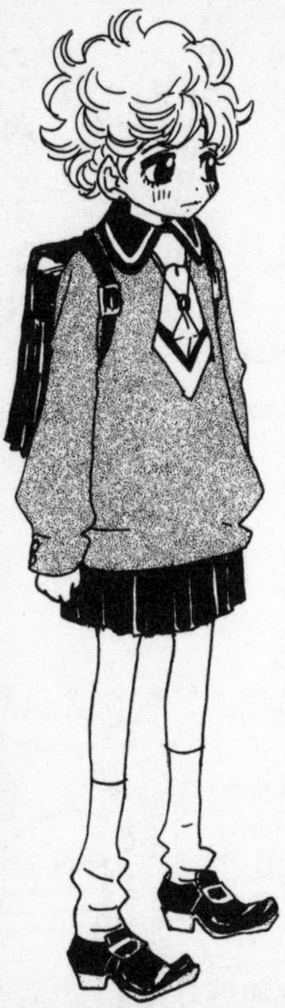

VANILLA MIEUX
(VANILLA ICE)

HEIGHT: 150CM

AGE: 10 HUMAN YEARS OLD

HOBBY: BAKING

SPECIALTY: TALKING WITH SENIOR CITIZENS

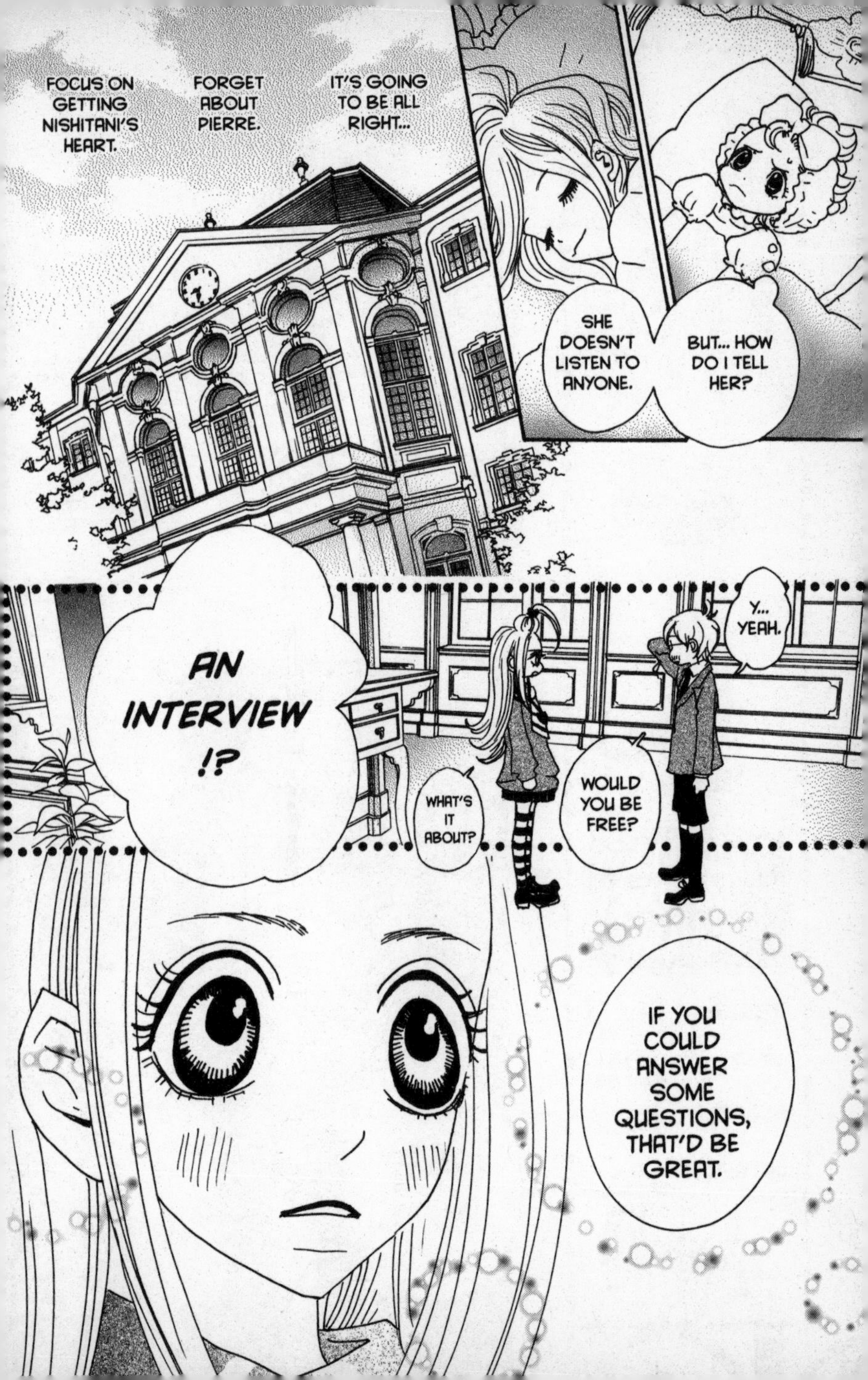
BUT... HOW DO I TELL HER?
SHE DOESN'T LISTEN TO ANYONE.
IT'S GOING TO BE ALL RIGHT...
FORGET ABOUT PIERRE.
FOCUS ON GETTING NISHITANI'S HEART.
Y... YEAH.
WOULD YOU BE FREE?
WHAT'S IT ABOUT?
IF YOU COULD ANSWER SOME QUESTIONS, THAT'D BE GREAT.
AN INTERVIEW !?

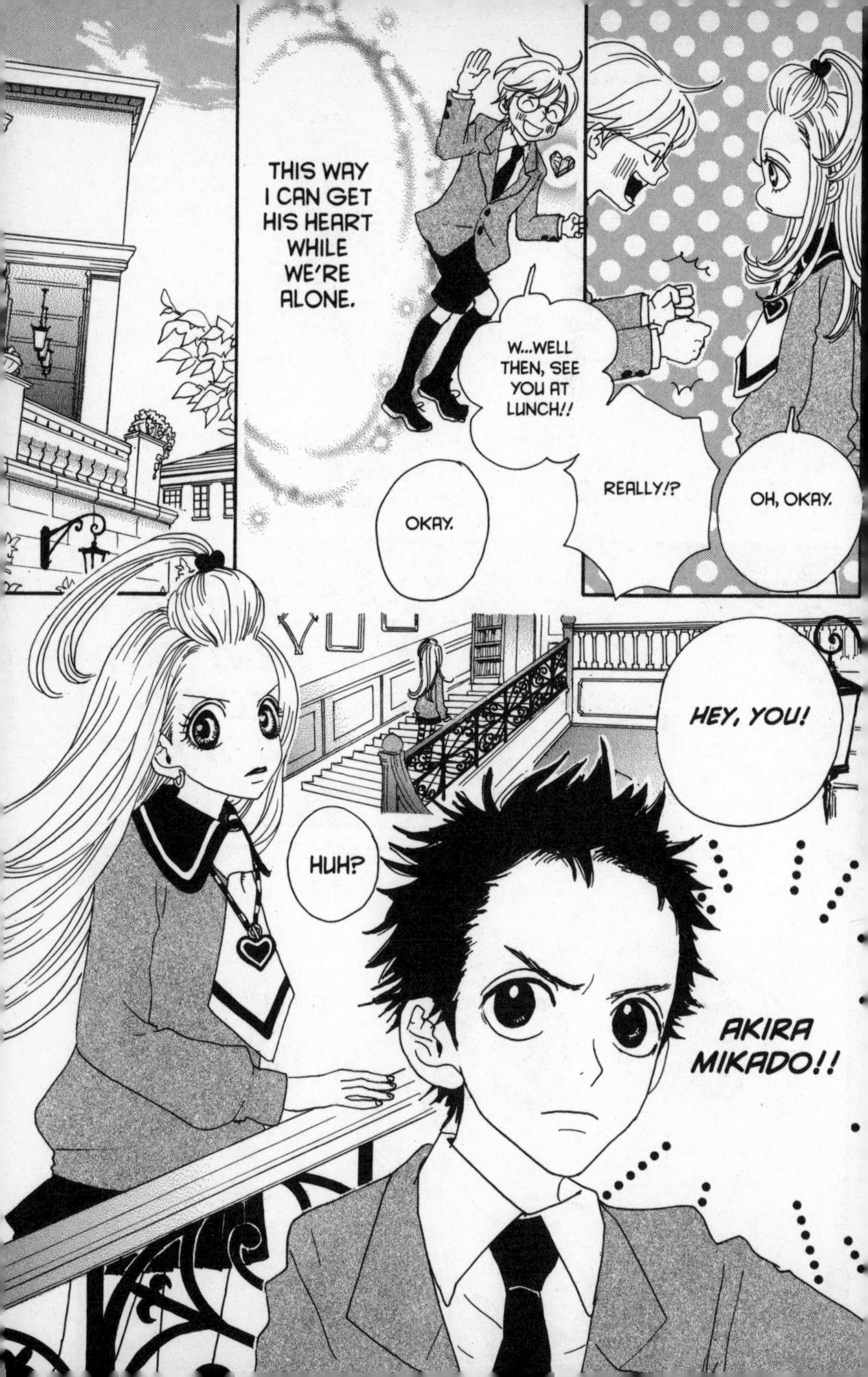

OH, OKAY.
REALLY!?
W...WELL THEN, SEE YOU AT LUNCH!!
OKAY.
THIS WAY I CAN GET HIS HEART WHILE WE'RE ALONE.
HEY, YOU!
HUH?
AKIRA MIKADO!!

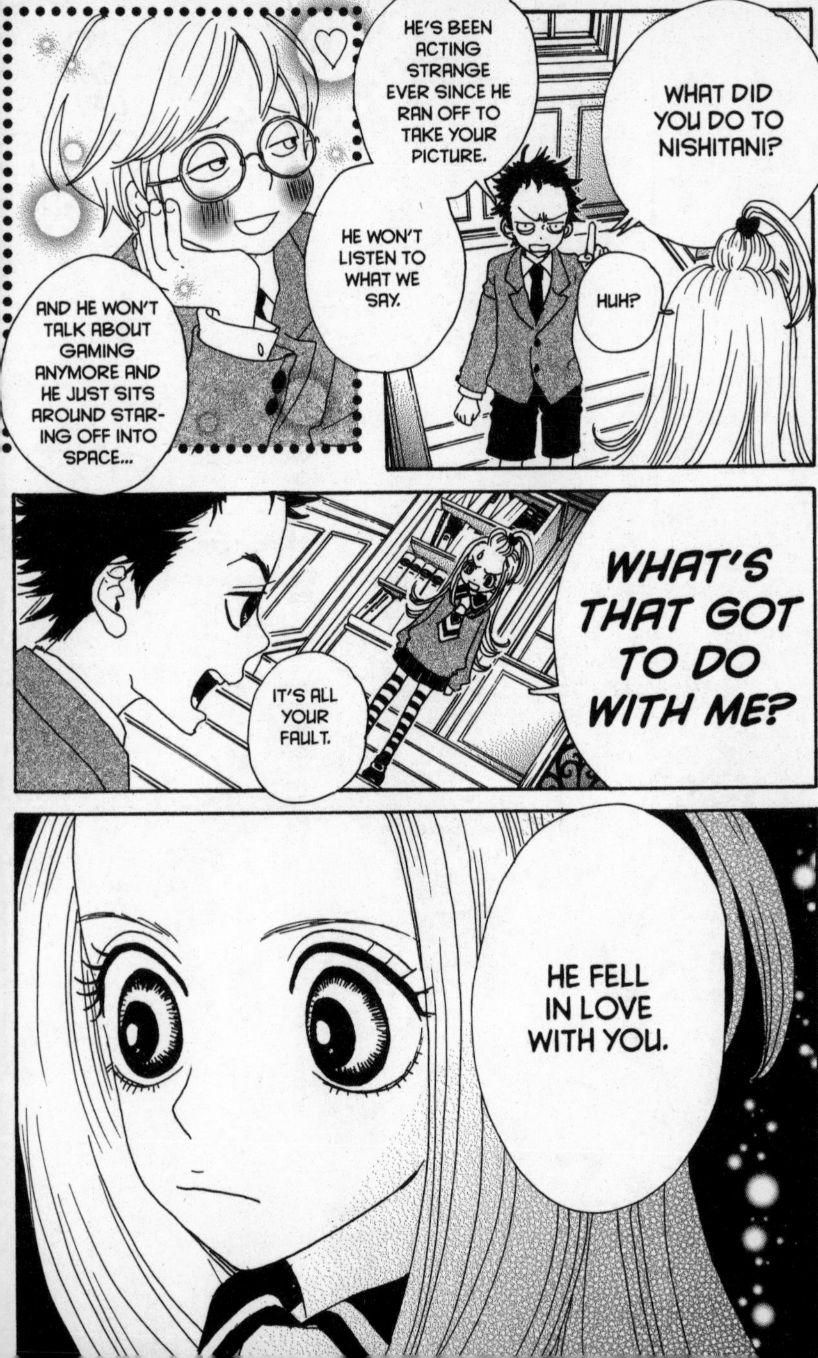
WHAT DID YOU DO TO NISHITANI?
HUH?
HE'S BEEN ACTING STRANGE EVER SINCE HE RAN OFF TO TAKE YOUR PICTURE.
HE WON'T LISTEN TO WHAT WE SAY.
AND HE WON'T TALK ABOUT GAMING ANYMORE AND HE JUST SITS AROUND STAR-ING OFF INTO SPACE...
WHAT'S THAT GOT TO DO WITH ME?
IT'S ALL YOUR FAULT.
HE FELL IN LOVE WITH YOU.

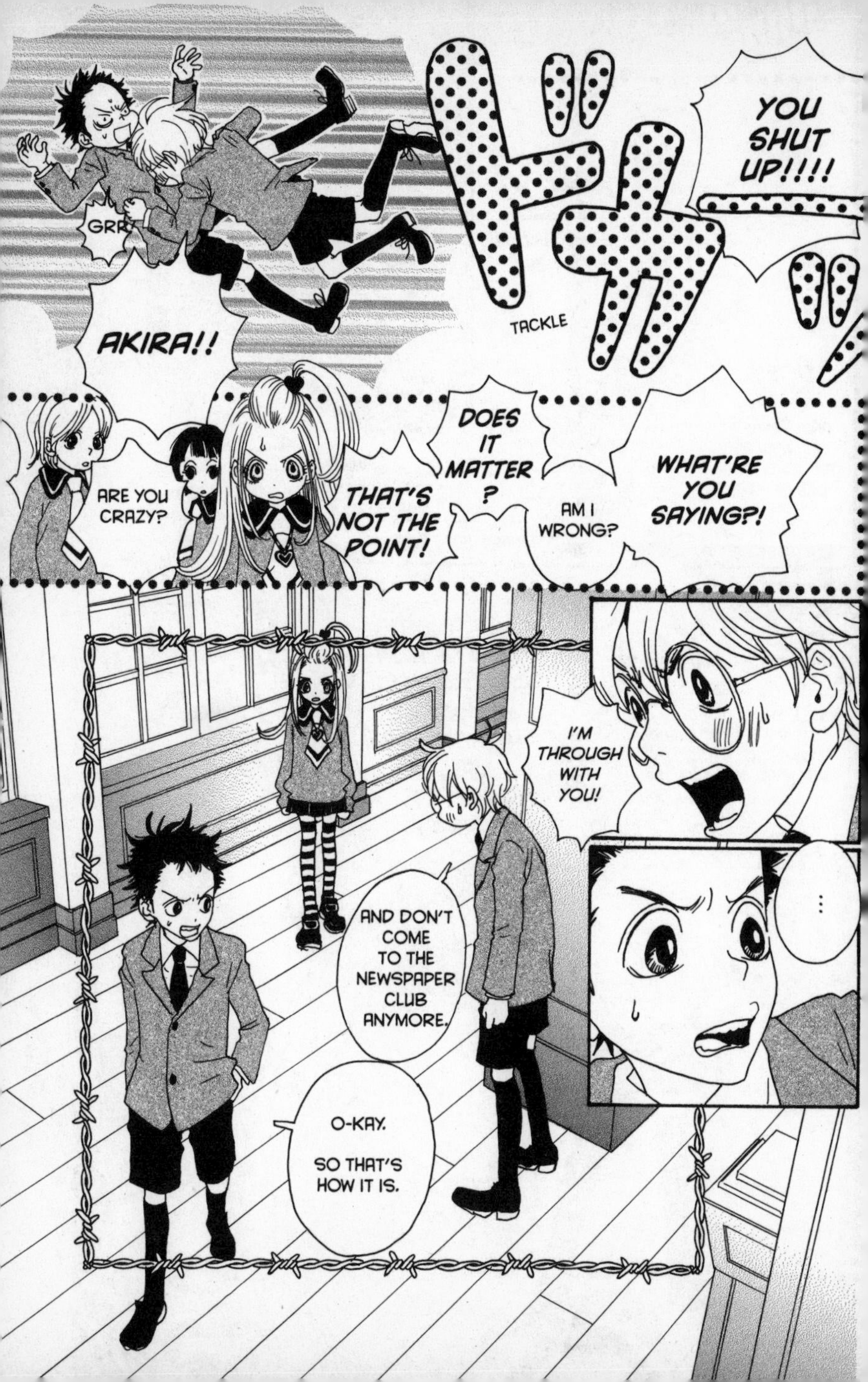
YOU SHUT UP!!!!
TACKLE
GRR
AKIRA!!
WHAT'RE YOU SAYING?!
AM I WRONG?
DOES IT MATTER?
THAT'S NOT THE POINT!
ARE YOU CRAZY?
I'M THROUGH WITH YOU!
...
AND DON'T COME TO THE NEWSPAPER CLUB ANYMORE.
O-KAY.
SO THAT'S HOW IT IS.

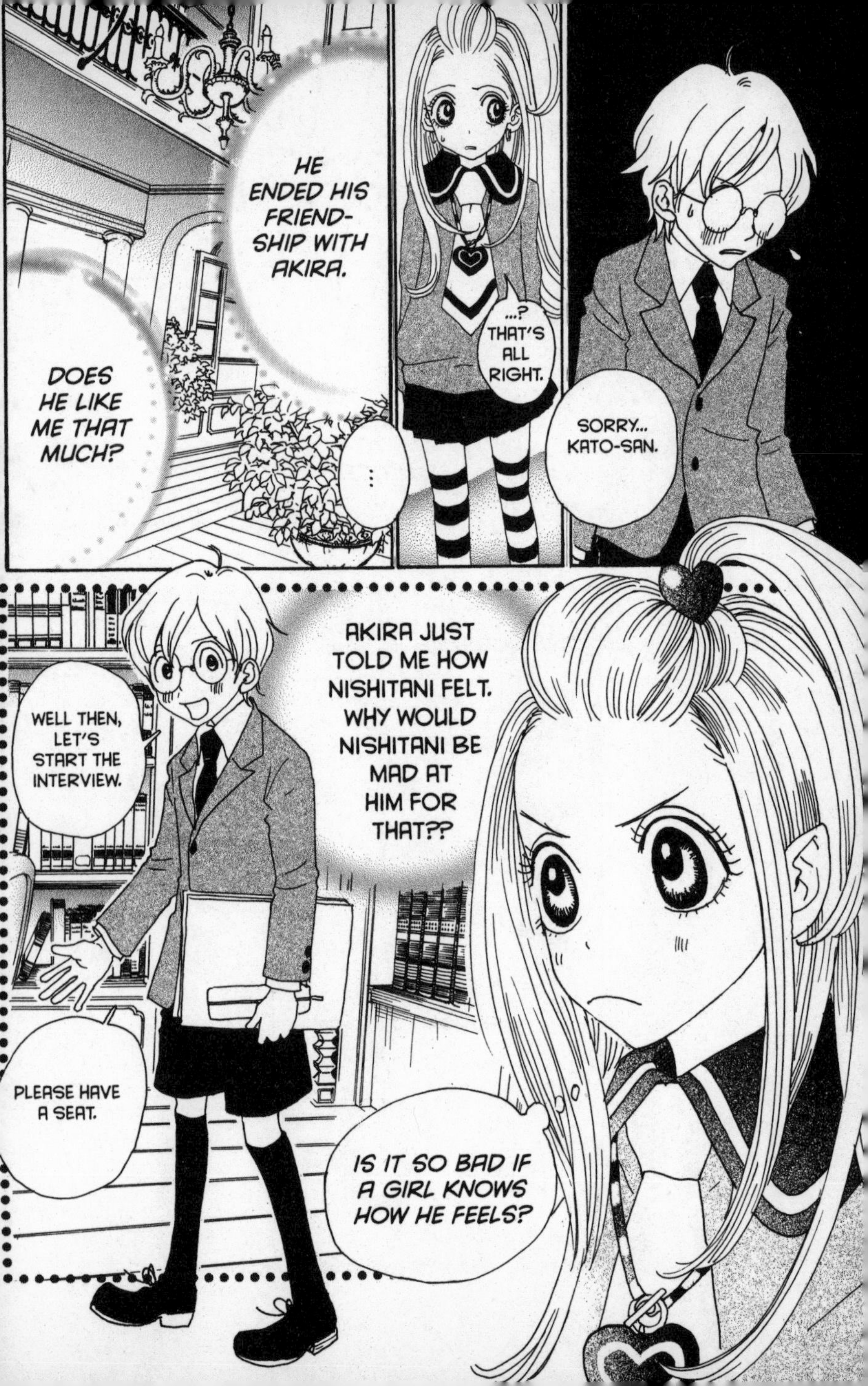
SORRY... KATO-SAN.
...? THAT'S ALL RIGHT.
...
HE ENDED HIS FRIEND-SHIP WITH AKIRA.
DOES HE LIKE ME THAT MUCH?
AKIRA JUST TOLD ME HOW NISHITANI FELT. WHY WOULD NISHITANI BE MAD AT HIM FOR THAT??
IS IT SO BAD IF A GIRL KNOWS HOW HE FEELS?
WELL THEN, LET'S START THE INTERVIEW.
PLEASE HAVE A SEAT.

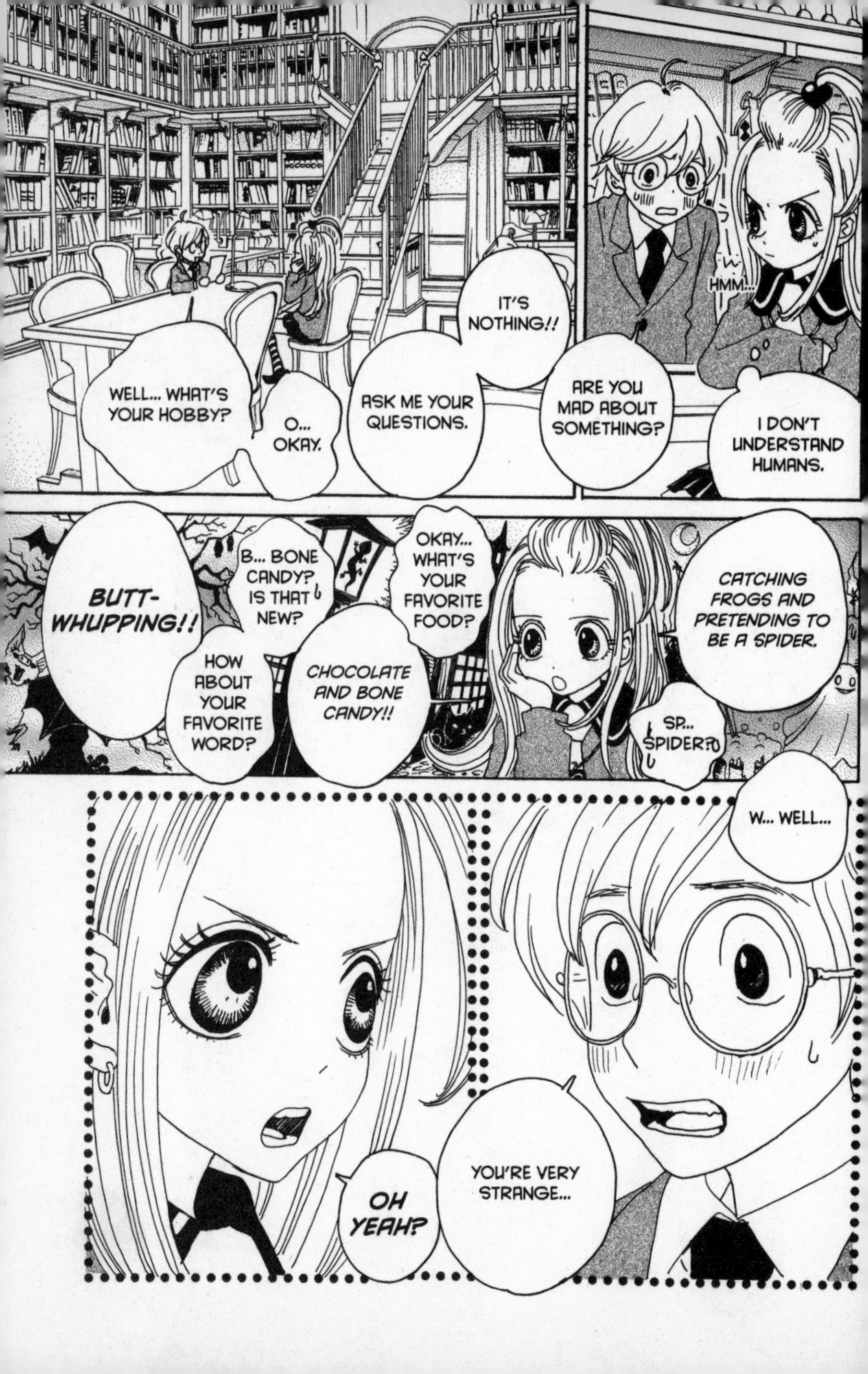
I DON'T UNDERSTAND HUMANS.
HMM...
ARE YOU MAD ABOUT SOMETHING?
IT'S NOTHING!!
ASK ME YOUR QUESTIONS.
O... OKAY.
WELL... WHAT'S YOUR HOBBY?
CATCHING FROGS AND PRETENDING TO BE A SPIDER.
SP... SPIDER?!
OKAY... WHAT'S YOUR FAVORITE FOOD?
CHOCOLATE AND BONE CANDY!!
B... BONE CANDY? IS THAT NEW?
HOW ABOUT YOUR FAVORITE WORD?
BUTT-WHUPPING!!
W... WELL...
YOU'RE VERY STRANGE...
OH YEAH?

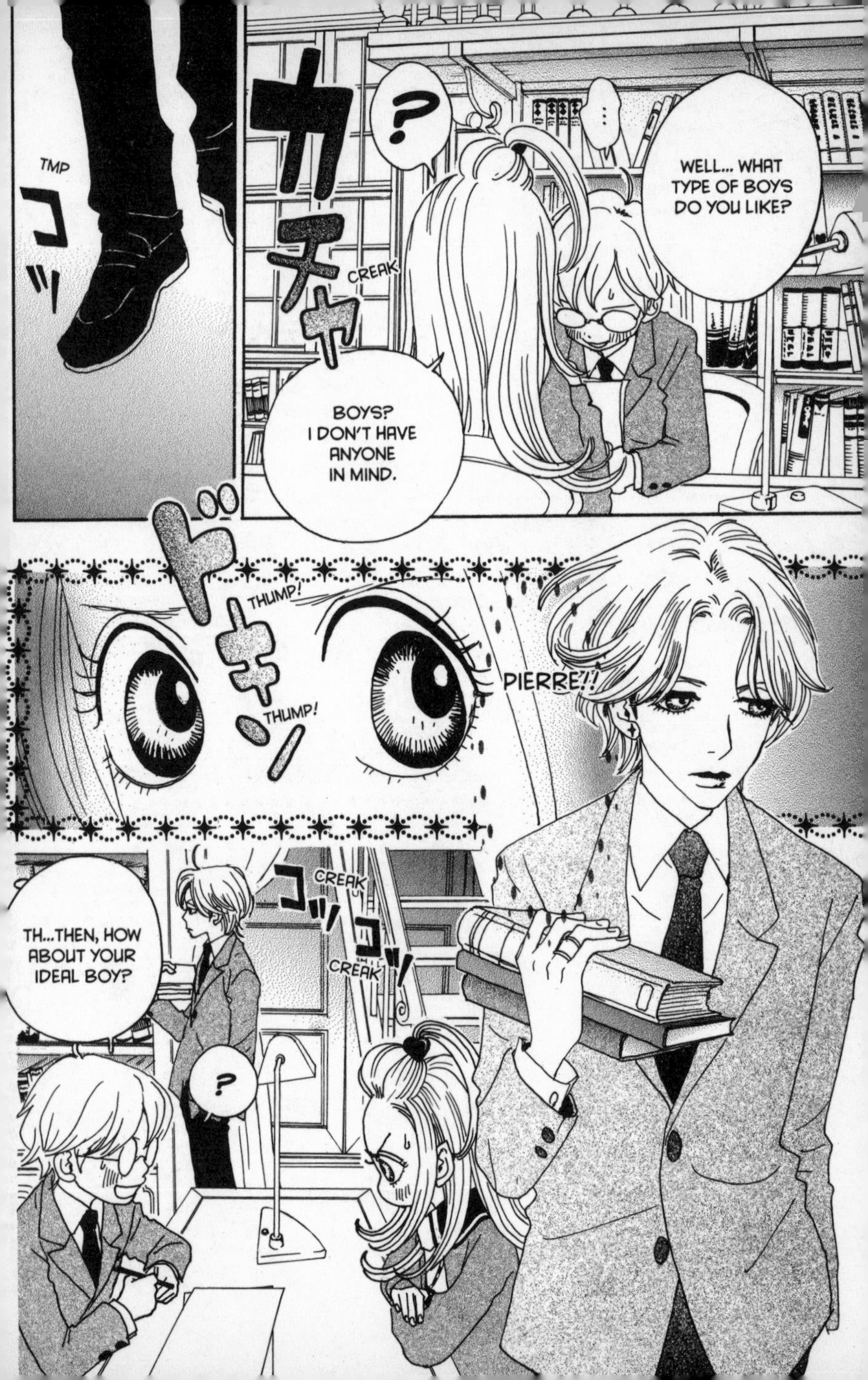
WELL... WHAT TYPE OF BOYS DO YOU LIKE?
...
?
CREAK
BOYS? I DON'T HAVE ANYONE IN MIND.
TMP
THUMP!
THUMP!
PIERRE!!
CREAK
CREAK
TH...THEN, HOW ABOUT YOUR IDEAL BOY?
?

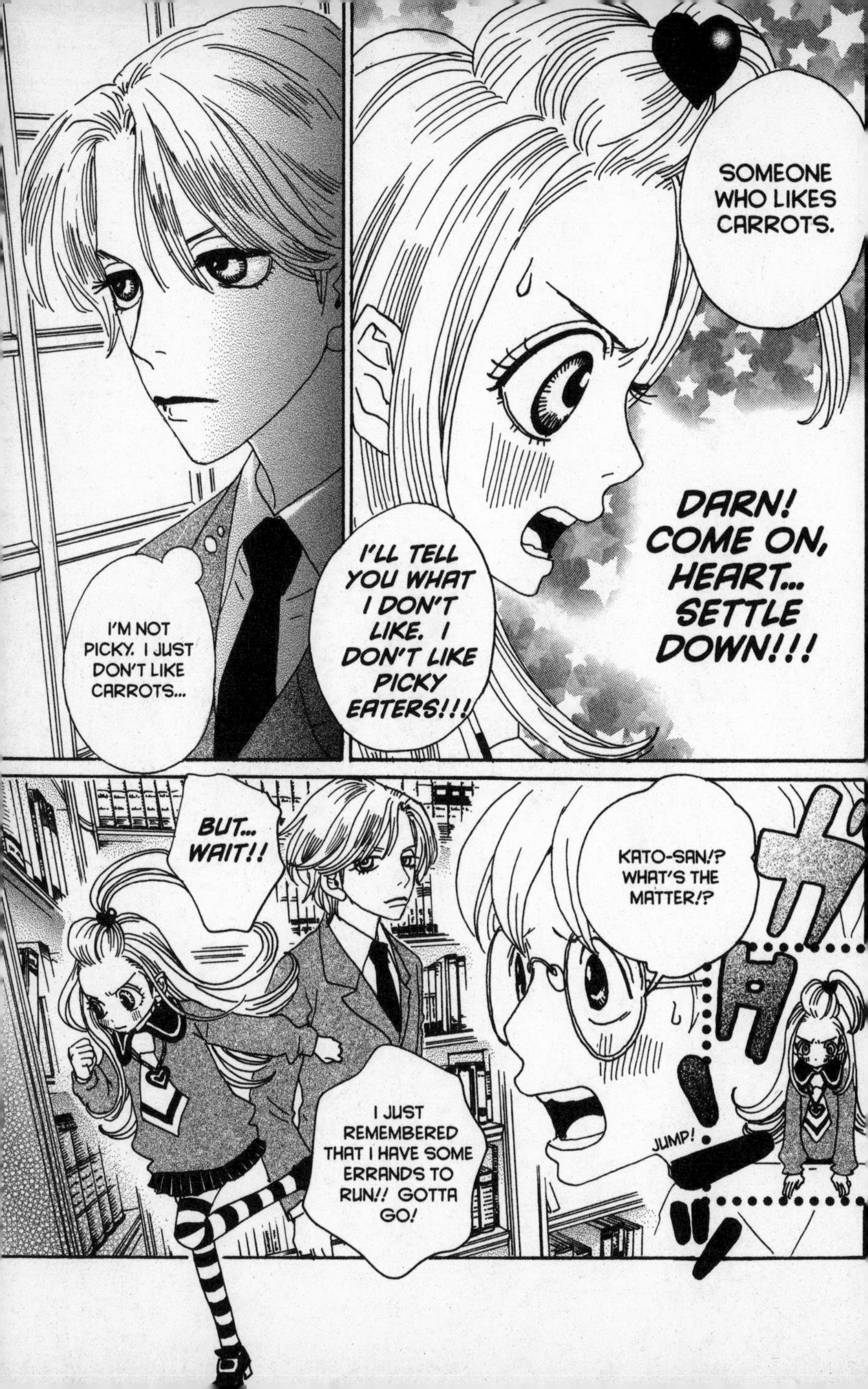
SOMEONE WHO LIKES CARROTS.
DARN! COME ON, HEART... SETTLE DOWN!!!
I'LL TELL YOU WHAT I DON'T LIKE. I DON'T LIKE PICKY EATERS!!!
I'M NOT PICKY. I JUST DON'T LIKE CARROTS...
KATO-SAN!? WHAT'S THE MATTER!?
JUMP!
I JUST REMEMBERED THAT I HAVE SOME ERRANDS TO RUN!! GOTTA GO!
BUT... WAIT!!

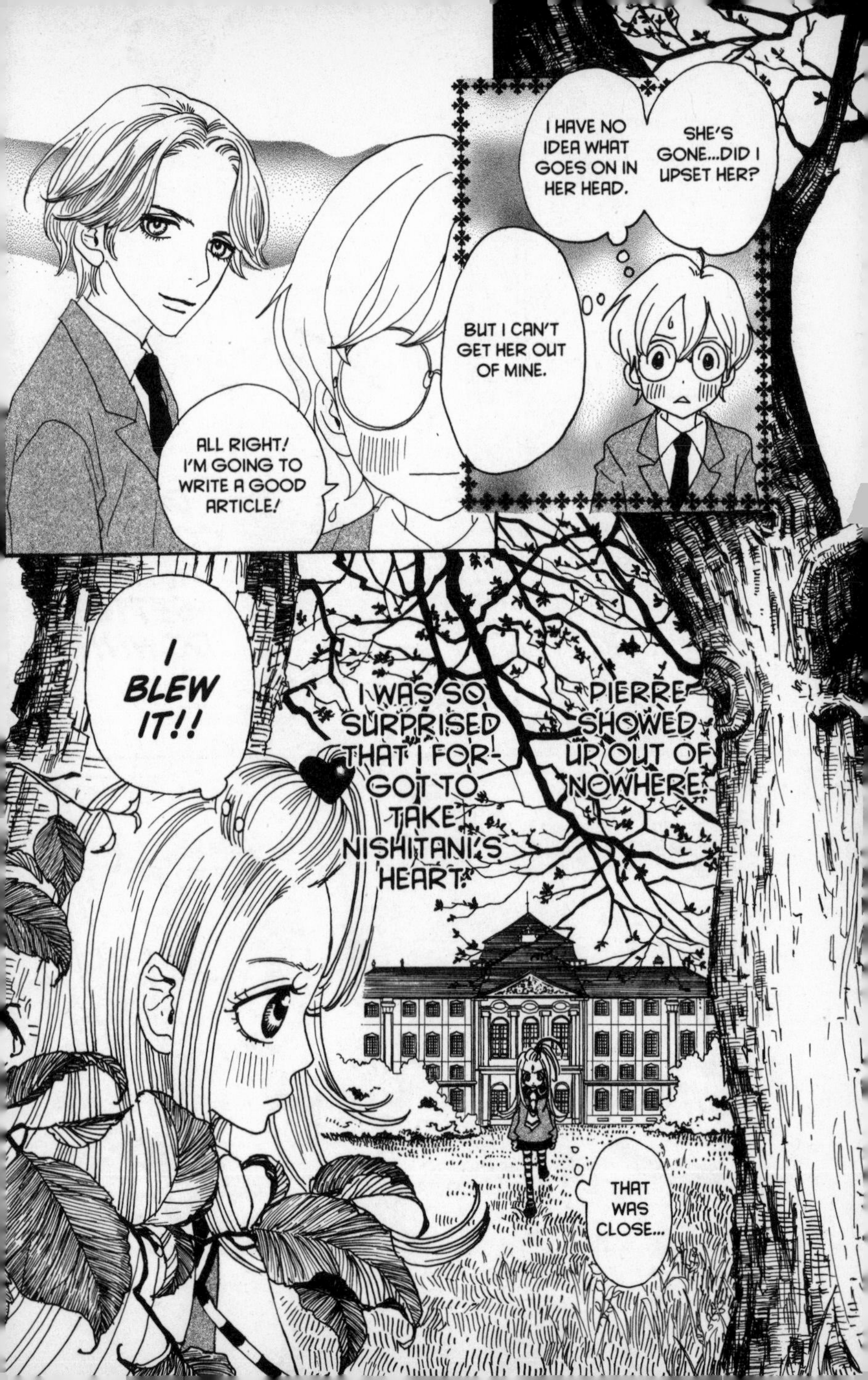
SHE'S GONE...DID I UPSET HER?
I HAVE NO IDEA WHAT GOES ON IN HER HEAD.
BUT I CAN'T GET HER OUT OF MINE.
ALL RIGHT! I'M GOING TO WRITE A GOOD ARTICLE!
PIERRE SHOWED UP OUT OF NOWHERE.
THAT WAS CLOSE...
I WAS SO SURPRISED THAT I FORGOT TO TAKE NISHITANI'S HEART.
I BLEW IT!!

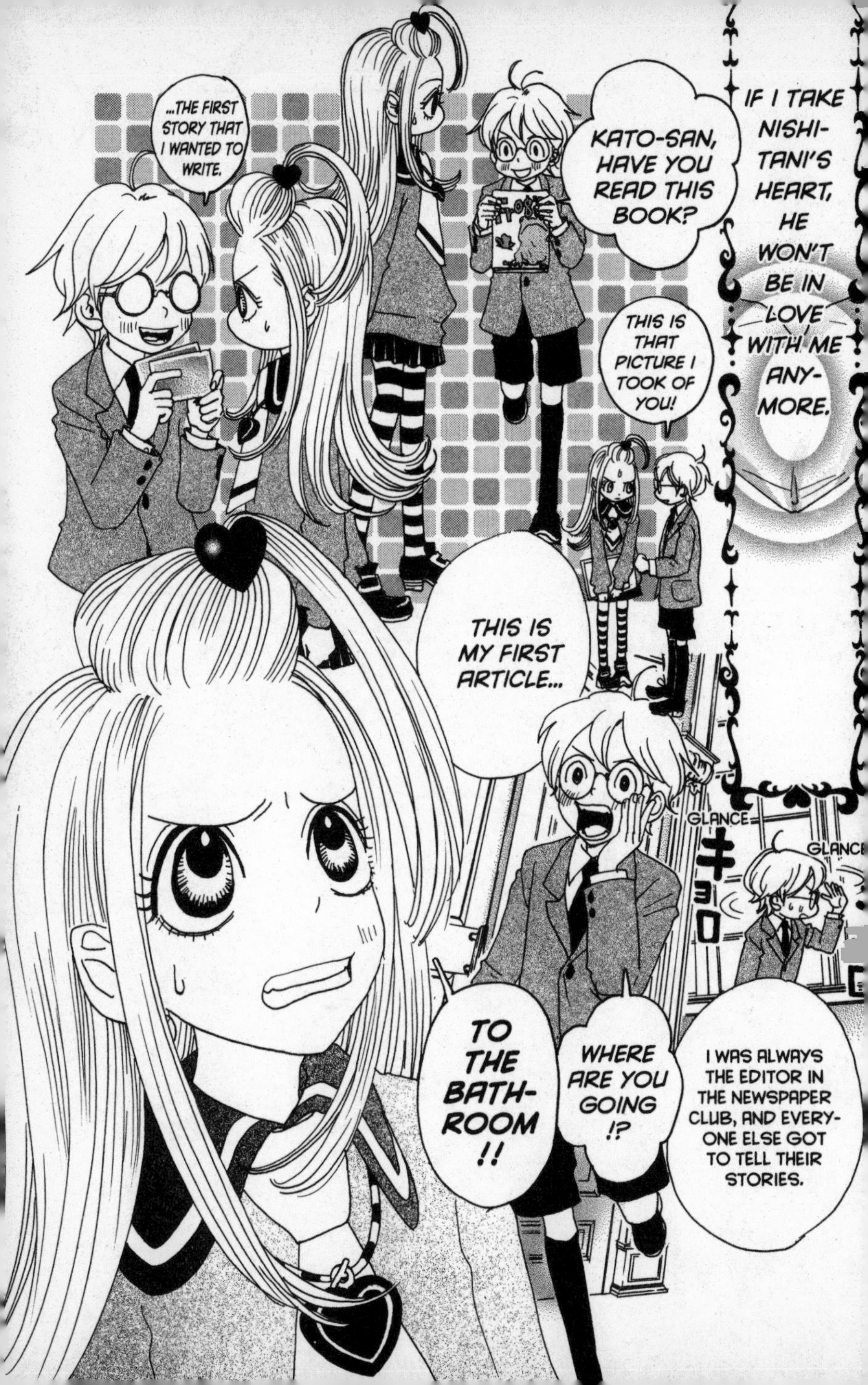
IF I TAKE NISHITANI'S HEART, HE WON'T BE IN LOVE WITH ME ANYMORE.
KATO-SAN, HAVE YOU READ THIS BOOK?
...THE FIRST STORY THAT I WANTED TO WRITE.
THIS IS THAT PICTURE I TOOK OF YOU!
THIS IS MY FIRST ARTICLE...
GLANC
キョロ
GLANCE
I WAS ALWAYS THE EDITOR IN THE NEWSPAPER CLUB, AND EVERYONE ELSE GOT TO TELL THEIR STORIES.
WHERE ARE YOU GOING!?
TO THE BATHROOM!!

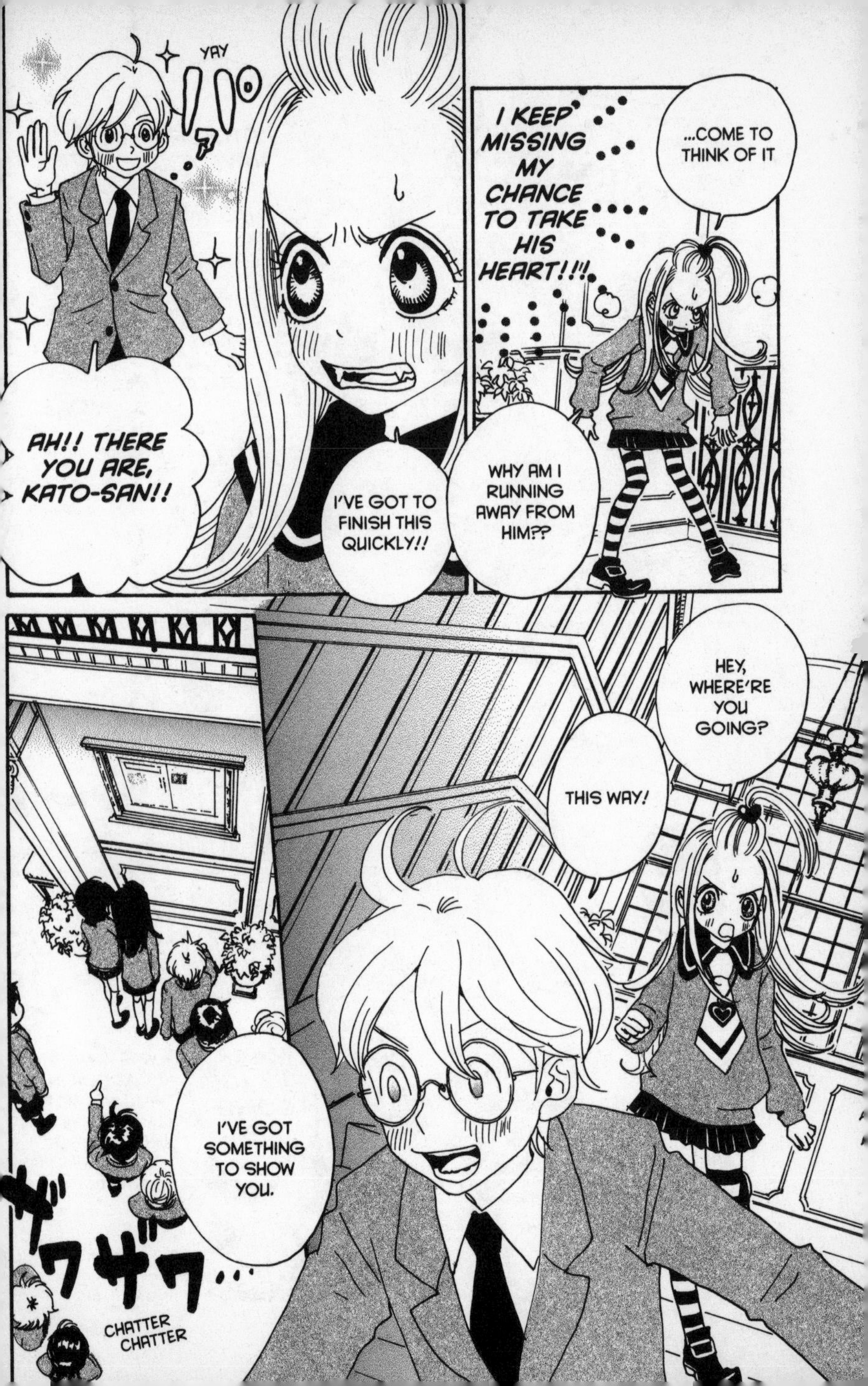
...COME TO THINK OF IT
I KEEP MISSING MY CHANCE TO TAKE HIS HEART!!!
WHY AM I RUNNING AWAY FROM HIM??
YAY
AH!! THERE YOU ARE, KATO-SAN!!
I'VE GOT TO FINISH THIS QUICKLY!!
HEY, WHERE'RE YOU GOING?
THIS WAY!
I'VE GOT SOMETHING TO SHOW YOU.
ザワザワ…
CHATTER CHATTER

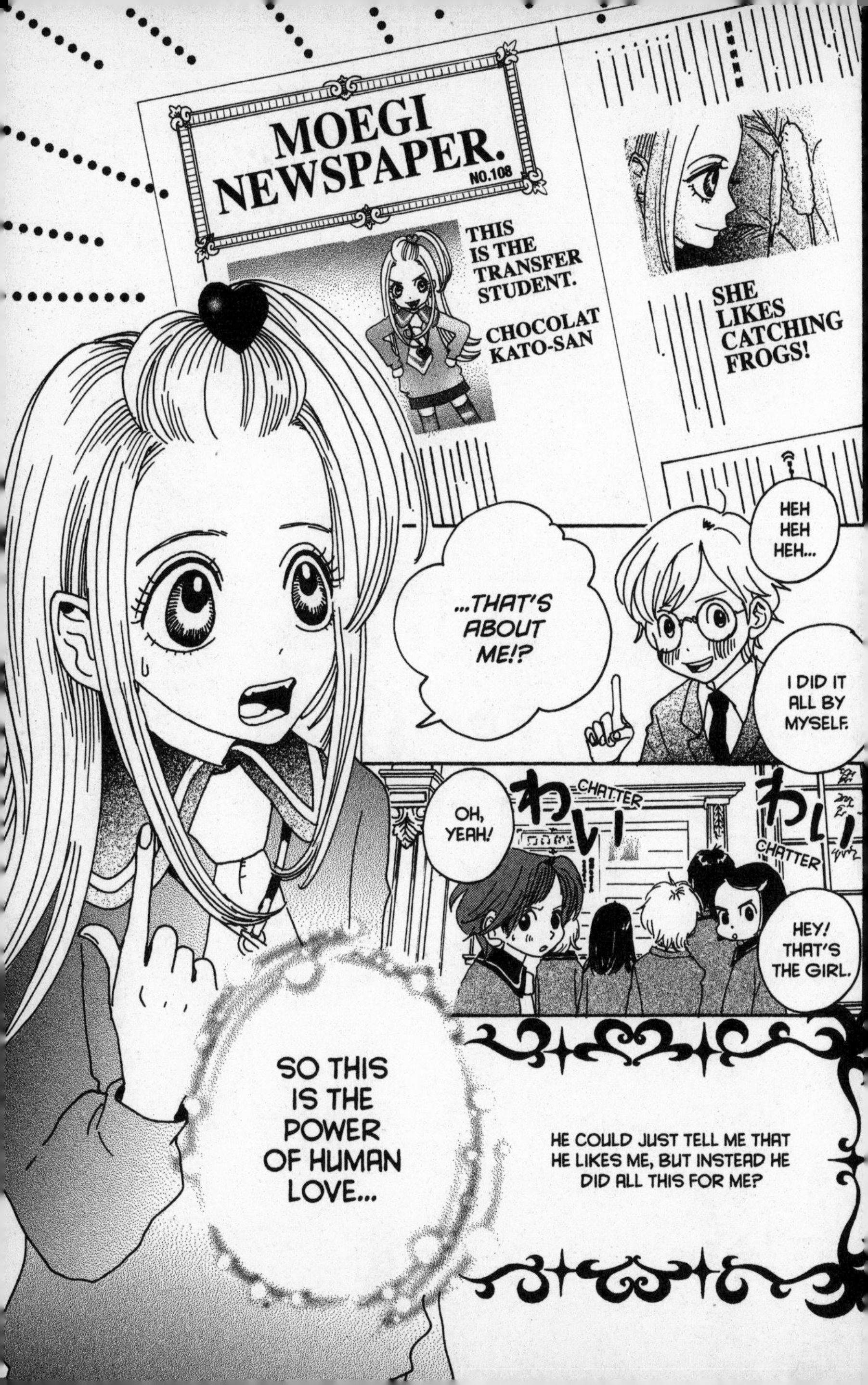
MOEGI NEWSPAPER.
NO.108
THIS IS THE TRANSFER STUDENT.
CHOCOLAT KATO-SAN
SHE LIKES CATCHING FROGS!
HEH HEH HEH...
...THAT'S ABOUT ME!?
I DID IT ALL BY MYSELF.
わい
CHATTER
わい
CHATTER
OH, YEAH!
HEY! THAT'S THE GIRL.
HE COULD JUST TELL ME THAT HE LIKES ME, BUT INSTEAD HE DID ALL THIS FOR ME?
SO THIS IS THE POWER OF HUMAN LOVE...

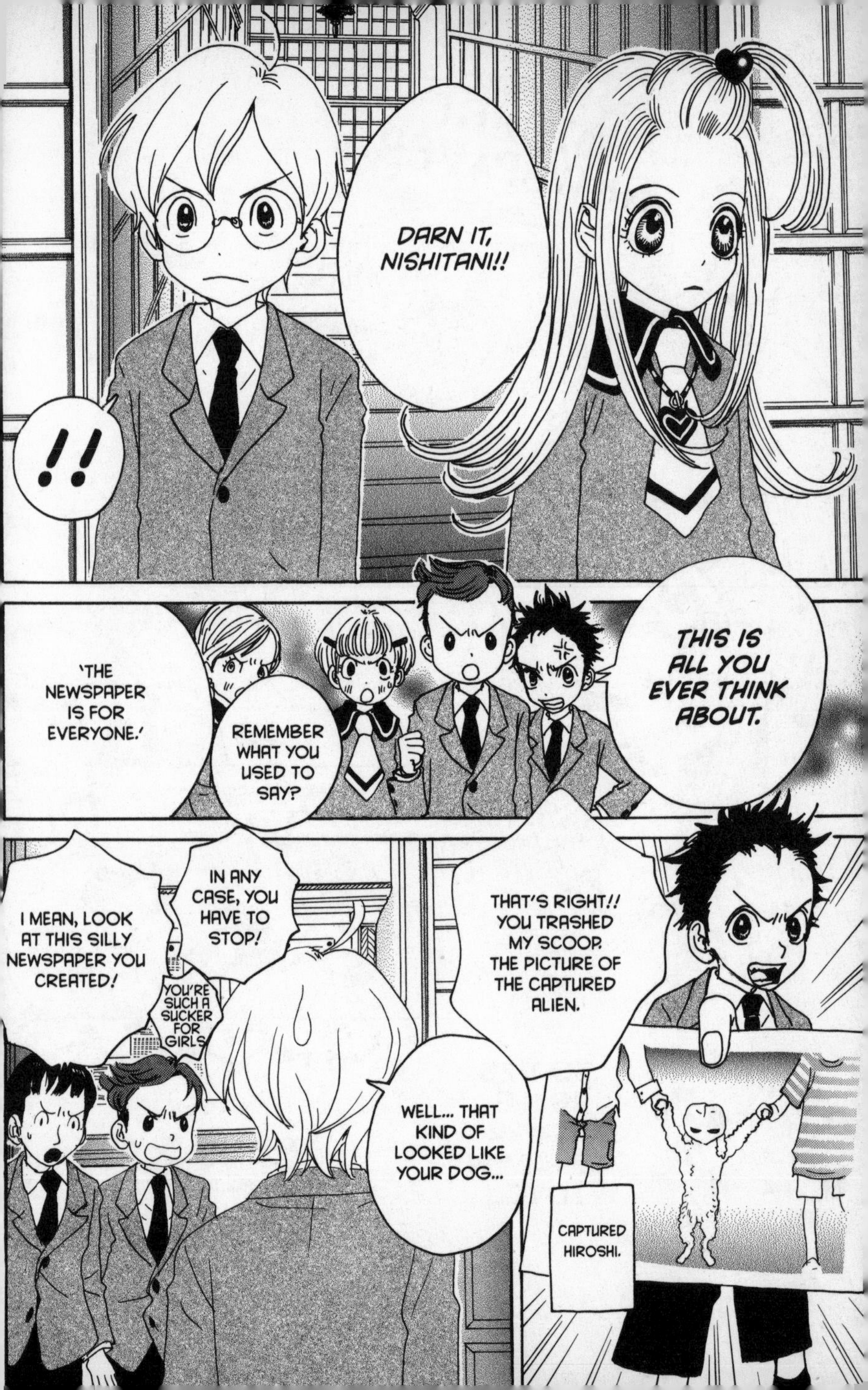
DARN IT, NISHITANI!!
!!
THIS IS ALL YOU EVER THINK ABOUT.
REMEMBER WHAT YOU USED TO SAY?
'THE NEWSPAPER IS FOR EVERYONE.'
THAT'S RIGHT!! YOU TRASHED MY SCOOP. THE PICTURE OF THE CAPTURED ALIEN.
CAPTURED HIROSHI.
WELL... THAT KIND OF LOOKED LIKE YOUR DOG...
IN ANY CASE, YOU HAVE TO STOP!
I MEAN, LOOK AT THIS SILLY NEWSPAPER YOU CREATED!
YOU'RE SUCH A SUCKER FOR GIRLS

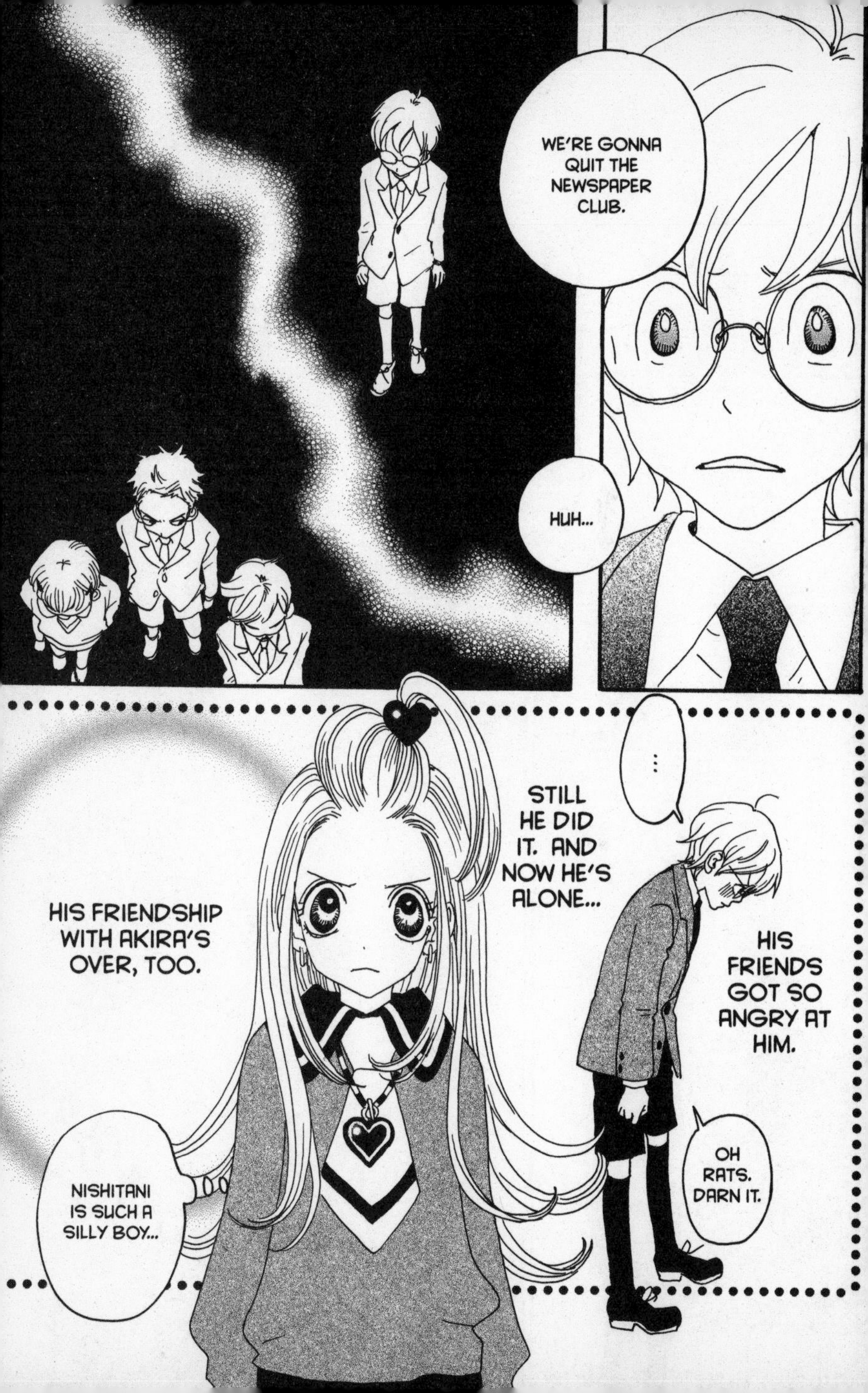
WE'RE GONNA QUIT THE NEWSPAPER CLUB.
HUH...
...
HIS FRIENDS GOT SO ANGRY AT HIM.
STILL HE DID IT. AND NOW HE'S ALONE...
HIS FRIENDSHIP WITH AKIRA'S OVER, TOO.
OH RATS. DARN IT.
NISHITANI IS SUCH A SILLY BOY...

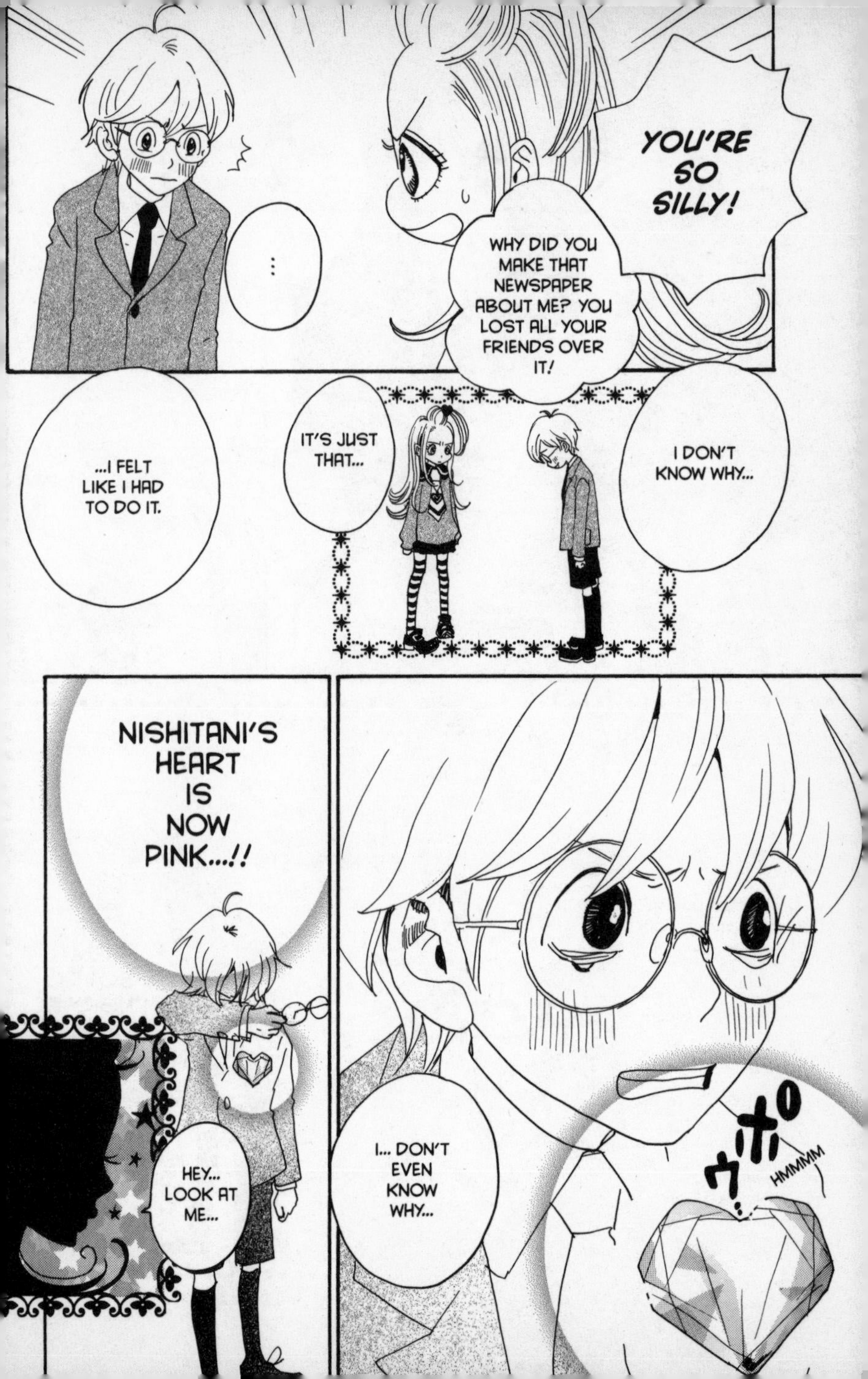
YOU'RE SO SILLY!
WHY DID YOU MAKE THAT NEWSPAPER ABOUT ME? YOU LOST ALL YOUR FRIENDS OVER IT!
...
I DON'T KNOW WHY...
IT'S JUST THAT...
...I FELT LIKE I HAD TO DO IT.
I... DON'T EVEN KNOW WHY...
HMMMM
NISHITANI'S HEART IS NOW PINK...!!
HEY... LOOK AT ME...

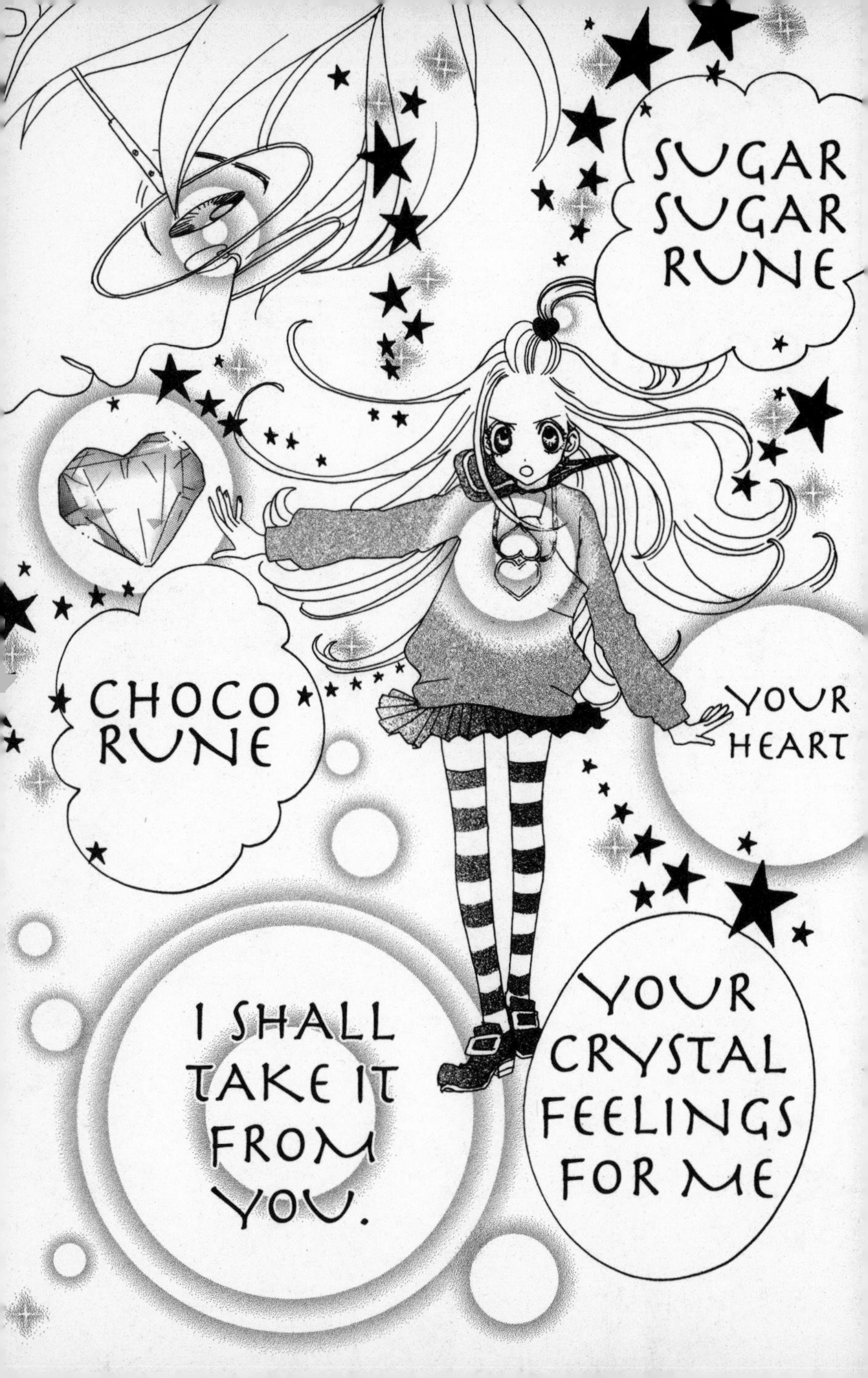
SUGAR SUGAR RUNE
CHOCO RUNE
YOUR HEART
YOUR CRYSTAL FEELINGS FOR ME
I SHALL TAKE IT FROM YOU.

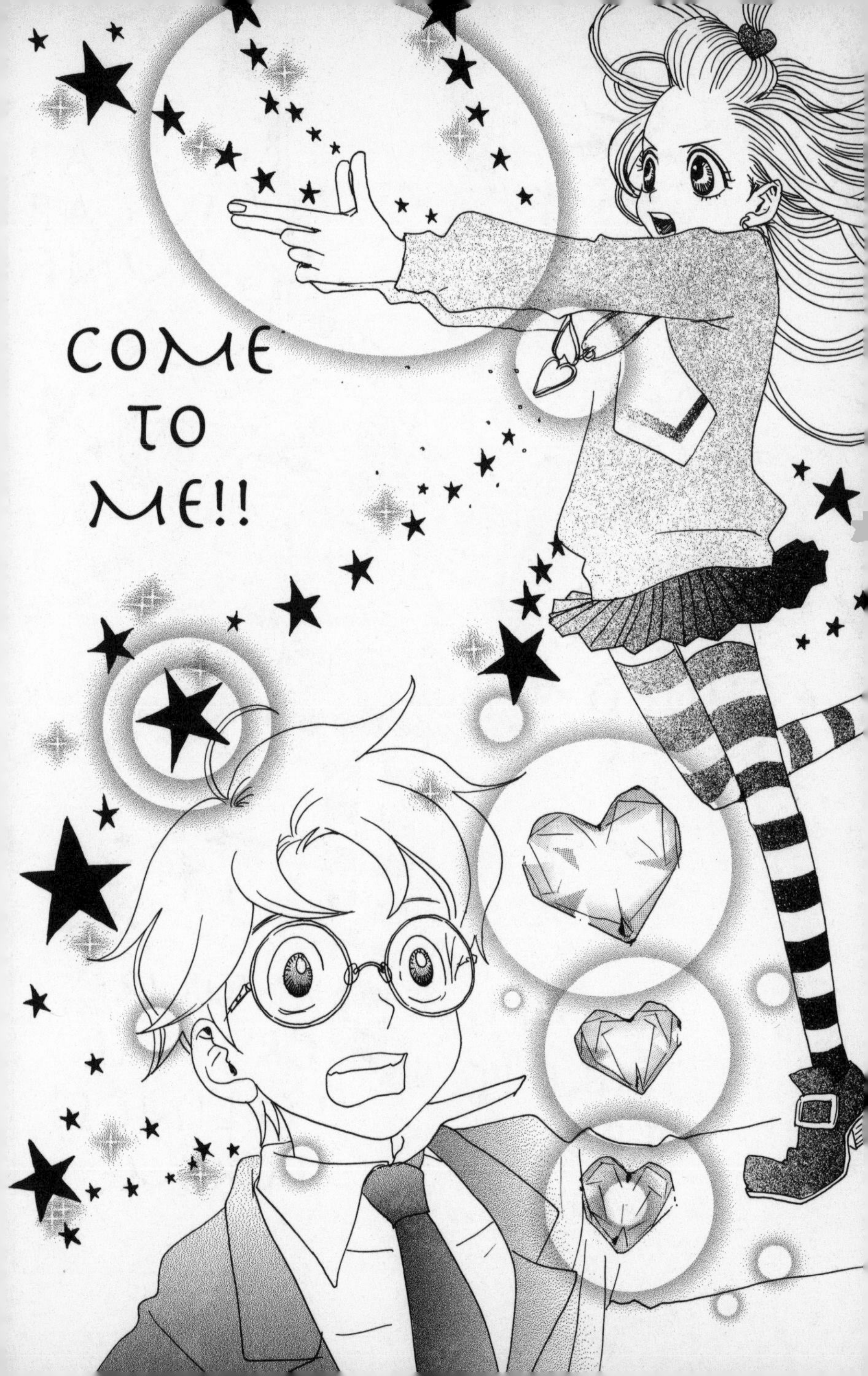
COME
TO
ME!!

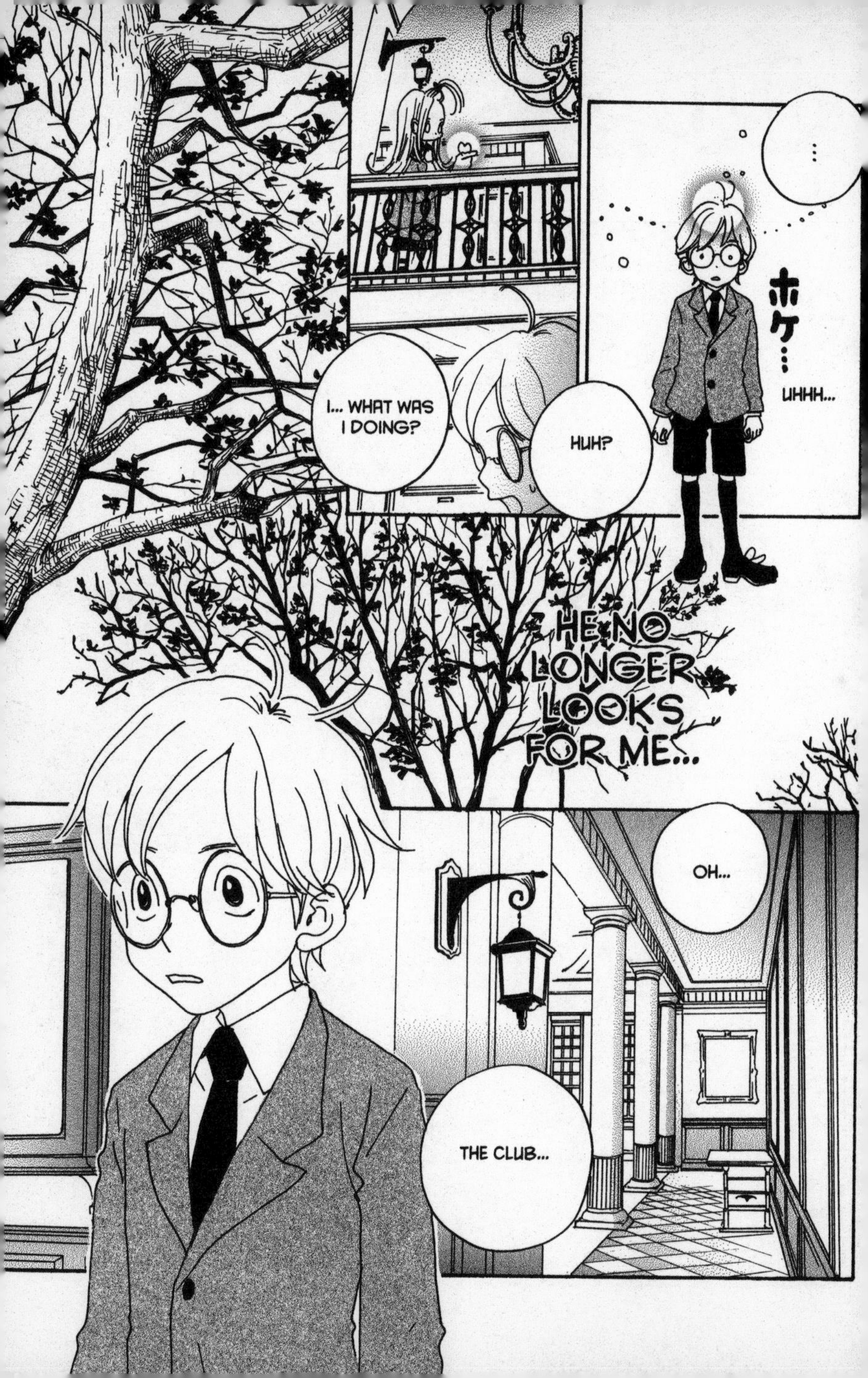
...
ホケ...
UHHH...
HUH?
I... WHAT WAS I DOING?
HE NO LONGER LOOKS FOR ME...
OH...
THE CLUB...

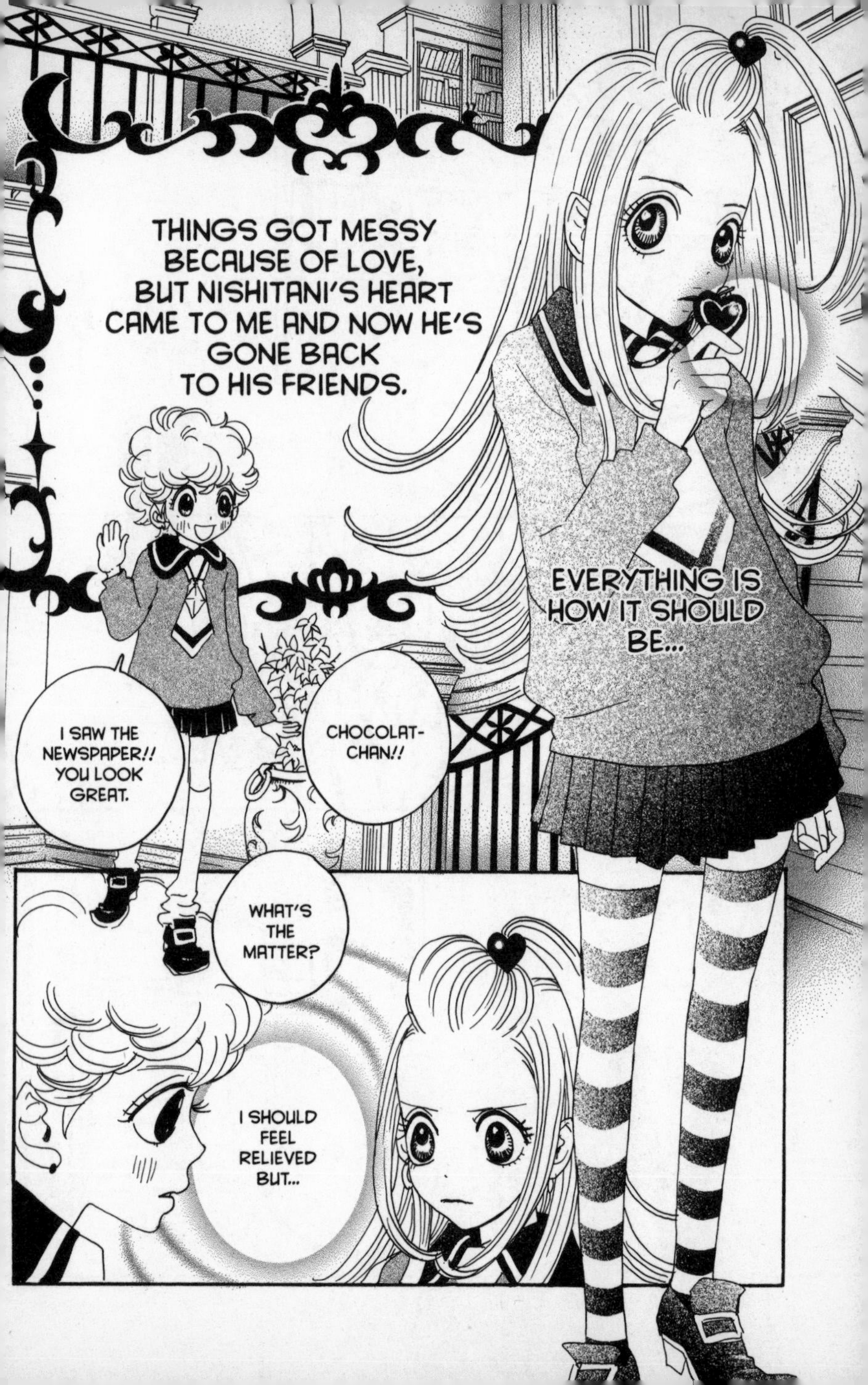
THINGS GOT MESSY BECAUSE OF LOVE, BUT NISHITANI'S HEART CAME TO ME AND NOW HE'S GONE BACK TO HIS FRIENDS.
EVERYTHING IS HOW IT SHOULD BE...
CHOCOLAT-CHAN!!
I SAW THE NEWSPAPER!! YOU LOOK GREAT.
WHAT'S THE MATTER?
I SHOULD FEEL RELIEVED BUT...

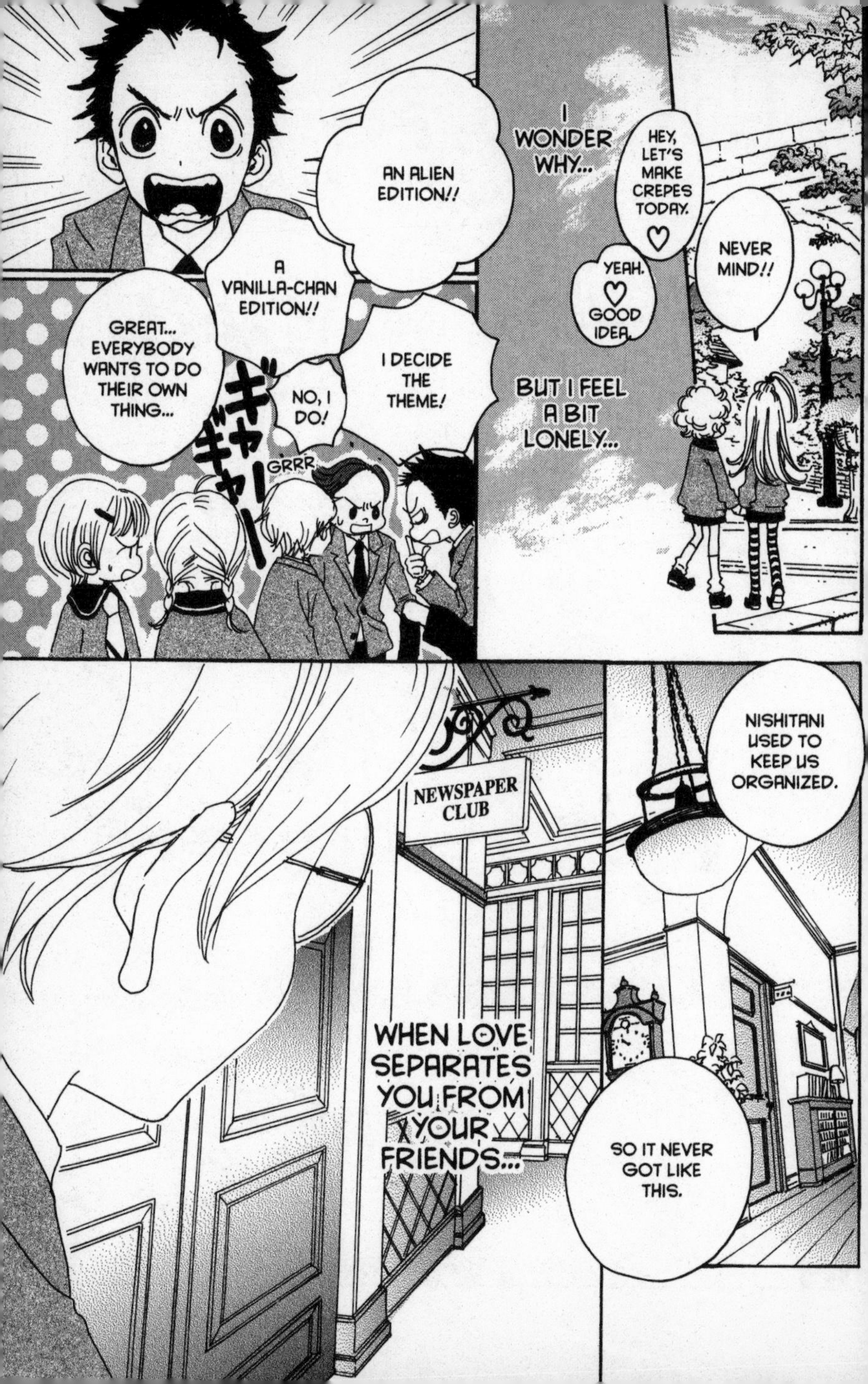
HEY, LET'S MAKE CREPES TODAY. ♡
I WONDER WHY...
YEAH. ♡ GOOD IDEA.
NEVER MIND!!
BUT I FEEL A BIT LONELY...
AN ALIEN EDITION!!
A VANILLA-CHAN EDITION!!
I DECIDE THE THEME!
NO, I DO!
GREAT... EVERYBODY WANTS TO DO THEIR OWN THING...
ギャーギャー
GRRR
NISHITANI USED TO KEEP US ORGANIZED.
SO IT NEVER GOT LIKE THIS.
NEWSPAPER CLUB
WHEN LOVE SEPARATES YOU FROM YOUR FRIENDS...

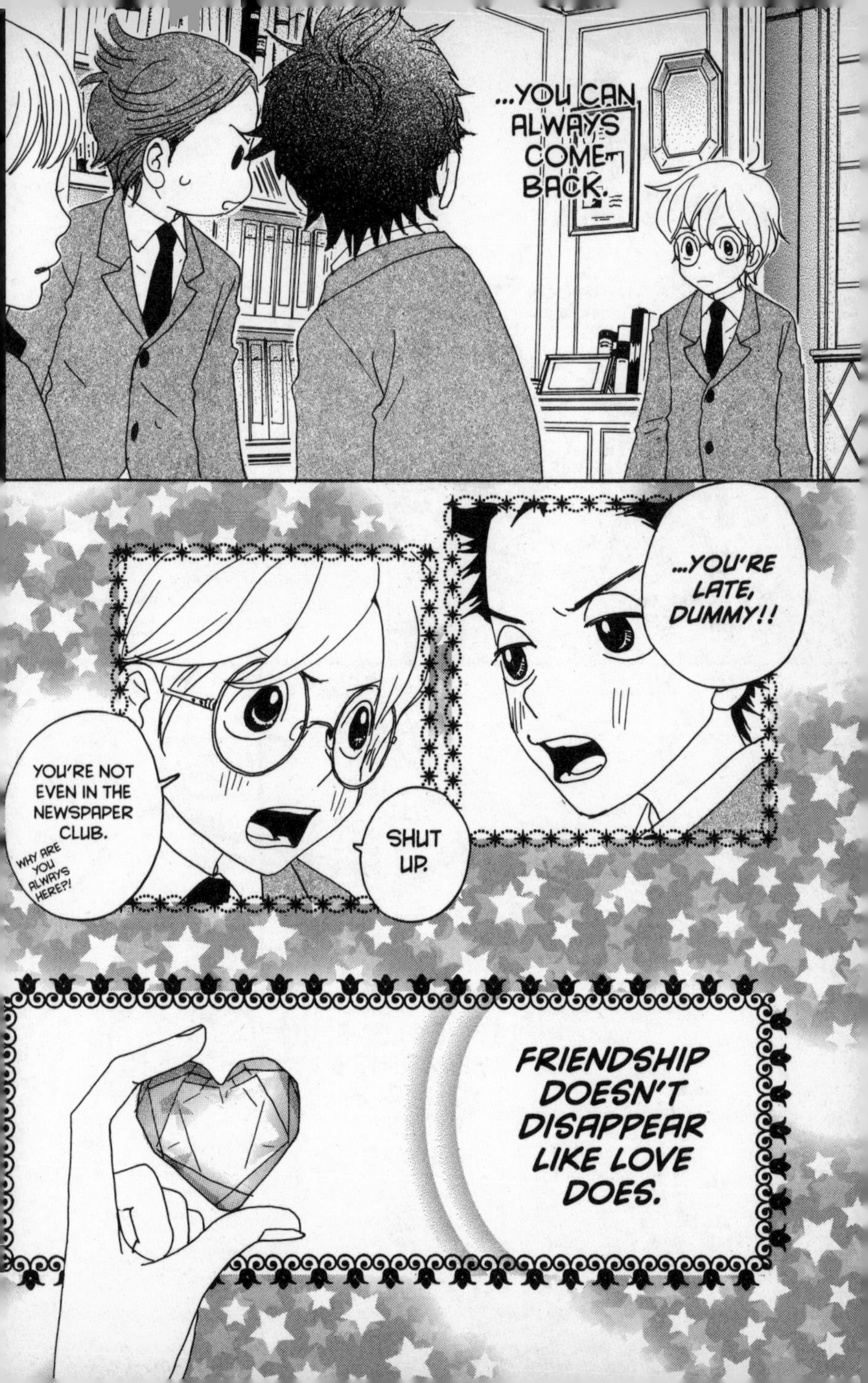
...YOU CAN ALWAYS COME BACK.
...YOU'RE LATE, DUMMY!!
SHUT UP.
YOU'RE NOT EVEN IN THE NEWSPAPER CLUB.
WHY ARE YOU ALWAYS HERE?!
FRIENDSHIP DOESN'T DISAPPEAR LIKE LOVE DOES.

THE DIFFERENCE BETWEEN WITCHES (OR WIZARDS) AND HUMANS.

NOW YOU CAN SEE THE DIFFERENCE BETWEEN HUMANS AND WITCHES LIKE CHOCOLAT WITH THIS EASY-TO-READ TABLE!

	WHERE THEY LIVE	MAGIC	HEART	LOVE
WITCHES (WIZARDS)	MAINLY IN THE MAGICAL WORLD. SOME LIVE IN THE HUMAN WORLD.	CAN USE MAGIC. BUT IN THE HUMAN WORLD, THEY NEED EXTRA ITEMS BECAUSE THEIR POWER IS WEAKER THAN IN THE MAGICAL WORLD.	IF THEIR HEART IS TAKEN, IT CAN'T BE REPLACED. IF THEIR HEART IS PINK OR HIGHER WHEN IT'S TAKEN, THEY MIGHT DIE.	SERIOUS LOVE WITH HUMANS IS FORBIDDEN. HEARTS ARE FREE TO BE EXCHANGED IN LOVE BETWEEN WITCHES AND WIZARDS.
HUMANS	IN THE HUMAN WORLD.	GENERALLY CANNOT USE ANY MAGIC.	AT ANY TIME, ANY KIND OF HEART IS POSSIBLE. THE POWER OF THE EMOTIONAL ENERGY IS HIGHER THAN IN THE HEARTS OF WITCHES (AND WIZARDS).	THEY ARE FREE TO FALL IN LOVE WITH ANYONE AT ANYTIME.

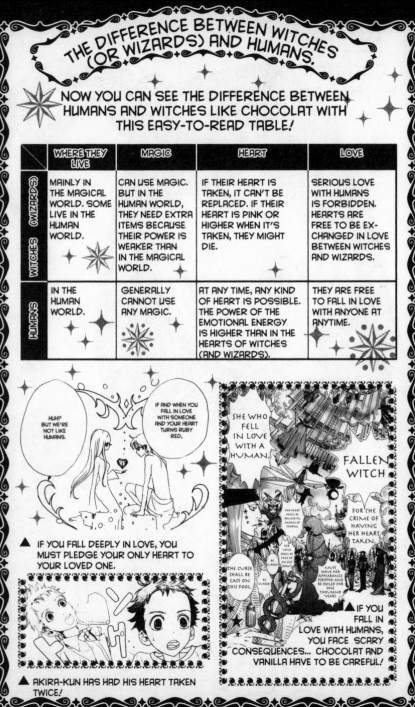

SHE WHO FELL IN LOVE WITH A HUMAN,
FALLEN WITCH
FOR THE CRIME OF HAVING HER HEART TAKEN,
HER HEART SHALL BE BOUND IN CHAINS OF THORNS.
HER VOICE SHALL BE THAT OF AN OLD CROW'S.
MUST HAVE HER APPEARANCE STRIPPED AND BE EXILED FOR ONE THOUSAND YEARS.
BE CURSED!
BE CURSED!
THE CURSE SHALL BE CAST ON THIS FOOL.

▲ IF YOU FALL IN LOVE WITH HUMANS, YOU FACE SCARY CONSEQUENCES... CHOCOLAT AND VANILLA HAVE TO BE CAREFUL!

IF AND WHEN YOU FALL IN LOVE WITH SOMEONE AND YOUR HEART TURNS RUBY RED,
HUH? BUT WE'RE NOT LIKE HUMANS.

▲ IF YOU FALL DEEPLY IN LOVE, YOU MUST PLEDGE YOUR ONLY HEART TO YOUR LOVED ONE.

▲ AKIRA-KUN HAS HAD HIS HEART TAKEN TWICE!

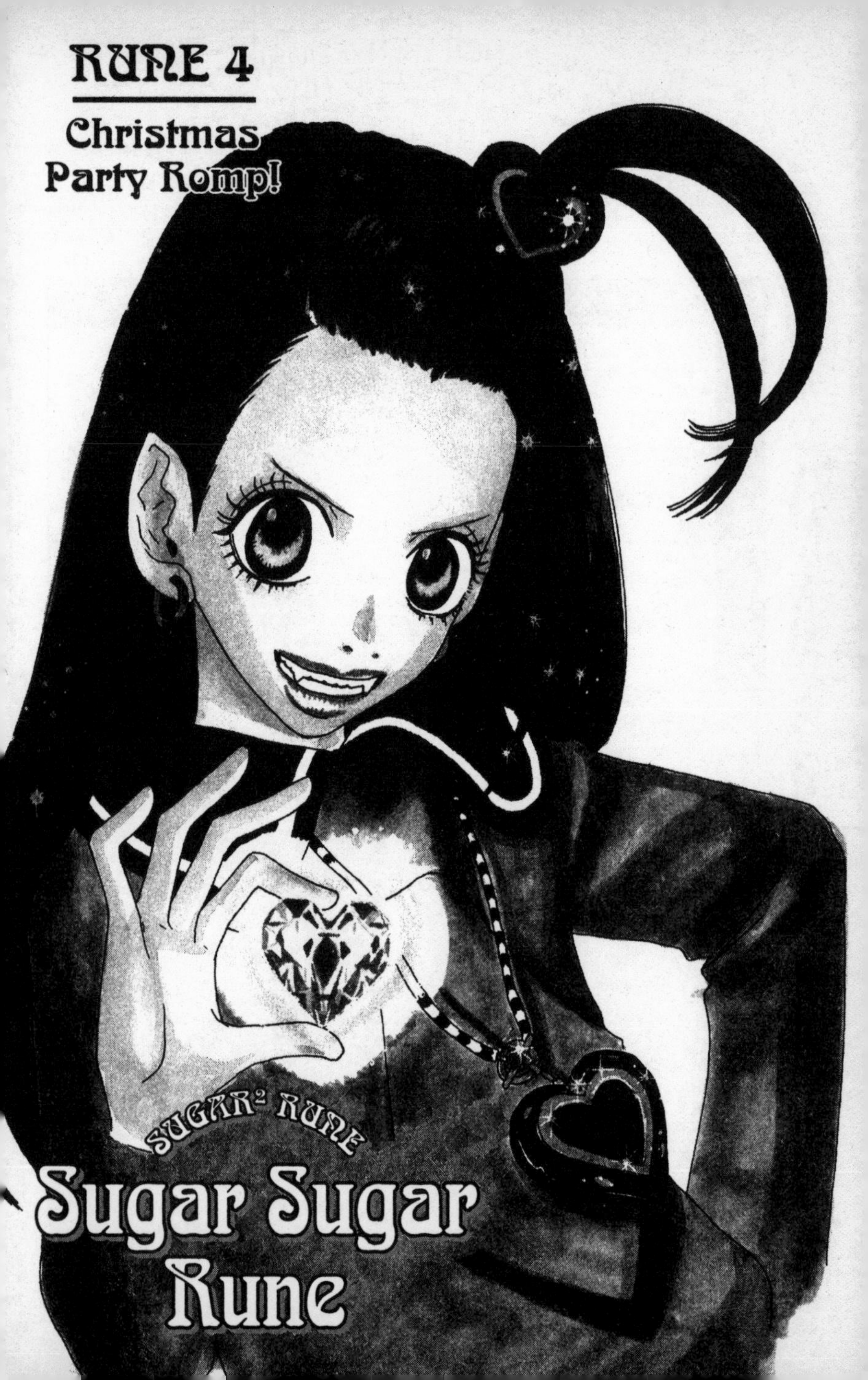
RUNE 4
Christmas Party Romp!
SUGAR² RUNE
Sugar Sugar Rune

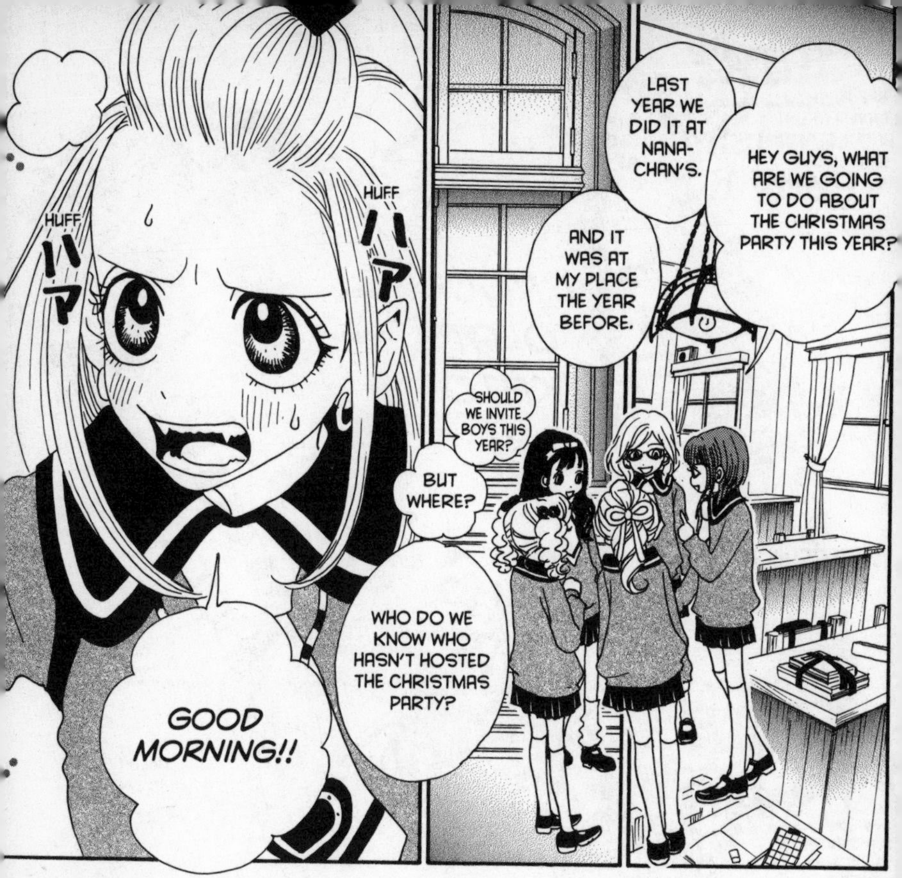
HEY GUYS, WHAT ARE WE GOING TO DO ABOUT THE CHRISTMAS PARTY THIS YEAR?
LAST YEAR WE DID IT AT NANA-CHAN'S.
AND IT WAS AT MY PLACE THE YEAR BEFORE.
SHOULD WE INVITE BOYS THIS YEAR?
BUT WHERE?
WHO DO WE KNOW WHO HASN'T HOSTED THE CHRISTMAS PARTY?
HUFF
ハア
HUFF
ハア
GOOD MORNING!!

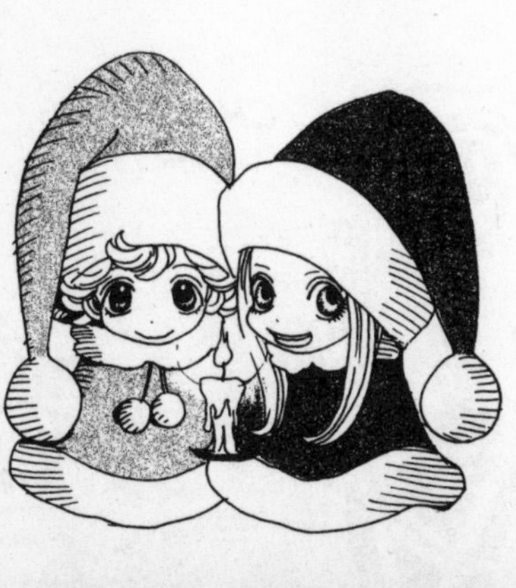

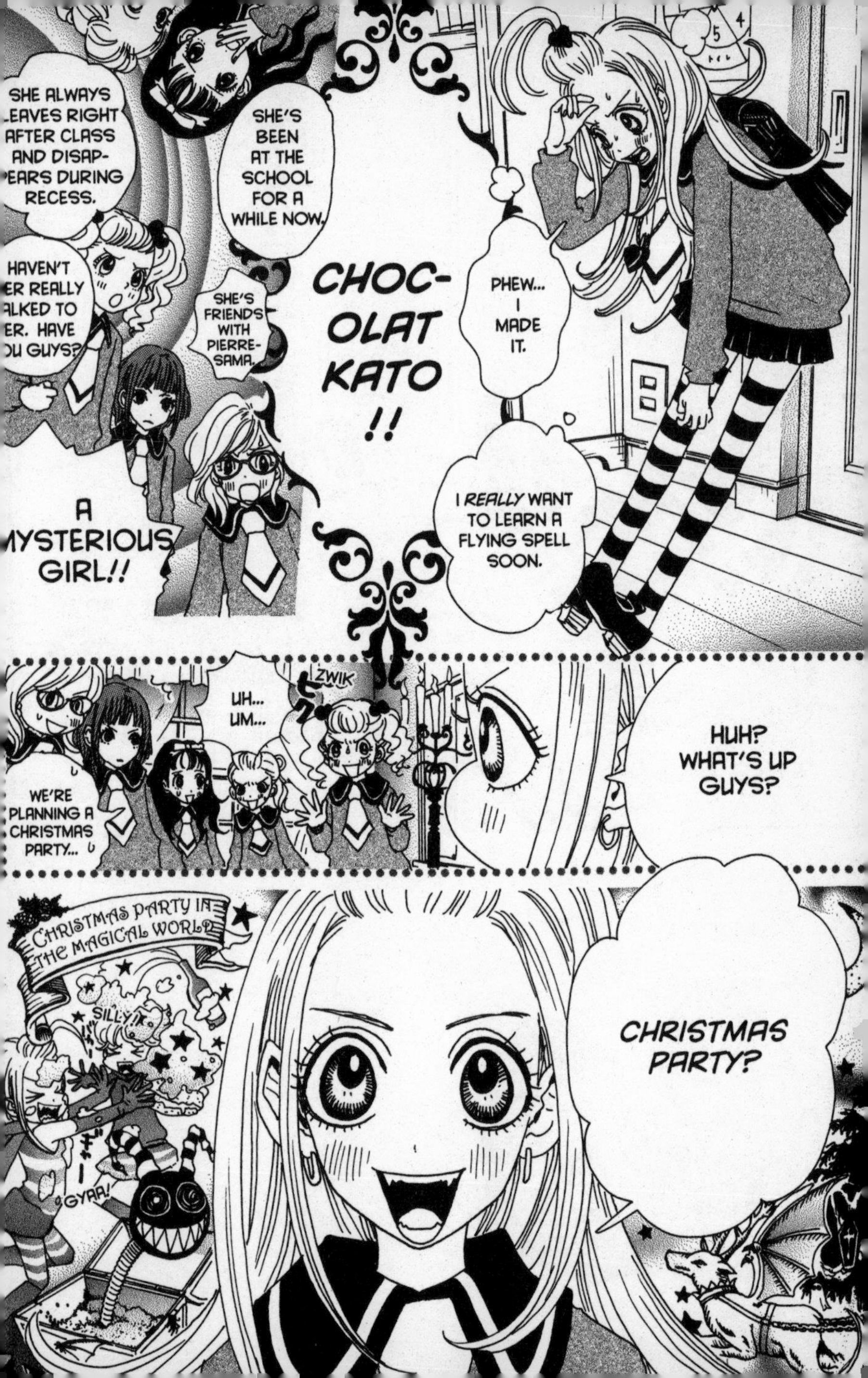
PHEW... I MADE IT.
I REALLY WANT TO LEARN A FLYING SPELL SOON.
CHOCOLAT KATO!!
SHE'S BEEN AT THE SCHOOL FOR A WHILE NOW.
SHE ALWAYS EAVES RIGHT AFTER CLASS AND DISAP- EARS DURING RECESS.
HAVEN'T ER REALLY ALKED TO ER. HAVE OU GUYS?
SHE'S FRIENDS WITH PIERRE-SAMA.
A MYSTERIOUS GIRL!!
HUH? WHAT'S UP GUYS?
ZWIK
UH... UM...
WE'RE PLANNING A CHRISTMAS PARTY...
CHRISTMAS PARTY?
CHRISTMAS PARTY IN THE MAGICAL WORLD
SILLY!
GYAA!

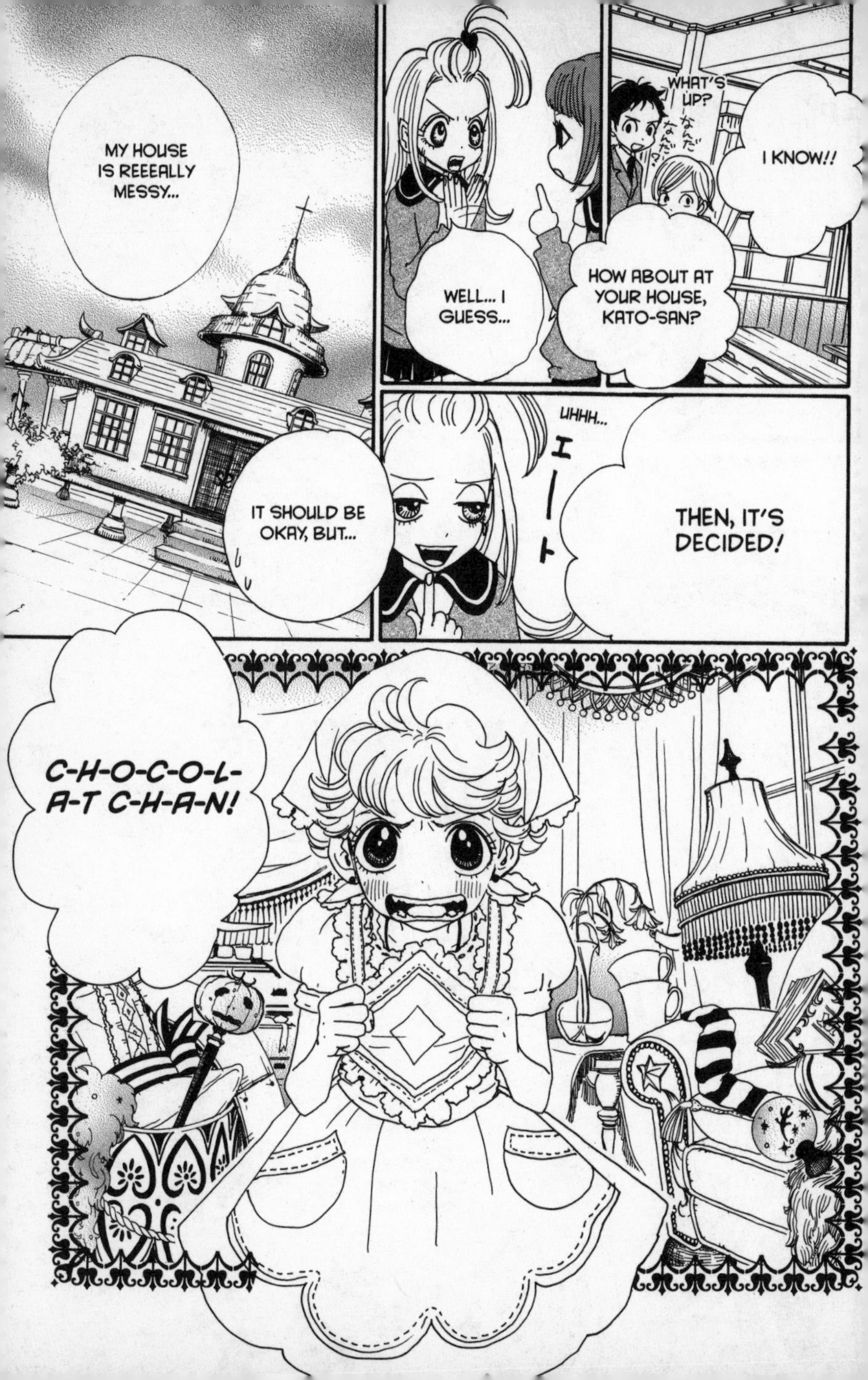
I KNOW!!
WHAT'S UP?
なんだ なんだ?
HOW ABOUT AT YOUR HOUSE, KATO-SAN?
WELL... I GUESS...
THEN, IT'S DECIDED!
UHHH...
エーート
IT SHOULD BE OKAY, BUT...
MY HOUSE IS REEEALLY MESSY...
C-H-O-C-O-L-A-T C-H-A-N!

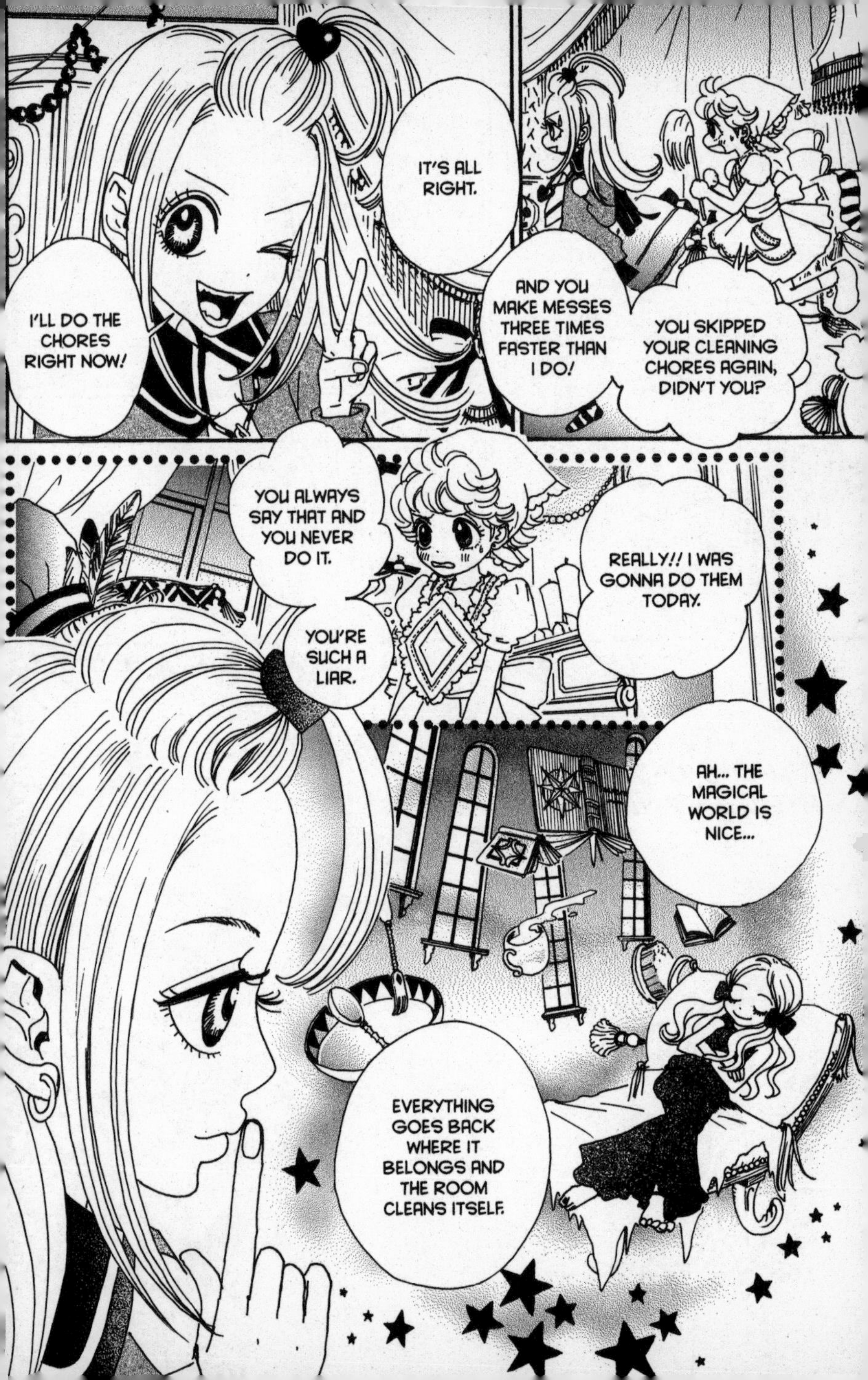
YOU SKIPPED YOUR CLEANING CHORES AGAIN, DIDN'T YOU?
AND YOU MAKE MESSES THREE TIMES FASTER THAN I DO!
IT'S ALL RIGHT.
I'LL DO THE CHORES RIGHT NOW!
REALLY!! I WAS GONNA DO THEM TODAY.
YOU ALWAYS SAY THAT AND YOU NEVER DO IT.
YOU'RE SUCH A LIAR.
AH... THE MAGICAL WORLD IS NICE...
EVERYTHING GOES BACK WHERE IT BELONGS AND THE ROOM CLEANS ITSELF.

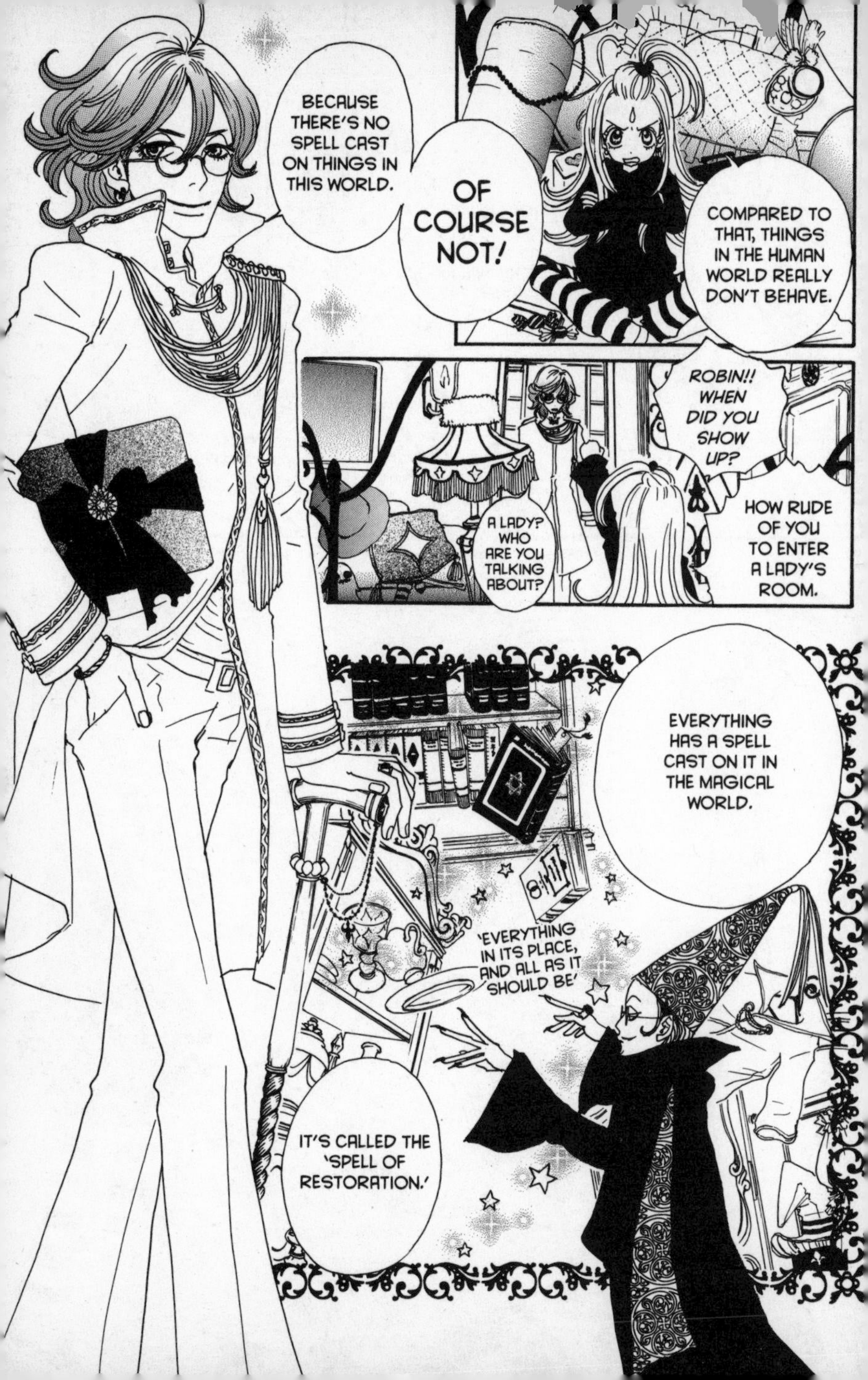
COMPARED TO THAT, THINGS IN THE HUMAN WORLD REALLY DON'T BEHAVE.
OF COURSE NOT!
BECAUSE THERE'S NO SPELL CAST ON THINGS IN THIS WORLD.
ROBIN!! WHEN DID YOU SHOW UP?
HOW RUDE OF YOU TO ENTER A LADY'S ROOM.
A LADY? WHO ARE YOU TALKING ABOUT?
EVERYTHING HAS A SPELL CAST ON IT IN THE MAGICAL WORLD.
'EVERYTHING IN ITS PLACE, AND ALL AS IT SHOULD BE'
IT'S CALLED THE 'SPELL OF RESTORATION.'

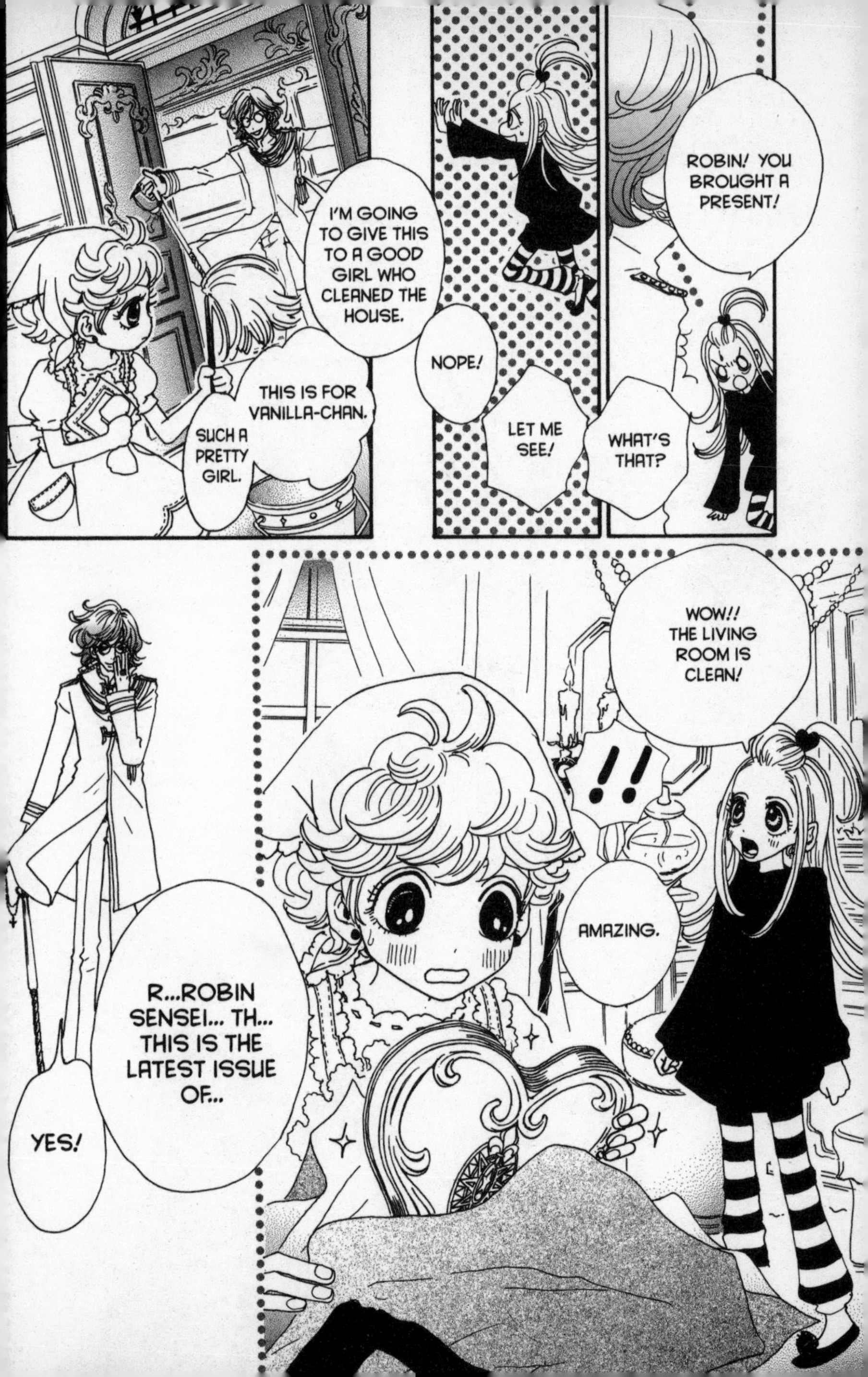
ROBIN! YOU BROUGHT A PRESENT!
WHAT'S THAT?
LET ME SEE!
NOPE!
I'M GOING TO GIVE THIS TO A GOOD GIRL WHO CLEANED THE HOUSE.
THIS IS FOR VANILLA-CHAN.
SUCH A PRETTY GIRL.
WOW!! THE LIVING ROOM IS CLEAN!
!!
AMAZING.
R...ROBIN SENSEI... TH... THIS IS THE LATEST ISSUE OF...
YES!

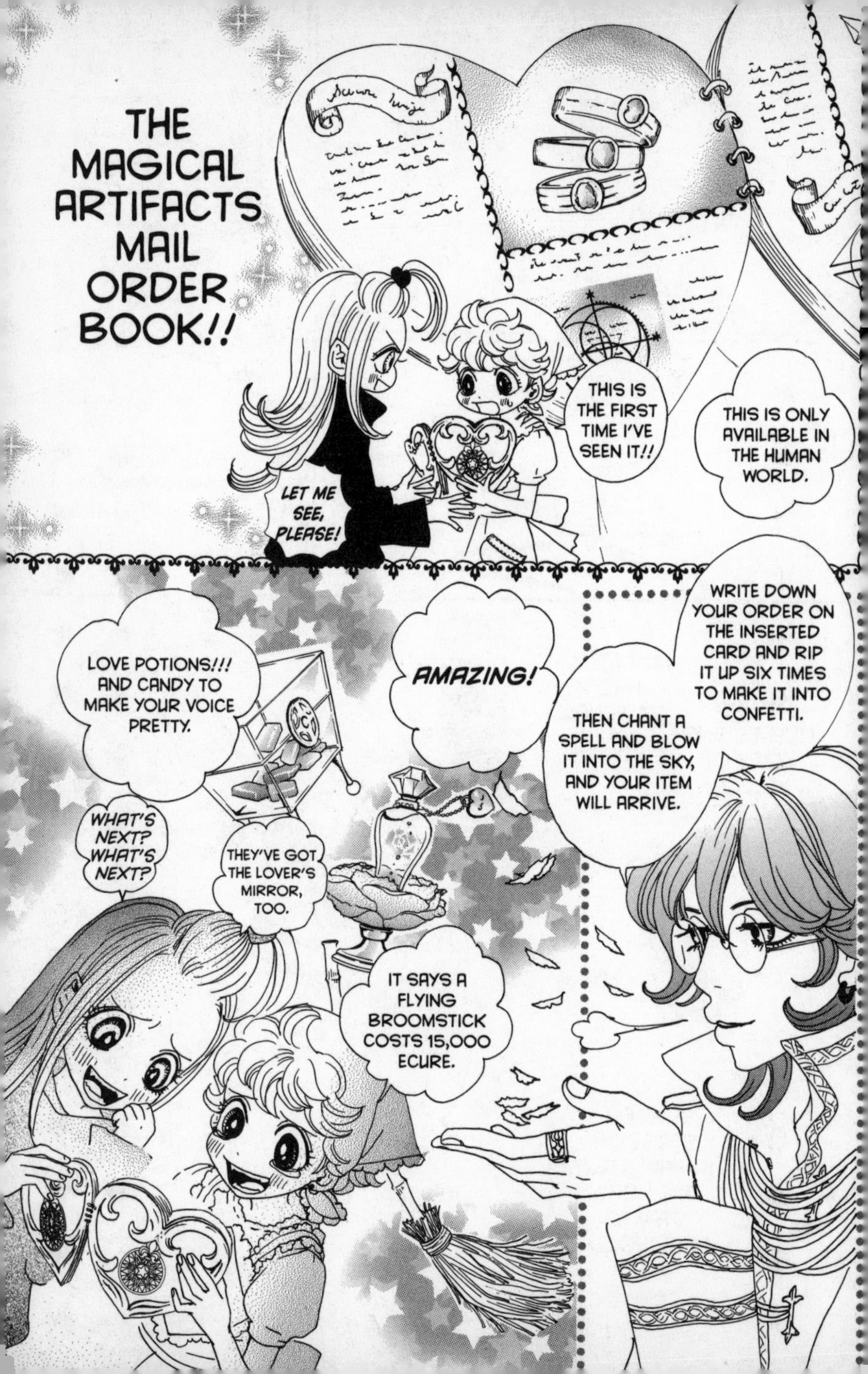
THE MAGICAL ARTIFACTS MAIL ORDER BOOK!!
THIS IS ONLY AVAILABLE IN THE HUMAN WORLD.
THIS IS THE FIRST TIME I'VE SEEN IT!!
LET ME SEE, PLEASE!
WRITE DOWN YOUR ORDER ON THE INSERTED CARD AND RIP IT UP SIX TIMES TO MAKE IT INTO CONFETTI.
THEN CHANT A SPELL AND BLOW IT INTO THE SKY, AND YOUR ITEM WILL ARRIVE.
AMAZING!
LOVE POTIONS!!! AND CANDY TO MAKE YOUR VOICE PRETTY.
THEY'VE GOT THE LOVER'S MIRROR, TOO.
WHAT'S NEXT? WHAT'S NEXT?
IT SAYS A FLYING BROOMSTICK COSTS 15,000 ECURE.

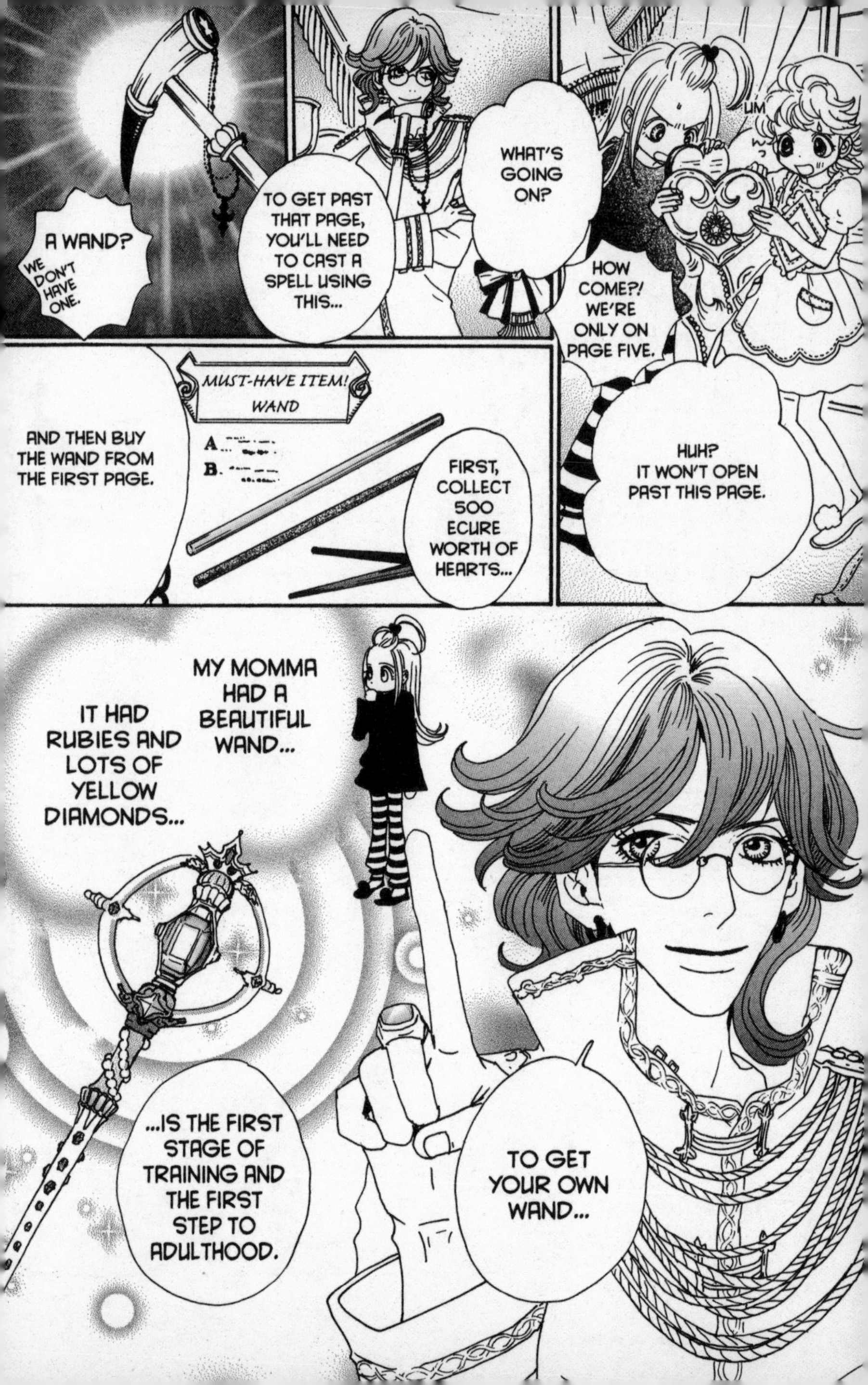
UM
WHAT'S GOING ON?
HOW COME?! WE'RE ONLY ON PAGE FIVE.
HUH? IT WON'T OPEN PAST THIS PAGE.
TO GET PAST THAT PAGE, YOU'LL NEED TO CAST A SPELL USING THIS...
A WAND?
WE DON'T HAVE ONE.
FIRST, COLLECT 500 ECURE WORTH OF HEARTS...
MUST-HAVE ITEM! WAND
AND THEN BUY THE WAND FROM THE FIRST PAGE.
TO GET YOUR OWN WAND...
...IS THE FIRST STAGE OF TRAINING AND THE FIRST STEP TO ADULTHOOD.
MY MOMMA HAD A BEAUTIFUL WAND...
IT HAD RUBIES AND LOTS OF YELLOW DIAMONDS...

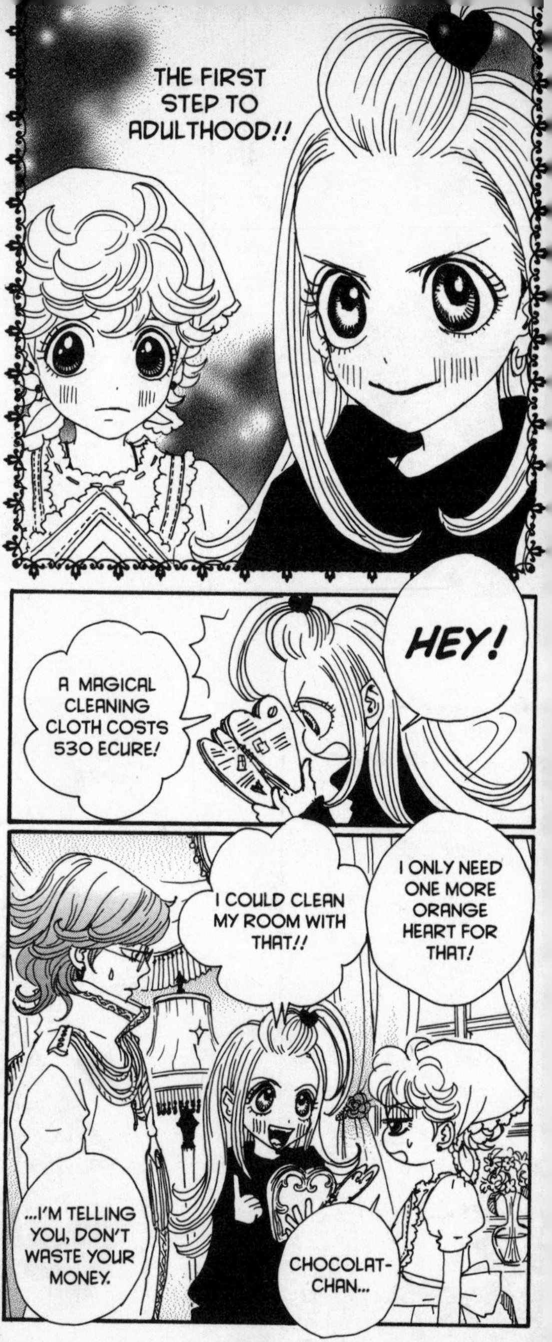
THE FIRST STEP TO ADULTHOOD!!
HEY!
A MAGICAL CLEANING CLOTH COSTS 530 ECURE!
I ONLY NEED ONE MORE ORANGE HEART FOR THAT!
I COULD CLEAN MY ROOM WITH THAT!!
CHOCOLAT-CHAN...
...I'M TELLING YOU, DON'T WASTE YOUR MONEY.

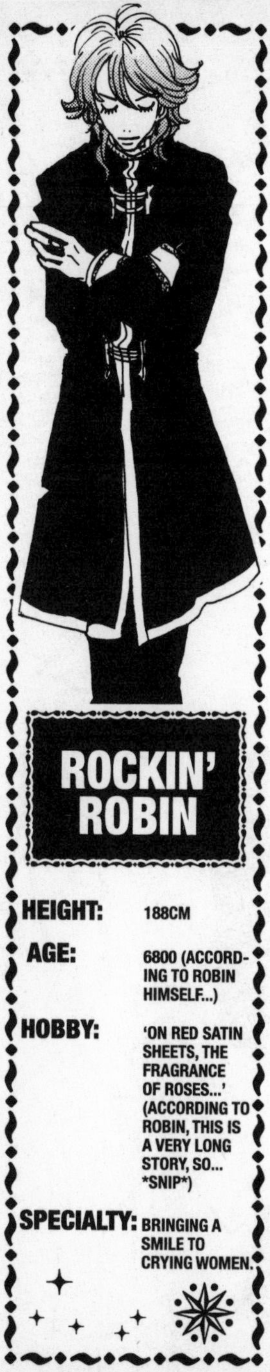

ROCKIN' ROBIN

HEIGHT: 188CM

AGE: 6800 (ACCORDING TO ROBIN HIMSELF...)

HOBBY: 'ON RED SATIN SHEETS, THE FRAGRANCE OF ROSES...' (ACCORDING TO ROBIN, THIS IS A VERY LONG STORY, SO... *SNIP*)

SPECIALTY: BRINGING A SMILE TO CRYING WOMEN.

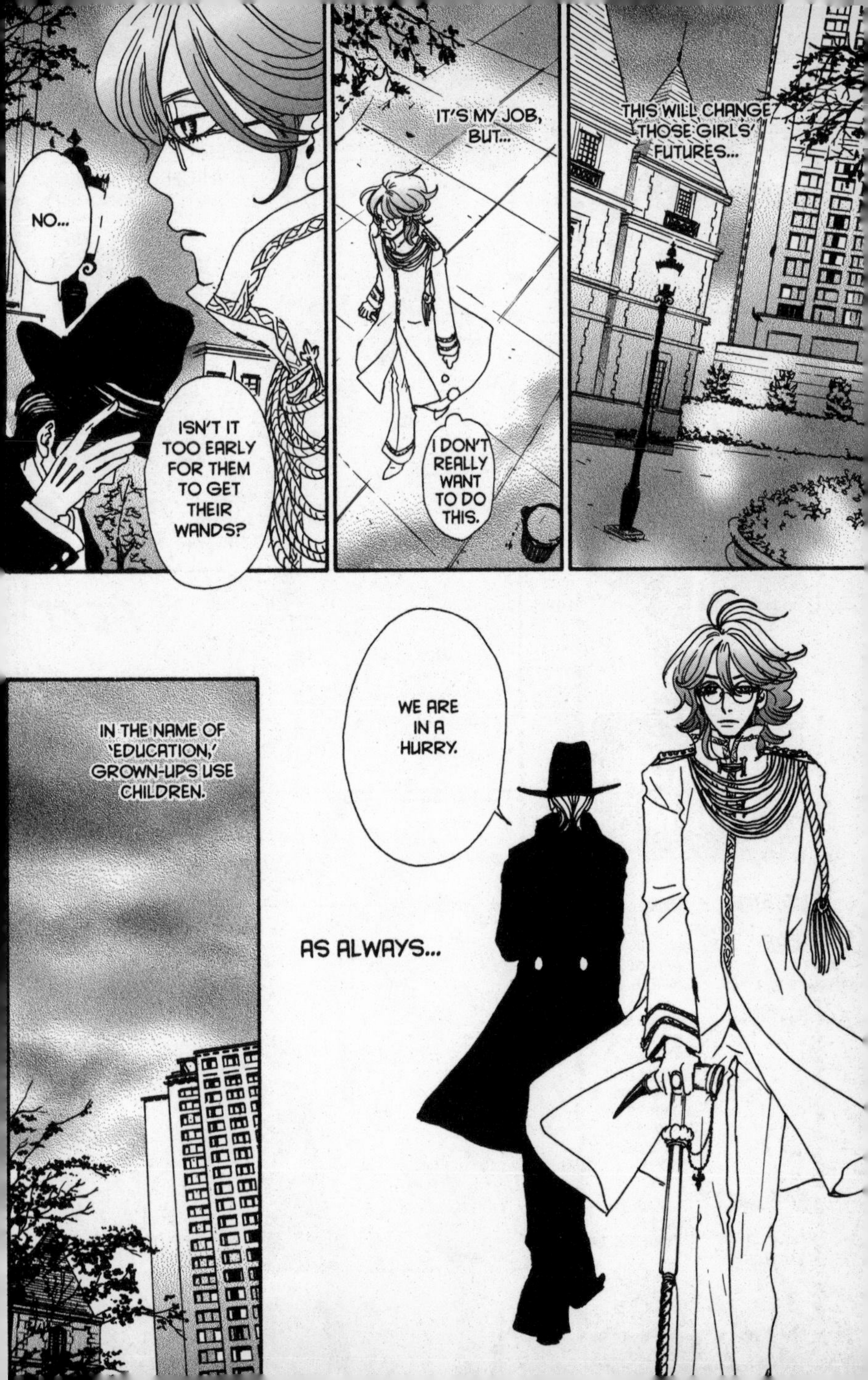
THIS WILL CHANGE THOSE GIRLS' FUTURES...
IT'S MY JOB, BUT...
I DON'T REALLY WANT TO DO THIS.
NO...
ISN'T IT TOO EARLY FOR THEM TO GET THEIR WANDS?
WE ARE IN A HURRY.
AS ALWAYS...
IN THE NAME OF 'EDUCATION,' GROWN-UPS USE CHILDREN.

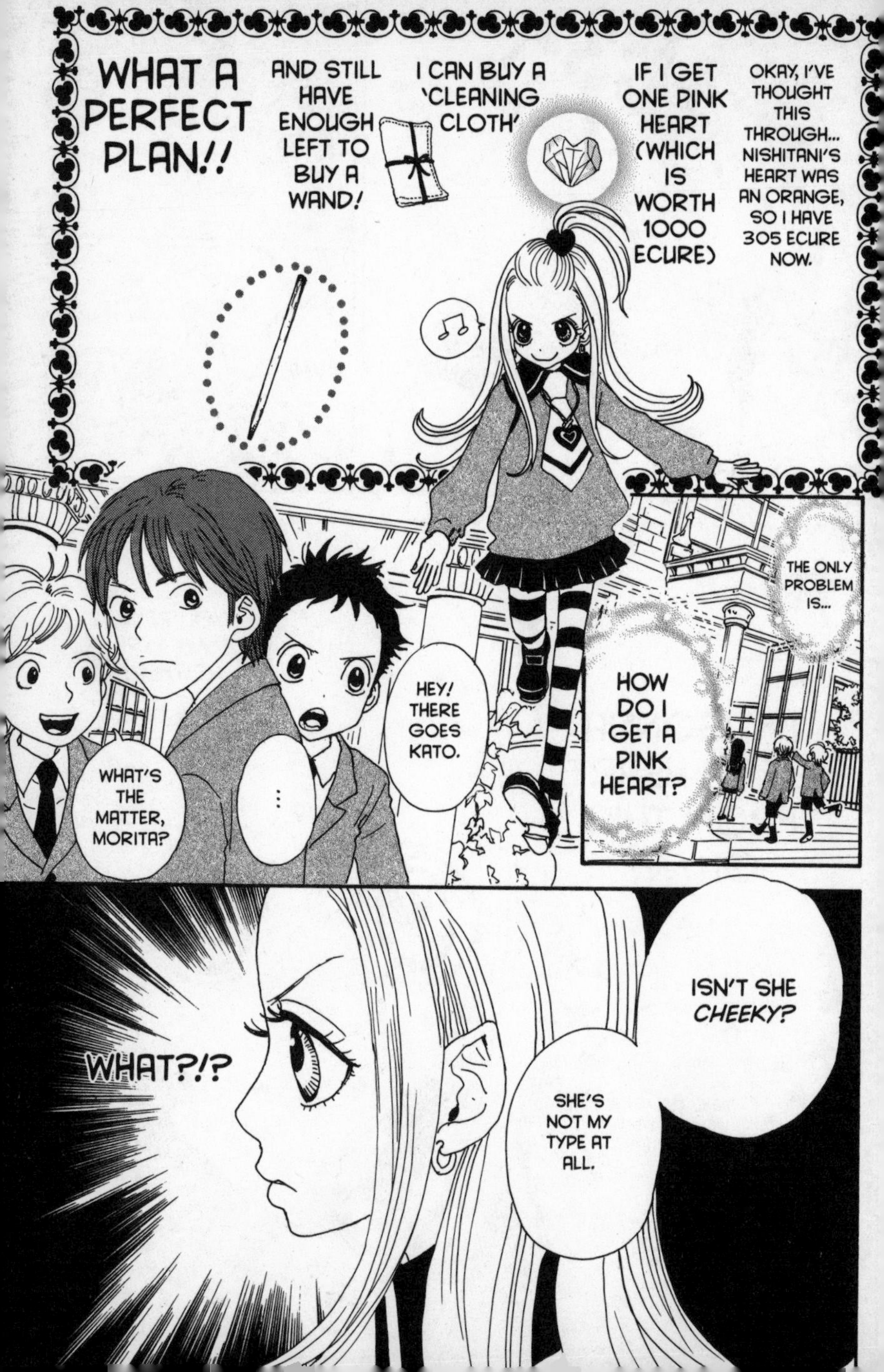
OKAY, I'VE THOUGHT THIS THROUGH... NISHITANI'S HEART WAS AN ORANGE, SO I HAVE 305 ECURE NOW.
IF I GET ONE PINK HEART (WHICH IS WORTH 1000 ECURE)
I CAN BUY A 'CLEANING CLOTH'
AND STILL HAVE ENOUGH LEFT TO BUY A WAND!
WHAT A PERFECT PLAN!!
THE ONLY PROBLEM IS...
HOW DO I GET A PINK HEART?
HEY! THERE GOES KATO.
...
WHAT'S THE MATTER, MORITA?
ISN'T SHE *CHEEKY*?
SHE'S NOT MY TYPE AT ALL.
WHAT?!?

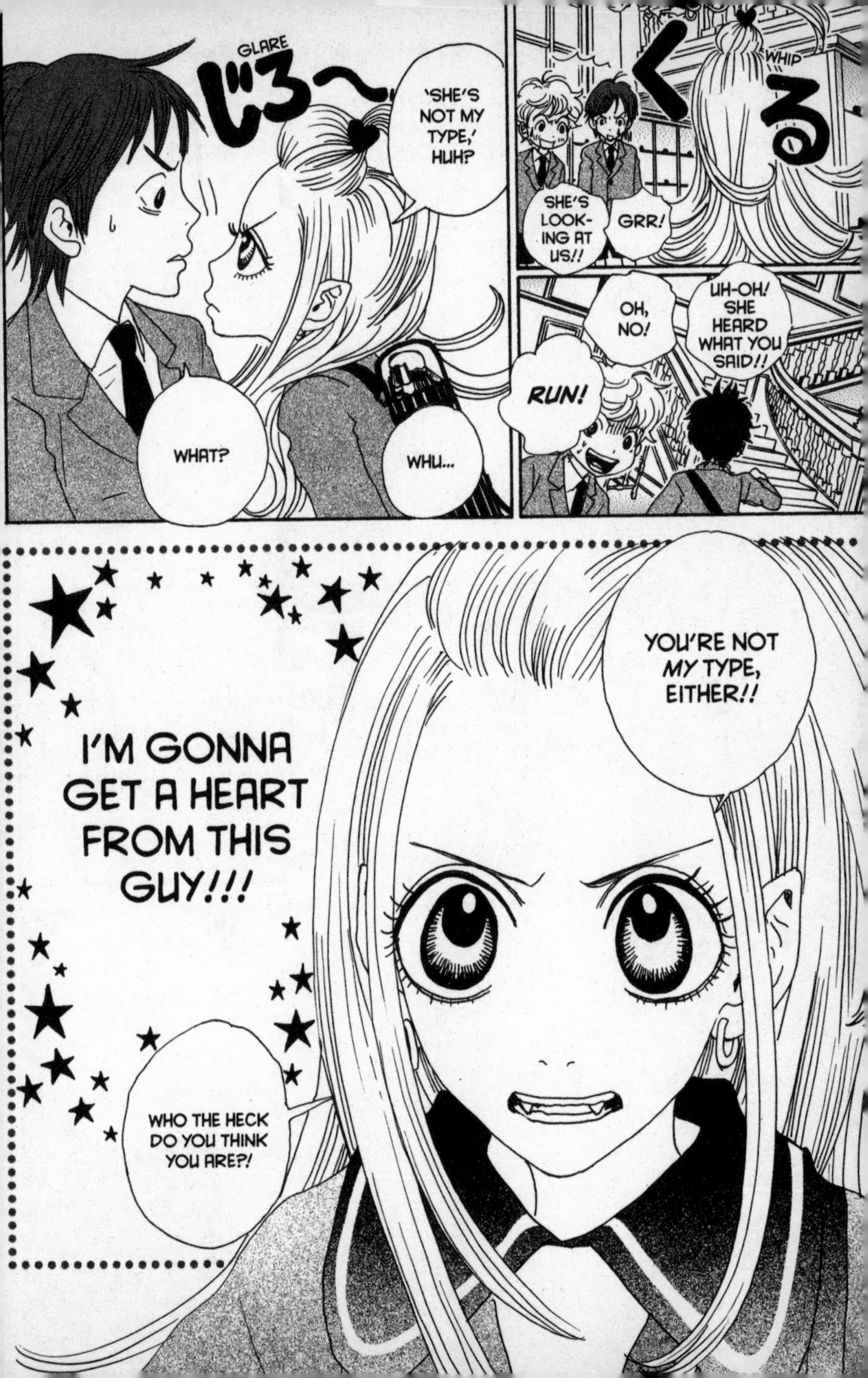
WHIP
くる
GRR!
SHE'S LOOKING AT US!!
UH-OH! SHE HEARD WHAT YOU SAID!!
OH, NO!
RUN!
GLARE
じろ〜
'SHE'S NOT MY TYPE,' HUH?
WHU...
WHAT?
YOU'RE NOT *MY TYPE*, EITHER!!
I'M GONNA GET A HEART FROM THIS GUY!!!
WHO THE HECK DO YOU THINK YOU ARE?!

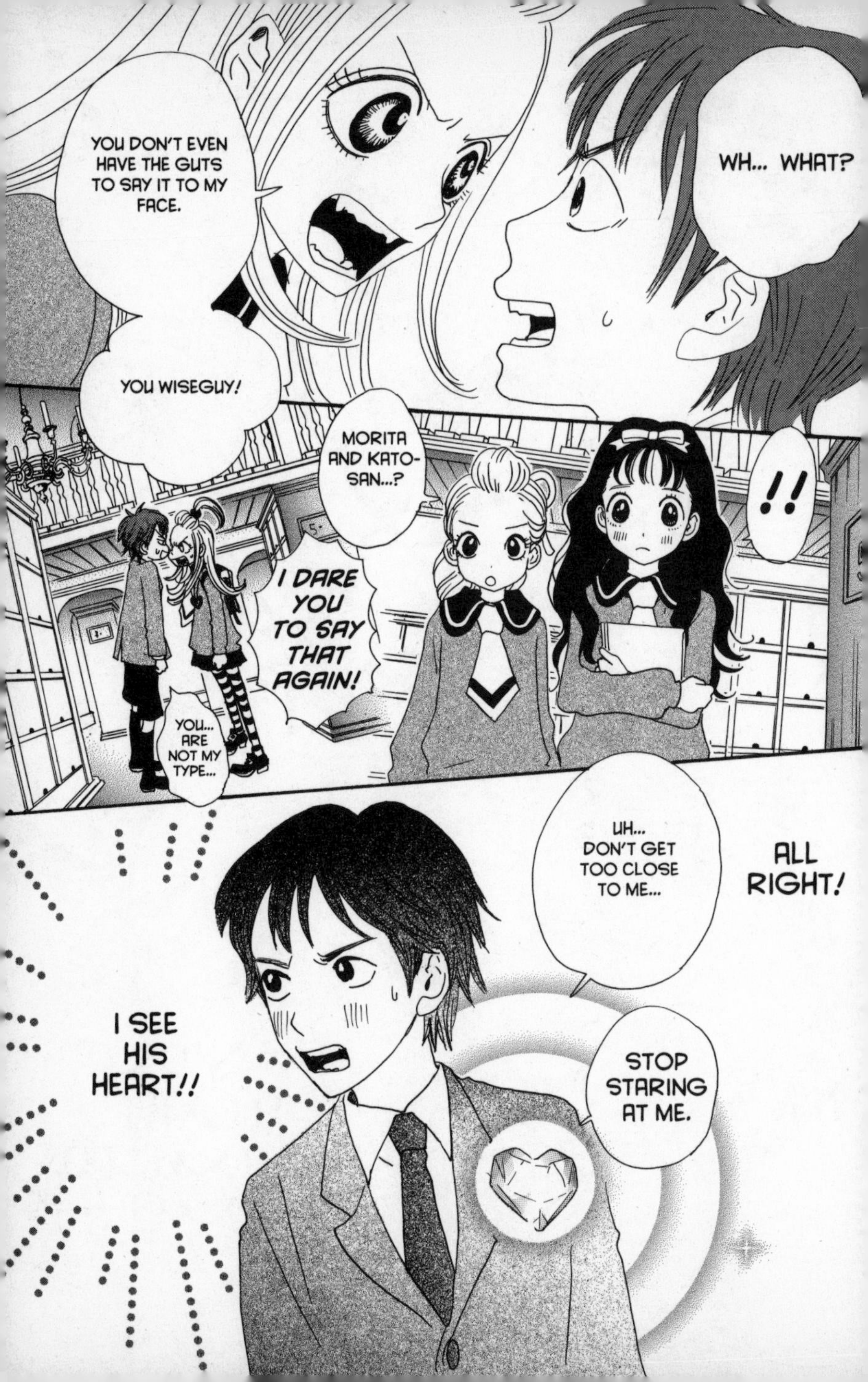
WH... WHAT?
YOU DON'T EVEN HAVE THE GUTS TO SAY IT TO MY FACE.
YOU WISEGUY!
!!
MORITA AND KATO-SAN...?
I DARE YOU TO SAY THAT AGAIN!
YOU... ARE NOT MY TYPE...
ALL RIGHT!
UH... DON'T GET TOO CLOSE TO ME...
STOP STARING AT ME.
I SEE HIS HEART!!

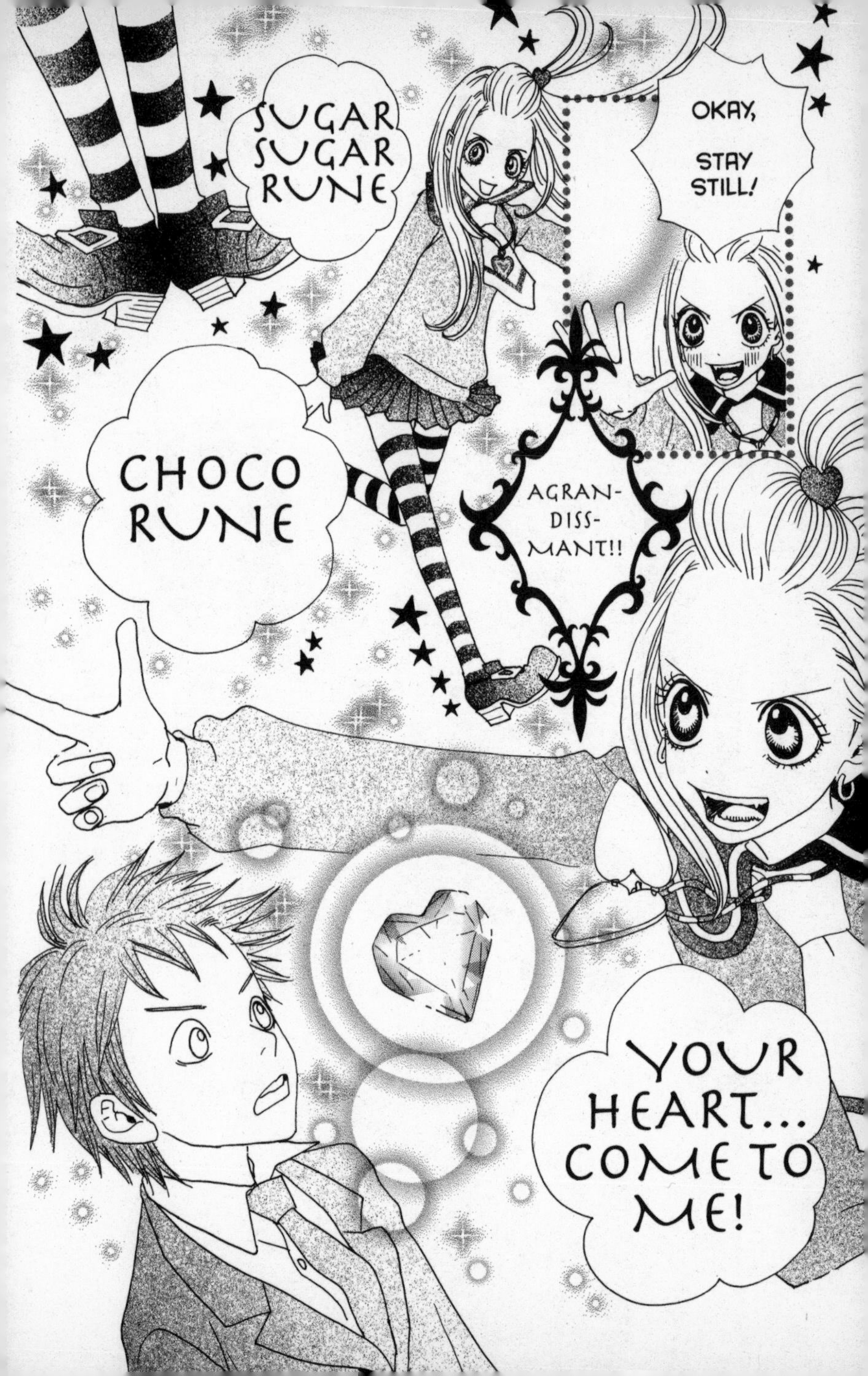
OKAY, STAY STILL!
SUGAR SUGAR RUNE
CHOCO RUNE
AGRAN-DISS-MANT!!
YOUR HEART... COME TO ME!

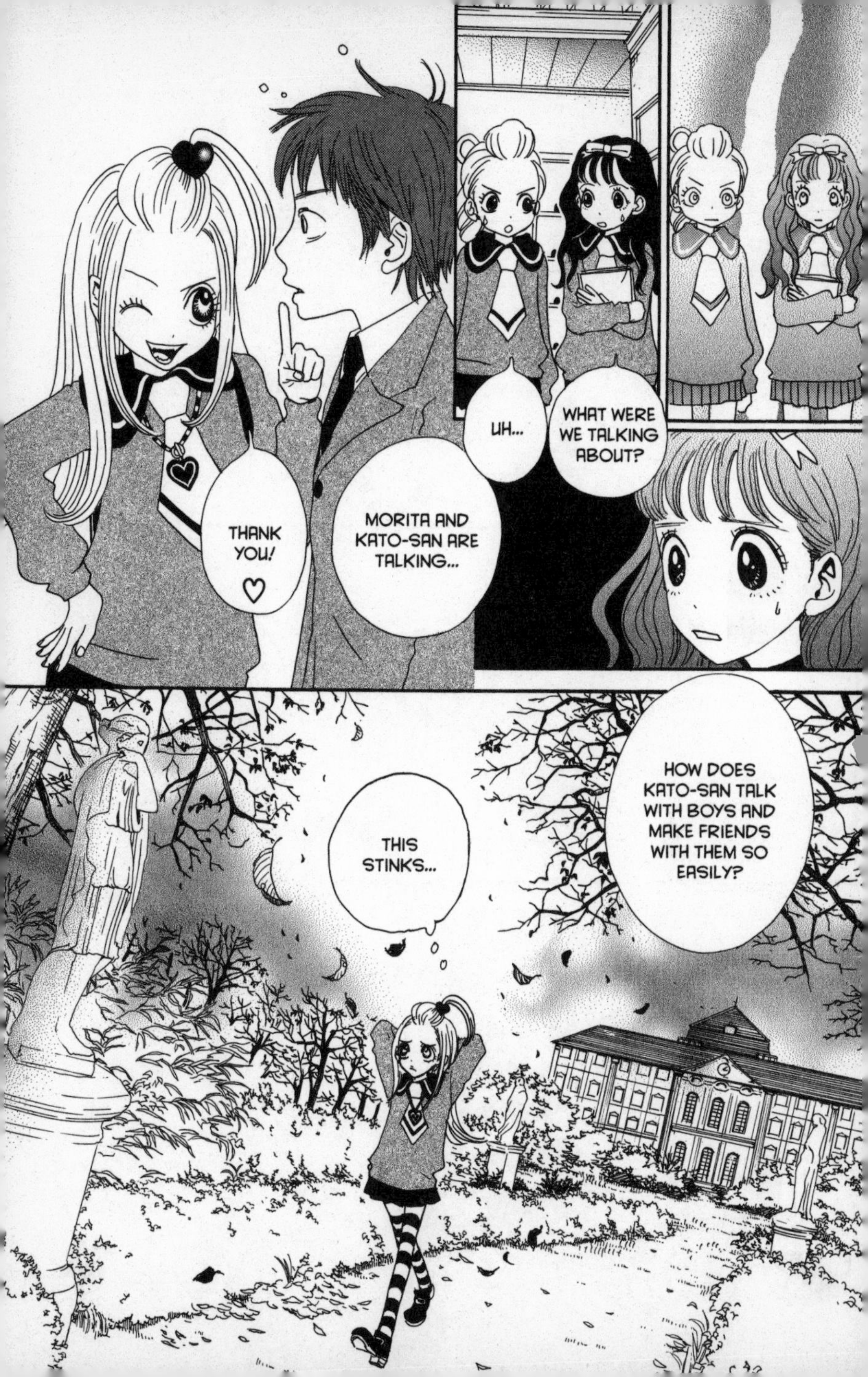
WHAT WERE WE TALKING ABOUT?
UH...
MORITA AND KATO-SAN ARE TALKING...
THANK YOU! ♡
HOW DOES KATO-SAN TALK WITH BOYS AND MAKE FRIENDS WITH THEM SO EASILY?
THIS STINKS...

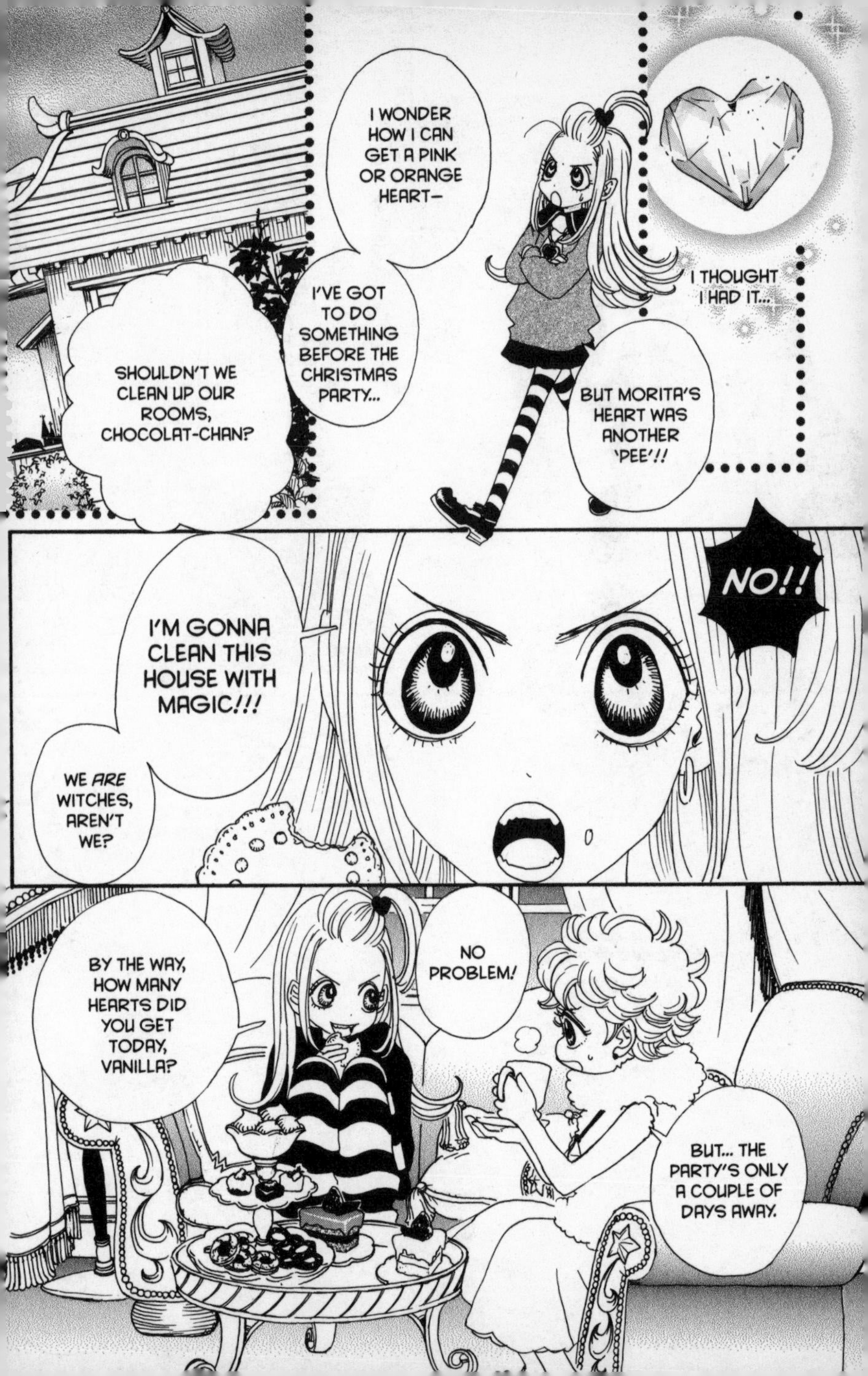
I THOUGHT I HAD IT...
BUT MORITA'S HEART WAS ANOTHER 'PEE'!!
I WONDER HOW I CAN GET A PINK OR ORANGE HEART—
I'VE GOT TO DO SOMETHING BEFORE THE CHRISTMAS PARTY...
SHOULDN'T WE CLEAN UP OUR ROOMS, CHOCOLAT-CHAN?
NO!!
I'M GONNA CLEAN THIS HOUSE WITH MAGIC!!!
WE *ARE* WITCHES, AREN'T WE?
BUT... THE PARTY'S ONLY A COUPLE OF DAYS AWAY.
NO PROBLEM!
BY THE WAY, HOW MANY HEARTS DID YOU GET TODAY, VANILLA?

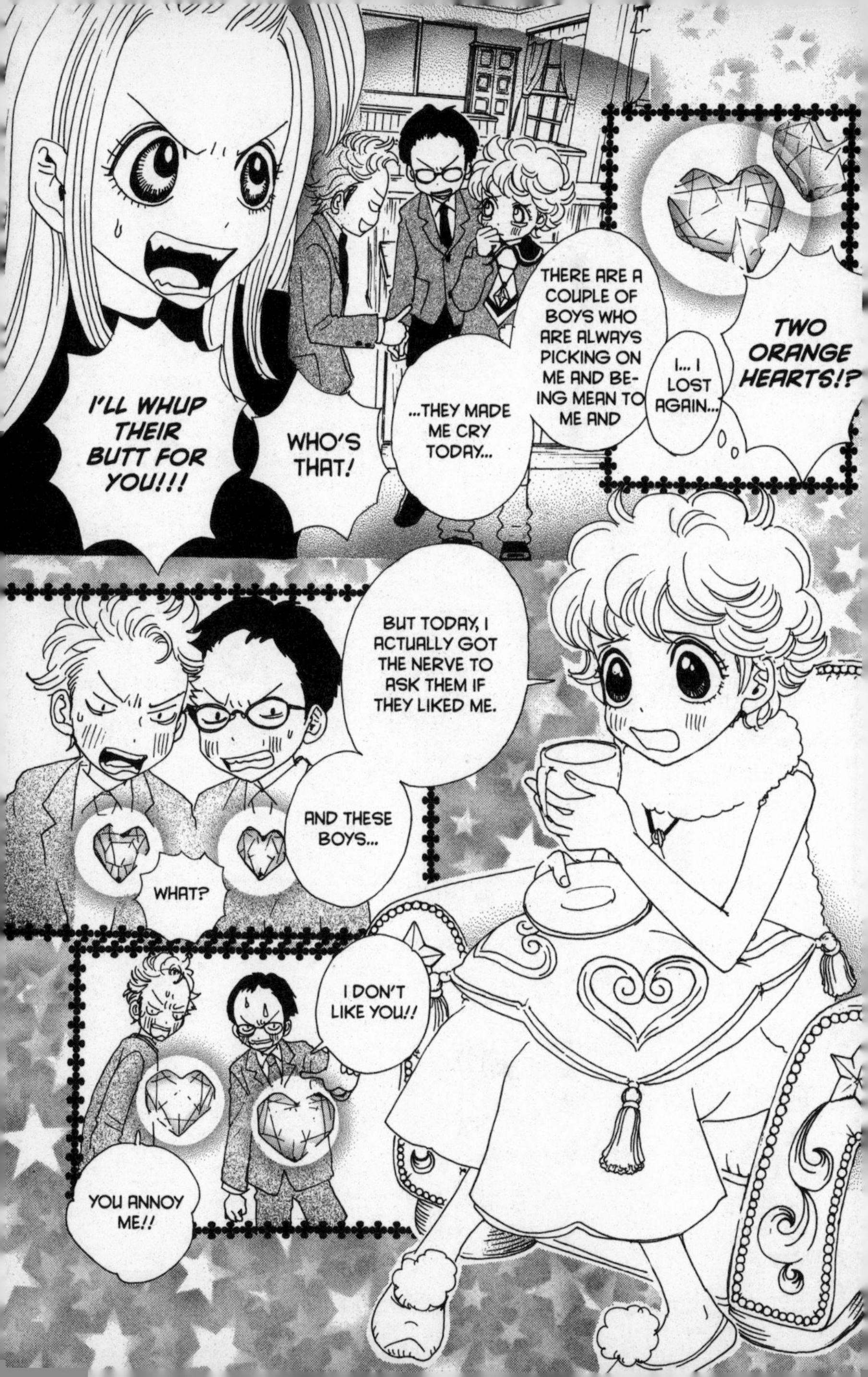
TWO ORANGE HEARTS!?
I... I LOST AGAIN...
THERE ARE A COUPLE OF BOYS WHO ARE ALWAYS PICKING ON ME AND BE-ING MEAN TO ME AND
...THEY MADE ME CRY TODAY...
WHO'S THAT!
I'LL WHUP THEIR BUTT FOR YOU!!!
BUT TODAY, I ACTUALLY GOT THE NERVE TO ASK THEM IF THEY LIKED ME.
AND THESE BOYS...
WHAT?
I DON'T LIKE YOU!!
YOU ANNOY ME!!

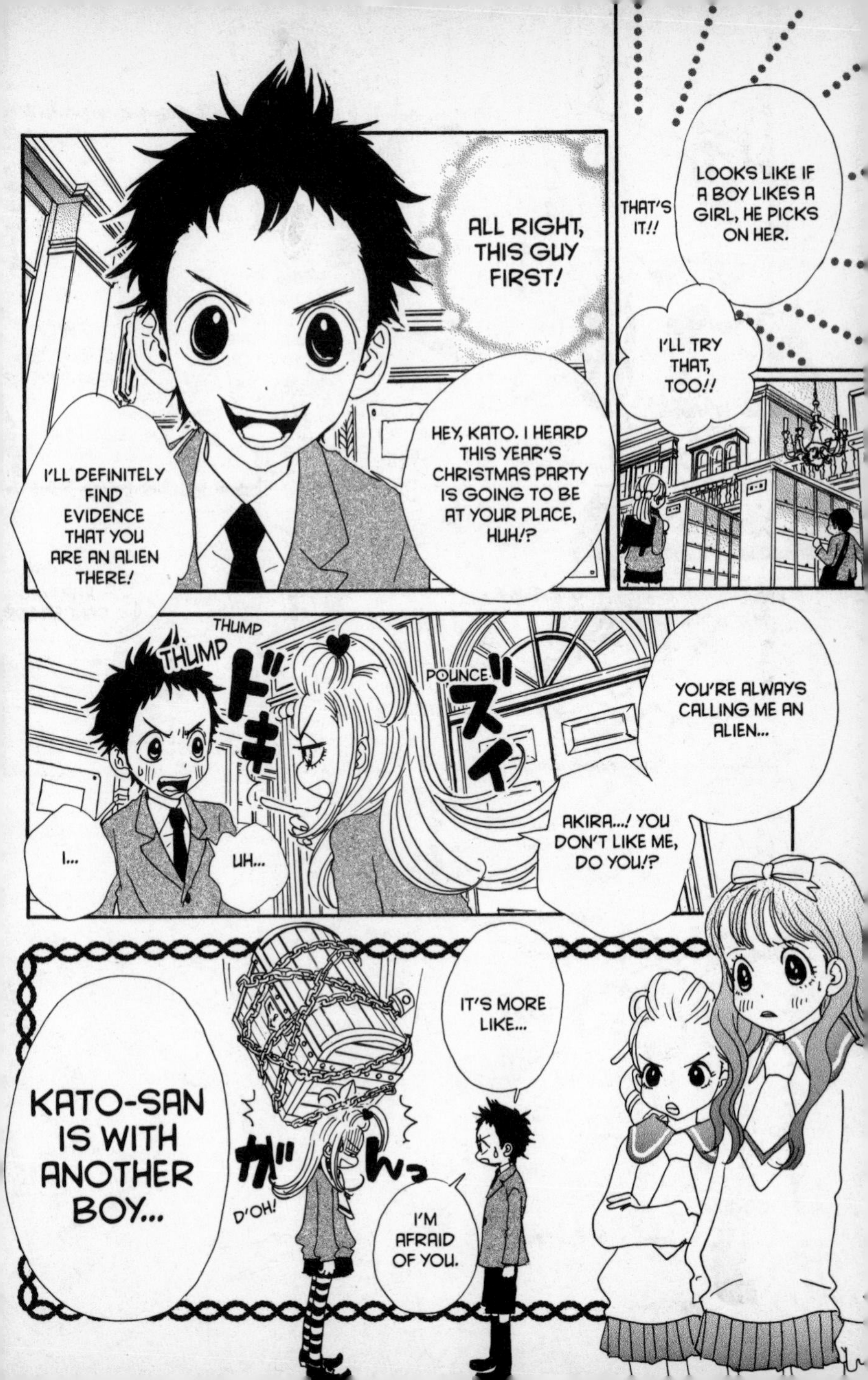
LOOKS LIKE IF A BOY LIKES A GIRL, HE PICKS ON HER.
THAT'S IT!!
I'LL TRY THAT, TOO!!
ALL RIGHT, THIS GUY FIRST!
HEY, KATO. I HEARD THIS YEAR'S CHRISTMAS PARTY IS GOING TO BE AT YOUR PLACE, HUH!?
I'LL DEFINITELY FIND EVIDENCE THAT YOU ARE AN ALIEN THERE!
YOU'RE ALWAYS CALLING ME AN ALIEN...
ズイ
POUNCE
AKIRA...! YOU DON'T LIKE ME, DO YOU!?
ドキ
THUMP THUMP
UH...
I...
IT'S MORE LIKE...
I'M AFRAID OF YOU.
がんっ
D'OH!
KATO-SAN IS WITH ANOTHER BOY...

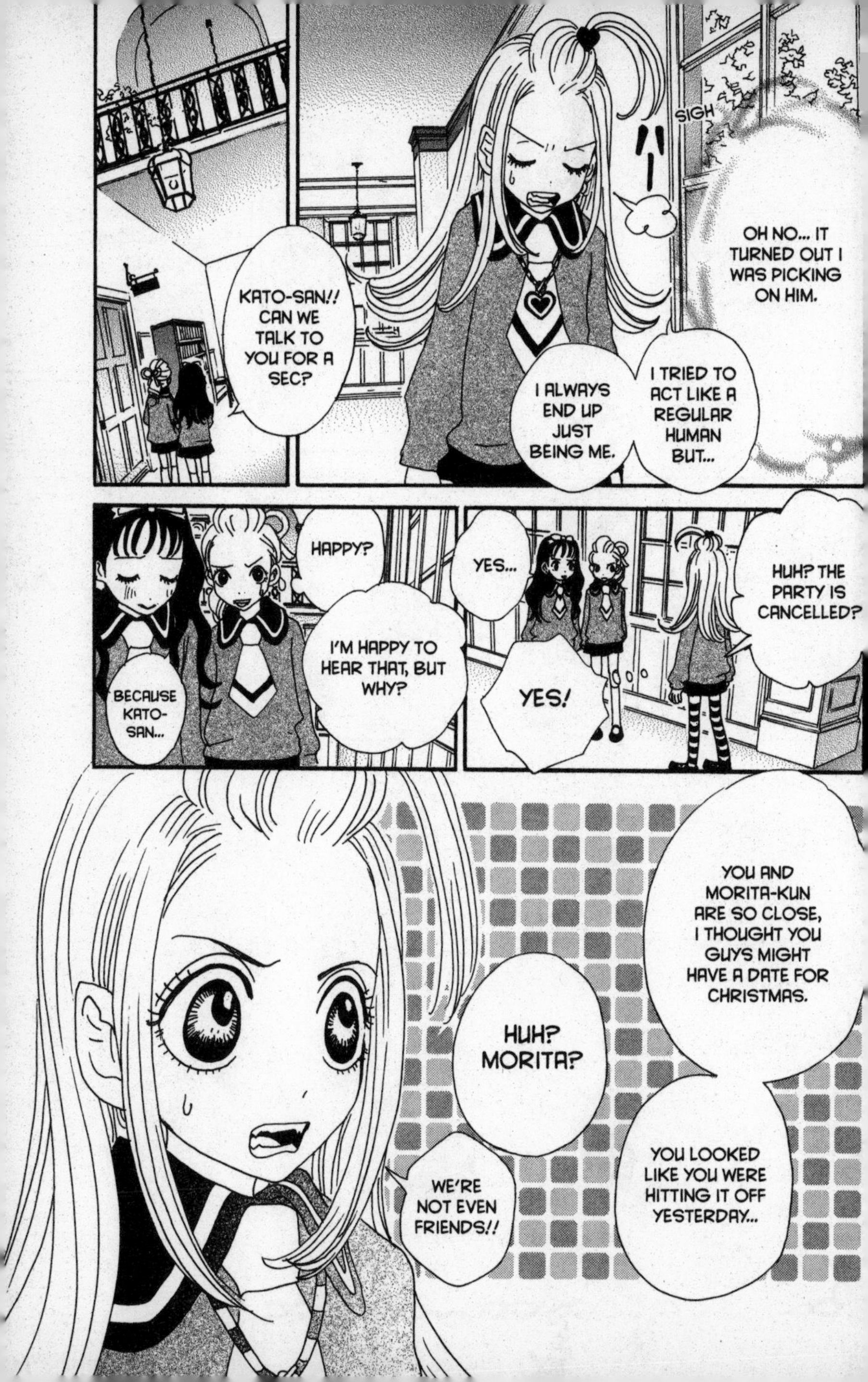
SIGH
OH NO... IT TURNED OUT I WAS PICKING ON HIM.
I TRIED TO ACT LIKE A REGULAR HUMAN BUT...
I ALWAYS END UP JUST BEING ME.
KATO-SAN!! CAN WE TALK TO YOU FOR A SEC?
HUH? THE PARTY IS CANCELLED?
YES...
YES!
HAPPY?
I'M HAPPY TO HEAR THAT, BUT WHY?
BECAUSE KATO-SAN...
YOU AND MORITA-KUN ARE SO CLOSE, I THOUGHT YOU GUYS MIGHT HAVE A DATE FOR CHRISTMAS.
YOU LOOKED LIKE YOU WERE HITTING IT OFF YESTERDAY...
HUH? MORITA?
WE'RE NOT EVEN FRIENDS!!

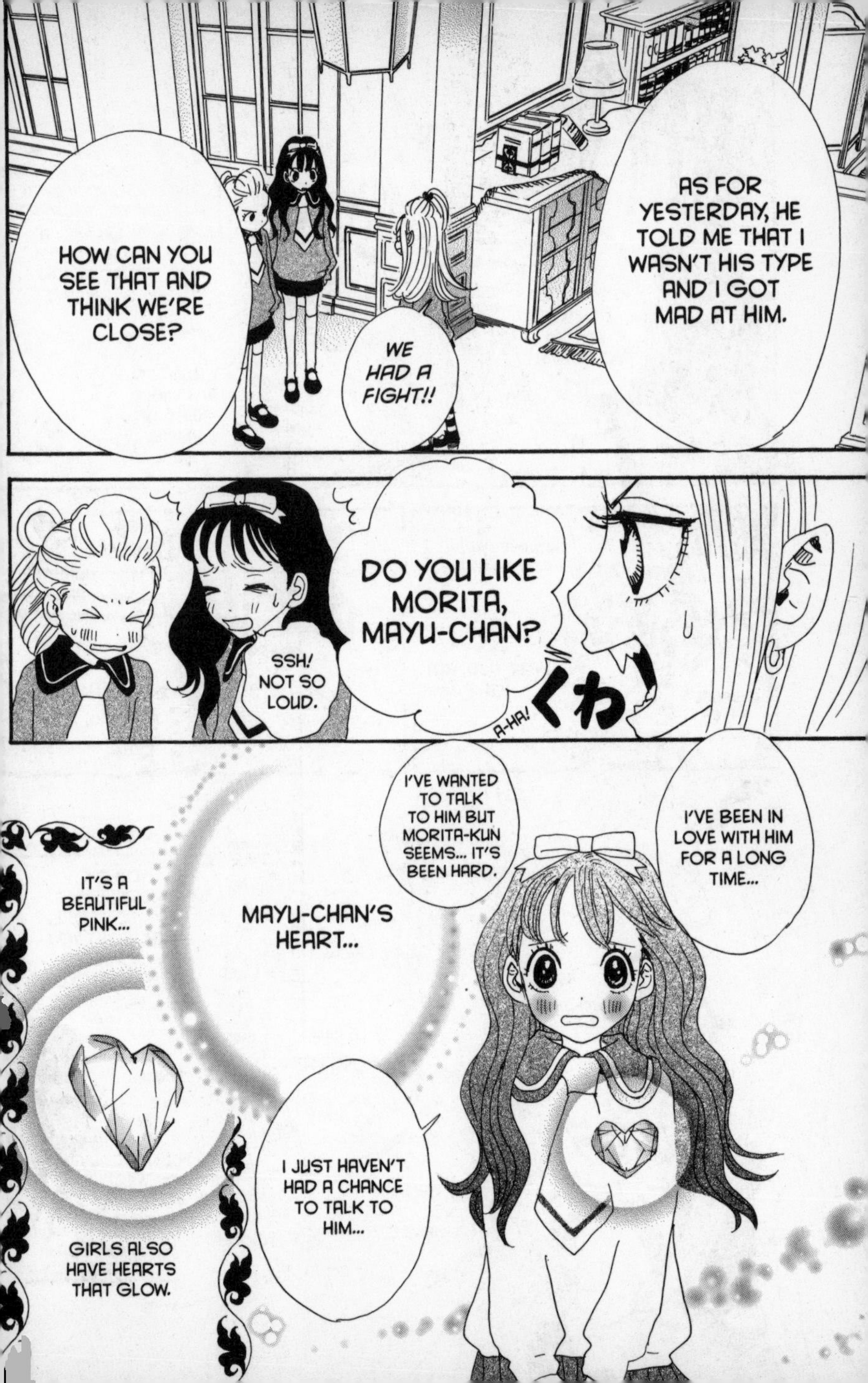
AS FOR YESTERDAY, HE TOLD ME THAT I WASN'T HIS TYPE AND I GOT MAD AT HIM.
WE HAD A FIGHT!!
HOW CAN YOU SEE THAT AND THINK WE'RE CLOSE?
DO YOU LIKE MORITA, MAYU-CHAN?
A-HA! くわ
SSH! NOT SO LOUD.
I'VE BEEN IN LOVE WITH HIM FOR A LONG TIME...
I'VE WANTED TO TALK TO HIM BUT MORITA-KUN SEEMS... IT'S BEEN HARD.
MAYU-CHAN'S HEART...
IT'S A BEAUTIFUL PINK...
I JUST HAVEN'T HAD A CHANCE TO TALK TO HIM...
GIRLS ALSO HAVE HEARTS THAT GLOW.

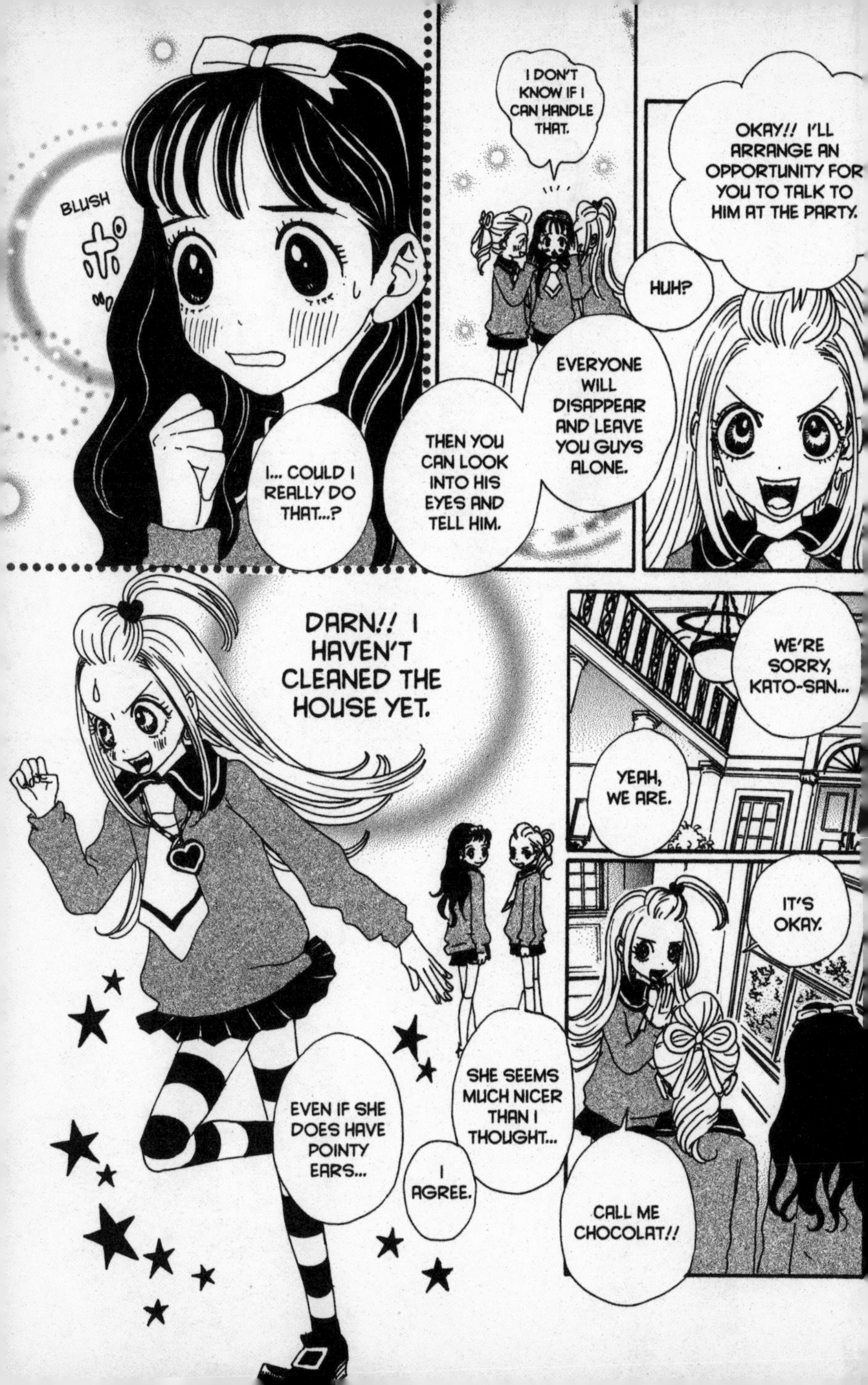
OKAY!! I'LL ARRANGE AN OPPORTUNITY FOR YOU TO TALK TO HIM AT THE PARTY.
HUH?
EVERYONE WILL DISAPPEAR AND LEAVE YOU GUYS ALONE.
THEN YOU CAN LOOK INTO HIS EYES AND TELL HIM.
I DON'T KNOW IF I CAN HANDLE THAT.
BLUSH
I... COULD I REALLY DO THAT...?
WE'RE SORRY, KATO-SAN...
YEAH, WE ARE.
IT'S OKAY.
CALL ME CHOCOLAT!!
SHE SEEMS MUCH NICER THAN I THOUGHT...
I AGREE.
EVEN IF SHE DOES HAVE POINTY EARS...
DARN!! I HAVEN'T CLEANED THE HOUSE YET.

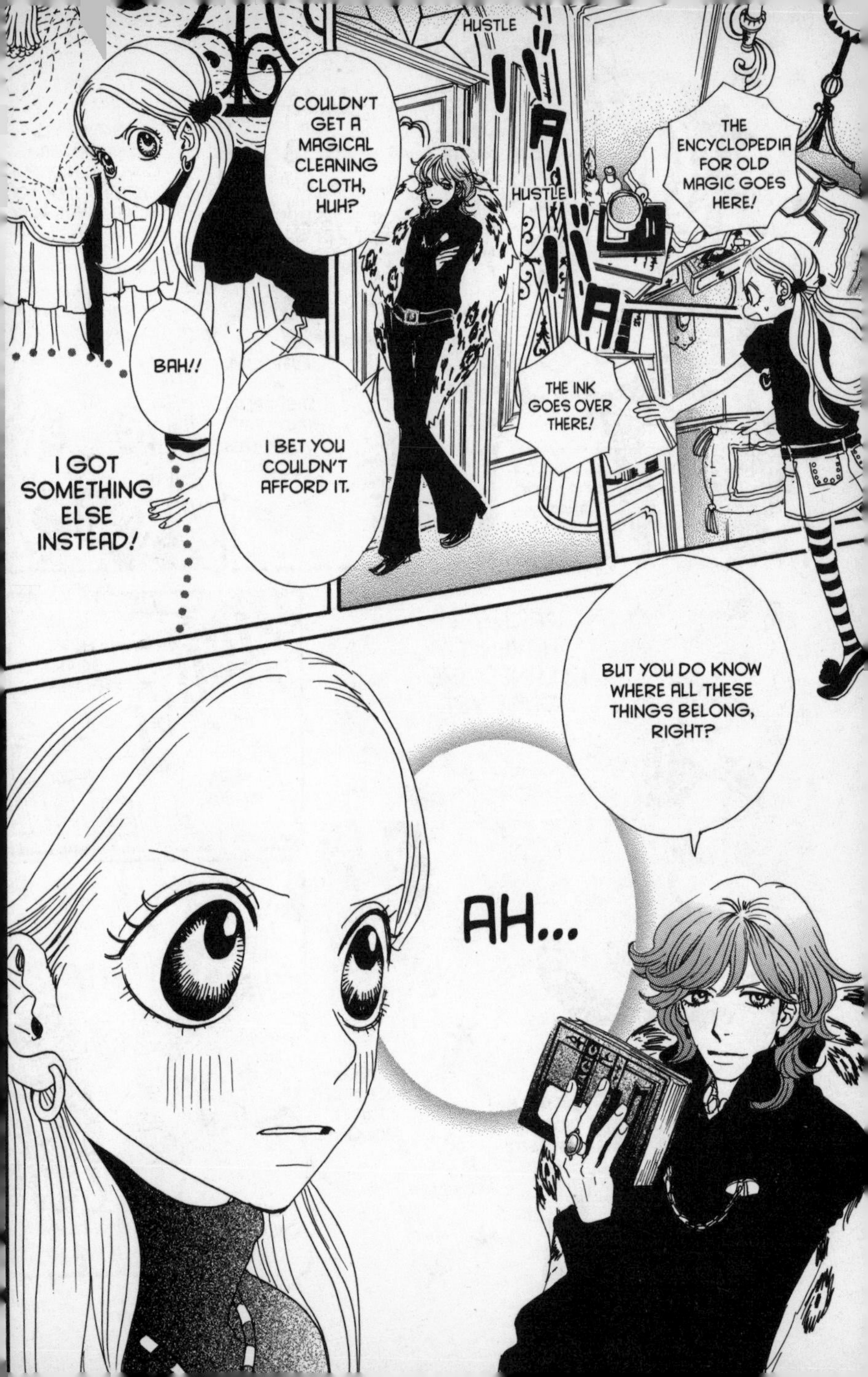
HUSTLE
HUSTLE
THE ENCYCLOPEDIA FOR OLD MAGIC GOES HERE!
THE INK GOES OVER THERE!
COULDN'T GET A MAGICAL CLEANING CLOTH, HUH?
I BET YOU COULDN'T AFFORD IT.
BAH!!
I GOT SOMETHING ELSE INSTEAD!
BUT YOU DO KNOW WHERE ALL THESE THINGS BELONG, RIGHT?
AH...

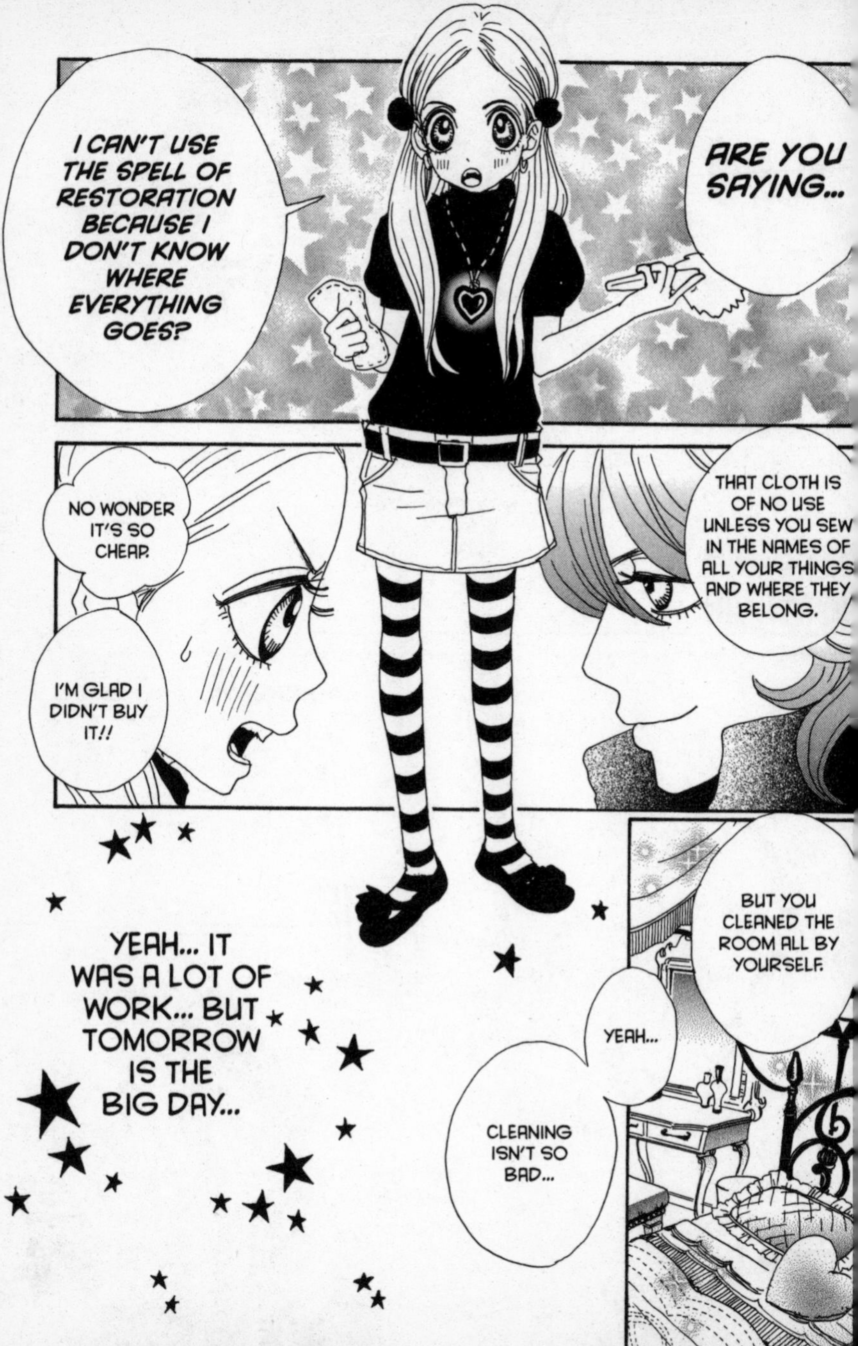
ARE YOU SAYING...
I CAN'T USE THE SPELL OF RESTORATION BECAUSE I DON'T KNOW WHERE EVERYTHING GOES?
THAT CLOTH IS OF NO USE UNLESS YOU SEW IN THE NAMES OF ALL YOUR THINGS AND WHERE THEY BELONG.
NO WONDER IT'S SO CHEAP.
I'M GLAD I DIDN'T BUY IT!!
BUT YOU CLEANED THE ROOM ALL BY YOURSELF.
YEAH...
CLEANING ISN'T SO BAD...
YEAH... IT WAS A LOT OF WORK... BUT TOMORROW IS THE BIG DAY...

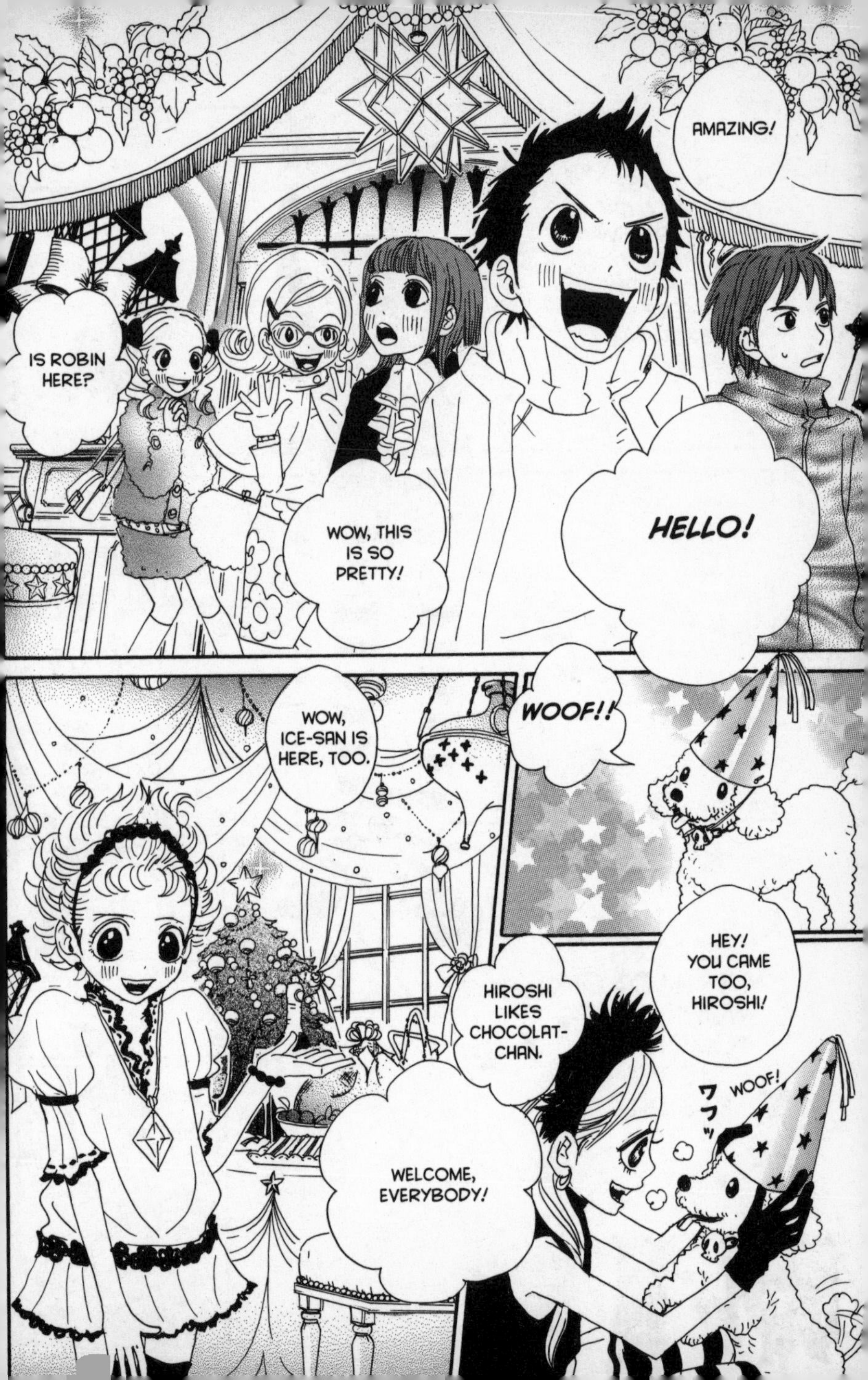
AMAZING!
HELLO!
WOW, THIS IS SO PRETTY!
IS ROBIN HERE?
WOOF!!
WOW, ICE-SAN IS HERE, TOO.
HEY! YOU CAME TOO, HIROSHI!
ワフッ
WOOF!
HIROSHI LIKES CHOCOLAT-CHAN.
WELCOME, EVERYBODY!

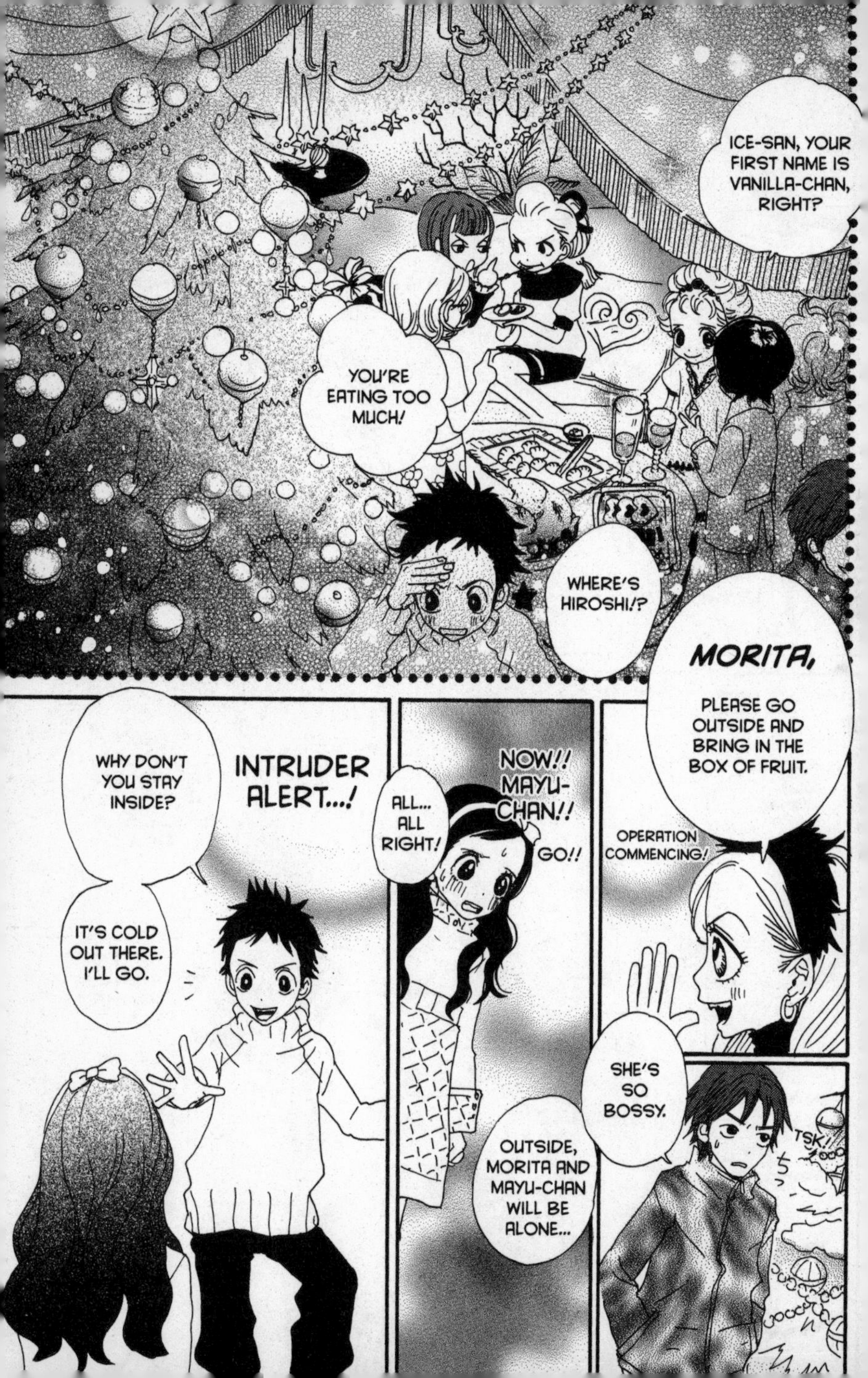
ICE-SAN, YOUR FIRST NAME IS VANILLA-CHAN, RIGHT?
YOU'RE EATING TOO MUCH!
WHERE'S HIROSHI!?
MORITA, PLEASE GO OUTSIDE AND BRING IN THE BOX OF FRUIT.
OPERATION COMMENCING!
SHE'S SO BOSSY.
TSK!!
OUTSIDE, MORITA AND MAYU-CHAN WILL BE ALONE...
NOW!! MAYU-CHAN!!
GO!!
ALL... ALL RIGHT!
INTRUDER ALERT...!
WHY DON'T YOU STAY INSIDE?
IT'S COLD OUT THERE. I'LL GO.

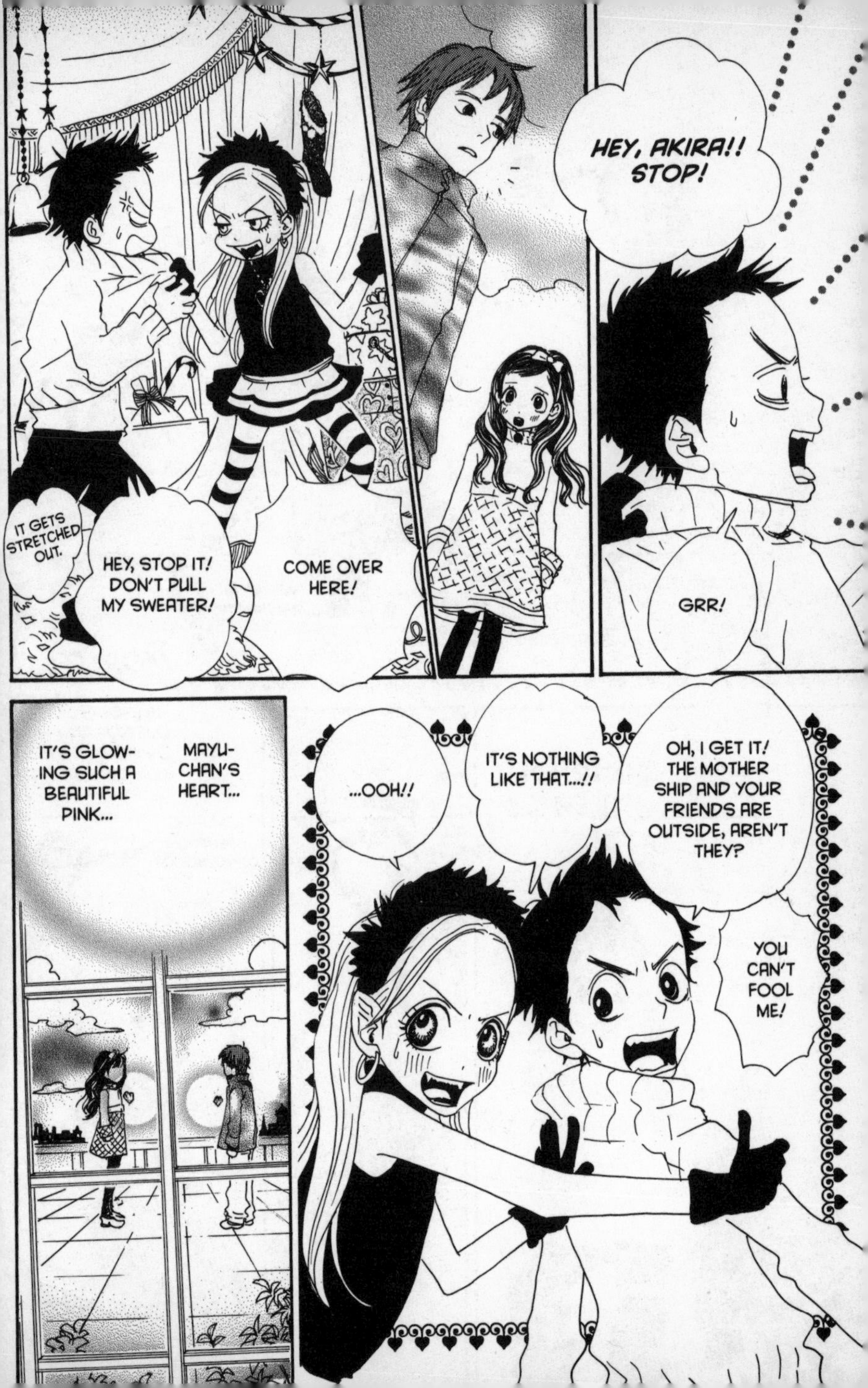
HEY, AKIRA!! STOP!
GRR!
COME OVER HERE!
HEY, STOP IT! DON'T PULL MY SWEATER!
IT GETS STRETCHED OUT.
OH, I GET IT! THE MOTHER SHIP AND YOUR FRIENDS ARE OUTSIDE, AREN'T THEY?
YOU CAN'T FOOL ME!
IT'S NOTHING LIKE THAT...!!
...OOH!!
MAYU-CHAN'S HEART...
IT'S GLOWING SUCH A BEAUTIFUL PINK...

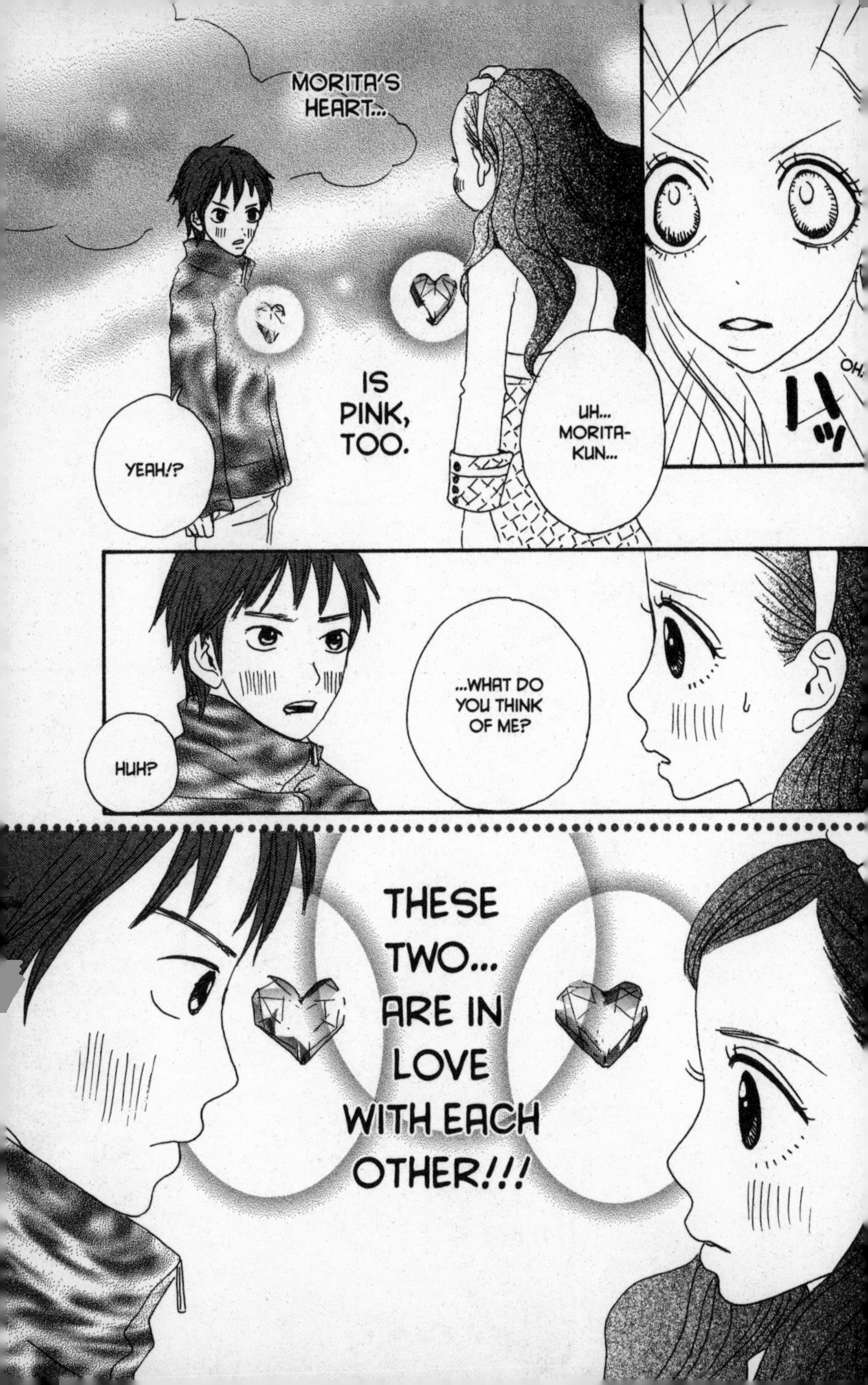
OH.
ハッ
MORITA'S HEART...
IS PINK, TOO.
UH... MORITA-KUN...
YEAH!?
...WHAT DO YOU THINK OF ME?
HUH?
THESE TWO... ARE IN LOVE WITH EACH OTHER!!!

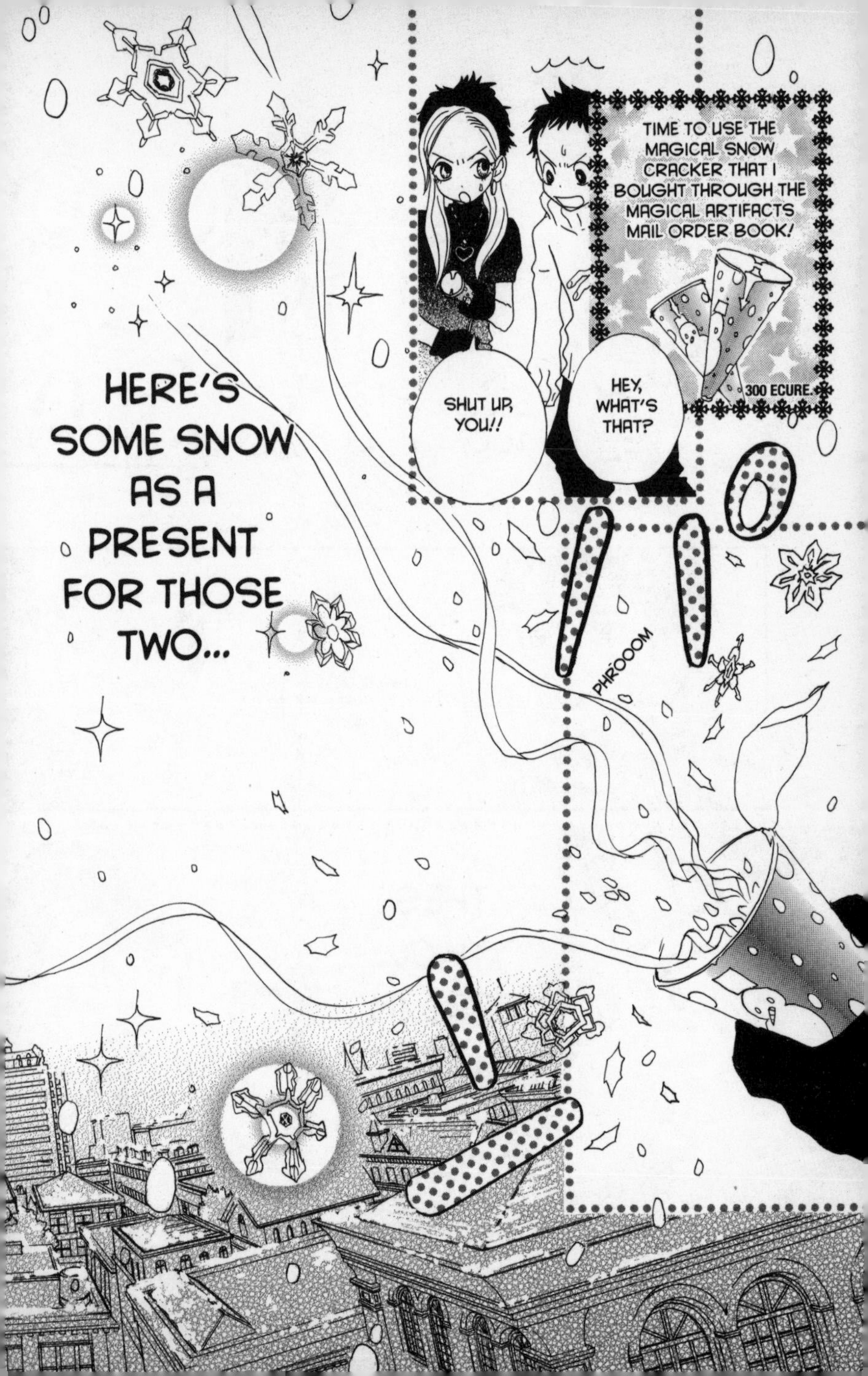
TIME TO USE THE MAGICAL SNOW CRACKER THAT I BOUGHT THROUGH THE MAGICAL ARTIFACTS MAIL ORDER BOOK!
300 ECURE.
HEY, WHAT'S THAT?
SHUT UP, YOU!!
PHROOOM
HERE'S SOME SNOW AS A PRESENT FOR THOSE TWO...

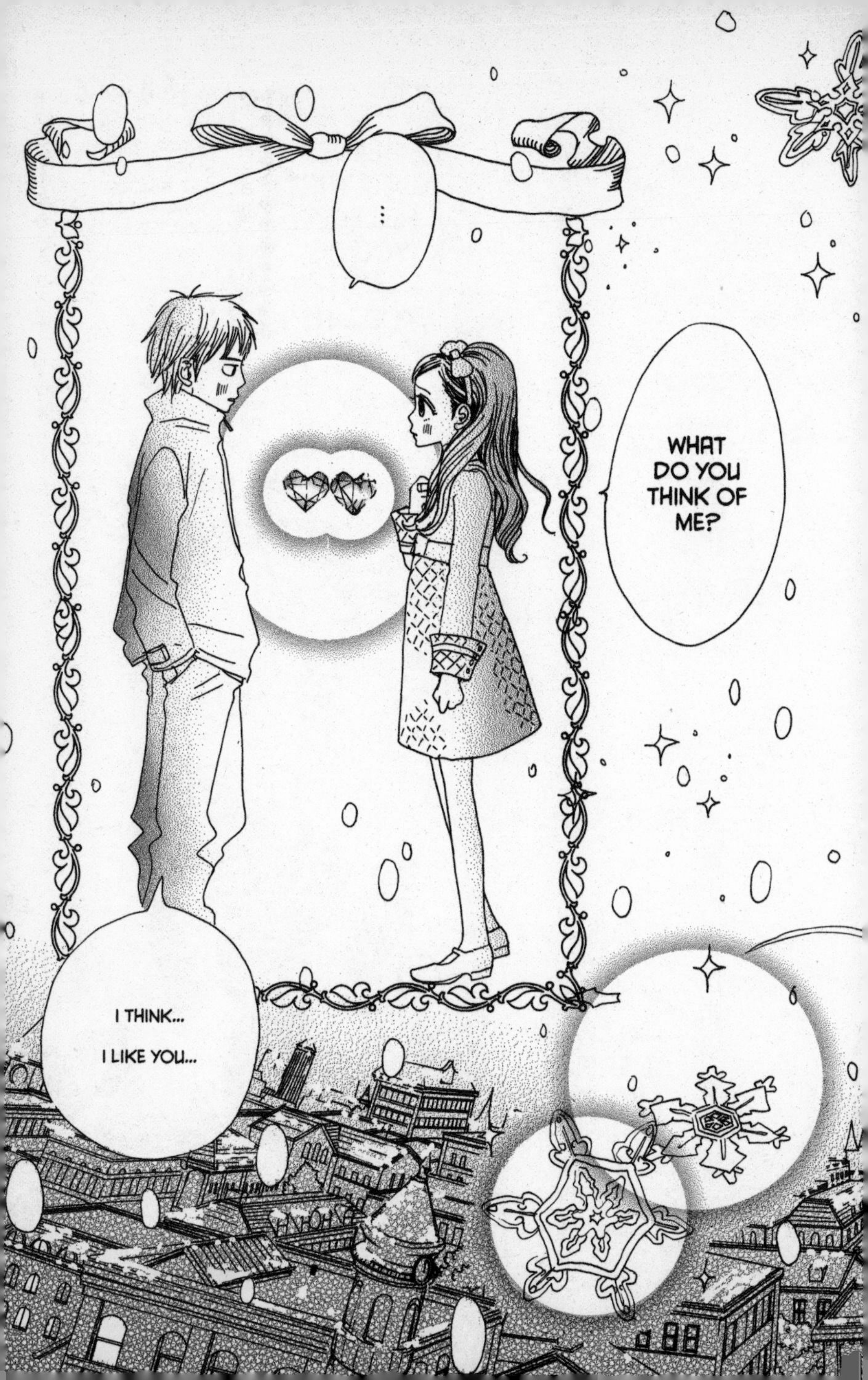
...
WHAT DO YOU THINK OF ME?
I THINK... I LIKE YOU...

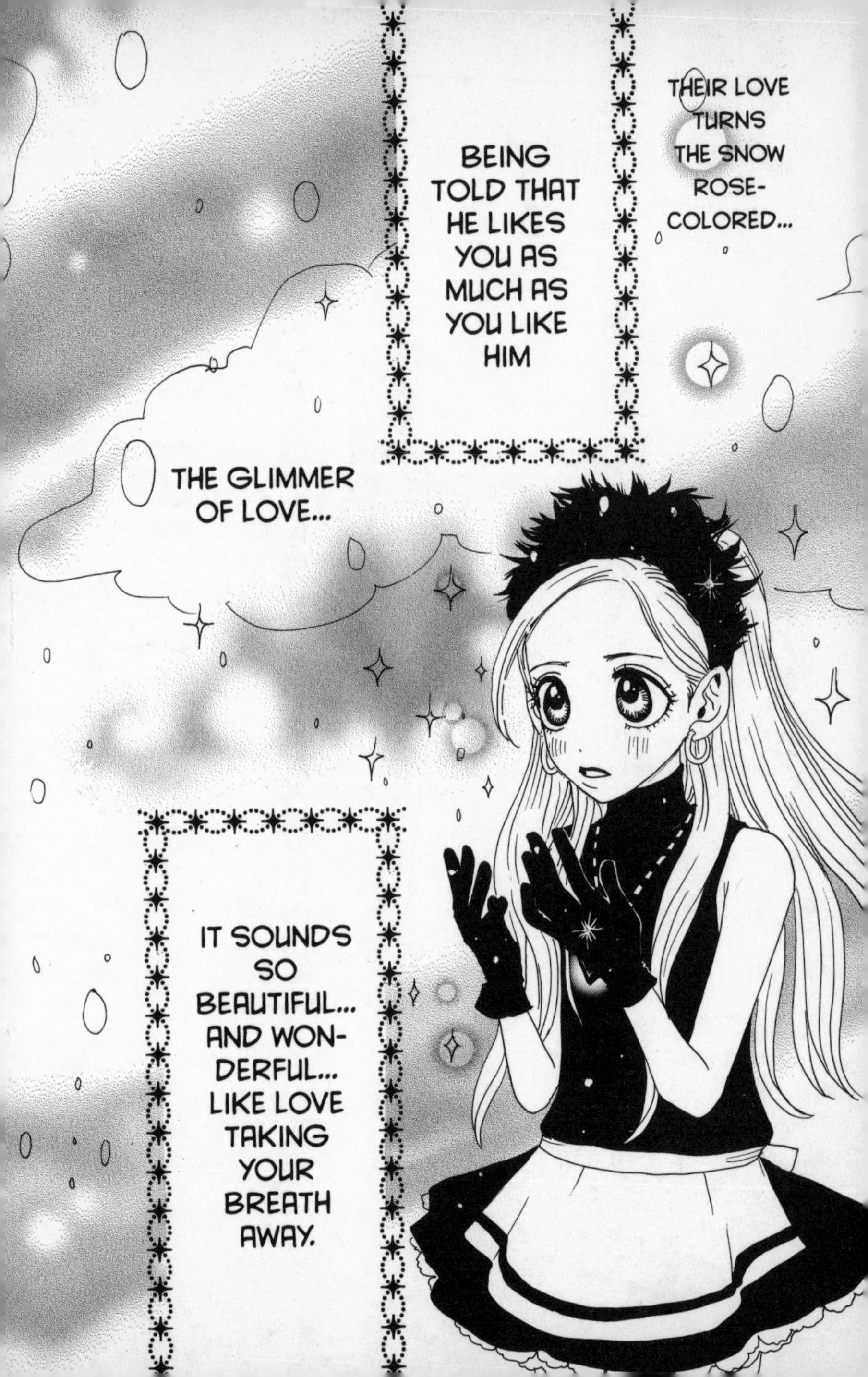
THEIR LOVE TURNS THE SNOW ROSE-COLORED...
BEING TOLD THAT HE LIKES YOU AS MUCH AS YOU LIKE HIM
THE GLIMMER OF LOVE...
IT SOUNDS SO BEAUTIFUL... AND WON-DERFUL... LIKE LOVE TAKING YOUR BREATH AWAY.

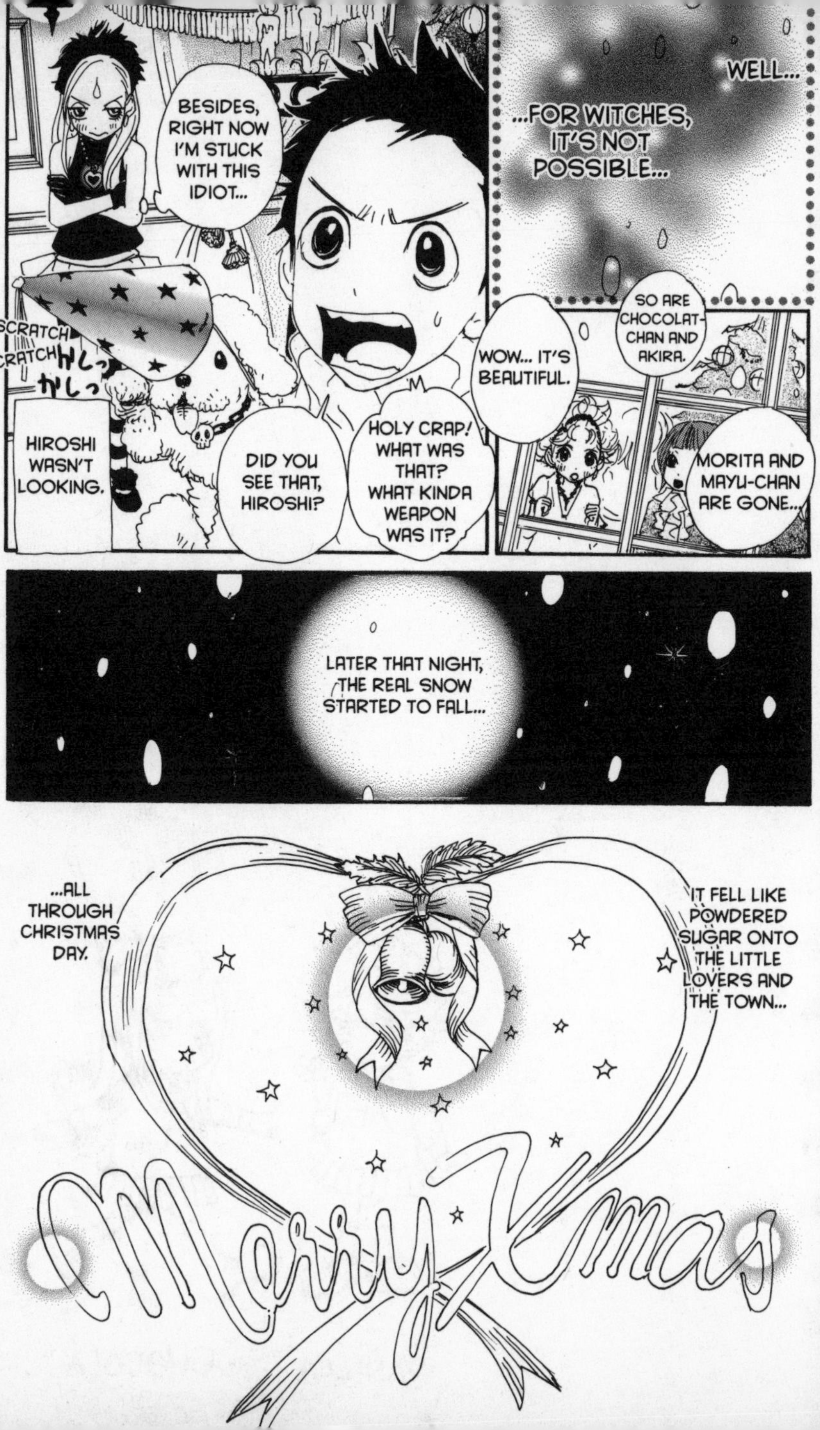
WELL...
...FOR WITCHES, IT'S NOT POSSIBLE...
SO ARE CHOCOLAT-CHAN AND AKIRA.
WOW... IT'S BEAUTIFUL.
MORITA AND MAYU-CHAN ARE GONE...
BESIDES, RIGHT NOW I'M STUCK WITH THIS IDIOT...
HOLY CRAP! WHAT WAS THAT? WHAT KINDA WEAPON WAS IT?
DID YOU SEE THAT, HIROSHI?
SCRATCH SCRATCH
かしっ かしっ
HIROSHI WASN'T LOOKING.
LATER THAT NIGHT, THE REAL SNOW STARTED TO FALL...
IT FELL LIKE POWDERED SUGAR ONTO THE LITTLE LOVERS AND THE TOWN...
...ALL THROUGH CHRISTMAS DAY.
Merry Xmas

VANILLA   CHOCOLA

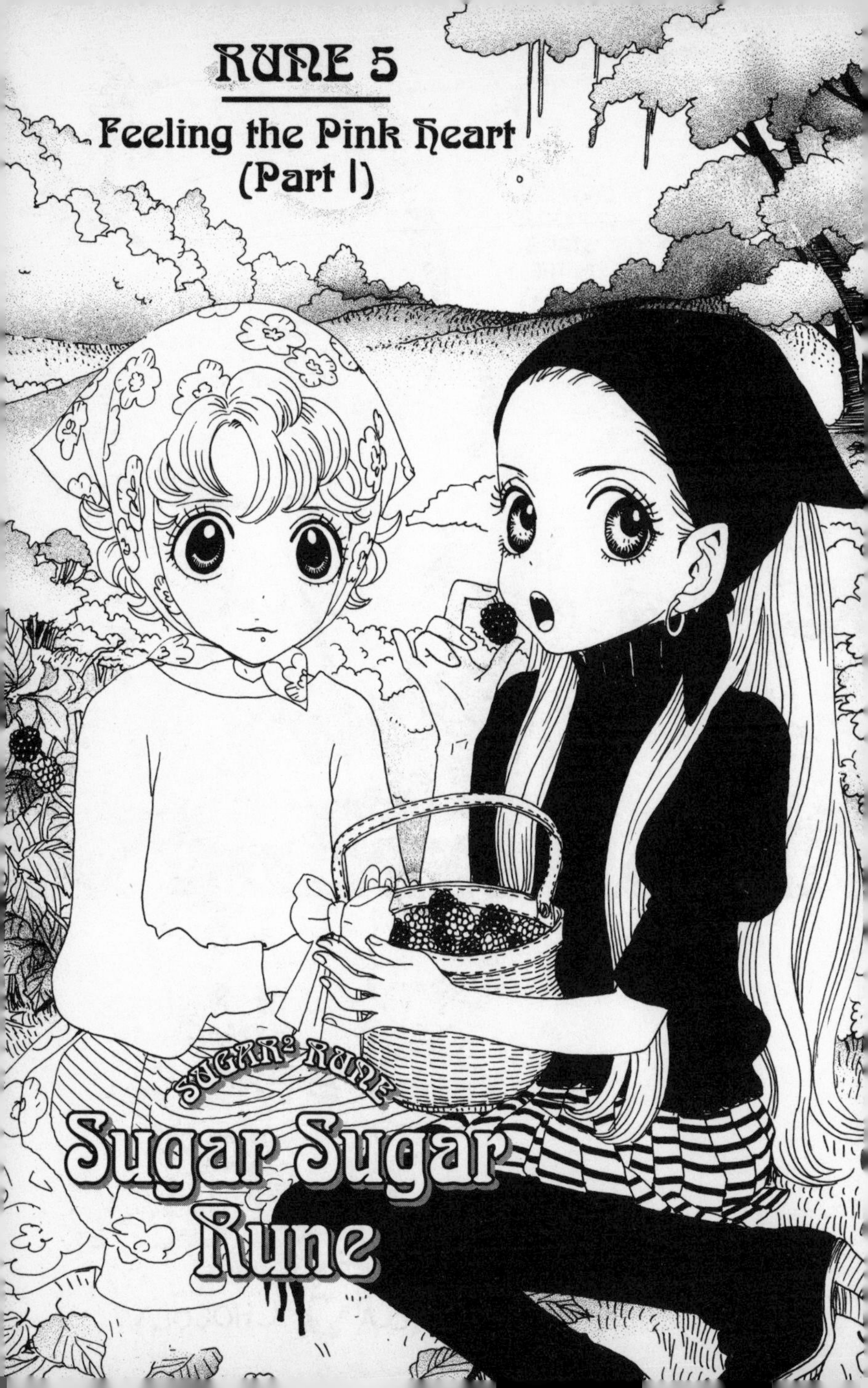
RUNE 5
Feeling the Pink Heart
(Part 1)
SUGAR² RUNE
Sugar Sugar
Rune

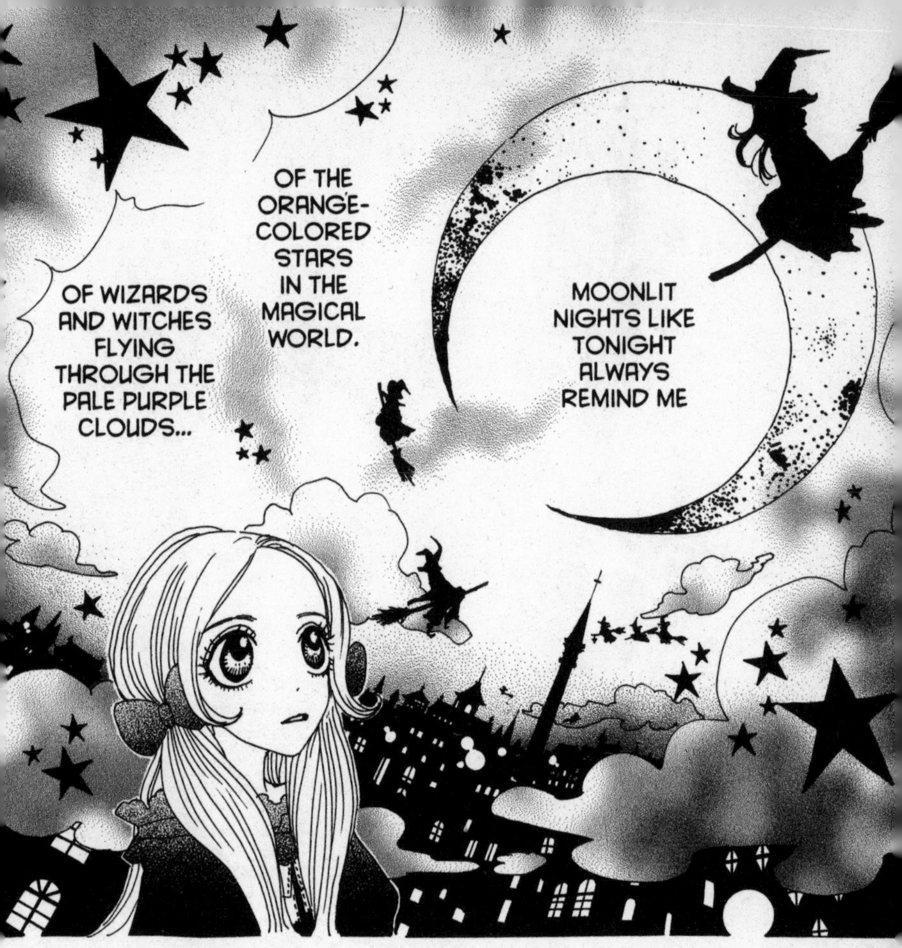
MOONLIT NIGHTS LIKE TONIGHT ALWAYS REMIND ME
OF THE ORANGE-COLORED STARS IN THE MAGICAL WORLD.
OF WIZARDS AND WITCHES FLYING THROUGH THE PALE PURPLE CLOUDS...

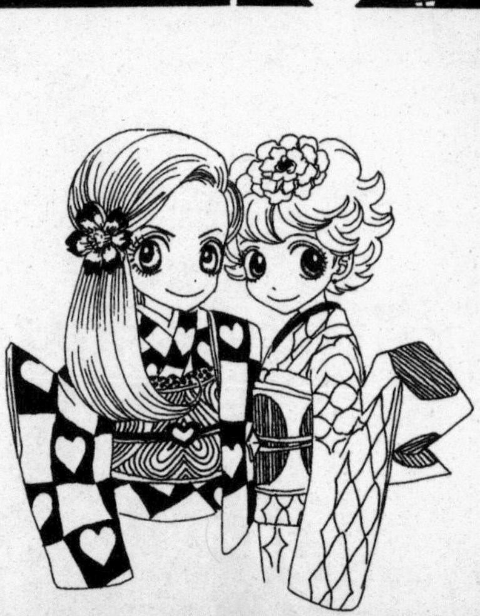

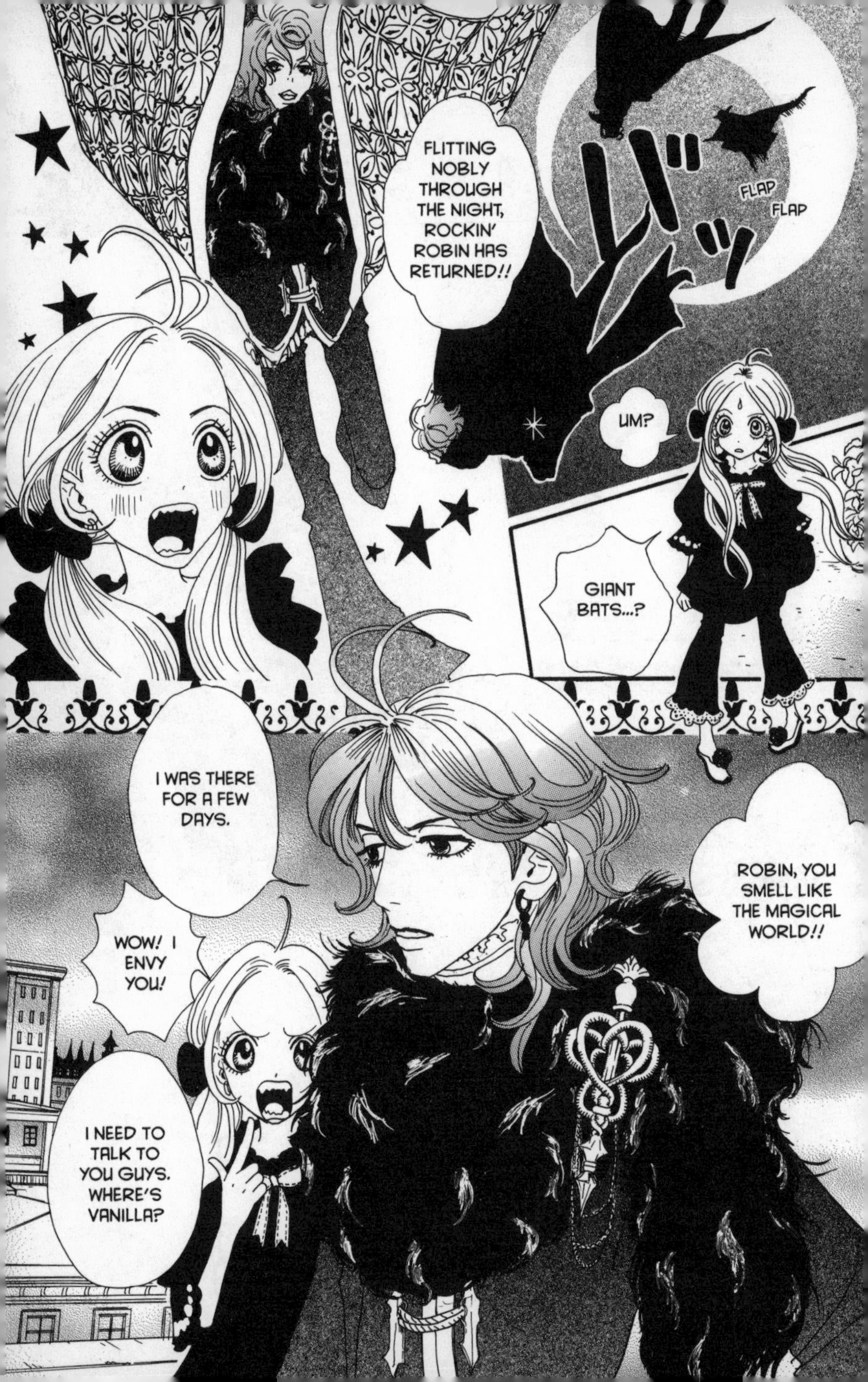
バッ
FLAP
FLAP
UM?
GIANT BATS...?
FLITTING NOBLY THROUGH THE NIGHT, ROCKIN' ROBIN HAS RETURNED!!
ROBIN, YOU SMELL LIKE THE MAGICAL WORLD!!
I WAS THERE FOR A FEW DAYS.
WOW! I ENVY YOU!
I NEED TO TALK TO YOU GUYS. WHERE'S VANILLA?

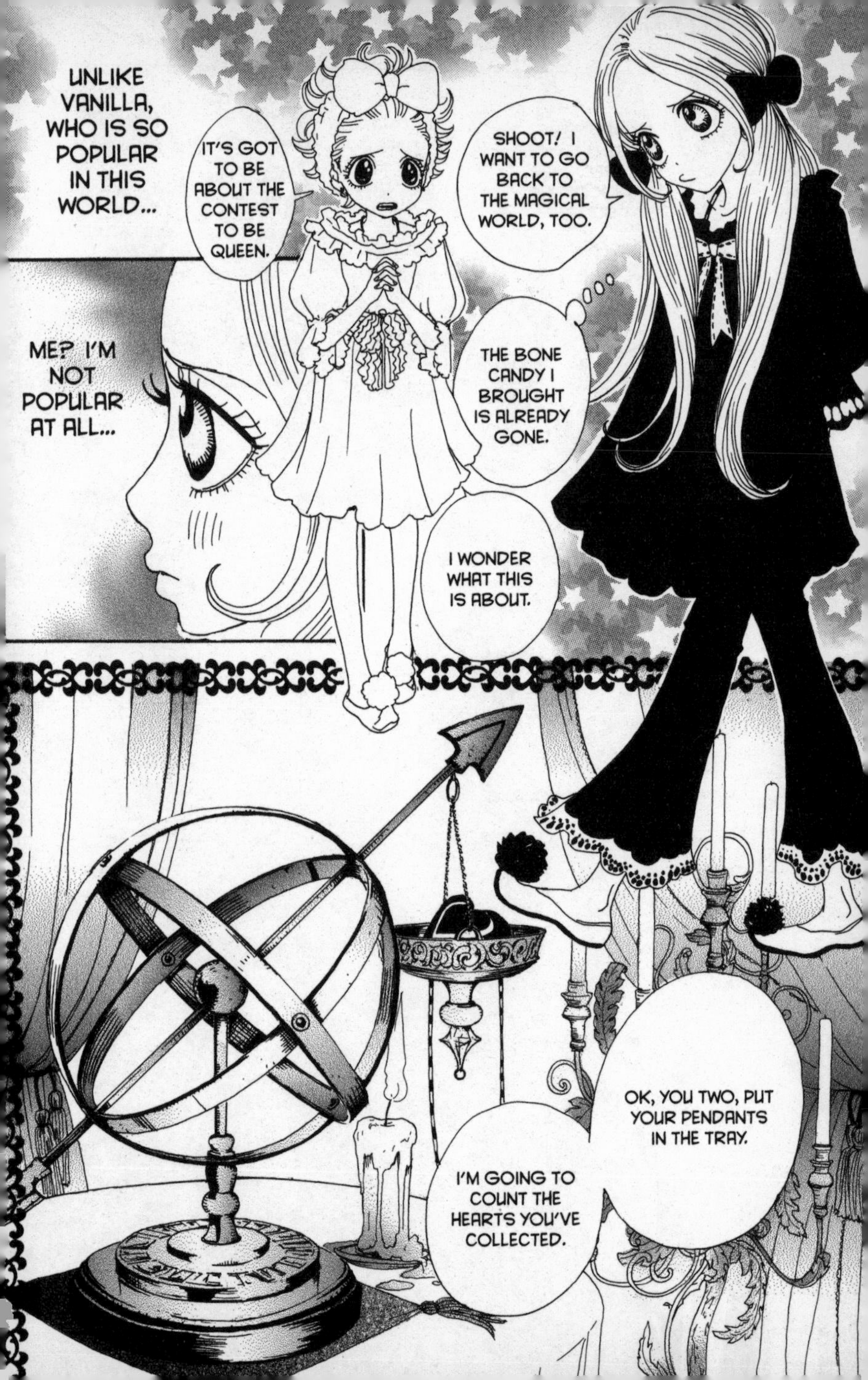
SHOOT! I WANT TO GO BACK TO THE MAGICAL WORLD, TOO.
IT'S GOT TO BE ABOUT THE CONTEST TO BE QUEEN.
UNLIKE VANILLA, WHO IS SO POPULAR IN THIS WORLD...
THE BONE CANDY I BROUGHT IS ALREADY GONE.
I WONDER WHAT THIS IS ABOUT.
ME? I'M NOT POPULAR AT ALL...
OK, YOU TWO, PUT YOUR PENDANTS IN THE TRAY.
I'M GOING TO COUNT THE HEARTS YOU'VE COLLECTED.

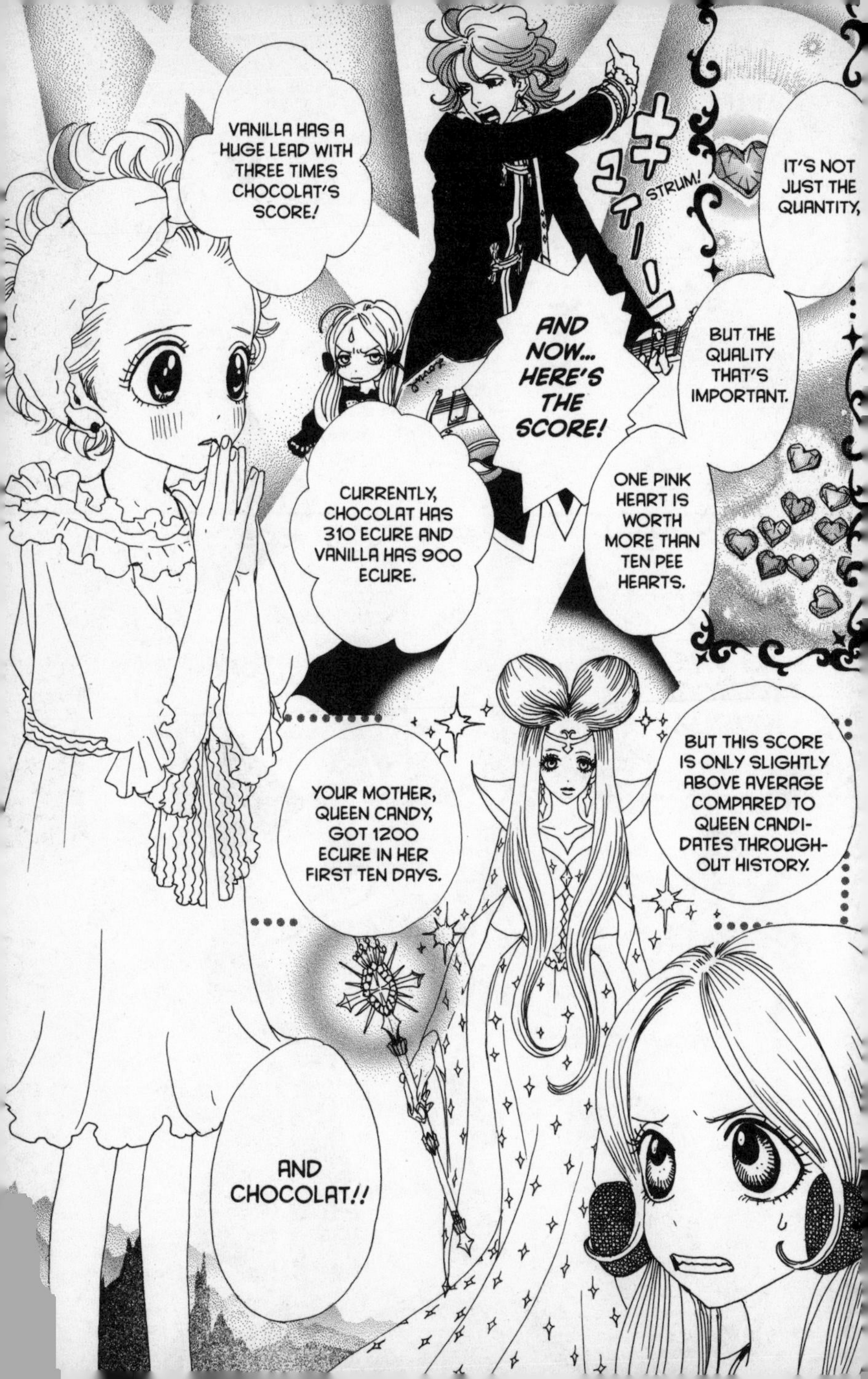
IT'S NOT JUST THE QUANTITY,
BUT THE QUALITY THAT'S IMPORTANT.
ONE PINK HEART IS WORTH MORE THAN TEN PEE HEARTS.
STRUM!
AND NOW... HERE'S THE SCORE!
CURRENTLY, CHOCOLAT HAS 310 ECURE AND VANILLA HAS 900 ECURE.
VANILLA HAS A HUGE LEAD WITH THREE TIMES CHOCOLAT'S SCORE!
BUT THIS SCORE IS ONLY SLIGHTLY ABOVE AVERAGE COMPARED TO QUEEN CANDI-DATES THROUGH-OUT HISTORY.
YOUR MOTHER, QUEEN CANDY, GOT 1200 ECURE IN HER FIRST TEN DAYS.
AND CHOCOLAT!!

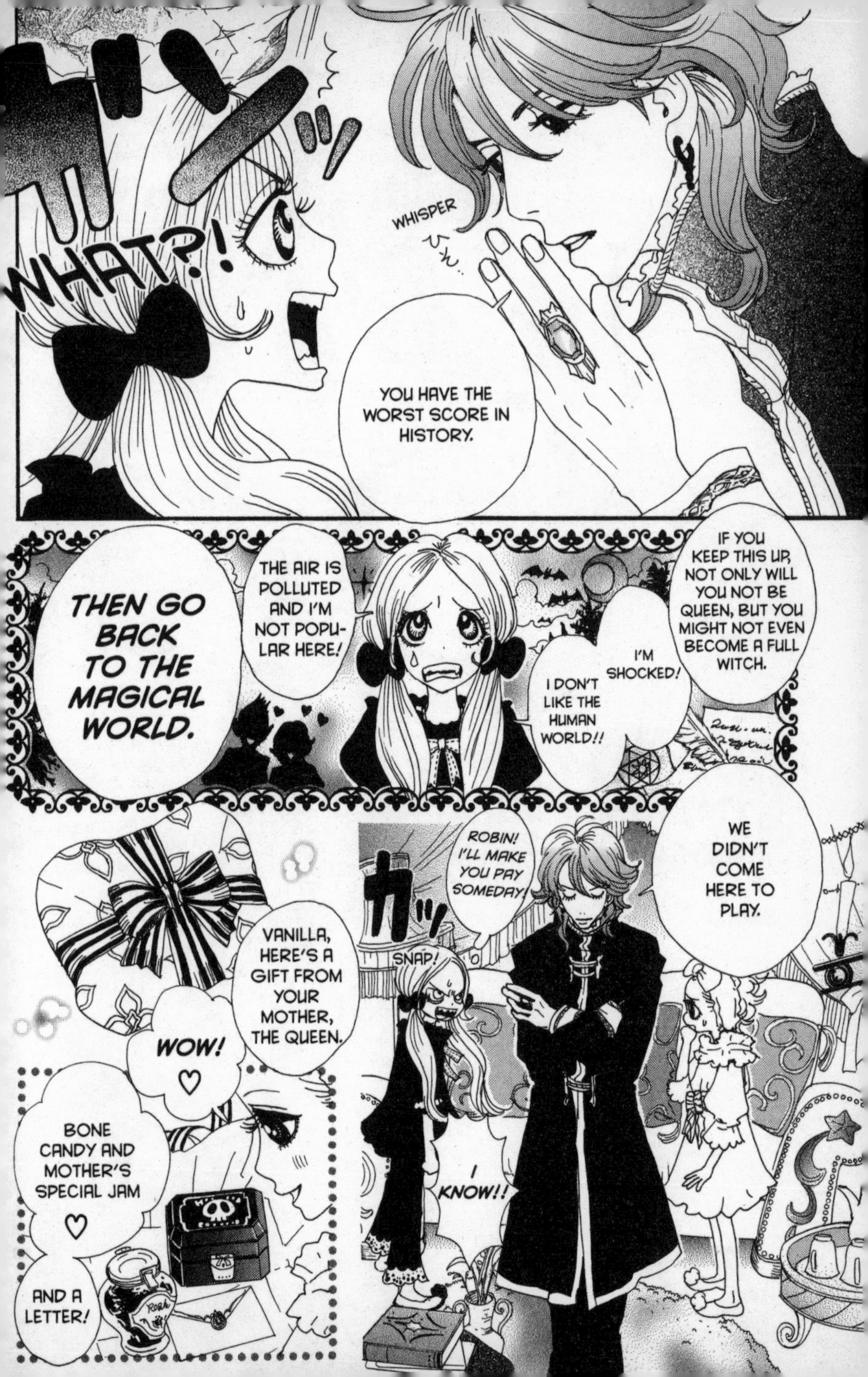
WHISPER
YOU HAVE THE WORST SCORE IN HISTORY.
WHAT?!
IF YOU KEEP THIS UP, NOT ONLY WILL YOU NOT BE QUEEN, BUT YOU MIGHT NOT EVEN BECOME A FULL WITCH.
I'M SHOCKED!
I DON'T LIKE THE HUMAN WORLD!!
THE AIR IS POLLUTED AND I'M NOT POPU-LAR HERE!
THEN GO BACK TO THE MAGICAL WORLD.
WE DIDN'T COME HERE TO PLAY.
ROBIN! I'LL MAKE YOU PAY SOMEDAY!
SNAP!
I KNOW!!
VANILLA, HERE'S A GIFT FROM YOUR MOTHER, THE QUEEN.
WOW! ♡
BONE CANDY AND MOTHER'S SPECIAL JAM ♡
AND A LETTER!

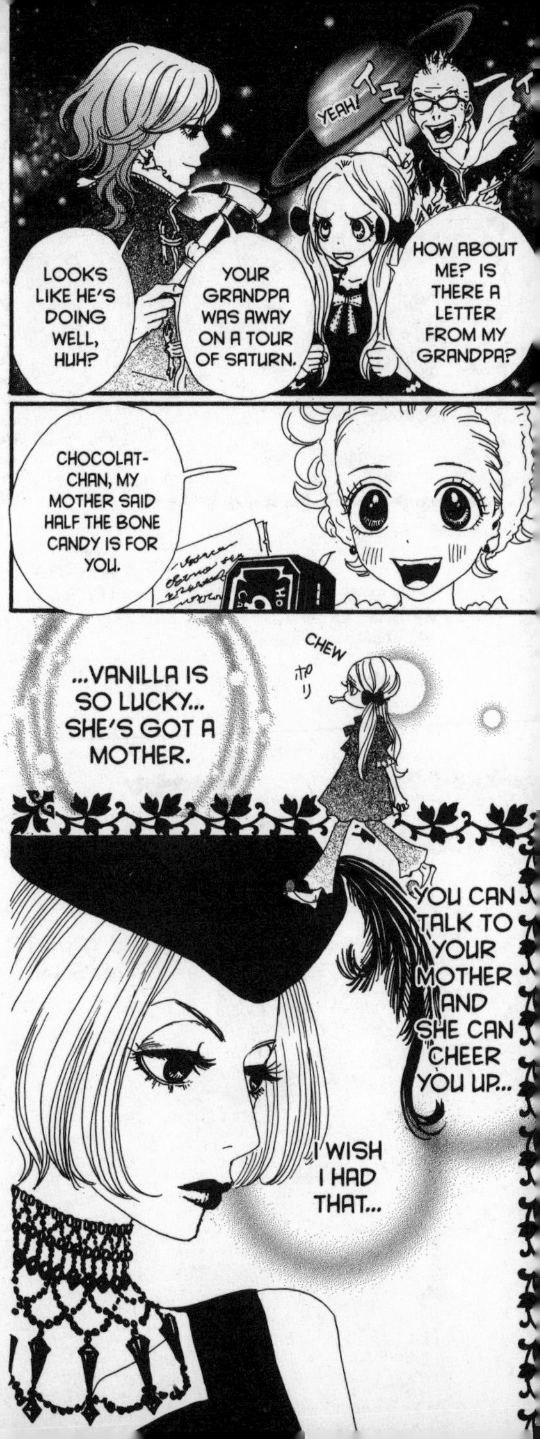
YEAH! イェーイ
HOW ABOUT ME? IS THERE A LETTER FROM MY GRANDPA?
YOUR GRANDPA WAS AWAY ON A TOUR OF SATURN.
LOOKS LIKE HE'S DOING WELL, HUH?
CHOCOLAT-CHAN, MY MOTHER SAID HALF THE BONE CANDY IS FOR YOU.
CHEW ポリ
...VANILLA IS SO LUCKY... SHE'S GOT A MOTHER.
YOU CAN TALK TO YOUR MOTHER AND SHE CAN CHEER YOU UP...
I WISH I HAD THAT...

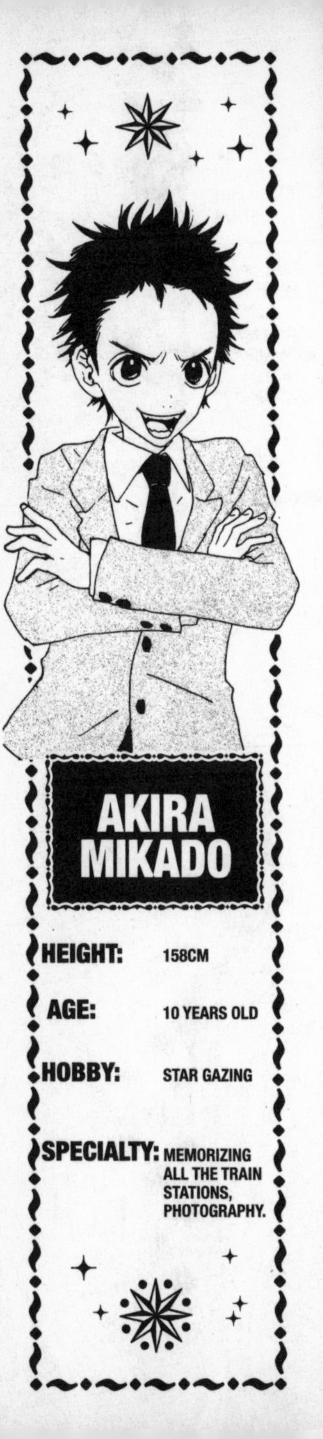

AKIRA MIKADO

HEIGHT: 158CM

AGE: 10 YEARS OLD

HOBBY: STAR GAZING

SPECIALTY: MEMORIZING ALL THE TRAIN STATIONS, PHOTOGRAPHY.

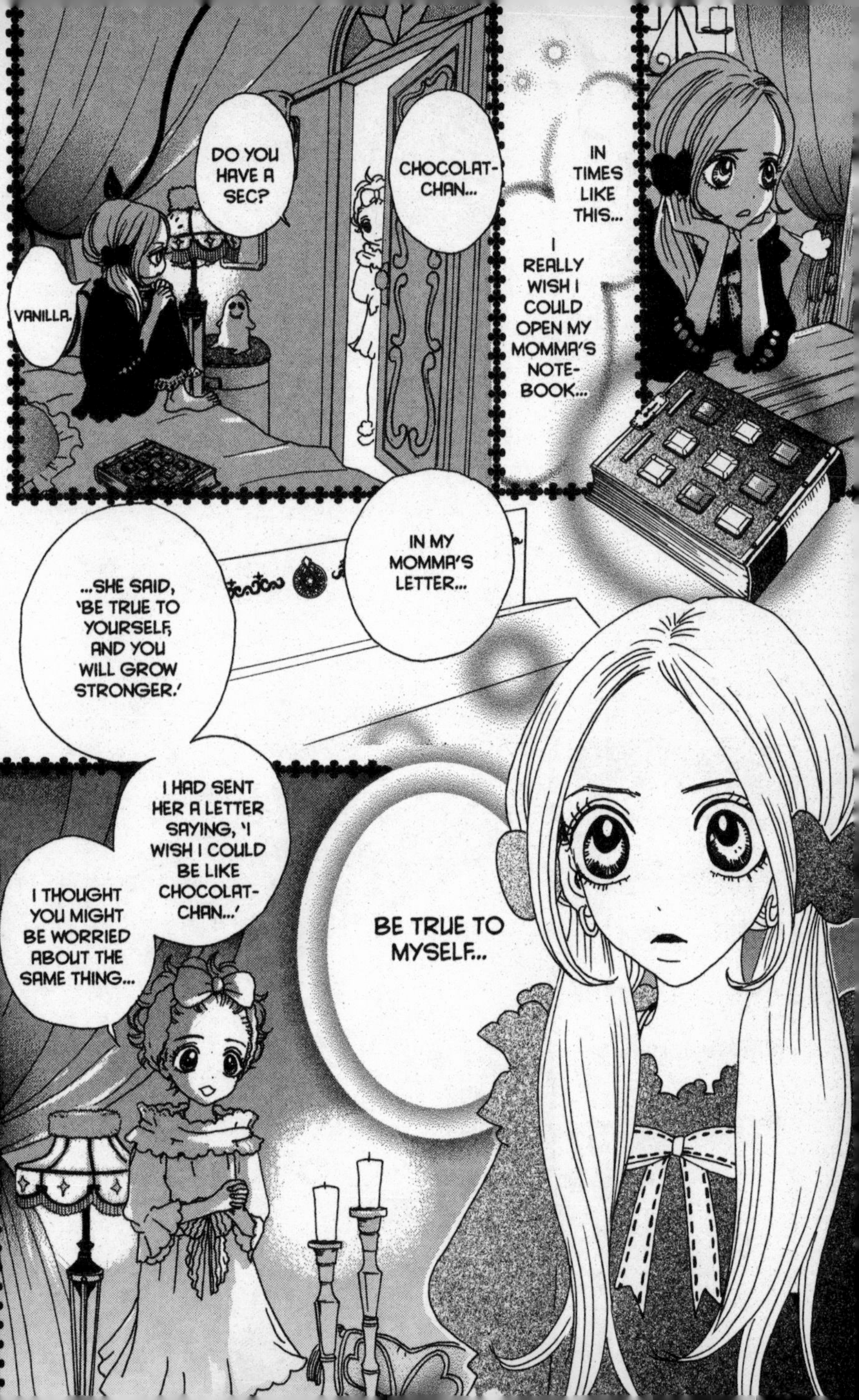
IN TIMES LIKE THIS...
I REALLY WISH I COULD OPEN MY MOMMA'S NOTE-BOOK...
CHOCOLAT-CHAN...
DO YOU HAVE A SEC?
VANILLA.
IN MY MOMMA'S LETTER...
...SHE SAID, 'BE TRUE TO YOURSELF, AND YOU WILL GROW STRONGER.'
BE TRUE TO MYSELF...
I HAD SENT HER A LETTER SAYING, 'I WISH I COULD BE LIKE CHOCOLAT-CHAN...'
I THOUGHT YOU MIGHT BE WORRIED ABOUT THE SAME THING...

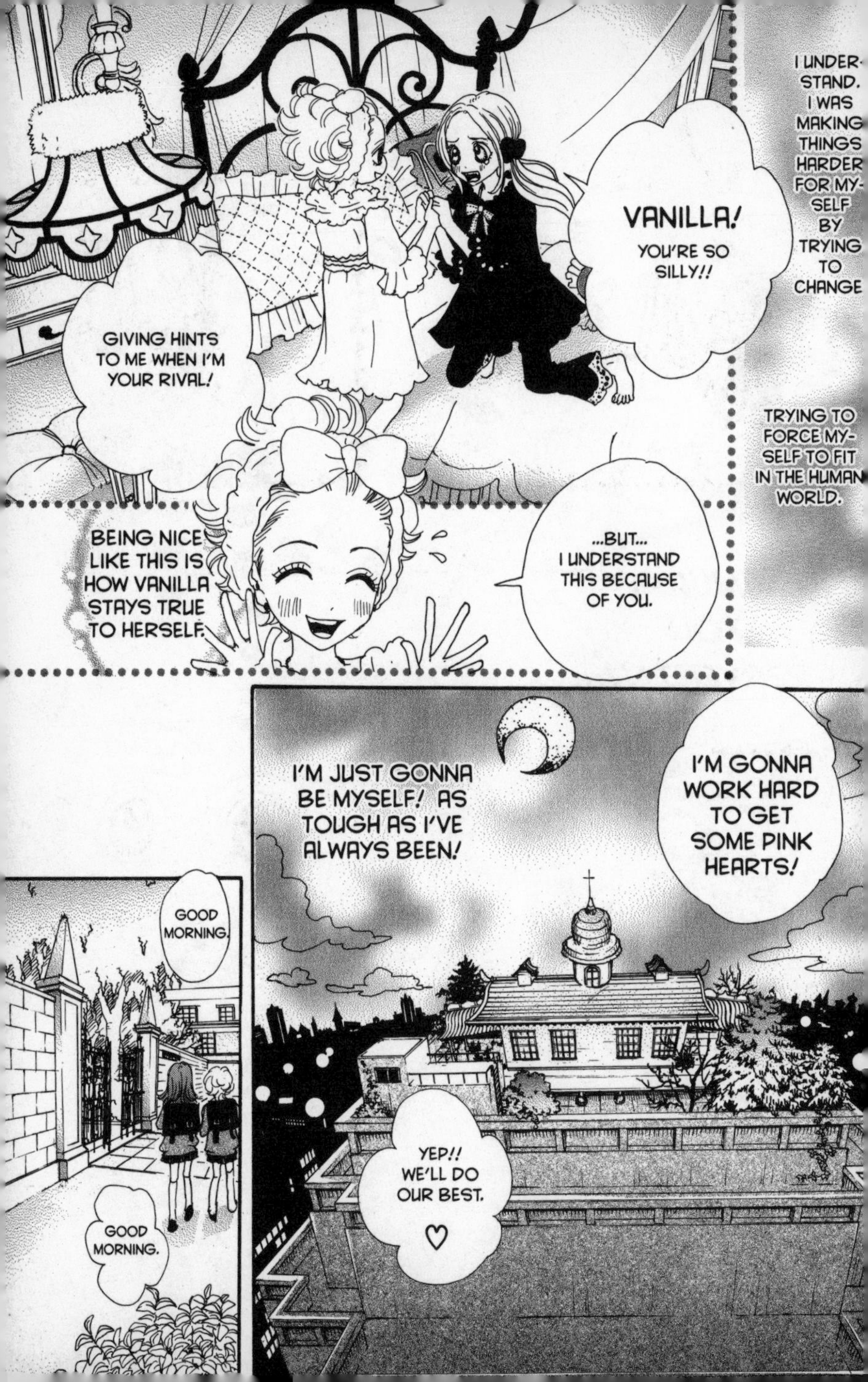
I UNDERSTAND. I WAS MAKING THINGS HARDER FOR MYSELF BY TRYING TO CHANGE
TRYING TO FORCE MYSELF TO FIT IN THE HUMAN WORLD.
VANILLA! YOU'RE SO SILLY!!
GIVING HINTS TO ME WHEN I'M YOUR RIVAL!
...BUT... I UNDERSTAND THIS BECAUSE OF YOU.
BEING NICE LIKE THIS IS HOW VANILLA STAYS TRUE TO HERSELF.
I'M GONNA WORK HARD TO GET SOME PINK HEARTS!
I'M JUST GONNA BE MYSELF! AS TOUGH AS I'VE ALWAYS BEEN!
YEP!! WE'LL DO OUR BEST. ♡
GOOD MORNING.
GOOD MORNING.

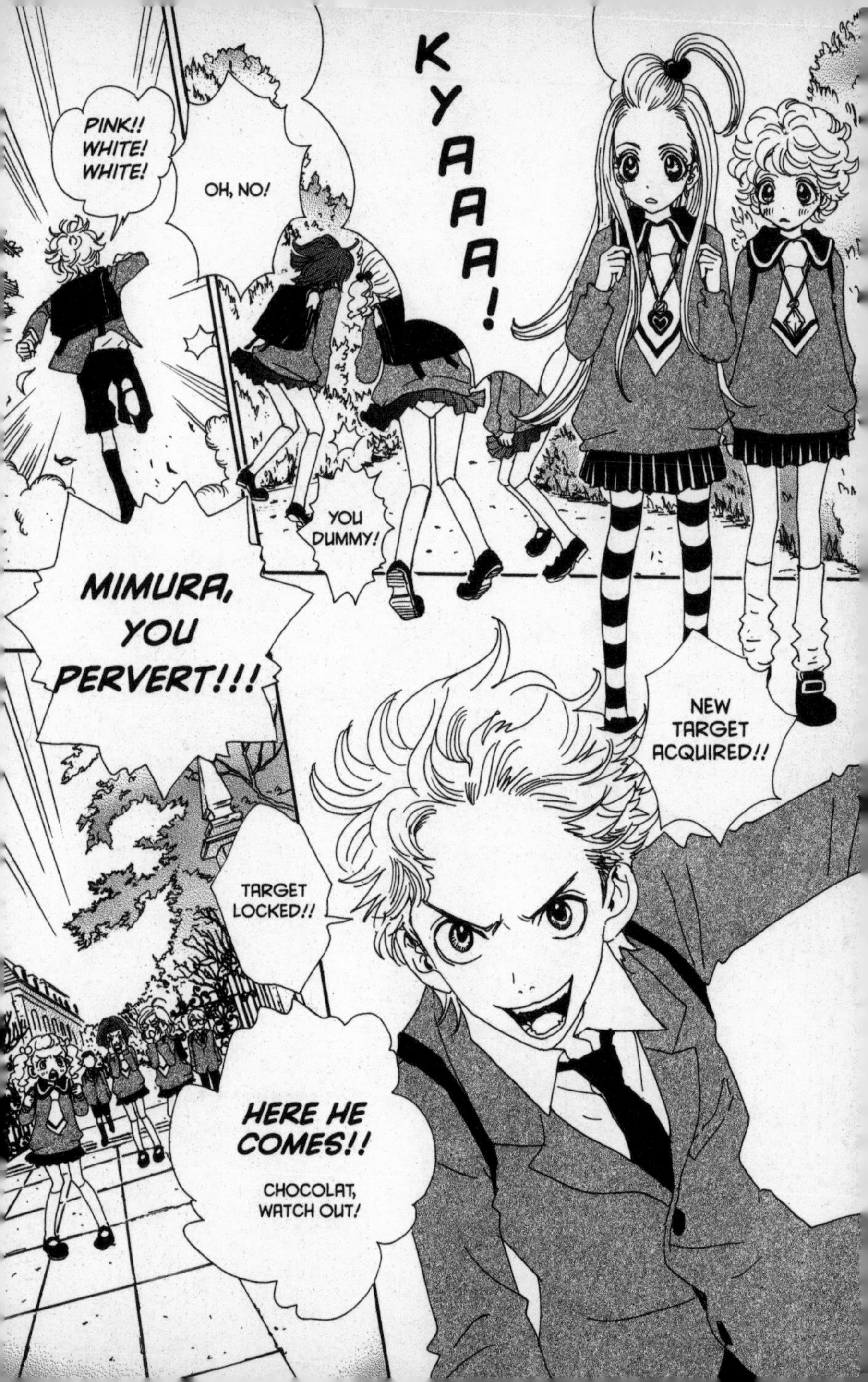
KYAAA!
OH, NO!
PINK!! WHITE! WHITE!
YOU DUMMY!
MIMURA, YOU PERVERT!!!
NEW TARGET ACQUIRED!!
TARGET LOCKED!!
HERE HE COMES!!
CHOCOLAT, WATCH OUT!

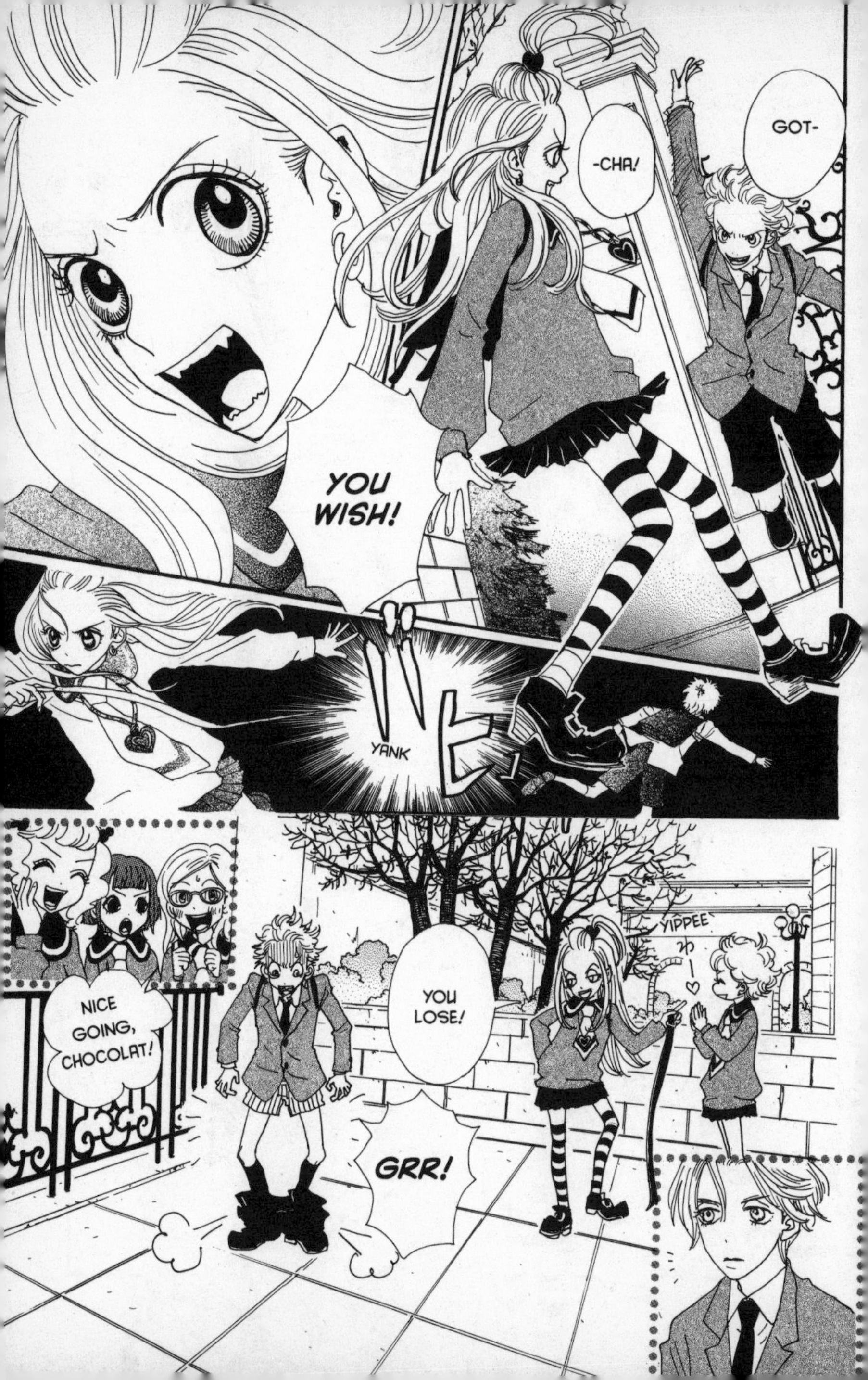
GOT-
-CHA!
YOU WISH!
YANK
YIPPEE
YOU LOSE!
GRR!
NICE GOING, CHOCOLAT!

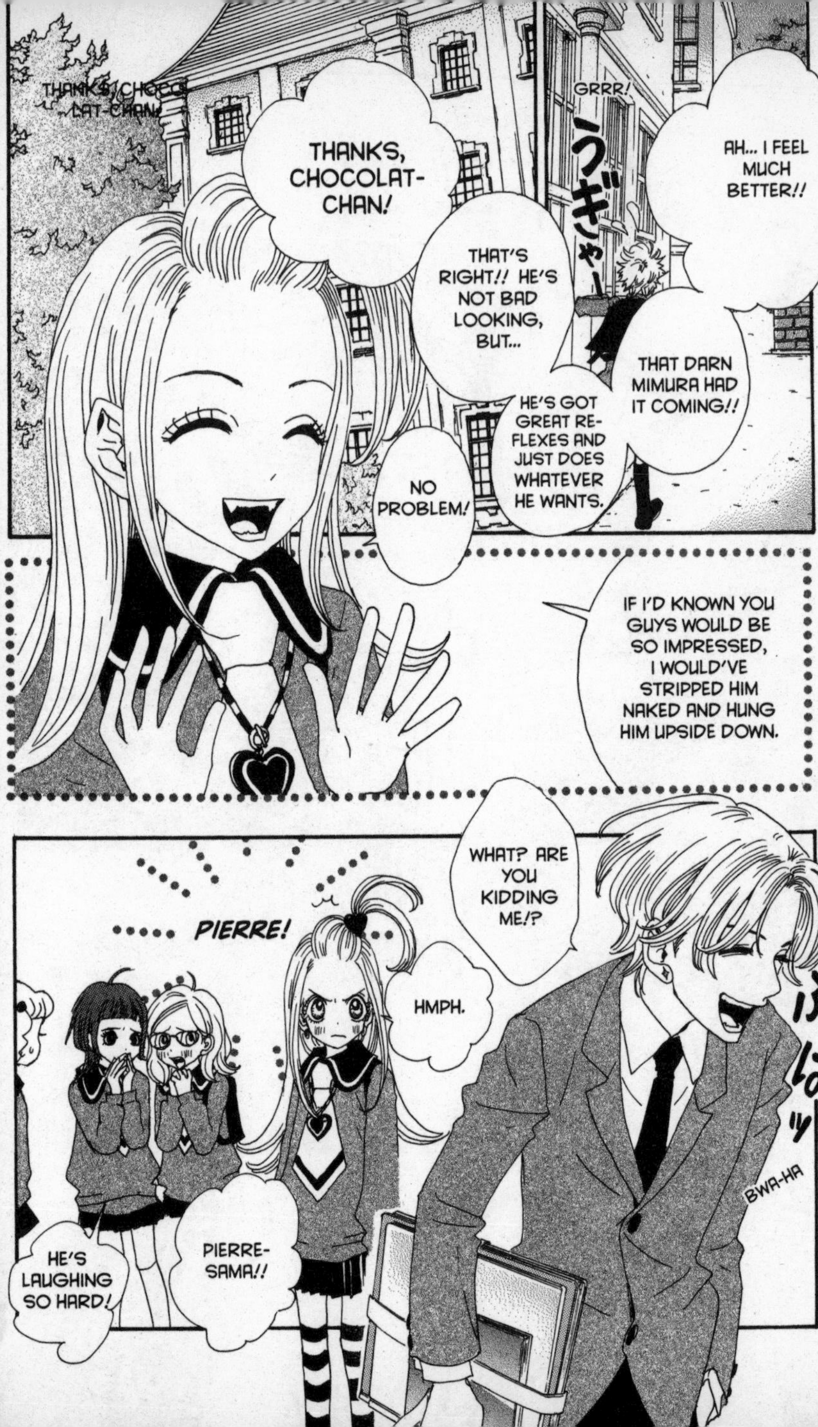
AH... I FEEL MUCH BETTER!!
GRRR!
うぎゃー
THANKS, CHOCOLAT-CHAN!
THANKS, CHOCO-LAT-CHAN!
THAT'S RIGHT!! HE'S NOT BAD LOOKING, BUT...
THAT DARN MIMURA HAD IT COMING!!
HE'S GOT GREAT RE-FLEXES AND JUST DOES WHATEVER HE WANTS.
NO PROBLEM!
IF I'D KNOWN YOU GUYS WOULD BE SO IMPRESSED, I WOULD'VE STRIPPED HIM NAKED AND HUNG HIM UPSIDE DOWN.
WHAT? ARE YOU KIDDING ME!?
ぶはッ
BWA-HA
..... PIERRE!
HMPH.
PIERRE-SAMA!!
HE'S LAUGHING SO HARD!

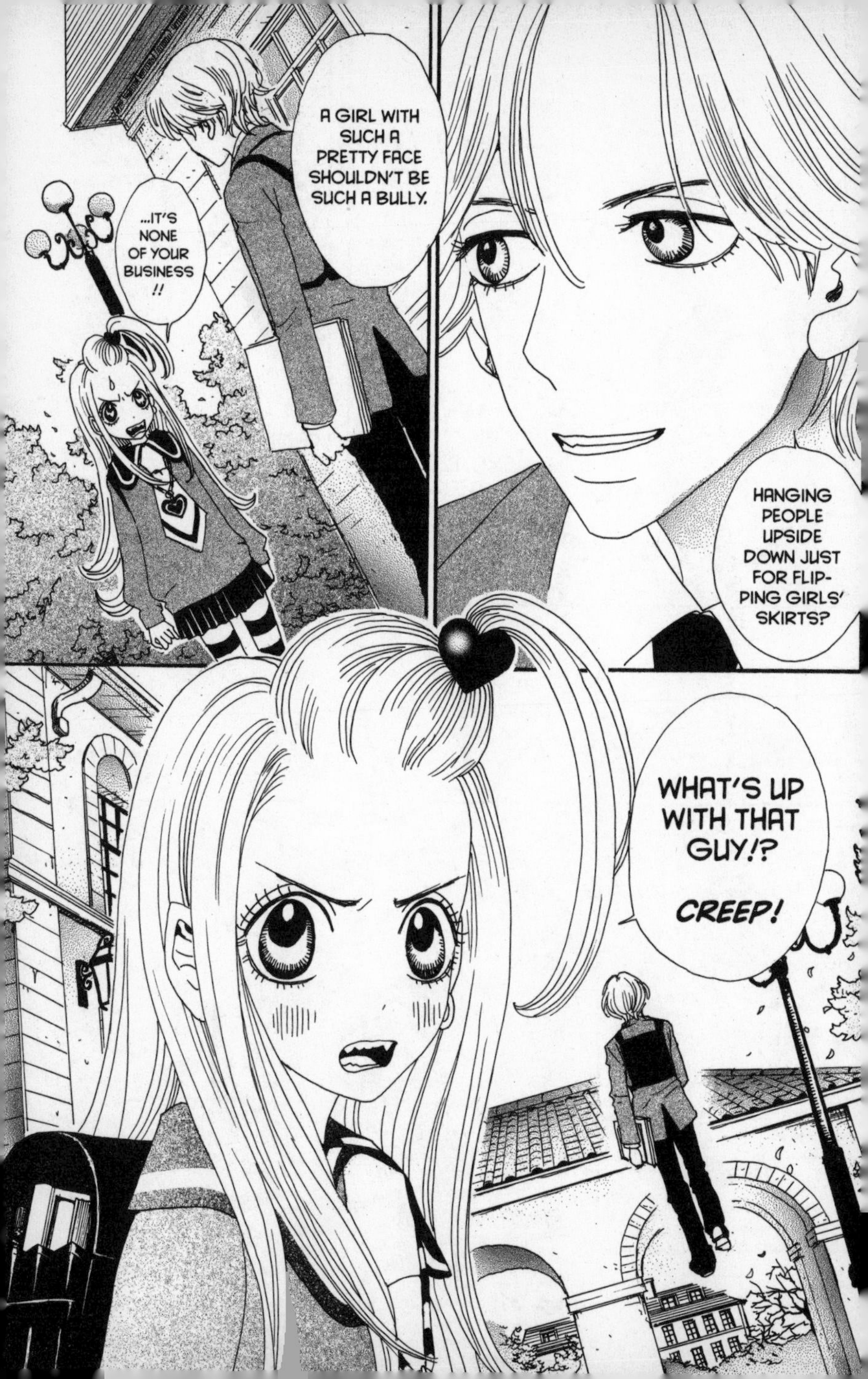
HANGING PEOPLE UPSIDE DOWN JUST FOR FLIP-PING GIRLS' SKIRTS?
A GIRL WITH SUCH A PRETTY FACE SHOULDN'T BE SUCH A BULLY.
...IT'S NONE OF YOUR BUSINESS!!
WHAT'S UP WITH THAT GUY!?
CREEP!

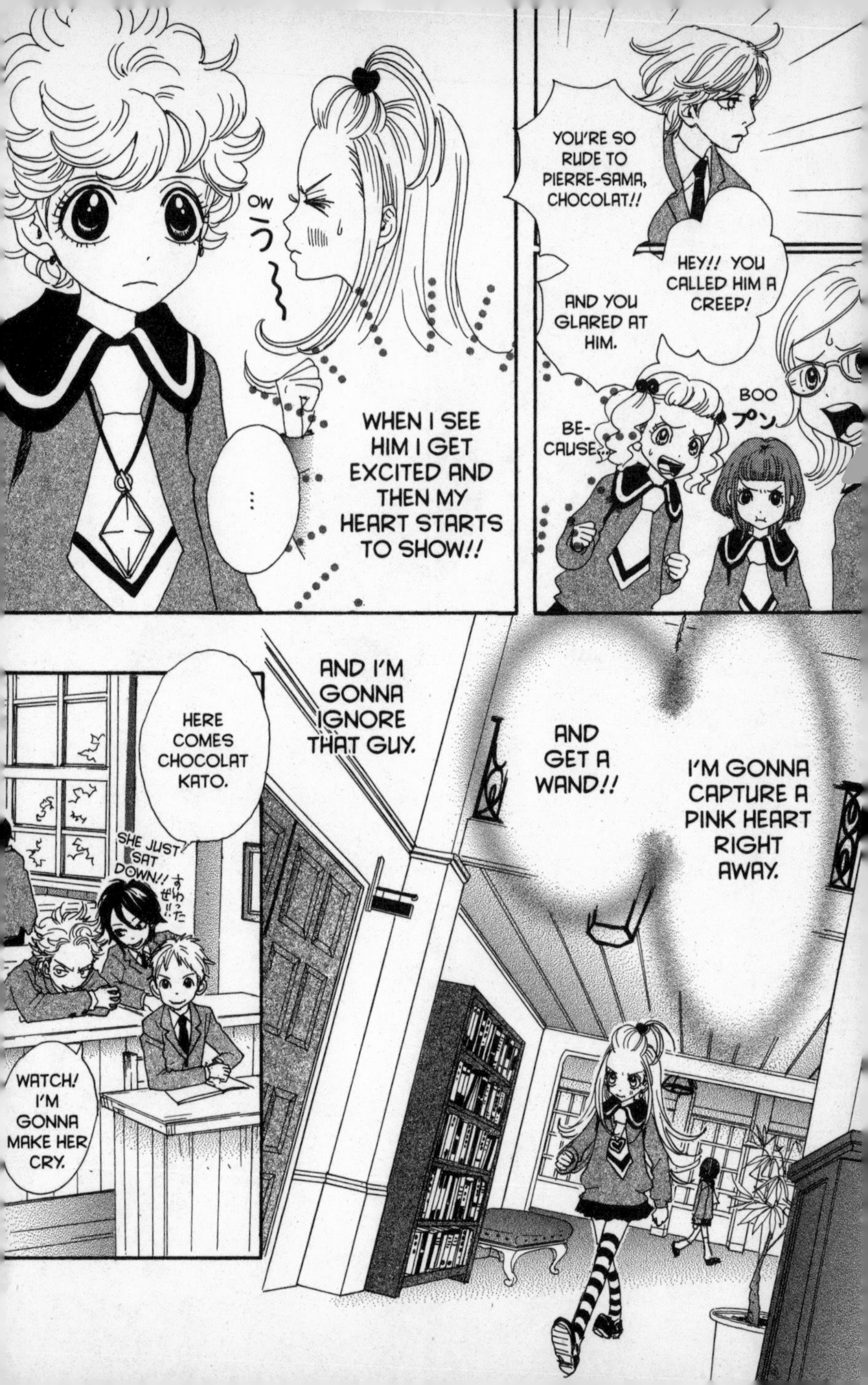
YOU'RE SO RUDE TO PIERRE-SAMA, CHOCOLAT!!
HEY!! YOU CALLED HIM A CREEP!
AND YOU GLARED AT HIM.
BOO プン
BE-CAUSE...
OW う~
WHEN I SEE HIM I GET EXCITED AND THEN MY HEART STARTS TO SHOW!!
...
I'M GONNA CAPTURE A PINK HEART RIGHT AWAY.
AND GET A WAND!!
AND I'M GONNA IGNORE THAT GUY.
HERE COMES CHOCOLAT KATO.
SHE JUST SAT DOWN!! すわった!!
WATCH! I'M GONNA MAKE HER CRY.

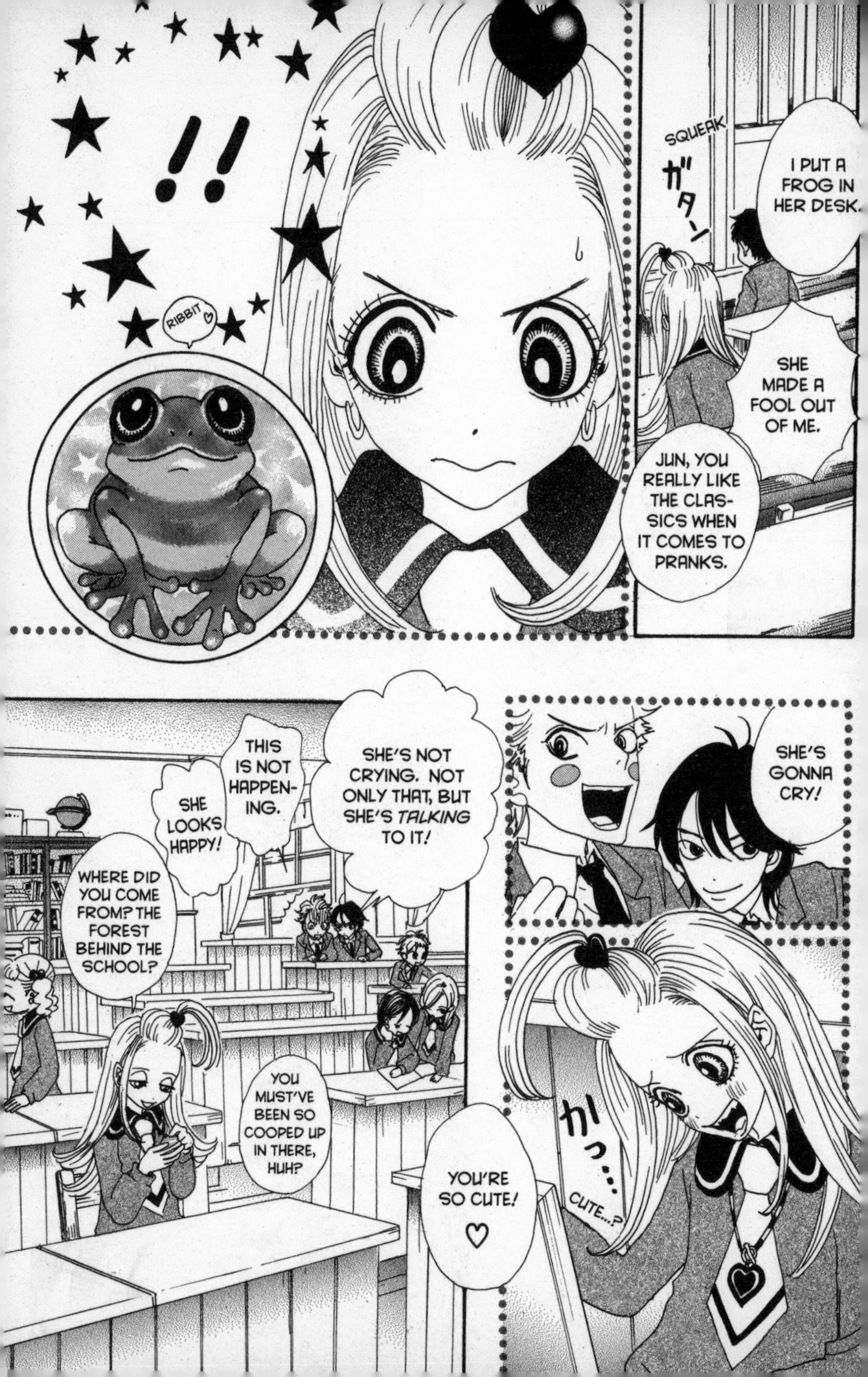
SQUEAK
ガタン
I PUT A FROG IN HER DESK.
SHE MADE A FOOL OUT OF ME.
JUN, YOU REALLY LIKE THE CLAS-SICS WHEN IT COMES TO PRANKS.
!!
RIBBIT ♡
SHE'S GONNA CRY!
SHE'S NOT CRYING. NOT ONLY THAT, BUT SHE'S *TALKING* TO IT!
THIS IS NOT HAPPEN-ING.
SHE LOOKS HAPPY!
WHERE DID YOU COME FROM? THE FOREST BEHIND THE SCHOOL?
YOU MUST'VE BEEN SO COOPED UP IN THERE, HUH?
YOU'RE SO CUTE! ♡
かっ…
CUTE...?

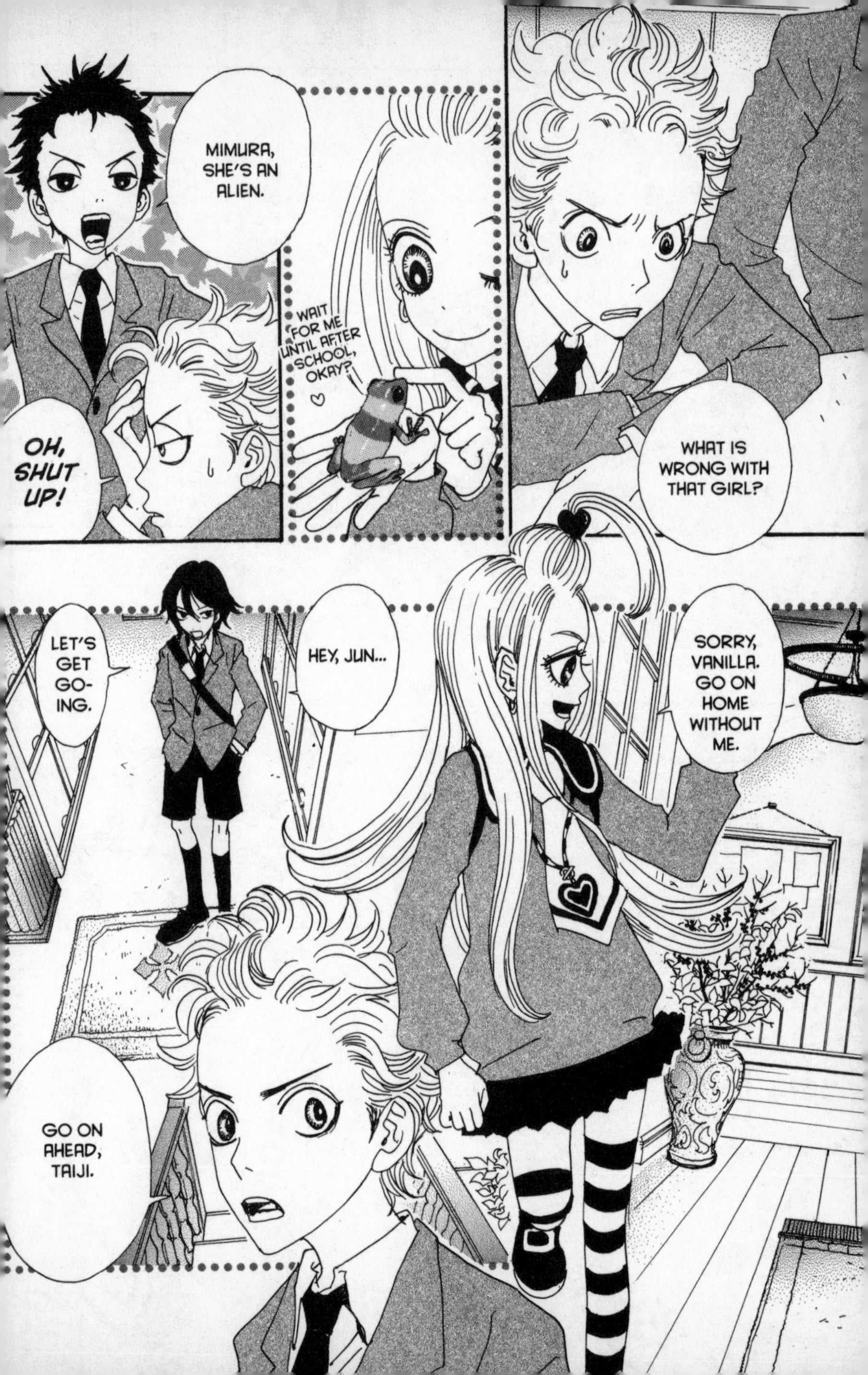
WHAT IS WRONG WITH THAT GIRL?
WAIT FOR ME UNTIL AFTER SCHOOL, OKAY?
MIMURA, SHE'S AN ALIEN.
OH, SHUT UP!
SORRY, VANILLA. GO ON HOME WITHOUT ME.
HEY, JUN...
LET'S GET GO-ING.
GO ON AHEAD, TAIJI.

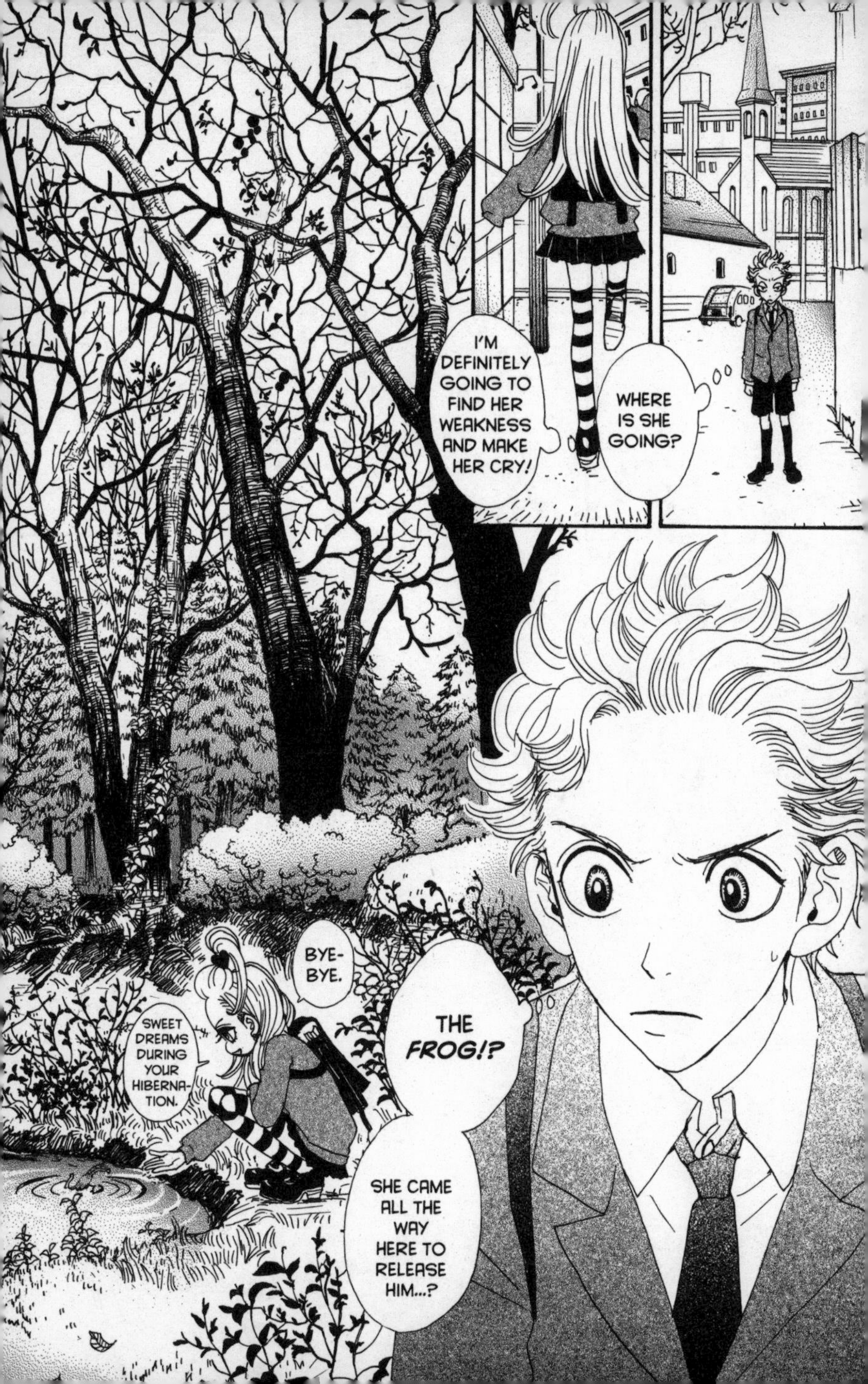
WHERE IS SHE GOING?
I'M DEFINITELY GOING TO FIND HER WEAKNESS AND MAKE HER CRY!
THE FROG!?
SHE CAME ALL THE WAY HERE TO RELEASE HIM...?
BYE-BYE.
SWEET DREAMS DURING YOUR HIBERNA-TION.

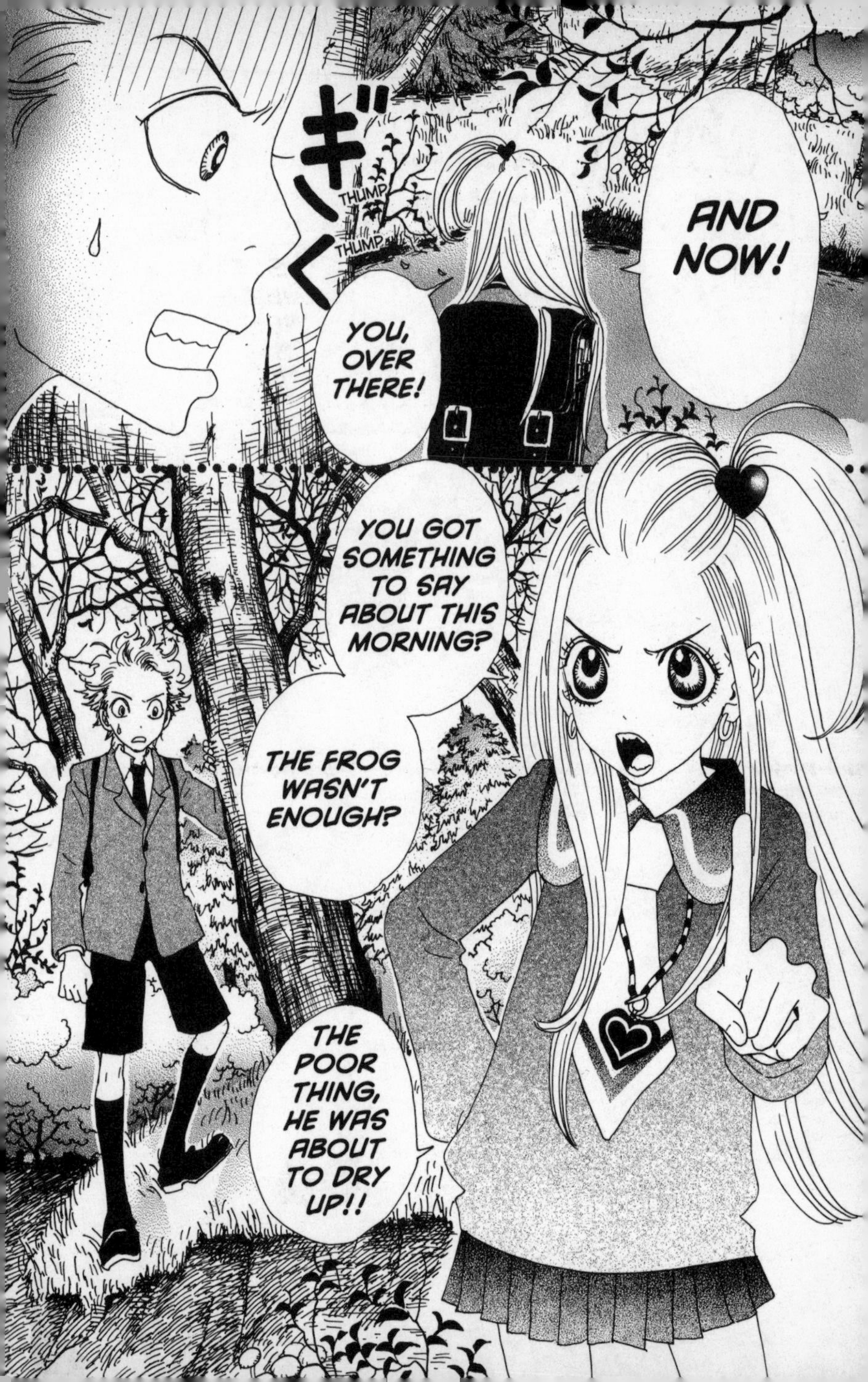
AND NOW!
YOU, OVER THERE!
ぎく
THUMP
THUMP
YOU GOT SOMETHING TO SAY ABOUT THIS MORNING?
THE FROG WASN'T ENOUGH?
THE POOR THING, HE WAS ABOUT TO DRY UP!!

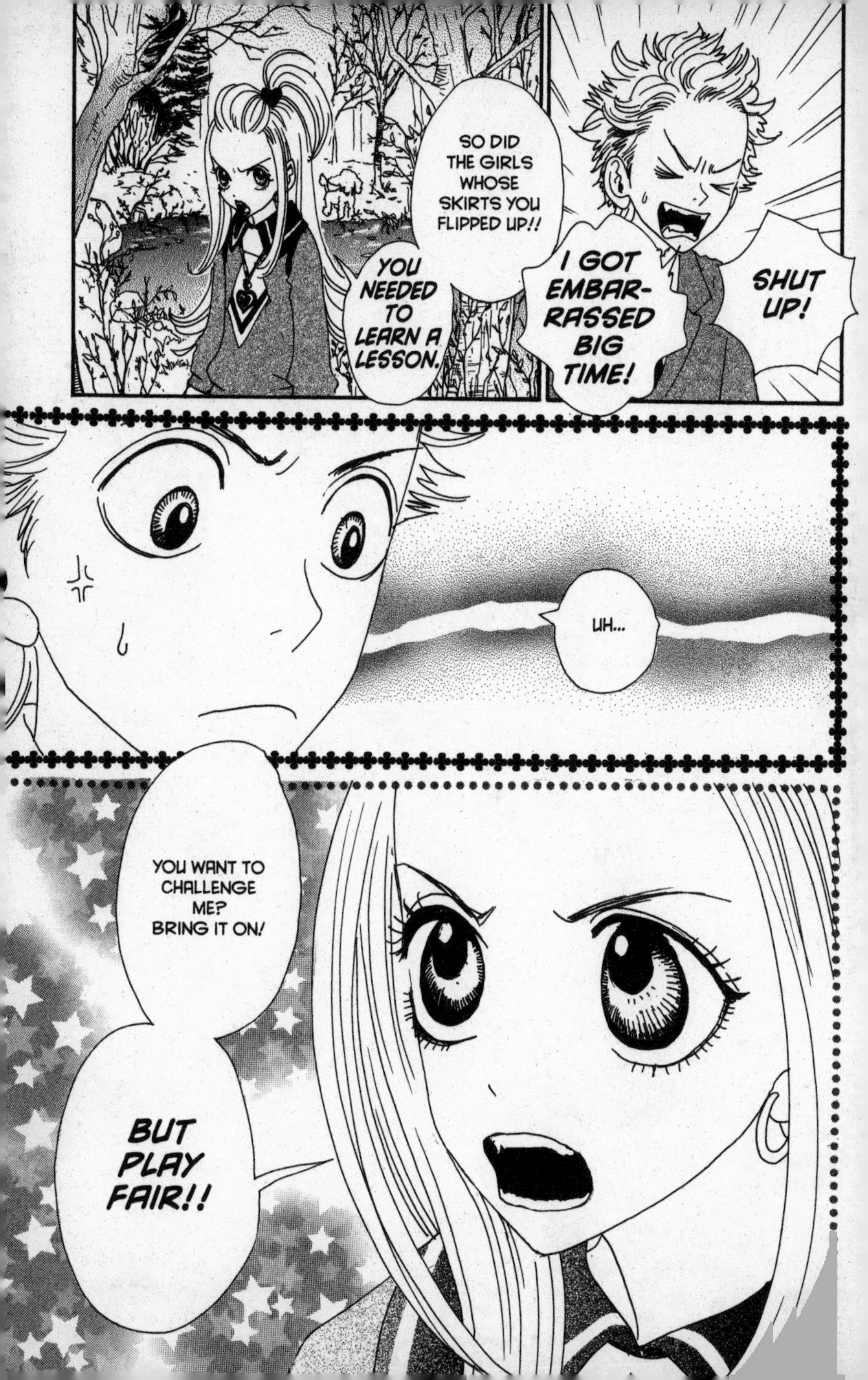
SHUT UP!
I GOT EMBAR-RASSED BIG TIME!
SO DID THE GIRLS WHOSE SKIRTS YOU FLIPPED UP!!
YOU NEEDED TO LEARN A LESSON.
UH...
YOU WANT TO CHALLENGE ME? BRING IT ON!
BUT PLAY FAIR!!

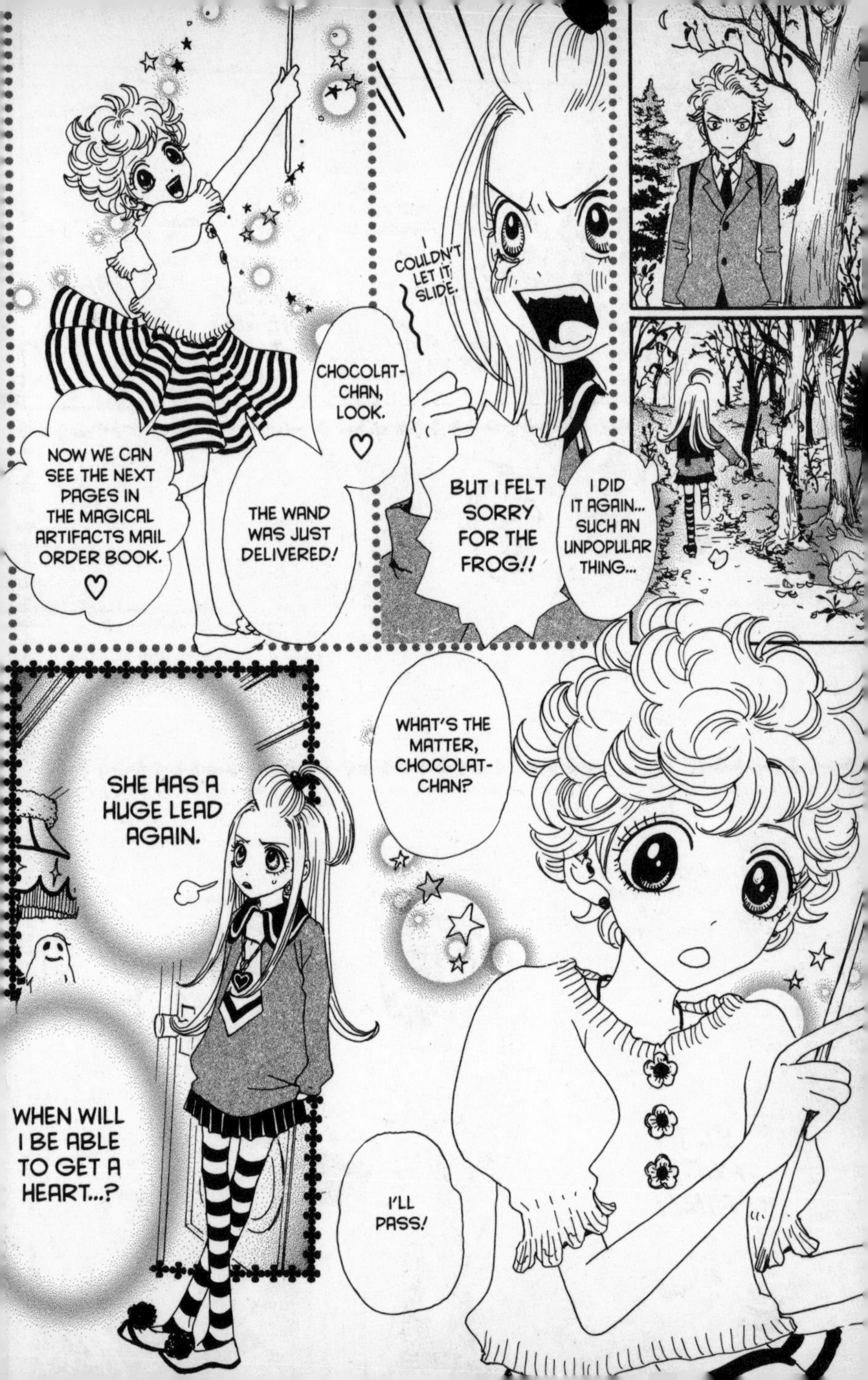
I DID IT AGAIN... SUCH AN UNPOPULAR THING...
I COULDN'T LET IT SLIDE.
BUT I FELT SORRY FOR THE FROG!!
CHOCOLAT-CHAN, LOOK. ♡
THE WAND WAS JUST DELIVERED!
NOW WE CAN SEE THE NEXT PAGES IN THE MAGICAL ARTIFACTS MAIL ORDER BOOK. ♡
WHAT'S THE MATTER, CHOCOLAT-CHAN?
I'LL PASS!
SHE HAS A HUGE LEAD AGAIN.
WHEN WILL I BE ABLE TO GET A HEART...?

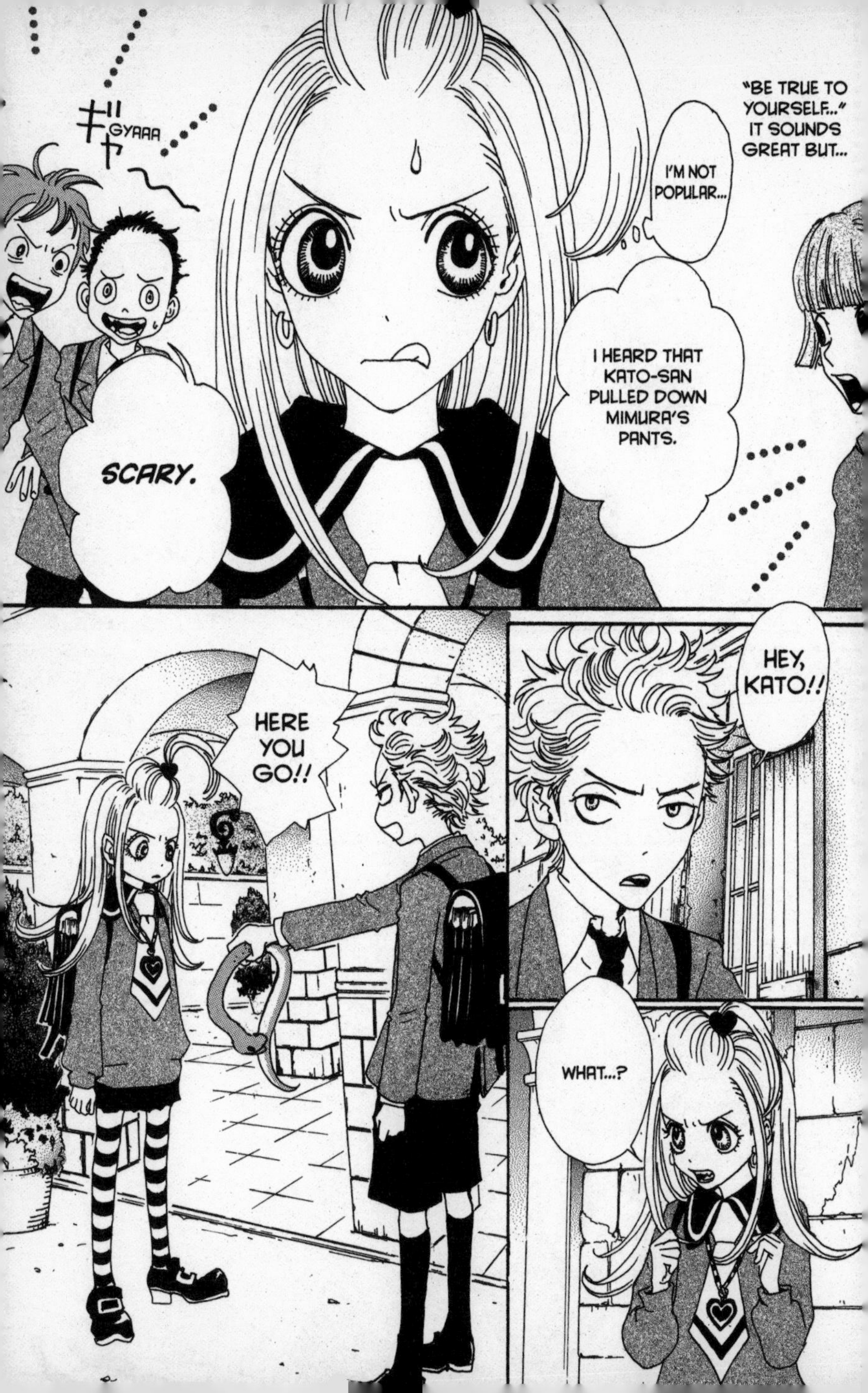
"BE TRUE TO YOURSELF..." IT SOUNDS GREAT BUT...
I'M NOT POPULAR...
I HEARD THAT KATO-SAN PULLED DOWN MIMURA'S PANTS.
SCARY.
GYAAA
HEY, KATO!!
WHAT...?
HERE YOU GO!!

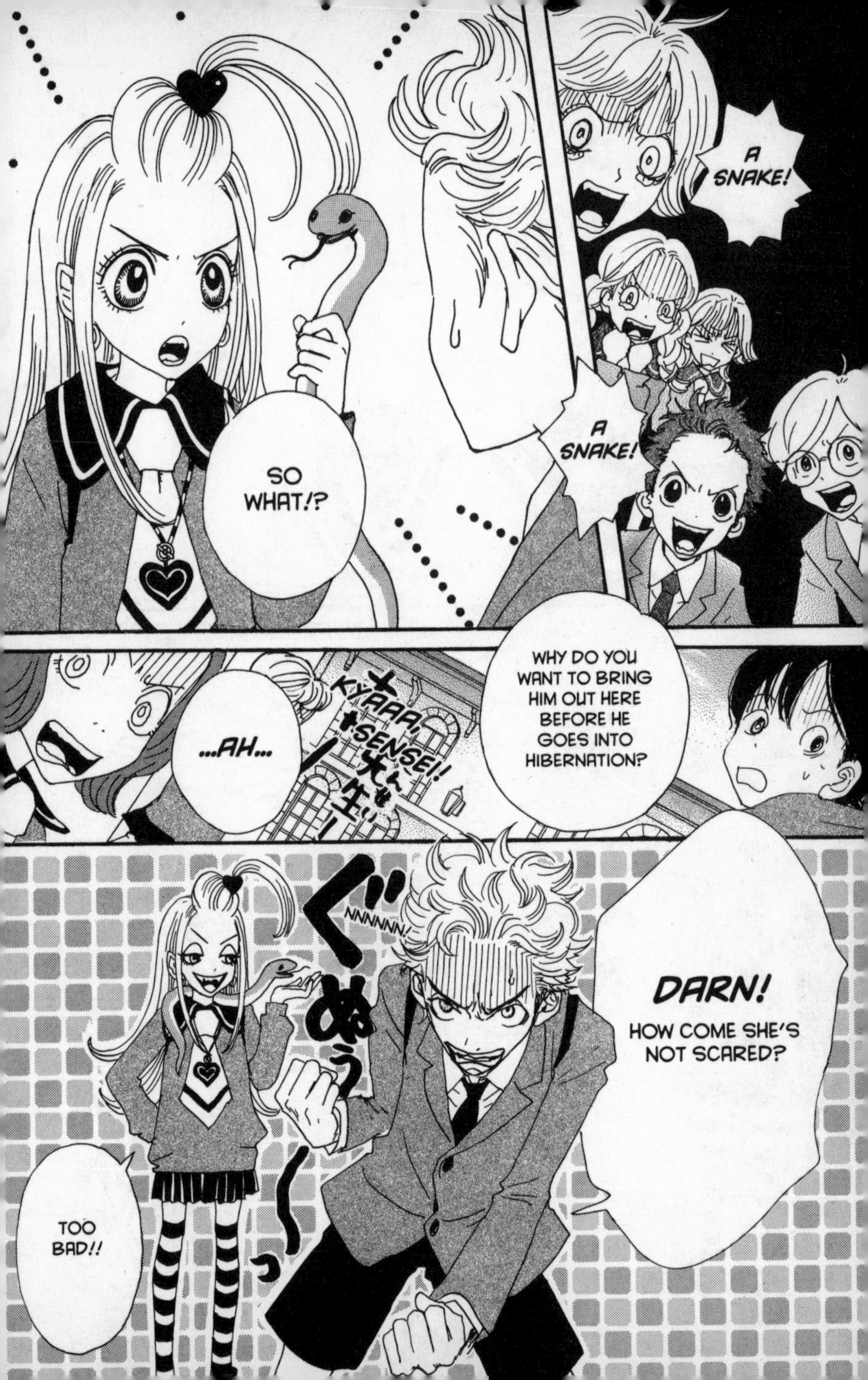
A SNAKE!
A SNAKE!
SO WHAT!?
WHY DO YOU WANT TO BRING HIM OUT HERE BEFORE HE GOES INTO HIBERNATION?
KYAAAA, SENSEI!
...AH...
DARN!
HOW COME SHE'S NOT SCARED?
GNNNNNN!
TOO BAD!!

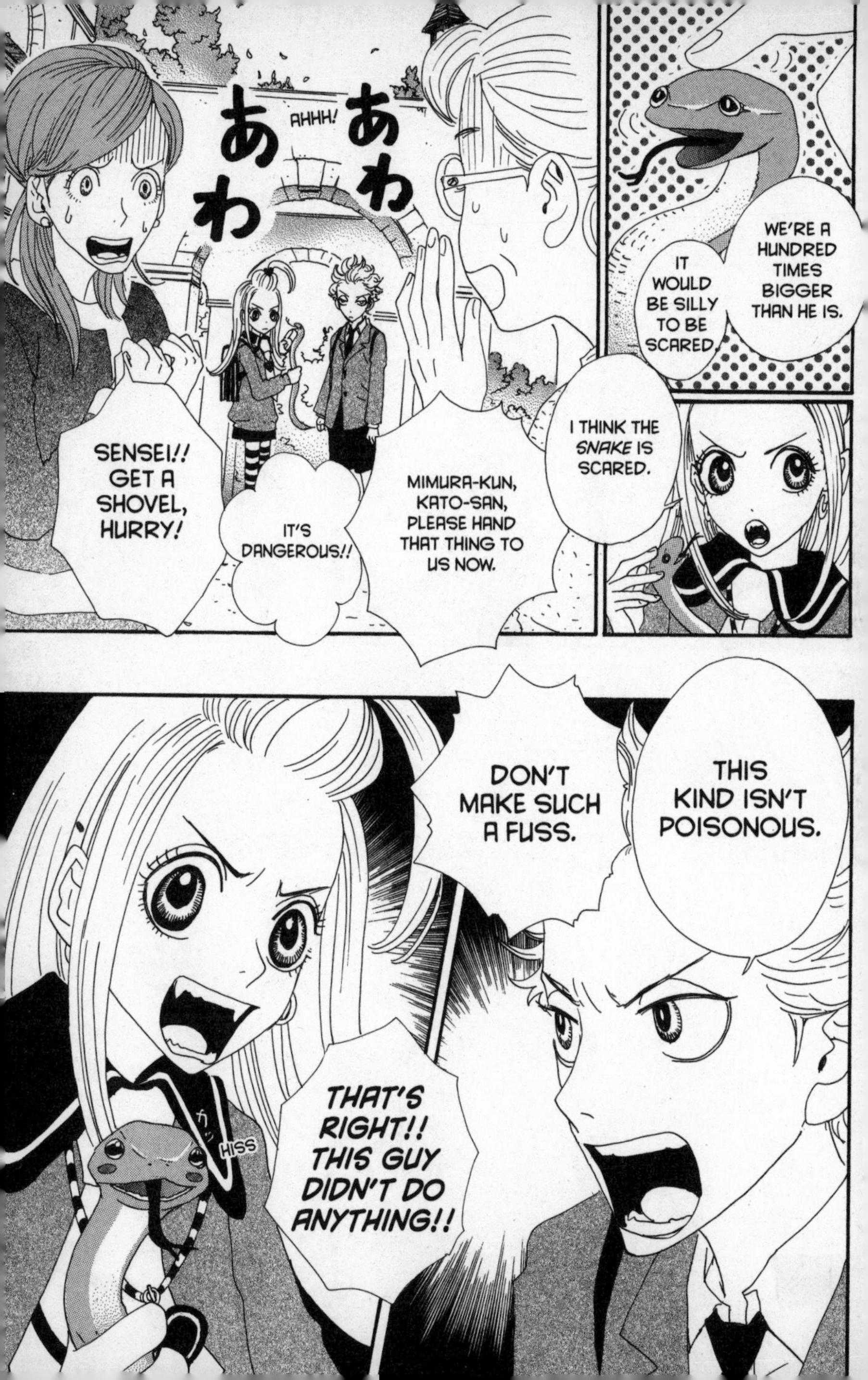
WE'RE A HUNDRED TIMES BIGGER THAN HE IS.
IT WOULD BE SILLY TO BE SCARED.
I THINK THE SNAKE IS SCARED.
MIMURA-KUN, KATO-SAN, PLEASE HAND THAT THING TO US NOW.
IT'S DANGEROUS!!
あわあわ
AHHH!
SENSEI!! GET A SHOVEL, HURRY!
THIS KIND ISN'T POISONOUS.
DON'T MAKE SUCH A FUSS.
THAT'S RIGHT!! THIS GUY DIDN'T DO ANYTHING!!
カッ
HISS

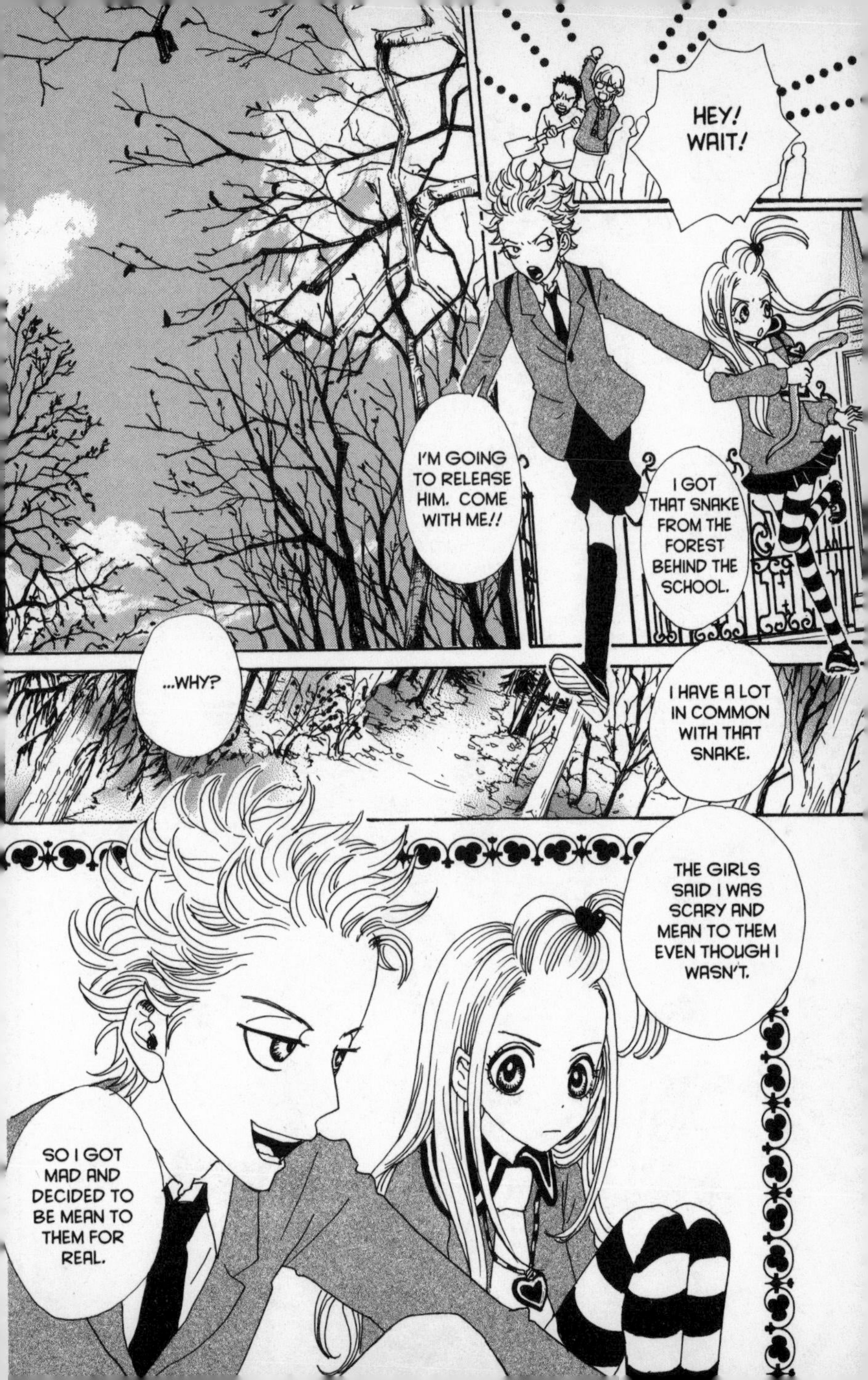
HEY! WAIT!
I'M GOING TO RELEASE HIM. COME WITH ME!!
I GOT THAT SNAKE FROM THE FOREST BEHIND THE SCHOOL.
...WHY?
I HAVE A LOT IN COMMON WITH THAT SNAKE.
THE GIRLS SAID I WAS SCARY AND MEAN TO THEM EVEN THOUGH I WASN'T.
SO I GOT MAD AND DECIDED TO BE MEAN TO THEM FOR REAL.

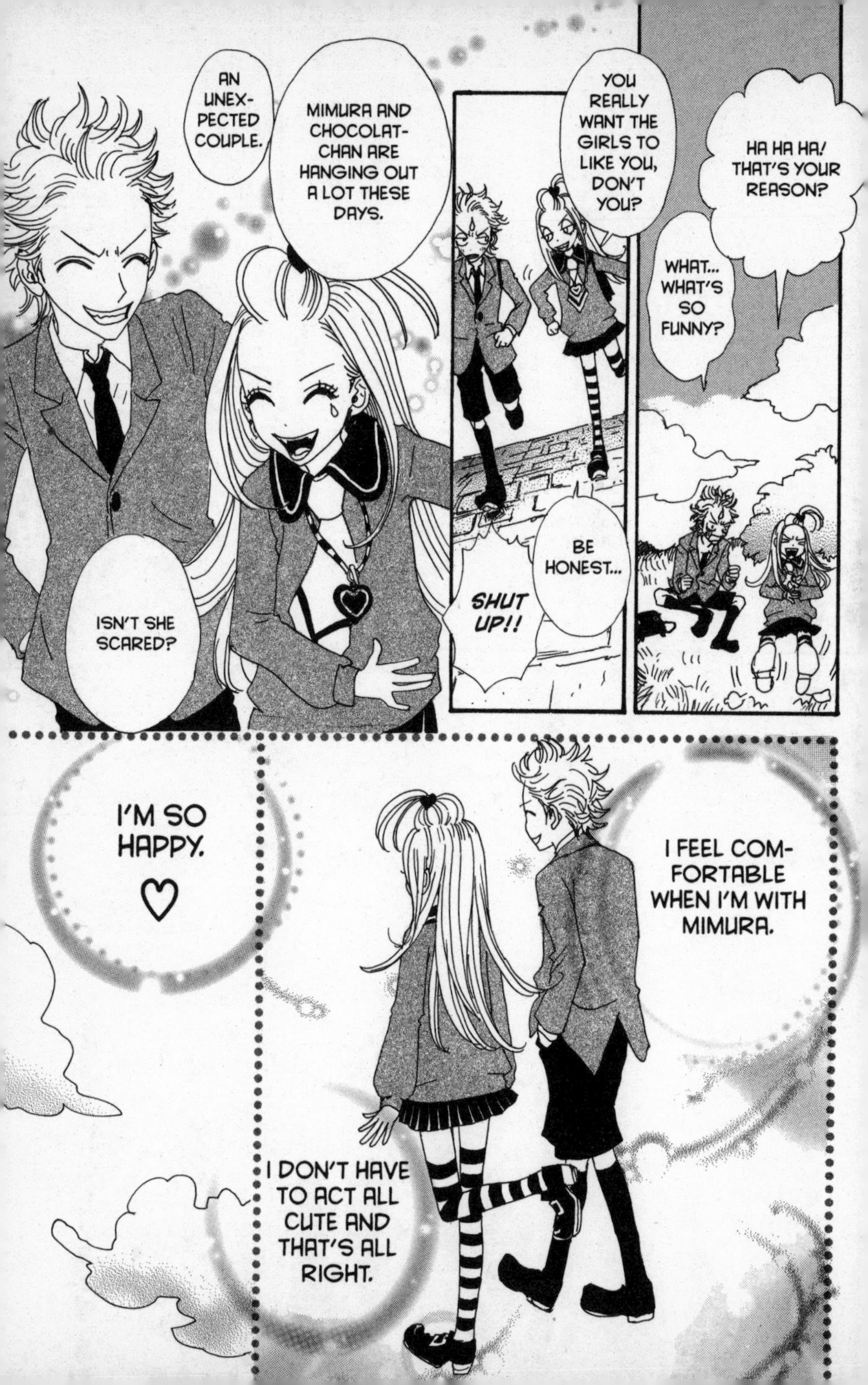
HA HA HA! THAT'S YOUR REASON?
WHAT... WHAT'S SO FUNNY?
YOU REALLY WANT THE GIRLS TO LIKE YOU, DON'T YOU?
BE HONEST...
SHUT UP!!
MIMURA AND CHOCOLAT-CHAN ARE HANGING OUT A LOT THESE DAYS.
AN UNEXPECTED COUPLE.
ISN'T SHE SCARED?
I FEEL COMFORTABLE WHEN I'M WITH MIMURA.
I DON'T HAVE TO ACT ALL CUTE AND THAT'S ALL RIGHT.
I'M SO HAPPY. ♡

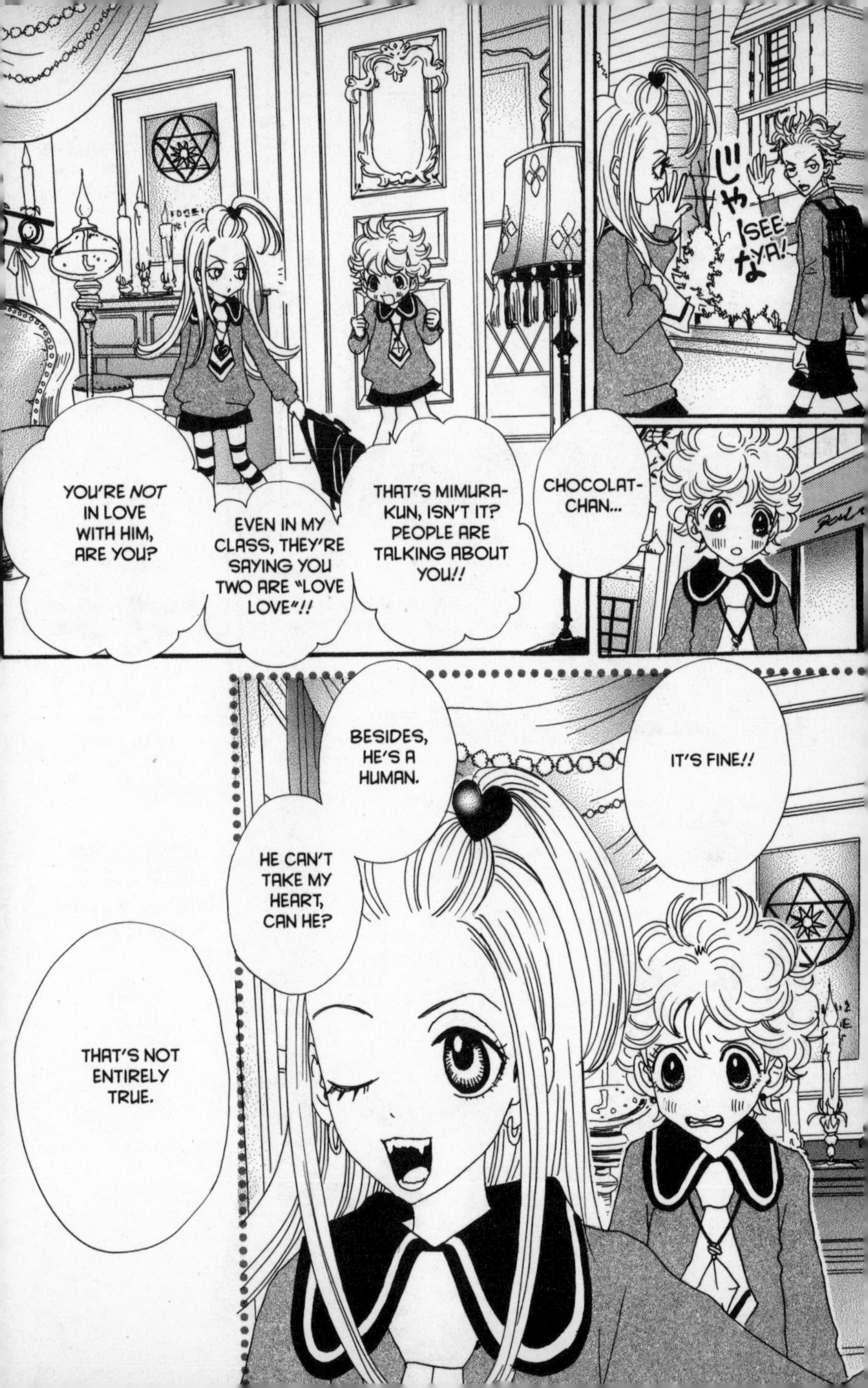
じゃな
SEE YA!
CHOCOLAT-CHAN...
THAT'S MIMURA-KUN, ISN'T IT? PEOPLE ARE TALKING ABOUT YOU!!
EVEN IN MY CLASS, THEY'RE SAYING YOU TWO ARE "LOVE LOVE"!!
YOU'RE *NOT* IN LOVE WITH HIM, ARE YOU?
IT'S FINE!!
BESIDES, HE'S A HUMAN.
HE CAN'T TAKE MY HEART, CAN HE?
THAT'S NOT ENTIRELY TRUE.

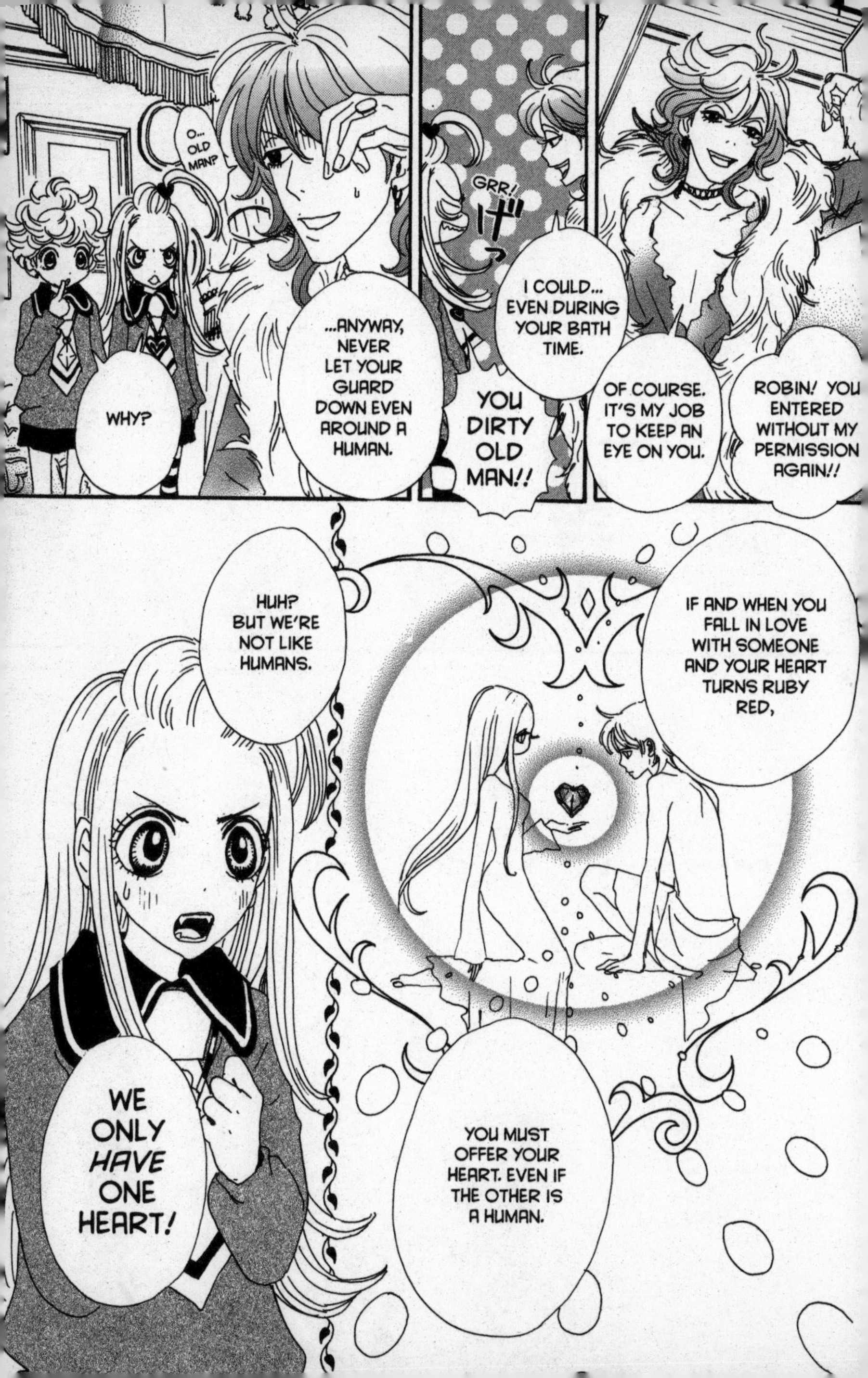
ROBIN! YOU ENTERED WITHOUT MY PERMISSION AGAIN!!
OF COURSE. IT'S MY JOB TO KEEP AN EYE ON YOU.
I COULD... EVEN DURING YOUR BATH TIME.
GRR! げ
YOU DIRTY OLD MAN!!
O... OLD MAN?
...ANYWAY, NEVER LET YOUR GUARD DOWN EVEN AROUND A HUMAN.
WHY?
HUH? BUT WE'RE NOT LIKE HUMANS.
IF AND WHEN YOU FALL IN LOVE WITH SOMEONE AND YOUR HEART TURNS RUBY RED,
YOU MUST OFFER YOUR HEART. EVEN IF THE OTHER IS A HUMAN.
WE ONLY *HAVE* ONE HEART!

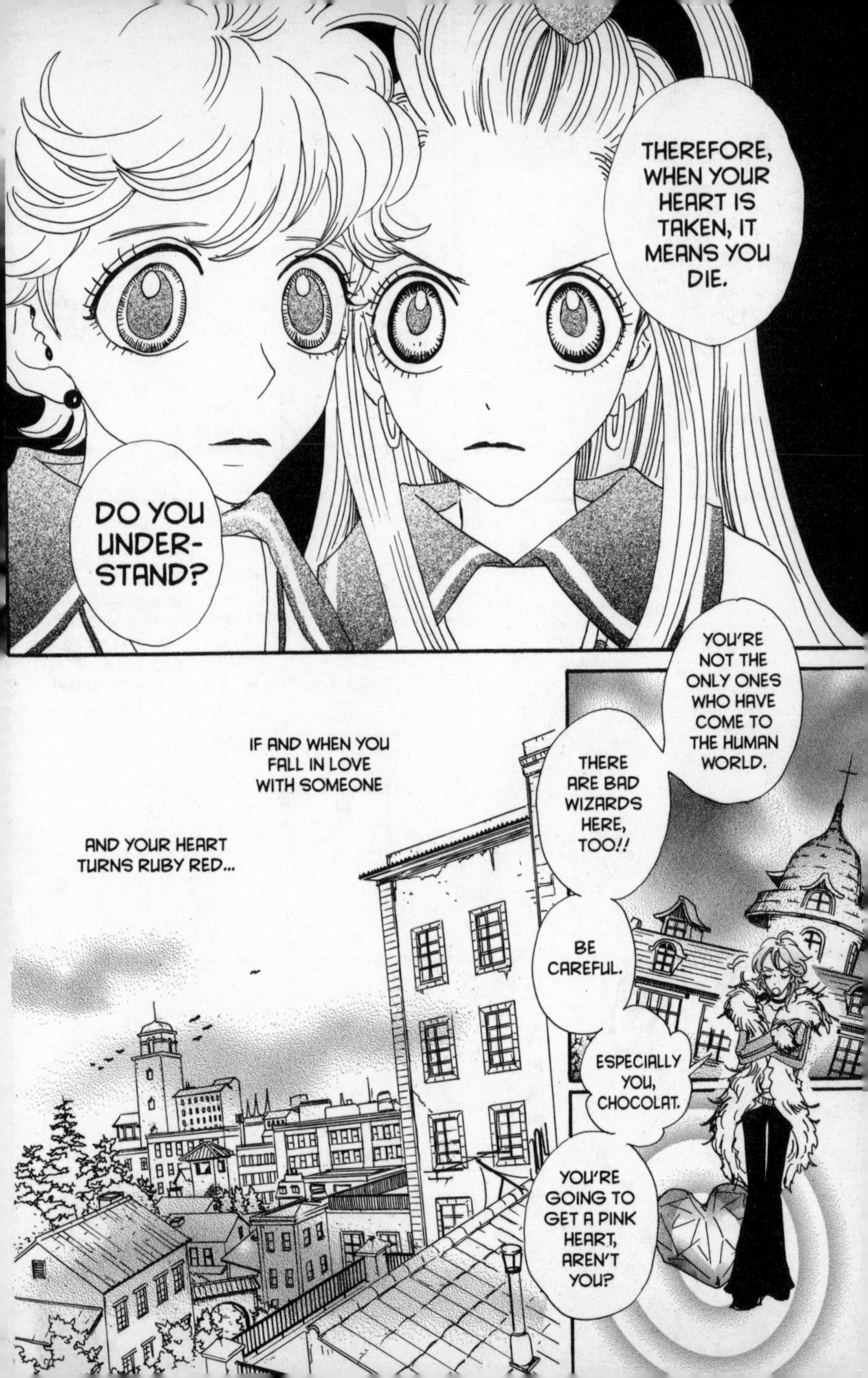
THEREFORE, WHEN YOUR HEART IS TAKEN, IT MEANS YOU DIE.
DO YOU UNDER-STAND?
YOU'RE NOT THE ONLY ONES WHO HAVE COME TO THE HUMAN WORLD.
THERE ARE BAD WIZARDS HERE, TOO!!
IF AND WHEN YOU FALL IN LOVE WITH SOMEONE
AND YOUR HEART TURNS RUBY RED...
BE CAREFUL.
ESPECIALLY YOU, CHOCOLAT.
YOU'RE GOING TO GET A PINK HEART, AREN'T YOU?

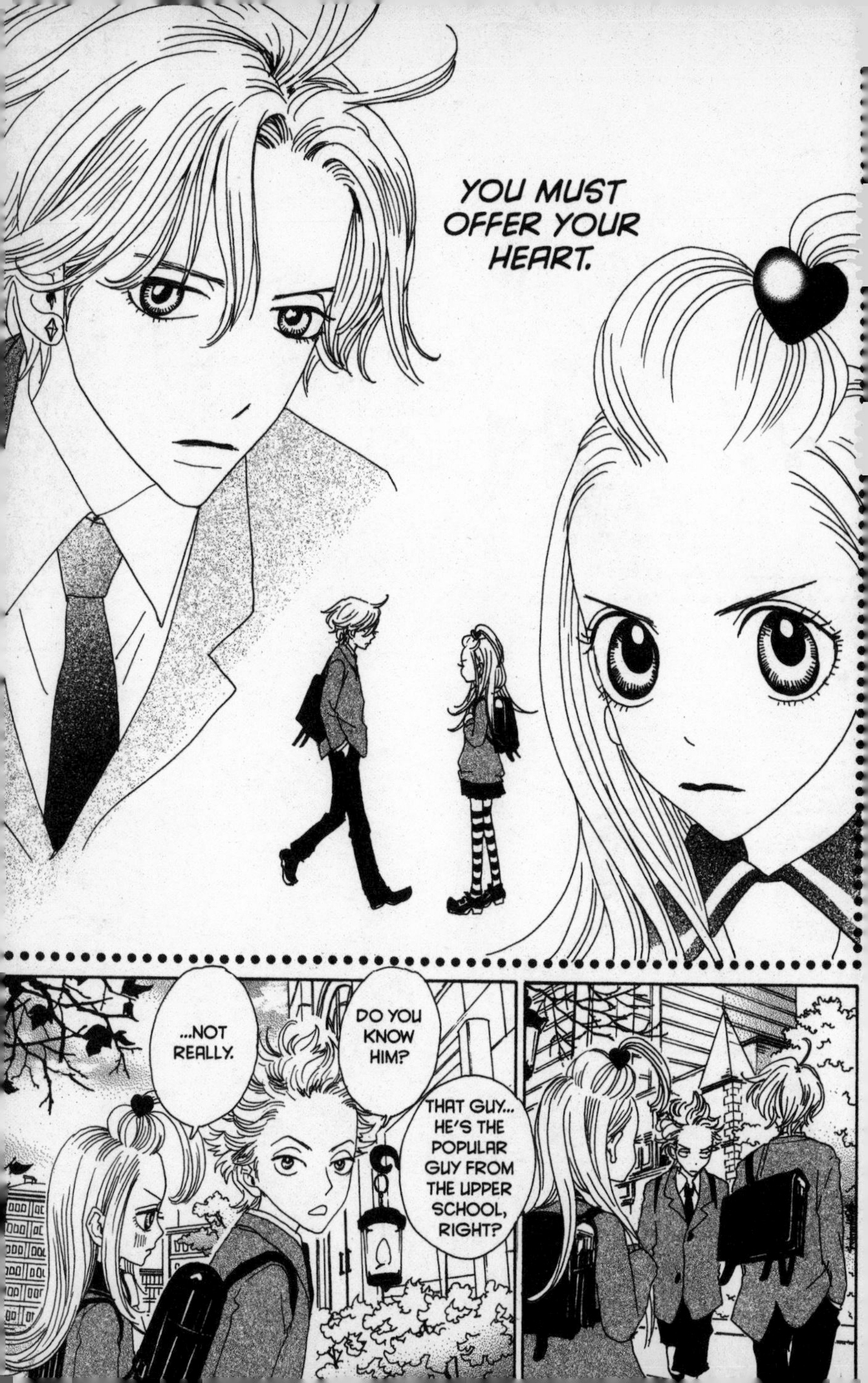
YOU MUST OFFER YOUR HEART.
THAT GUY... HE'S THE POPULAR GUY FROM THE UPPER SCHOOL, RIGHT?
DO YOU KNOW HIM?
...NOT REALLY.

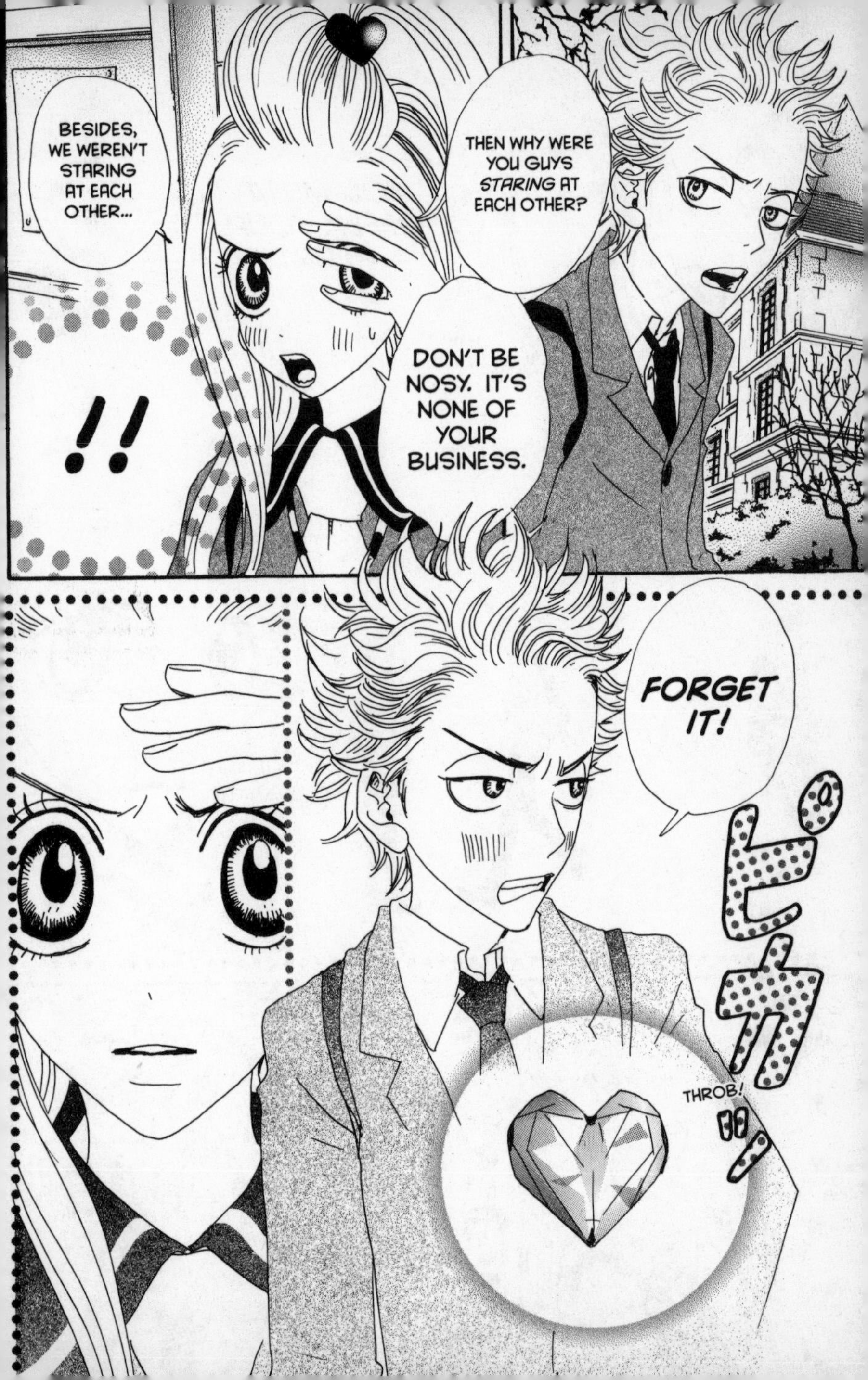
THEN WHY WERE YOU GUYS STARING AT EACH OTHER?
DON'T BE NOSY. IT'S NONE OF YOUR BUSINESS.
BESIDES, WE WEREN'T STARING AT EACH OTHER...
!!
FORGET IT!
ピカ
THROB!

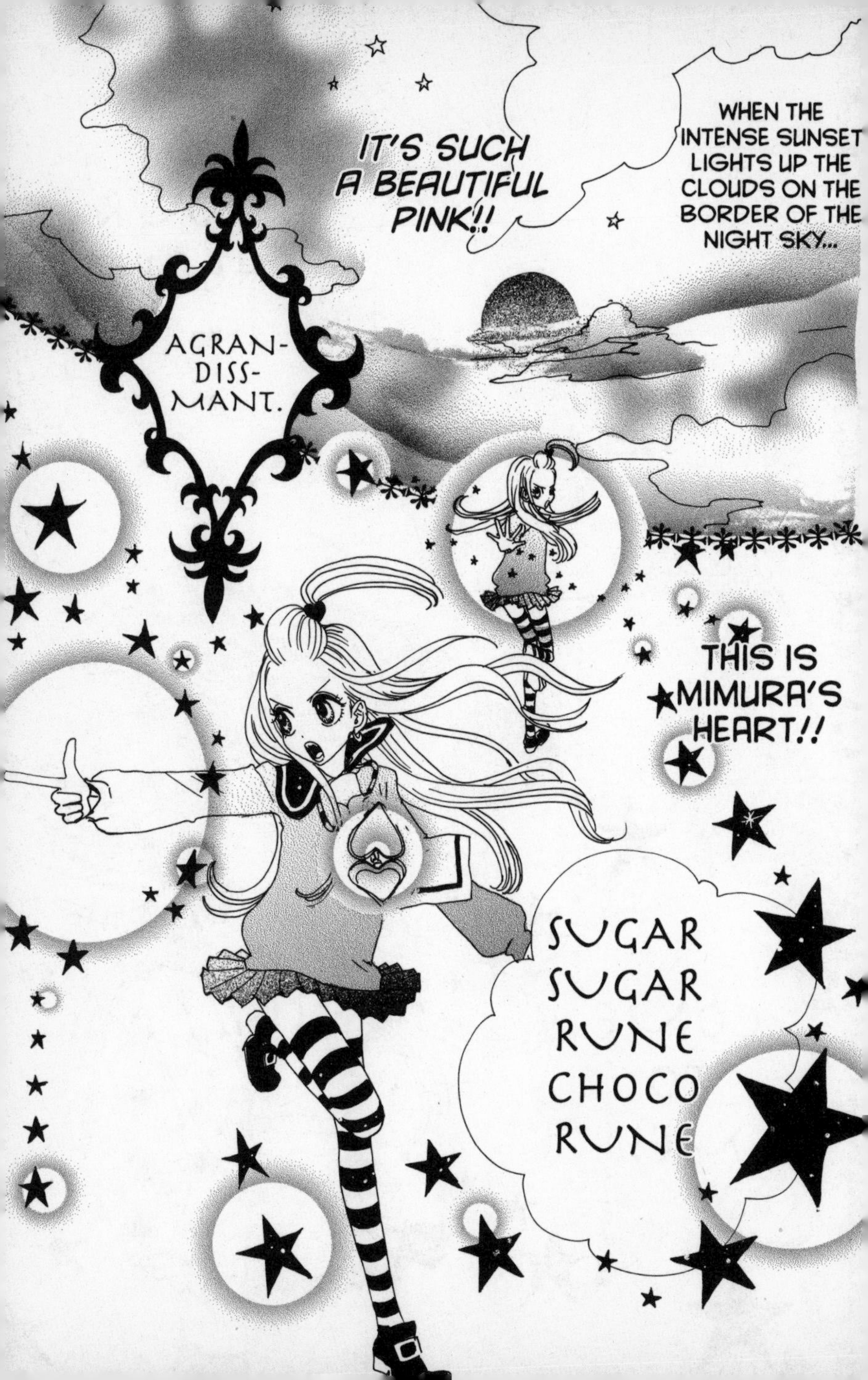
WHEN THE INTENSE SUNSET LIGHTS UP THE CLOUDS ON THE BORDER OF THE NIGHT SKY...
IT'S SUCH A BEAUTIFUL PINK!!
AGRAN-DISS-MANT.
THIS IS MIMURA'S HEART!!
SUGAR SUGAR RUNE CHOCO RUNE

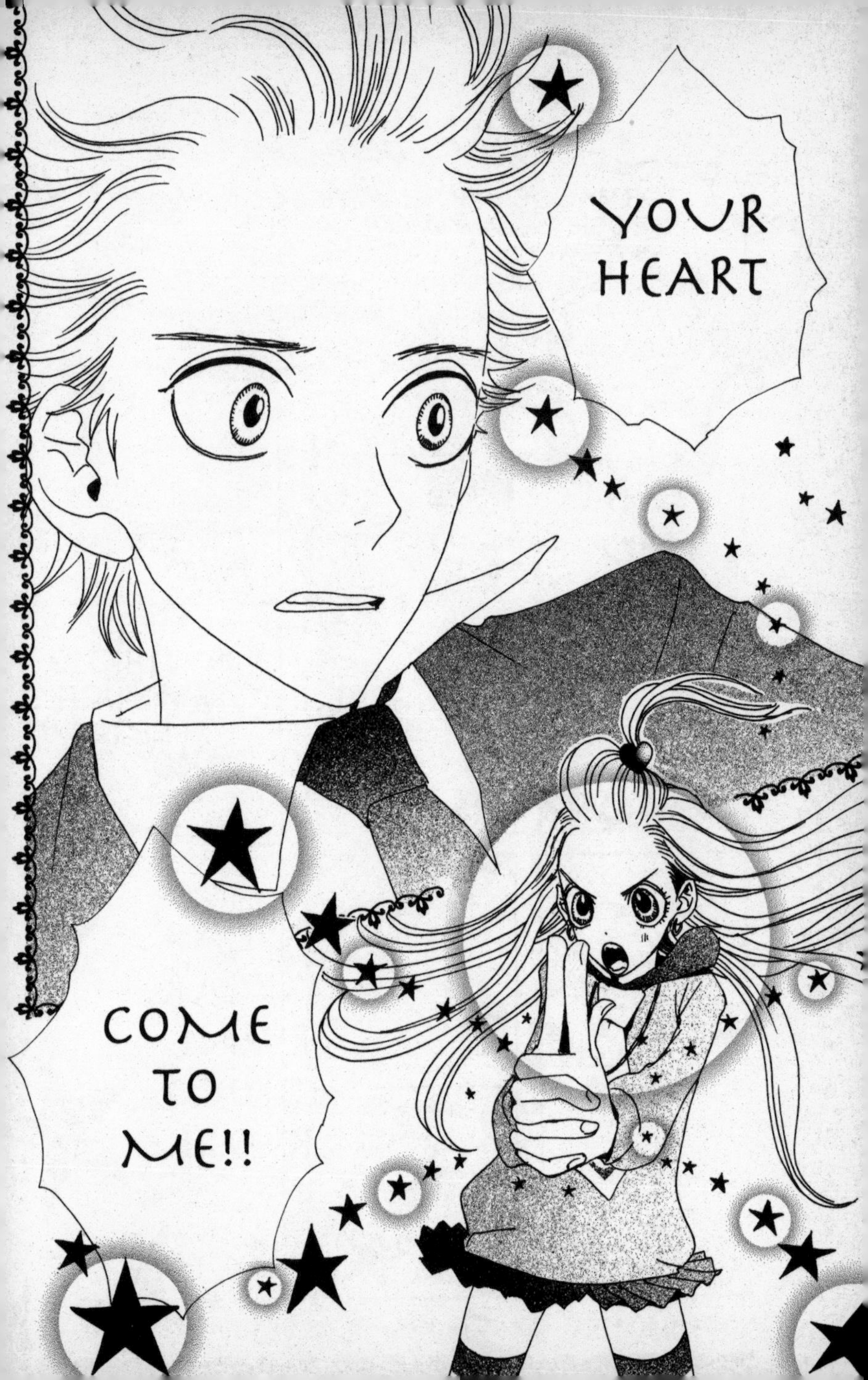
YOUR HEART
COME TO ME!!

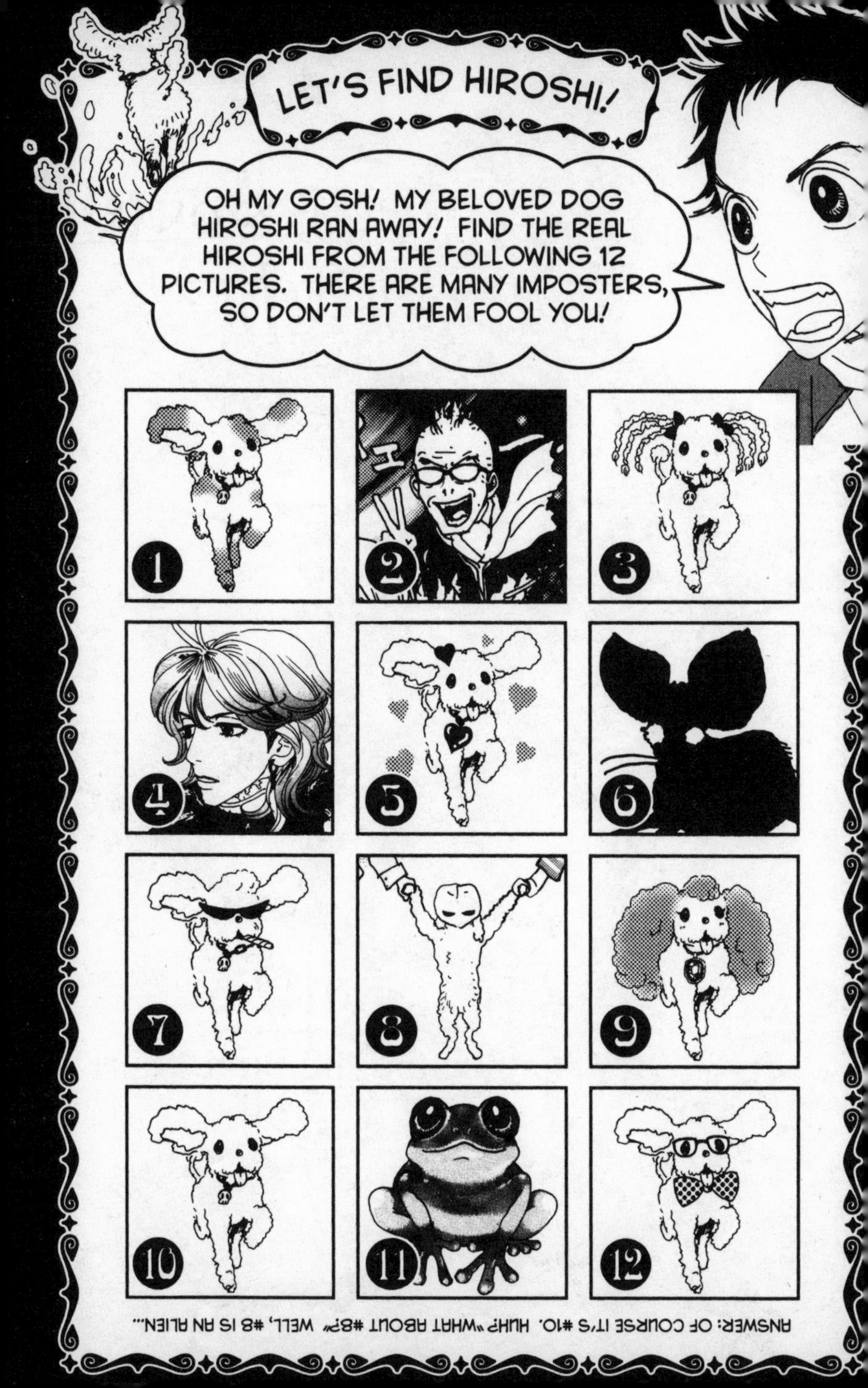
LET'S FIND HIROSHI!
OH MY GOSH! MY BELOVED DOG HIROSHI RAN AWAY! FIND THE REAL HIROSHI FROM THE FOLLOWING 12 PICTURES. THERE ARE MANY IMPOSTERS, SO DON'T LET THEM FOOL YOU!
1
2
3
4
5
6
7
8
9
10
11
12
ANSWER: OF COURSE IT'S #10. HUH? "WHAT ABOUT #8?" WELL, #8 IS AN ALIEN...

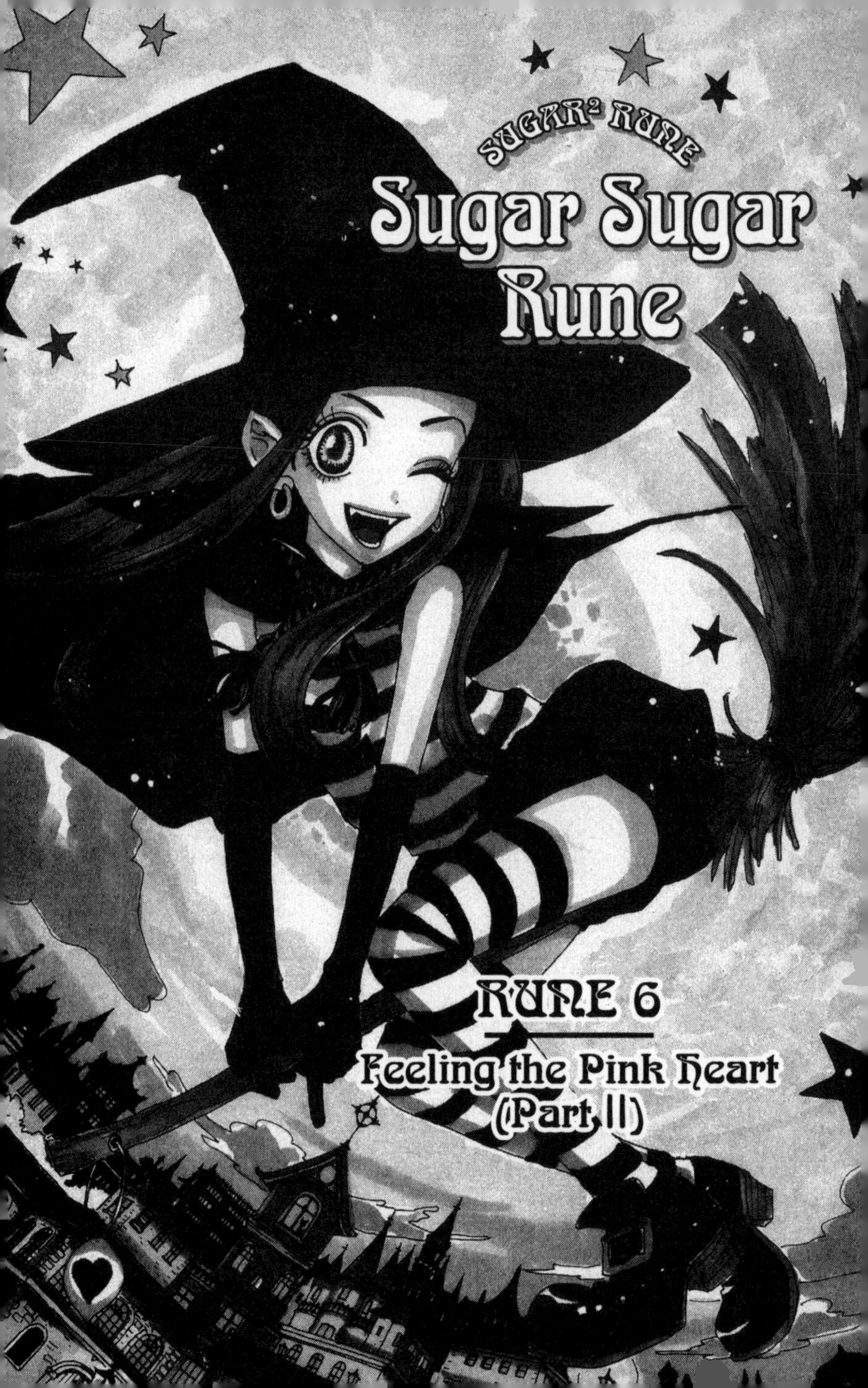
SUGAR² RUNE
Sugar Sugar Rune
RUNE 6
Feeling the Pink Heart
(Part II)

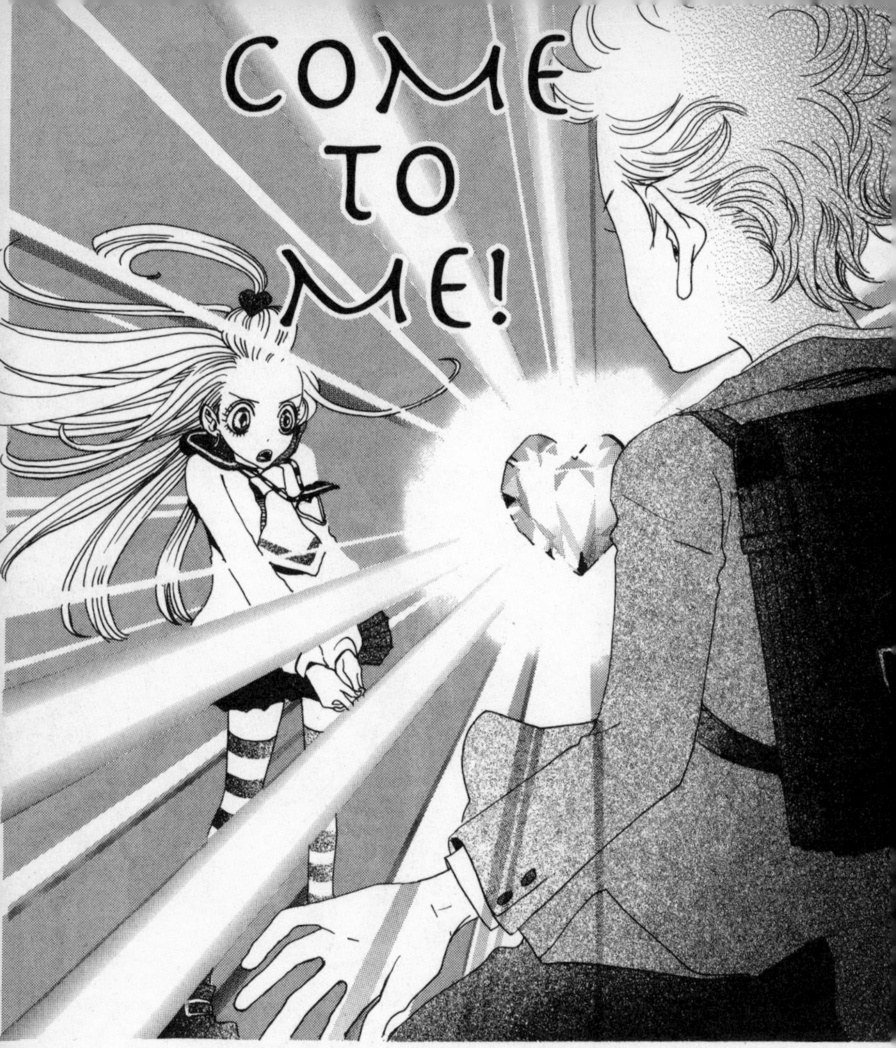
COME TO ME!
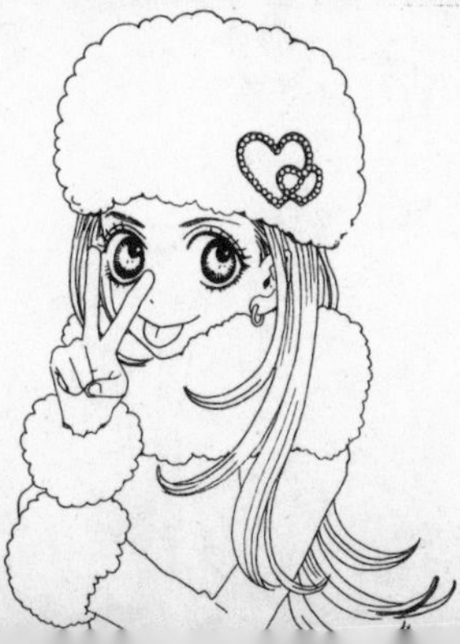

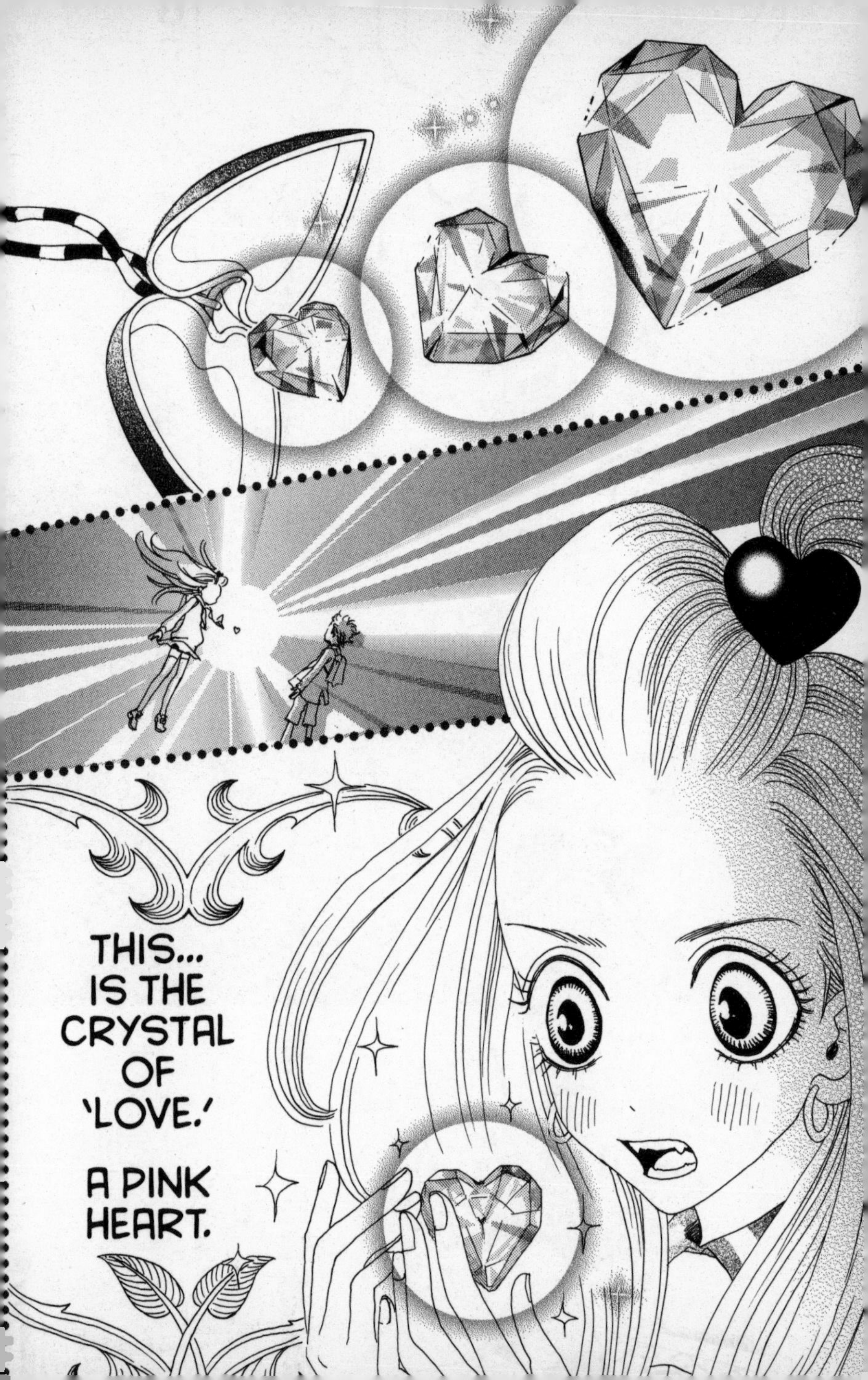
THIS... IS THE CRYSTAL OF 'LOVE.'
A PINK HEART.

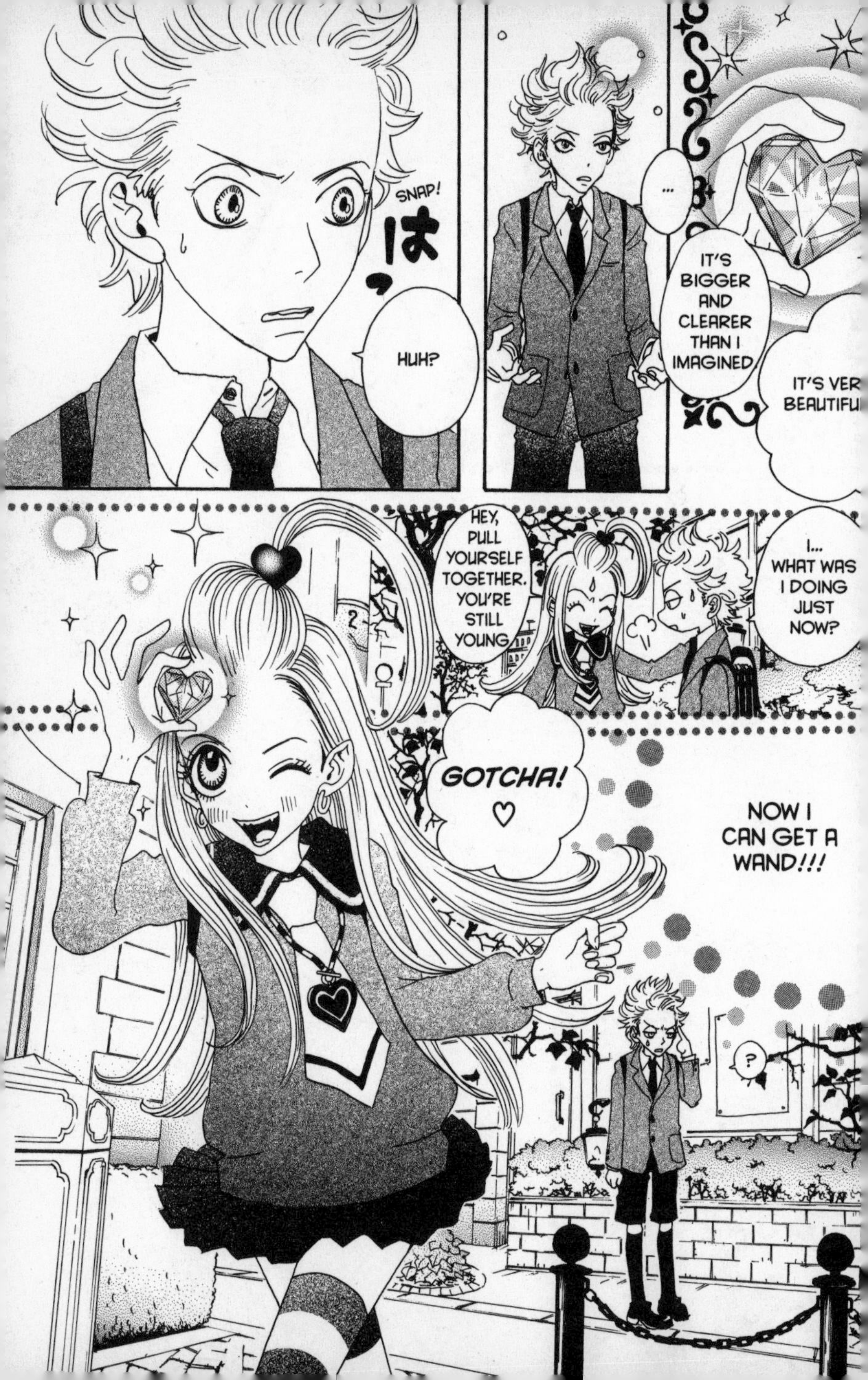
IT'S VER BEAUTIFU
...
IT'S BIGGER AND CLEARER THAN I IMAGINED
SNAP!
は
HUH?
I... WHAT WAS I DOING JUST NOW?
HEY, PULL YOURSELF TOGETHER. YOU'RE STILL YOUNG
GOTCHA! ♡
NOW I CAN GET A WAND!!!
?

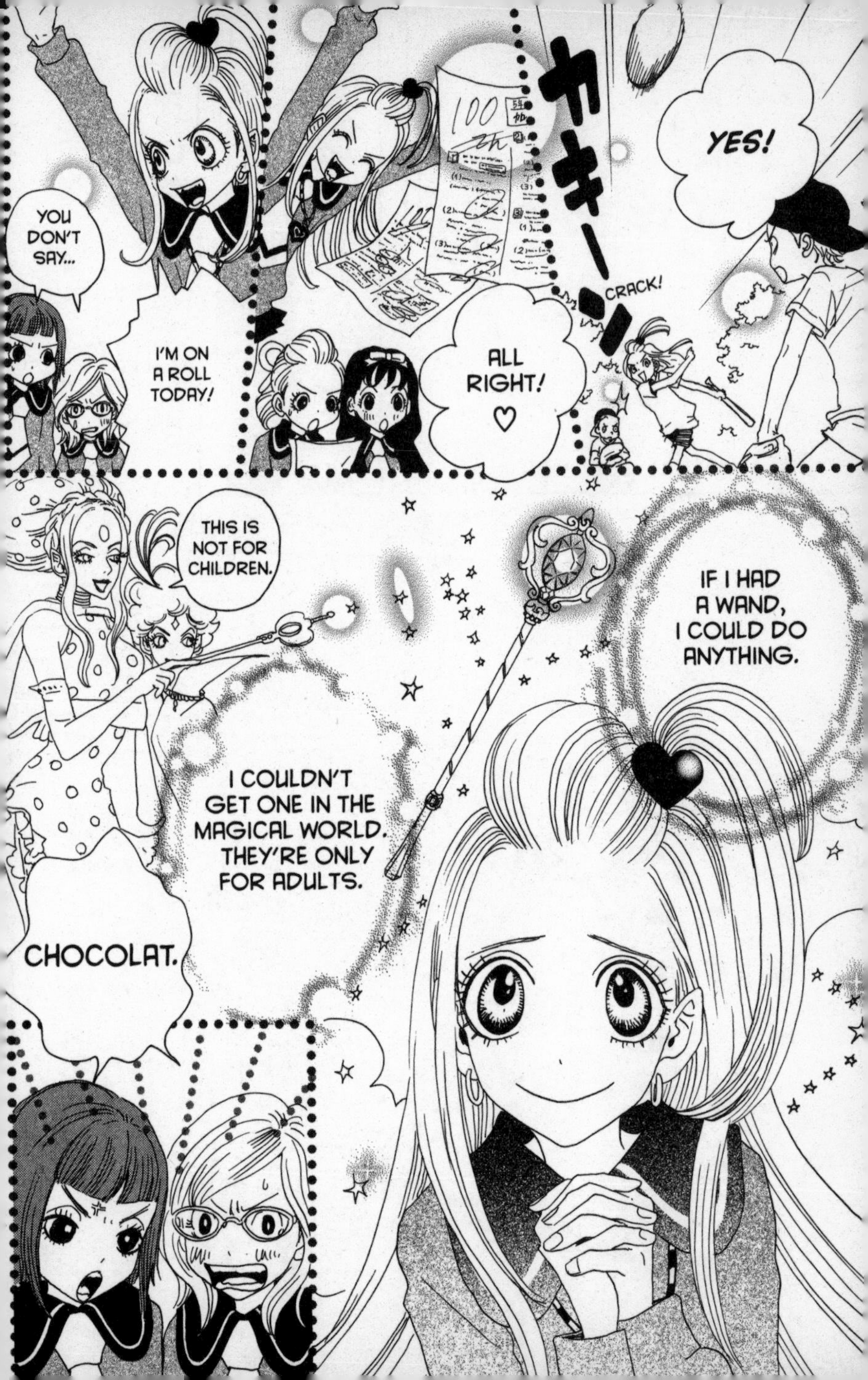
YES!
カキーン
CRACK!
ALL RIGHT! ♡
I'M ON A ROLL TODAY!
YOU DON'T SAY...
IF I HAD A WAND, I COULD DO ANYTHING.
THIS IS NOT FOR CHILDREN.
I COULDN'T GET ONE IN THE MAGICAL WORLD. THEY'RE ONLY FOR ADULTS.
CHOCOLAT.

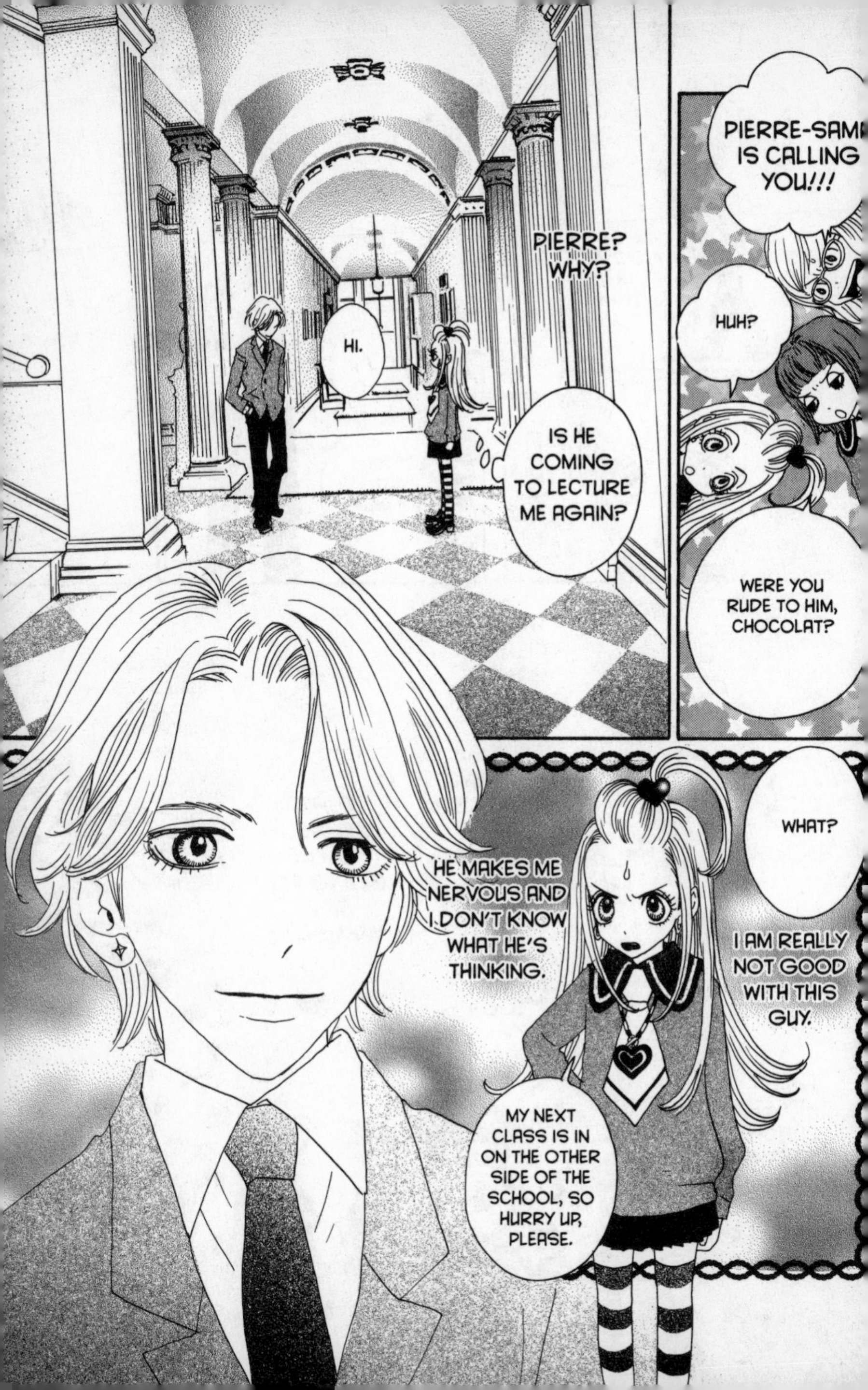
PIERRE-SAMA IS CALLING YOU!!!
HUH?
WERE YOU RUDE TO HIM, CHOCOLAT?
PIERRE? WHY?
HI.
IS HE COMING TO LECTURE ME AGAIN?
WHAT?
I AM REALLY NOT GOOD WITH THIS GUY.
HE MAKES ME NERVOUS AND I DON'T KNOW WHAT HE'S THINKING.
MY NEXT CLASS IS IN ON THE OTHER SIDE OF THE SCHOOL, SO HURRY UP, PLEASE.

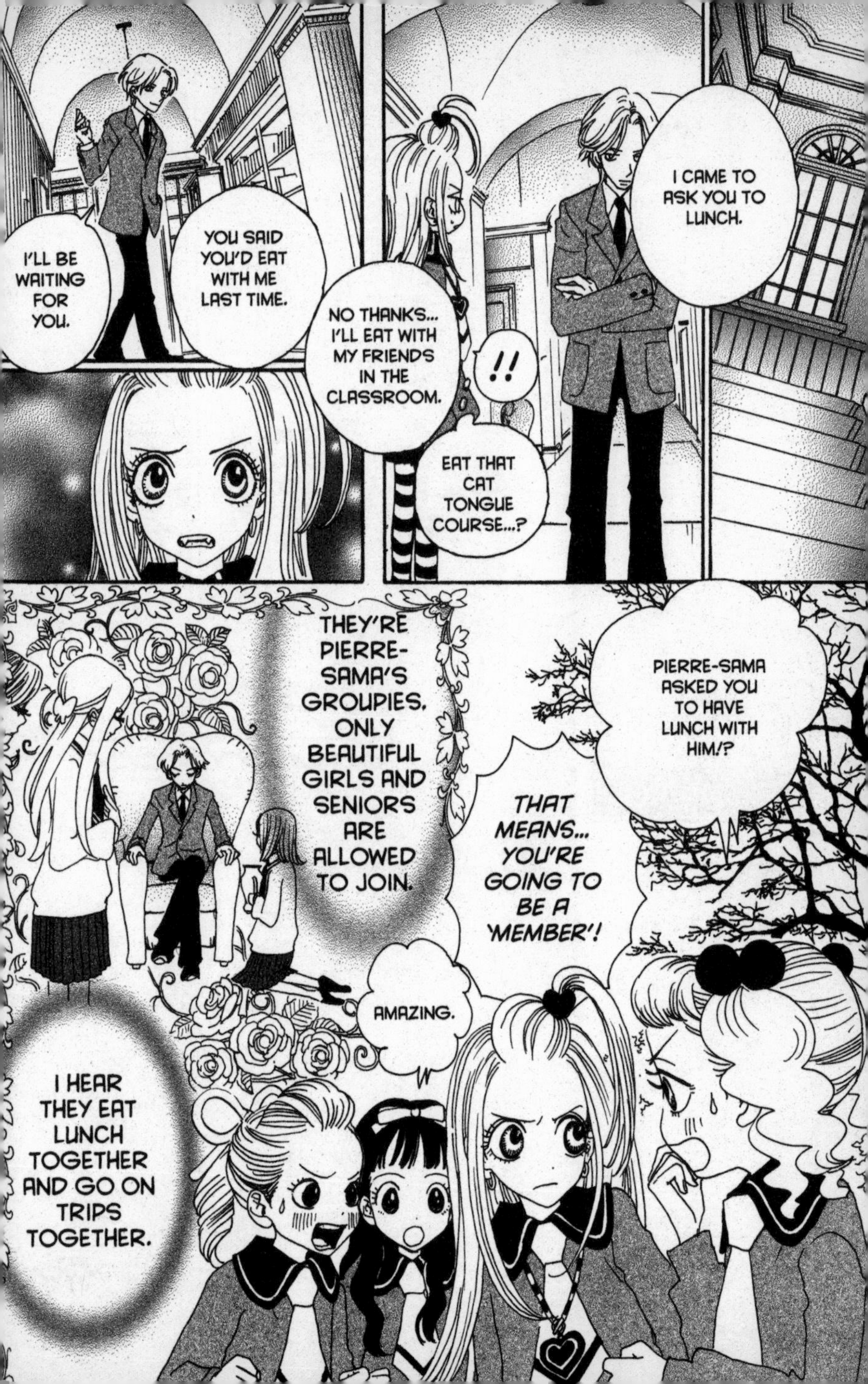
I CAME TO ASK YOU TO LUNCH.
NO THANKS... I'LL EAT WITH MY FRIENDS IN THE CLASSROOM.
!!
EAT THAT CAT TONGUE COURSE...?
YOU SAID YOU'D EAT WITH ME LAST TIME.
I'LL BE WAITING FOR YOU.
PIERRE-SAMA ASKED YOU TO HAVE LUNCH WITH HIM!?
THAT MEANS... YOU'RE GOING TO BE A 'MEMBER'!
THEY'RE PIERRE-SAMA'S GROUPIES. ONLY BEAUTIFUL GIRLS AND SENIORS ARE ALLOWED TO JOIN.
AMAZING.
I HEAR THEY EAT LUNCH TOGETHER AND GO ON TRIPS TOGETHER.

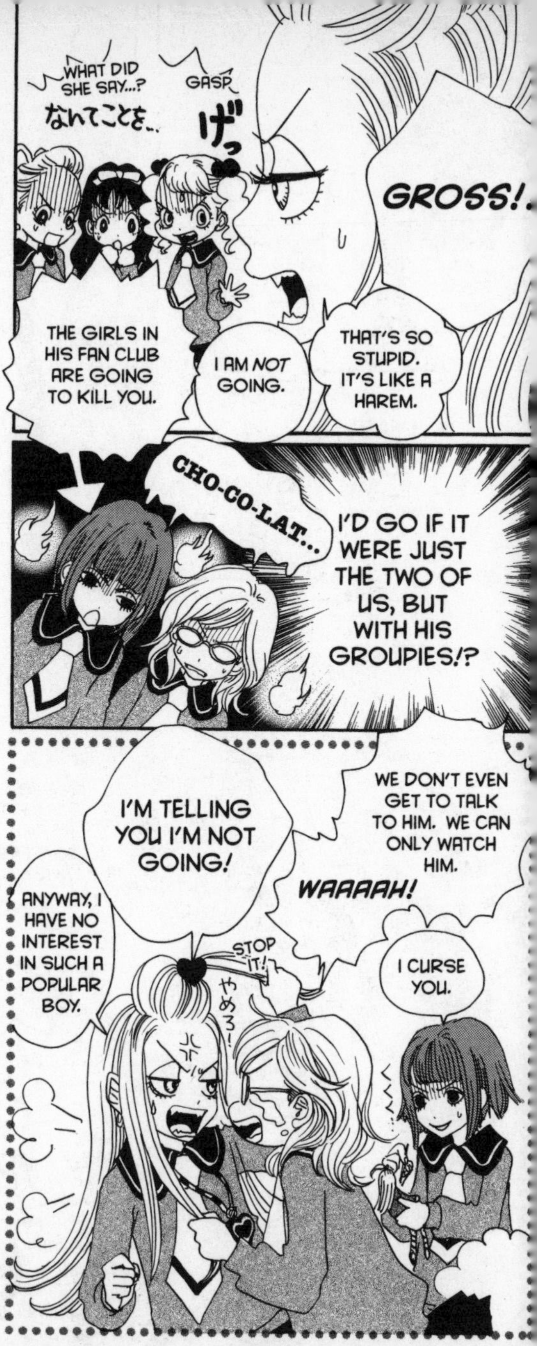
GROSS!..
GASP
げっ
WHAT DID SHE SAY...?
なんてことを..
THAT'S SO STUPID. IT'S LIKE A HAREM.
I AM *NOT* GOING.
THE GIRLS IN HIS FAN CLUB ARE GOING TO KILL YOU.
I'D GO IF IT WERE JUST THE TWO OF US, BUT WITH HIS GROUPIES!?
CHO-CO-LAT...
WE DON'T EVEN GET TO TALK TO HIM. WE CAN ONLY WATCH HIM.
WAAAAH!
I'M TELLING YOU I'M NOT GOING!
I CURSE YOU.
STOP IT!
やめろ!
ANYWAY, I HAVE NO INTEREST IN SUCH A POPULAR BOY.

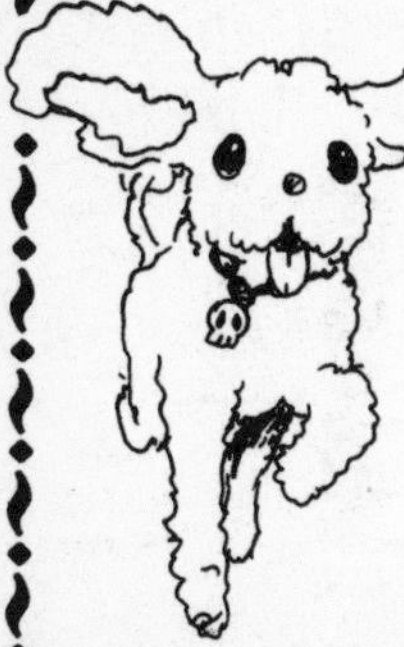

HIROSHI

HEIGHT: 80 CM

AGE: 36 IN HUMAN YEARS(!).

HOBBY: WANDERING ABOUT.

SPECIALTY: WIGGLING OUT OF HIS LEASH.

FAVORITE FOOD: FISH SAUSAGE.

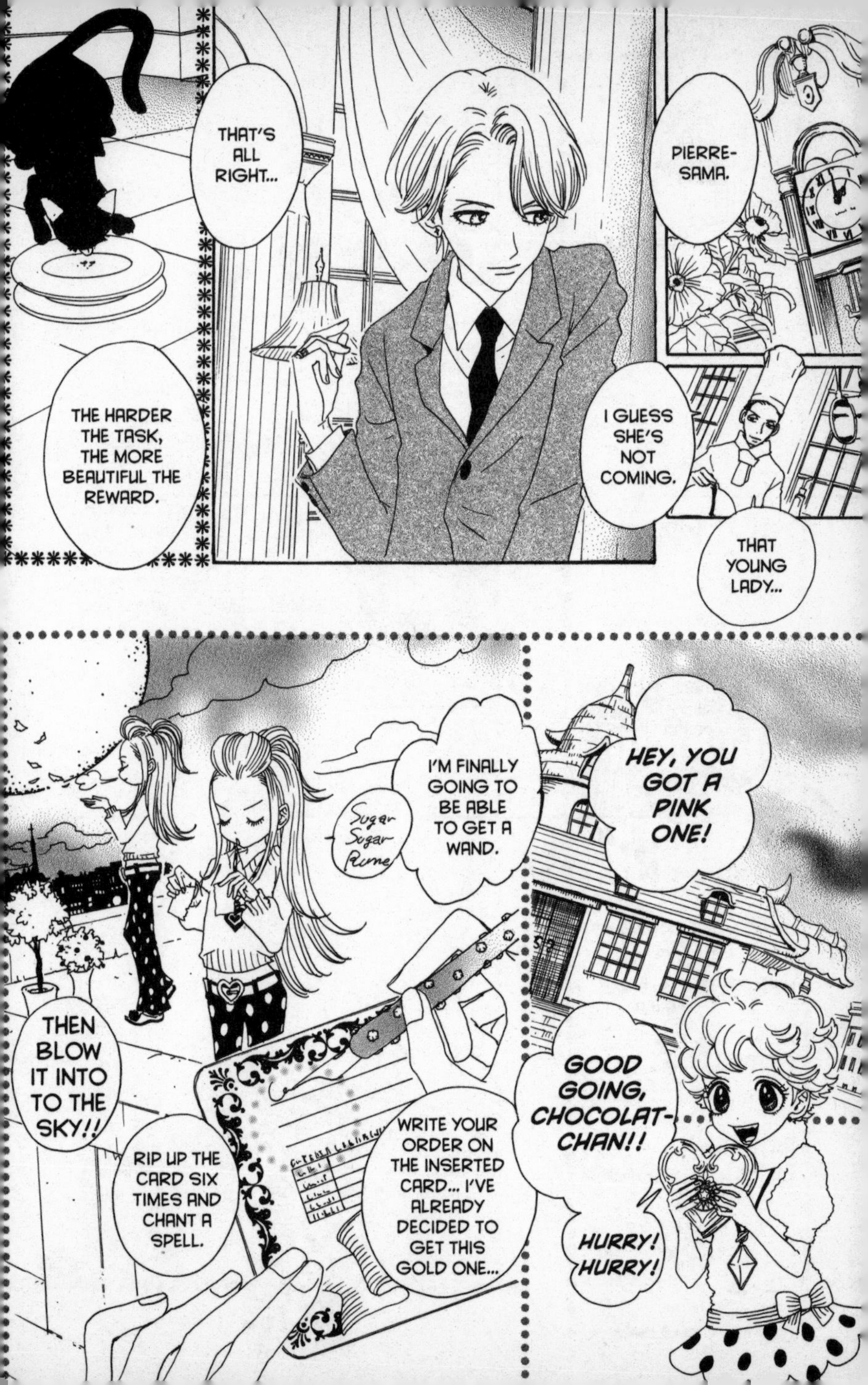
PIERRE-SAMA.
I GUESS SHE'S NOT COMING.
THAT YOUNG LADY...
THAT'S ALL RIGHT...
THE HARDER THE TASK, THE MORE BEAUTIFUL THE REWARD.
HEY, YOU GOT A PINK ONE!
GOOD GOING, CHOCOLAT-CHAN!!
HURRY! HURRY!
I'M FINALLY GOING TO BE ABLE TO GET A WAND.
Sugar Sugar Rune
WRITE YOUR ORDER ON THE INSERTED CARD... I'VE ALREADY DECIDED TO GET THIS GOLD ONE...
RIP UP THE CARD SIX TIMES AND CHANT A SPELL.
THEN BLOW IT INTO TO THE SKY!!

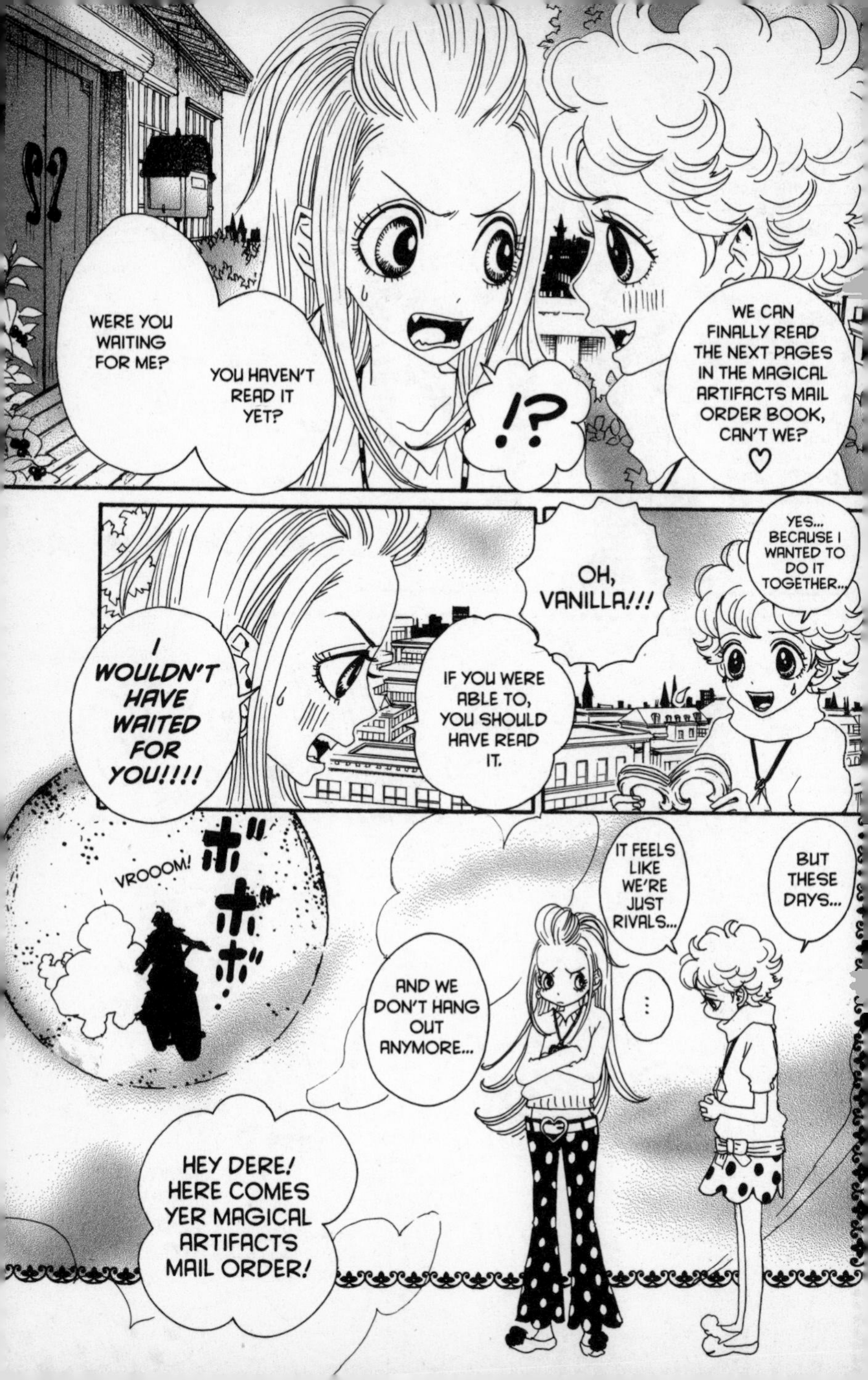
WE CAN FINALLY READ THE NEXT PAGES IN THE MAGICAL ARTIFACTS MAIL ORDER BOOK, CAN'T WE? ♡
!?
YOU HAVEN'T READ IT YET?
WERE YOU WAITING FOR ME?
YES... BECAUSE I WANTED TO DO IT TOGETHER...
OH, VANILLA!!!
IF YOU WERE ABLE TO, YOU SHOULD HAVE READ IT.
I WOULDN'T HAVE WAITED FOR YOU!!!!
BUT THESE DAYS...
IT FEELS LIKE WE'RE JUST RIVALS...
...
AND WE DON'T HANG OUT ANYMORE...
ボボボ
VROOOM!
HEY DERE! HERE COMES YER MAGICAL ARTIFACTS MAIL ORDER!

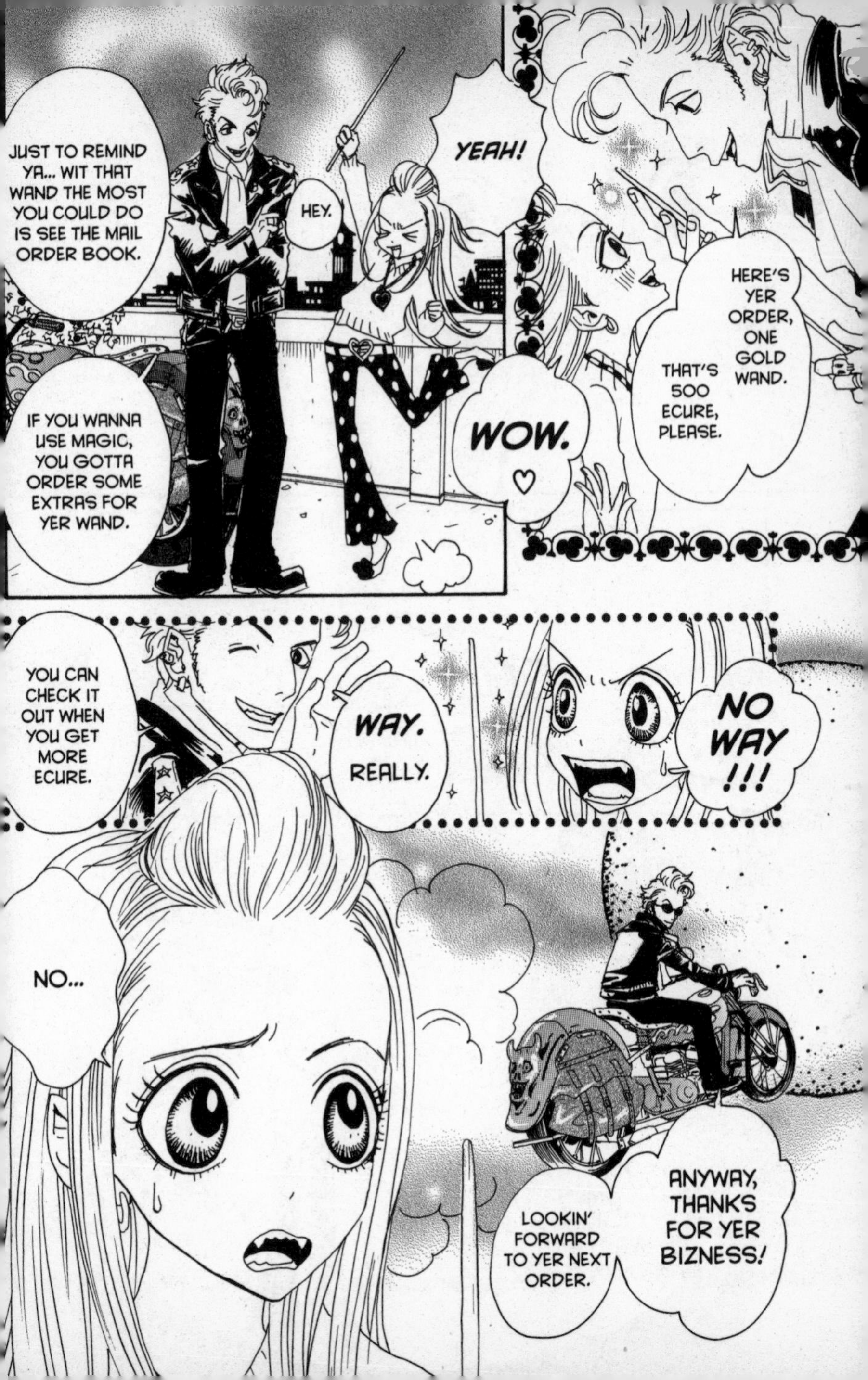
HERE'S YER ORDER, ONE GOLD WAND.
THAT'S 500 ECURE, PLEASE.
WOW. ♡
YEAH!
HEY.
JUST TO REMIND YA... WIT THAT WAND THE MOST YOU COULD DO IS SEE THE MAIL ORDER BOOK.
IF YOU WANNA USE MAGIC, YOU GOTTA ORDER SOME EXTRAS FOR YER WAND.
NO WAY!!!
WAY.
REALLY.
YOU CAN CHECK IT OUT WHEN YOU GET MORE ECURE.
ANYWAY, THANKS FOR YER BIZNESS!
LOOKIN' FORWARD TO YER NEXT ORDER.
NO...

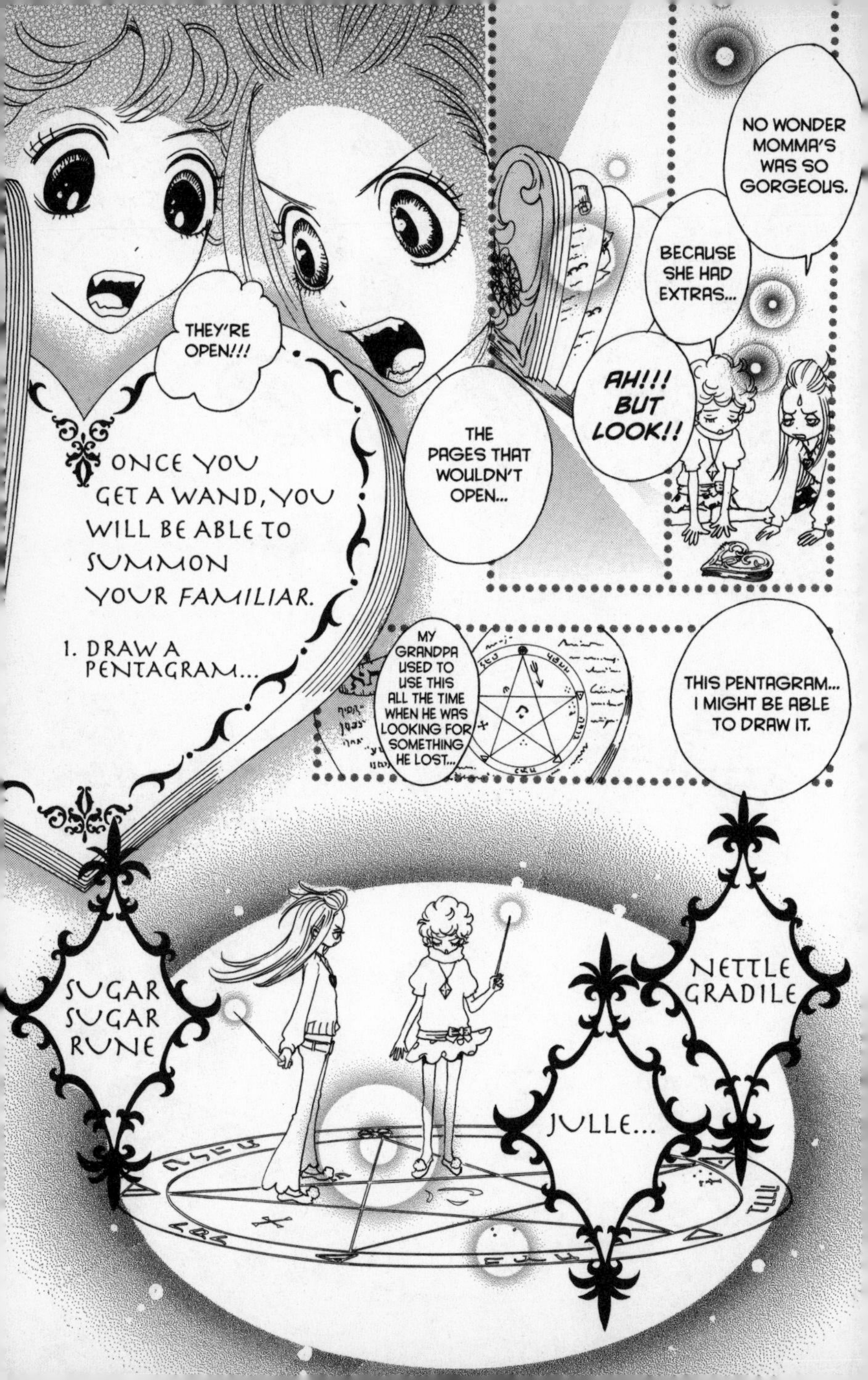
NO WONDER MOMMA'S WAS SO GORGEOUS.
BECAUSE SHE HAD EXTRAS...
AH!!! BUT LOOK!!
THE PAGES THAT WOULDN'T OPEN...
THEY'RE OPEN!!!
ONCE YOU GET A WAND, YOU WILL BE ABLE TO SUMMON YOUR FAMILIAR.
1. DRAW A PENTAGRAM...
THIS PENTAGRAM... I MIGHT BE ABLE TO DRAW IT.
MY GRANDPA USED TO USE THIS ALL THE TIME WHEN HE WAS LOOKING FOR SOMETHING HE LOST...
NETTLE GRADILE
JULLE...
SUGAR SUGAR RUNE

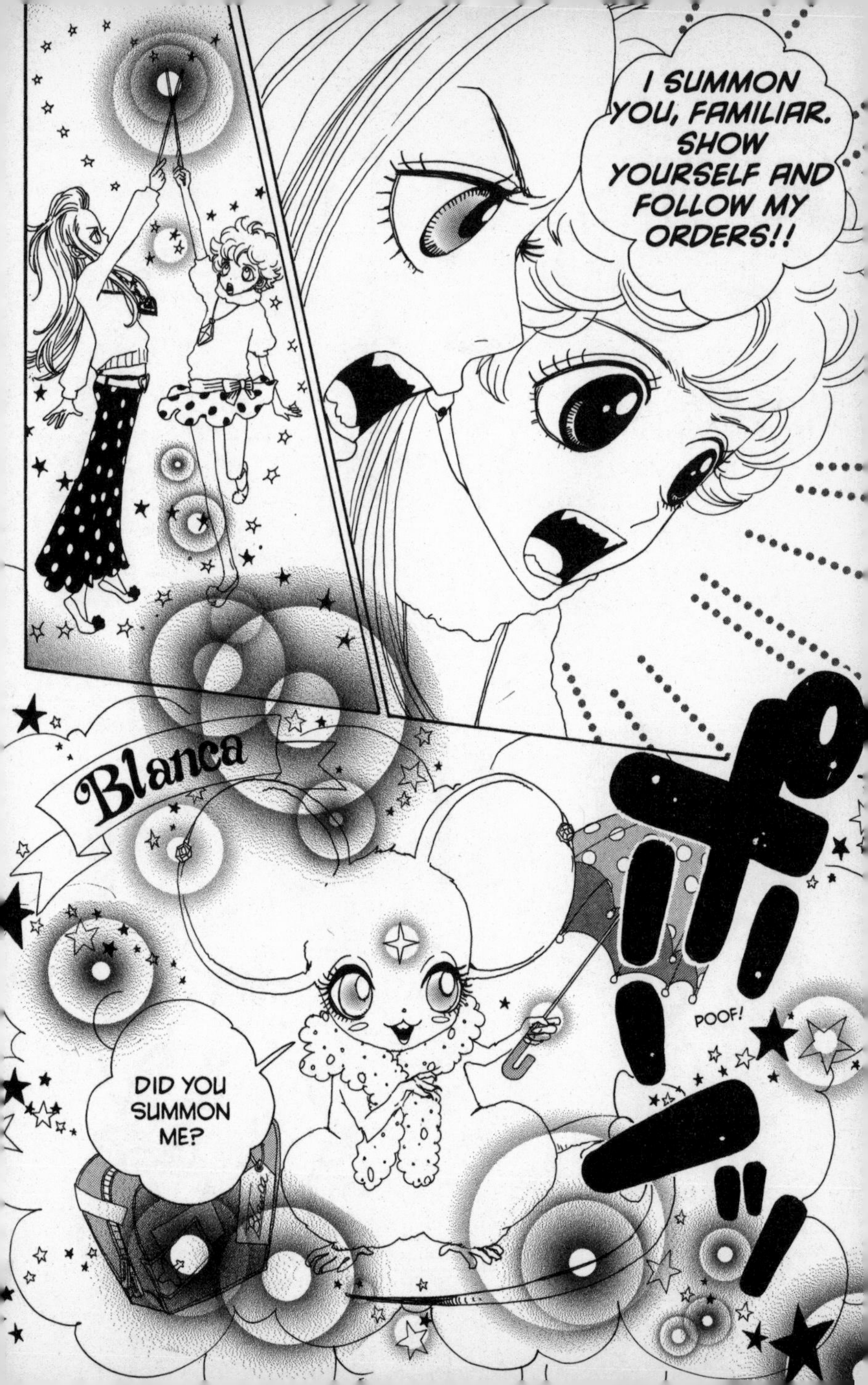
I SUMMON YOU, FAMILIAR. SHOW YOURSELF AND FOLLOW MY ORDERS!!
Blanca
POOF!
DID YOU SUMMON ME?

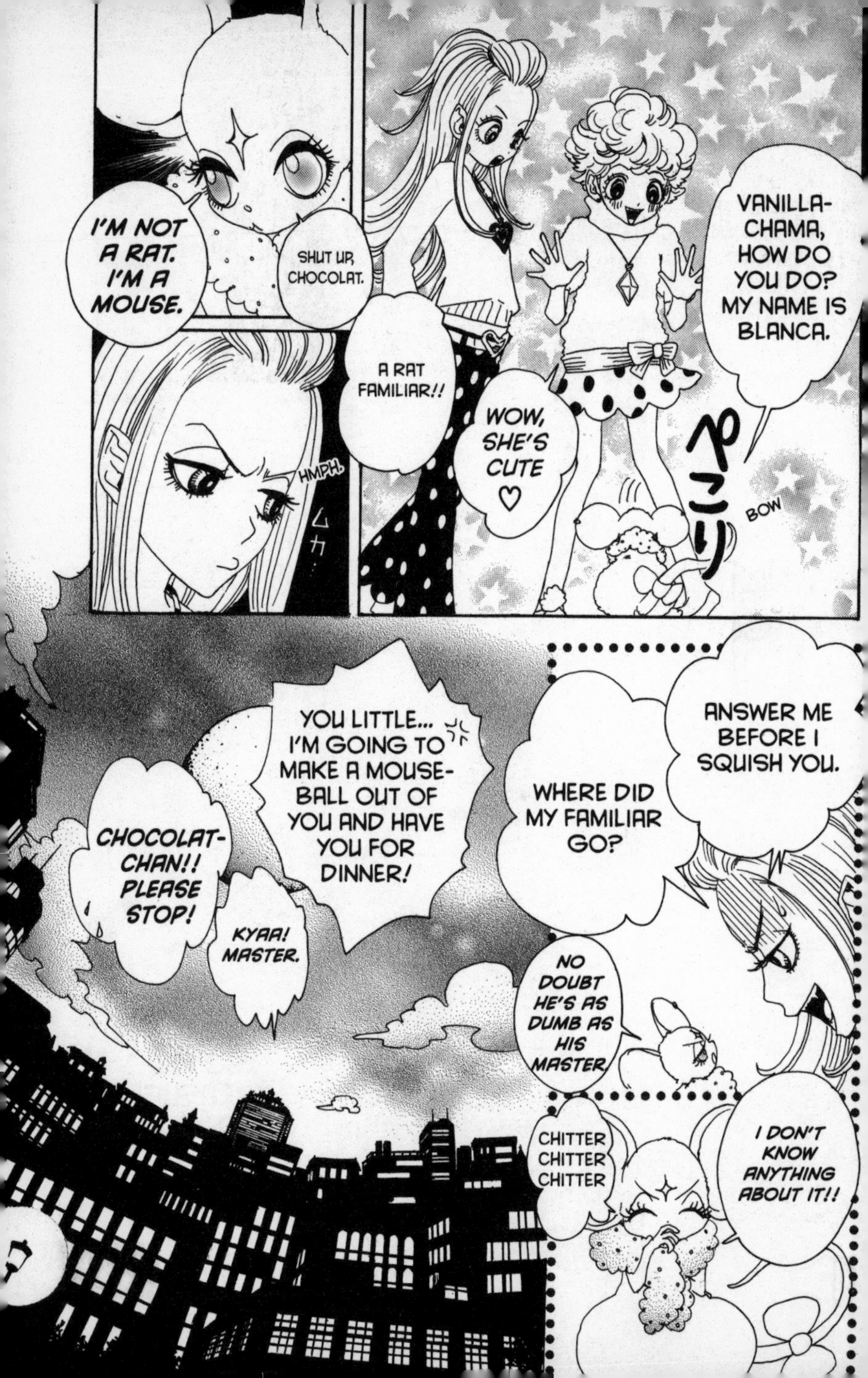
VANILLA-CHAMA, HOW DO YOU DO? MY NAME IS BLANCA.
ぺこり
BOW
WOW, SHE'S CUTE ♡
A RAT FAMILIAR!!
SHUT UP, CHOCOLAT.
I'M NOT A RAT. I'M A MOUSE.
HMPH.
ムカ
ANSWER ME BEFORE I SQUISH YOU.
WHERE DID MY FAMILIAR GO?
NO DOUBT HE'S AS DUMB AS HIS MASTER.
I DON'T KNOW ANYTHING ABOUT IT!!
CHITTER CHITTER CHITTER
YOU LITTLE... I'M GOING TO MAKE A MOUSE-BALL OUT OF YOU AND HAVE YOU FOR DINNER!
CHOCOLAT-CHAN!! PLEASE STOP!
KYAA! MASTER.

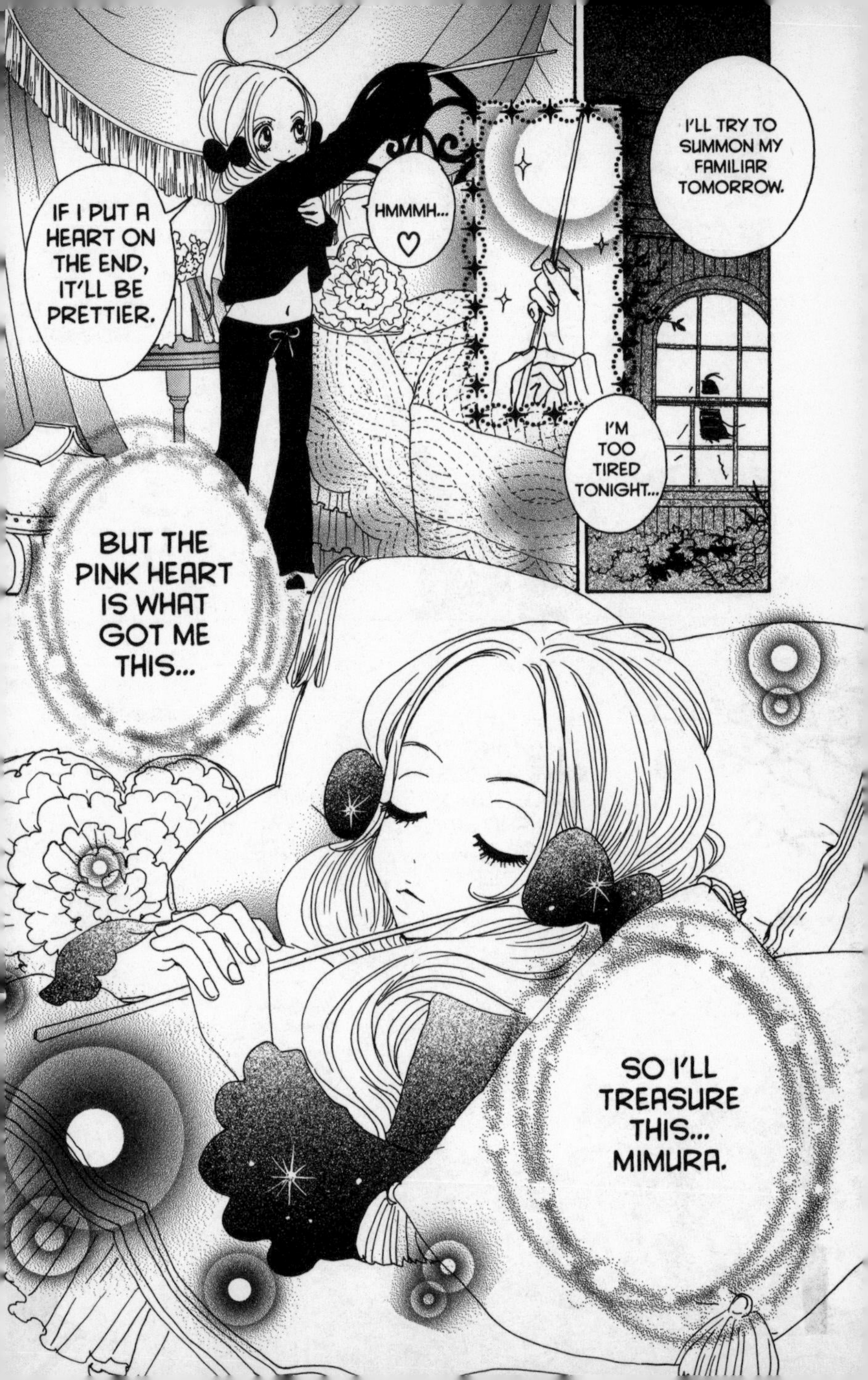
I'LL TRY TO SUMMON MY FAMILIAR TOMORROW.
I'M TOO TIRED TONIGHT...
HMMMH... ♡
IF I PUT A HEART ON THE END, IT'LL BE PRETTIER.
BUT THE PINK HEART IS WHAT GOT ME THIS...
SO I'LL TREASURE THIS... MIMURA.

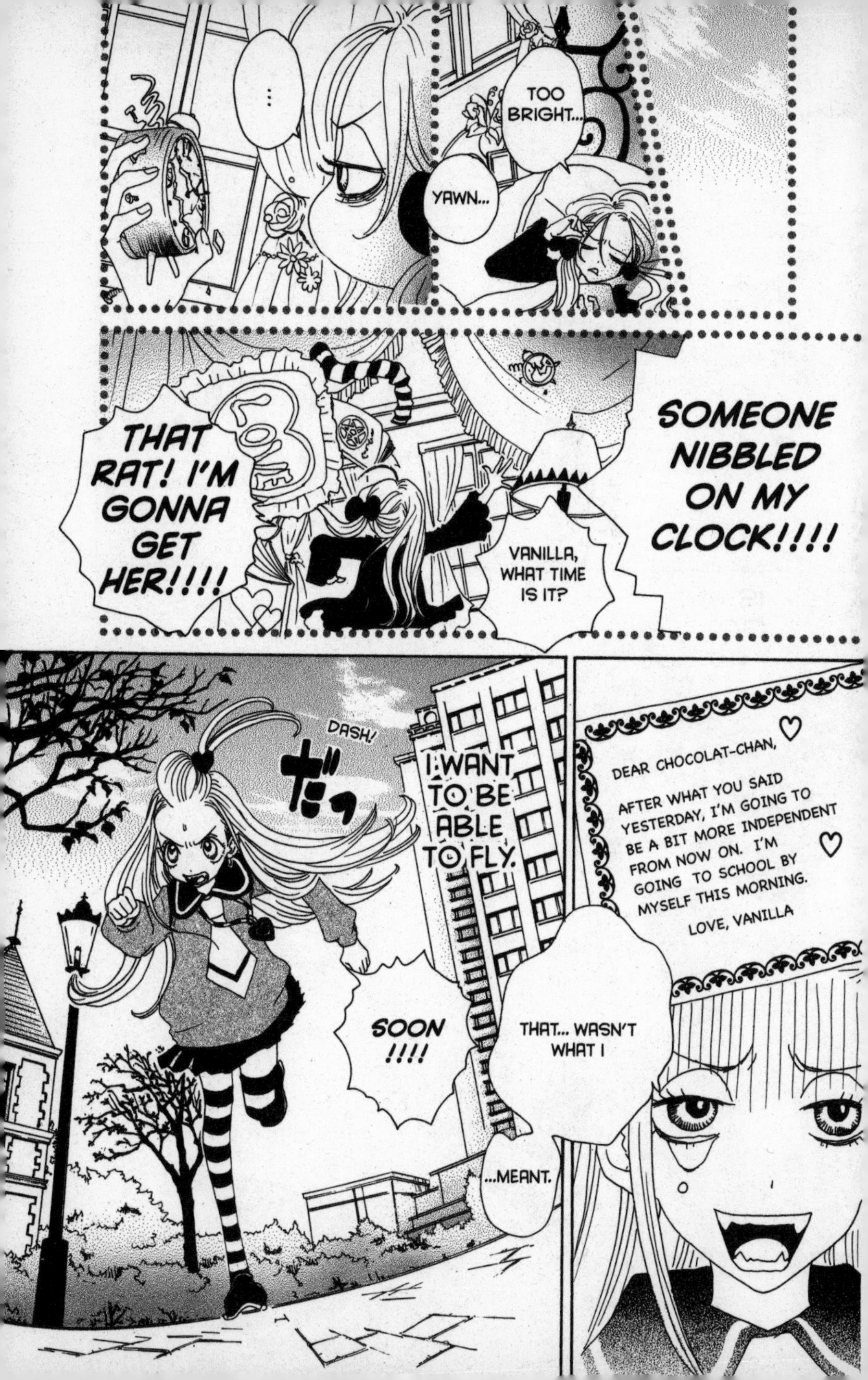
TOO BRIGHT...
YAWN...
...
VANILLA, WHAT TIME IS IT?
SOMEONE NIBBLED ON MY CLOCK!!!!
THAT RAT! I'M GONNA GET HER!!!!
DEAR CHOCOLAT-CHAN,
AFTER WHAT YOU SAID YESTERDAY, I'M GOING TO BE A BIT MORE INDEPENDENT FROM NOW ON. I'M GOING TO SCHOOL BY MYSELF THIS MORNING.
LOVE, VANILLA
THAT... WASN'T WHAT I
...MEANT.
DASH!
ダッ
I WANT TO BE ABLE TO FLY.
SOON!!!!

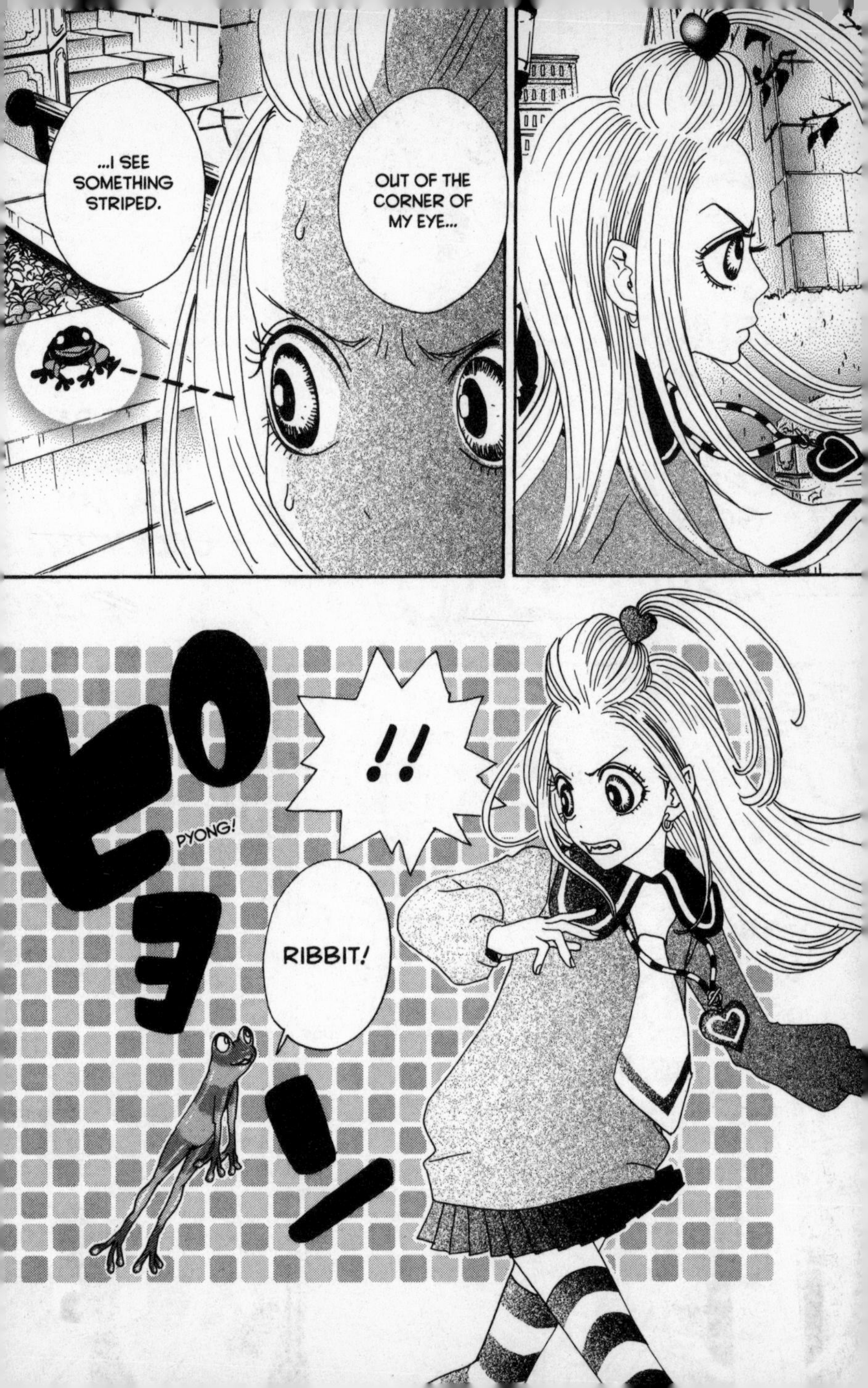
OUT OF THE CORNER OF MY EYE...
...I SEE SOMETHING STRIPED.
!!
PYONG!
RIBBIT!

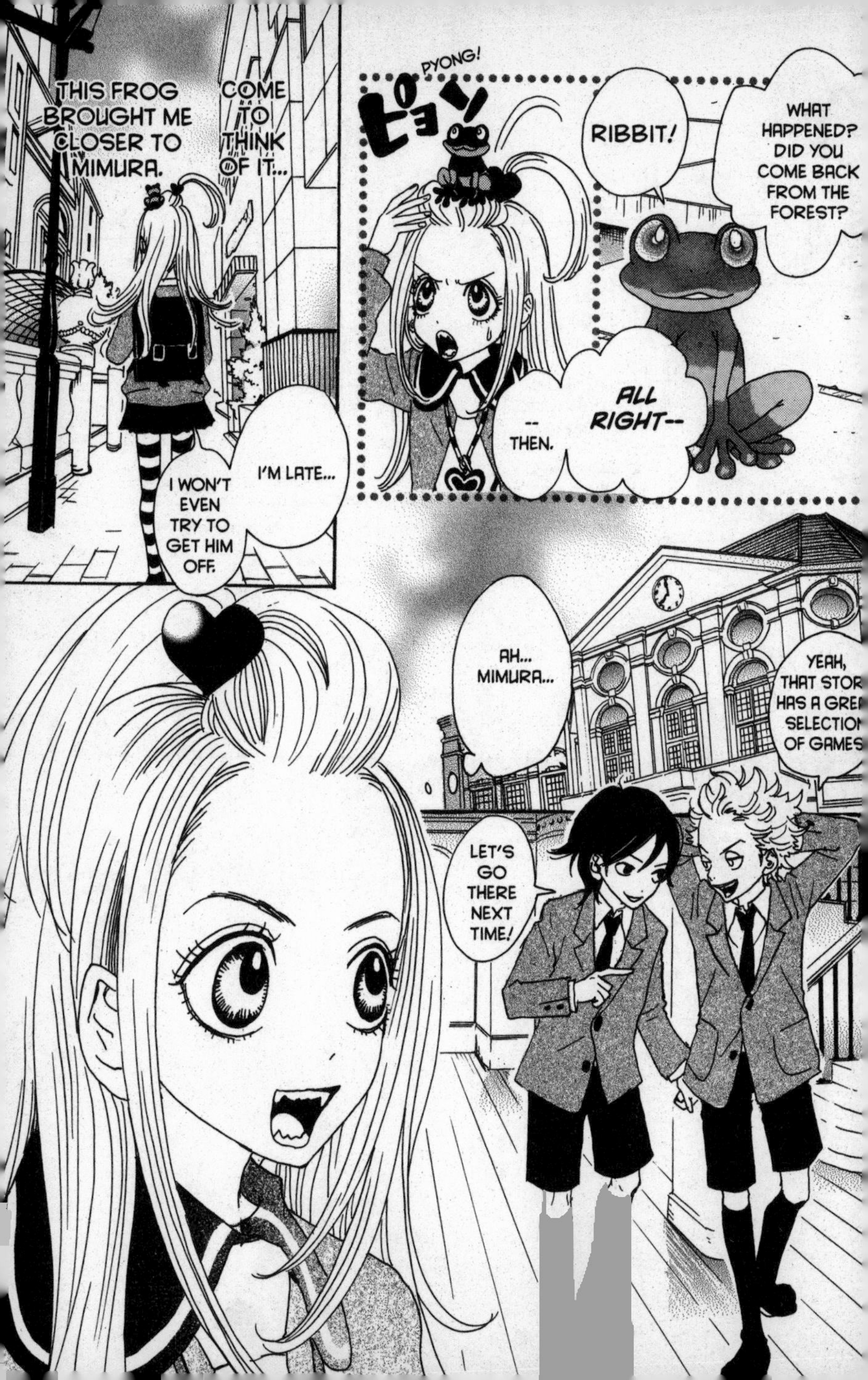
WHAT HAPPENED? DID YOU COME BACK FROM THE FOREST?
RIBBIT!
PYONG!
ピョン
ALL RIGHT-- -- THEN.
COME TO THINK OF IT...
THIS FROG BROUGHT ME CLOSER TO MIMURA.
I'M LATE...
I WON'T EVEN TRY TO GET HIM OFF.
YEAH, THAT STOR HAS A GRE SELECTIO OF GAMES
AH... MIMURA...
LET'S GO THERE NEXT TIME!

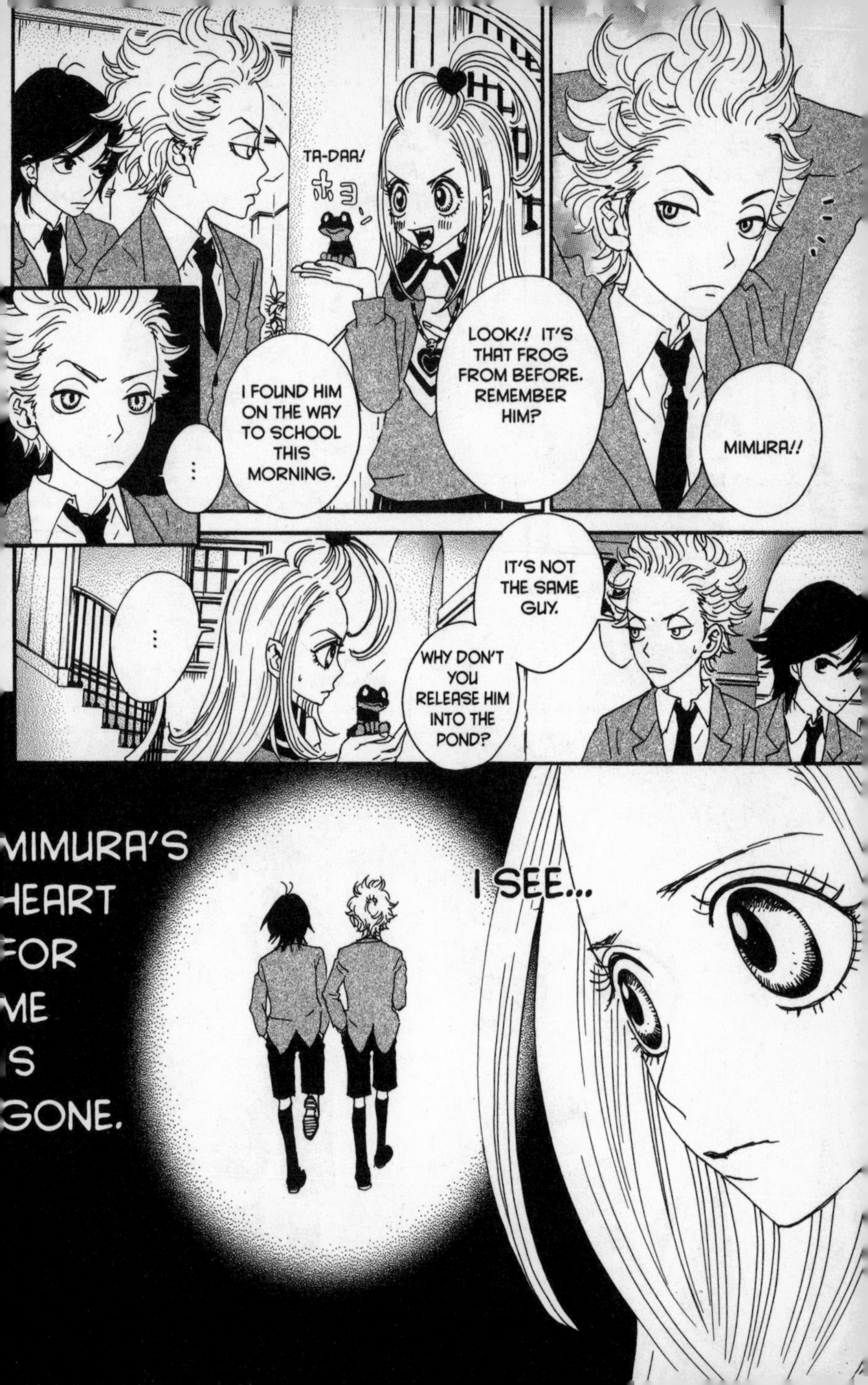
MIMURA!!
TA-DAA!
LOOK!! IT'S THAT FROG FROM BEFORE. REMEMBER HIM?
I FOUND HIM ON THE WAY TO SCHOOL THIS MORNING.
...
IT'S NOT THE SAME GUY.
WHY DON'T YOU RELEASE HIM INTO THE POND?
...
I SEE...
MIMURA'S HEART FOR ME IS GONE.

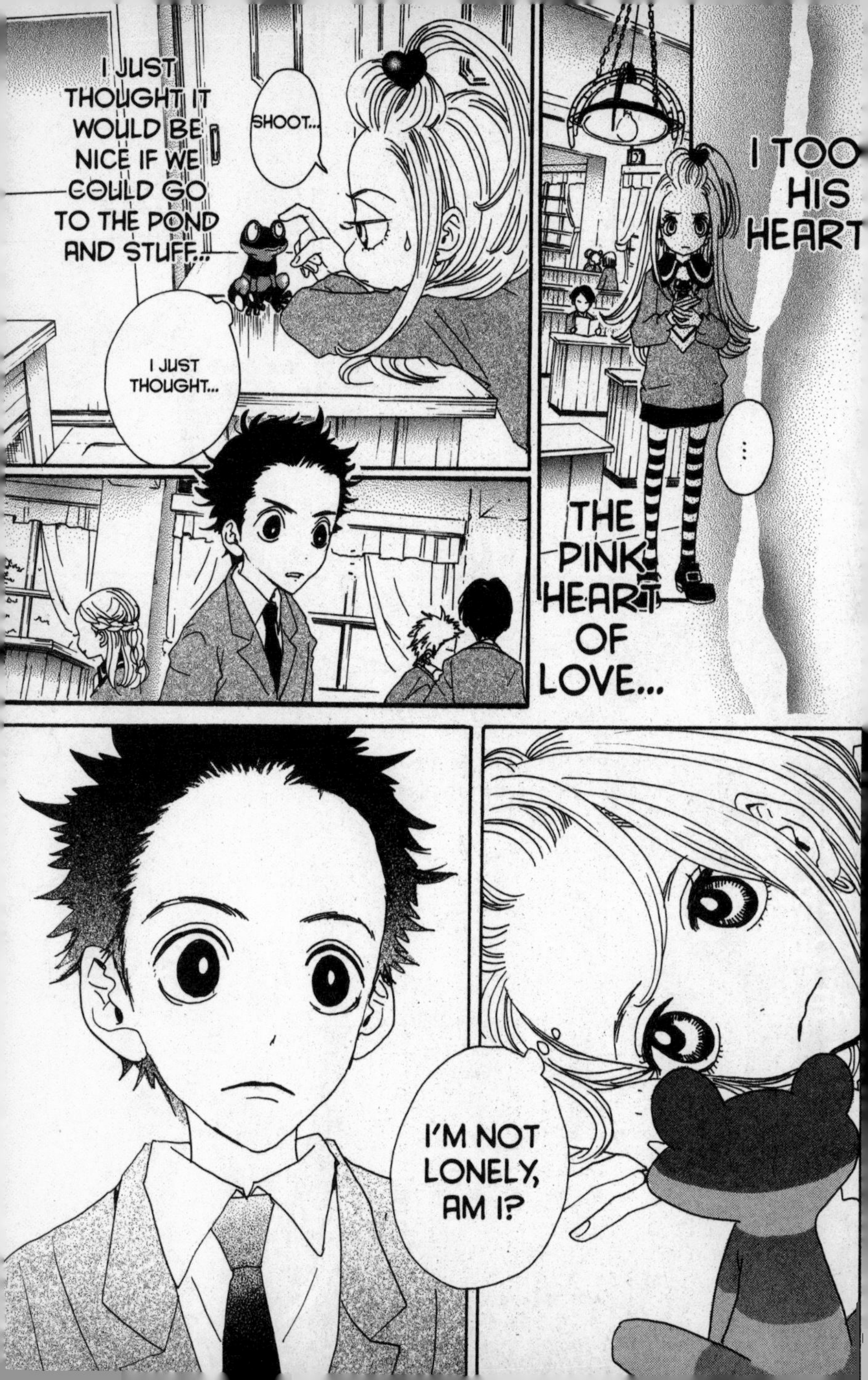
I TOO
HIS
HEART
...
THE PINK HEART OF LOVE...
SHOOT...
I JUST THOUGHT IT WOULD BE NICE IF WE COULD GO TO THE POND AND STUFF...
I JUST THOUGHT...
I'M NOT LONELY, AM I?

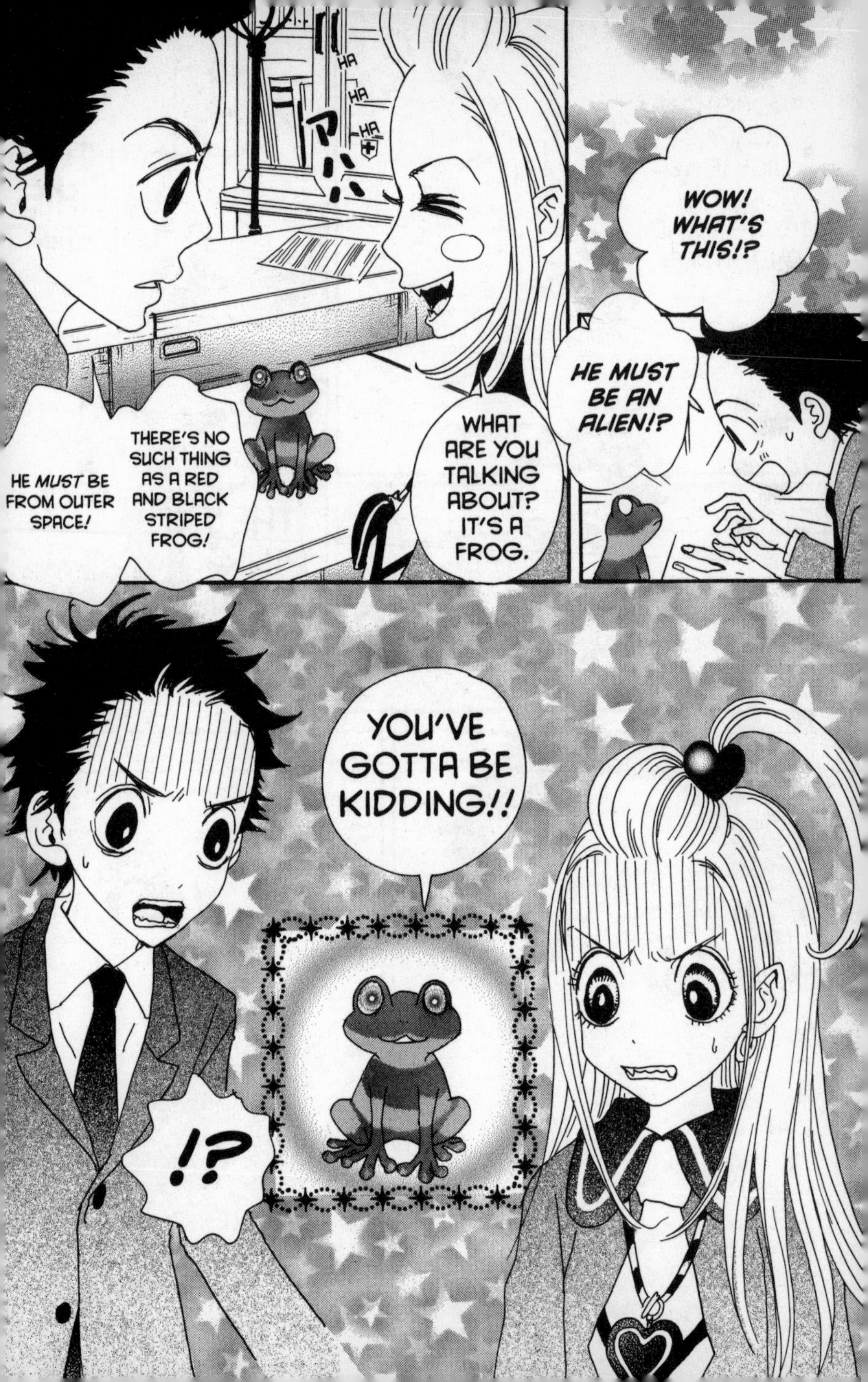
WOW! WHAT'S THIS!?
HE MUST BE AN ALIEN!?
HA HA HA
WHAT ARE YOU TALKING ABOUT? IT'S A FROG.
THERE'S NO SUCH THING AS A RED AND BLACK STRIPED FROG!
HE *MUST* BE FROM OUTER SPACE!
YOU'VE GOTTA BE KIDDING!!
!?

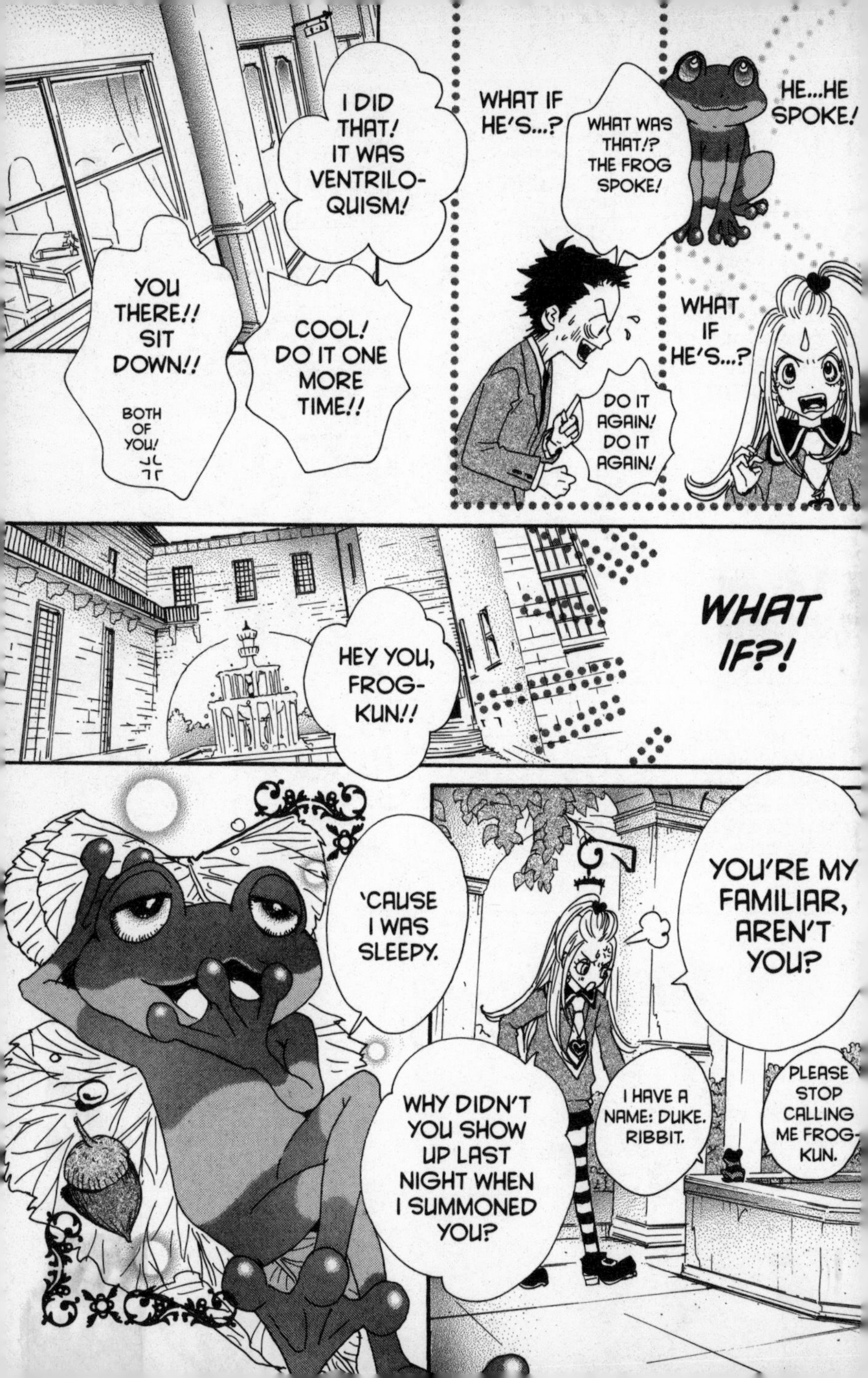
HE...HE SPOKE!
WHAT IF HE'S...?
WHAT WAS THAT!? THE FROG SPOKE!
WHAT IF HE'S...?
DO IT AGAIN! DO IT AGAIN!
I DID THAT! IT WAS VENTRILO-QUISM!
COOL! DO IT ONE MORE TIME!!
YOU THERE!! SIT DOWN!!
BOTH OF YOU!
WHAT IF?!
HEY YOU, FROG-KUN!!
YOU'RE MY FAMILIAR, AREN'T YOU?
PLEASE STOP CALLING ME FROG-KUN.
I HAVE A NAME: DUKE. RIBBIT.
WHY DIDN'T YOU SHOW UP LAST NIGHT WHEN I SUMMONED YOU?
'CAUSE I WAS SLEEPY.

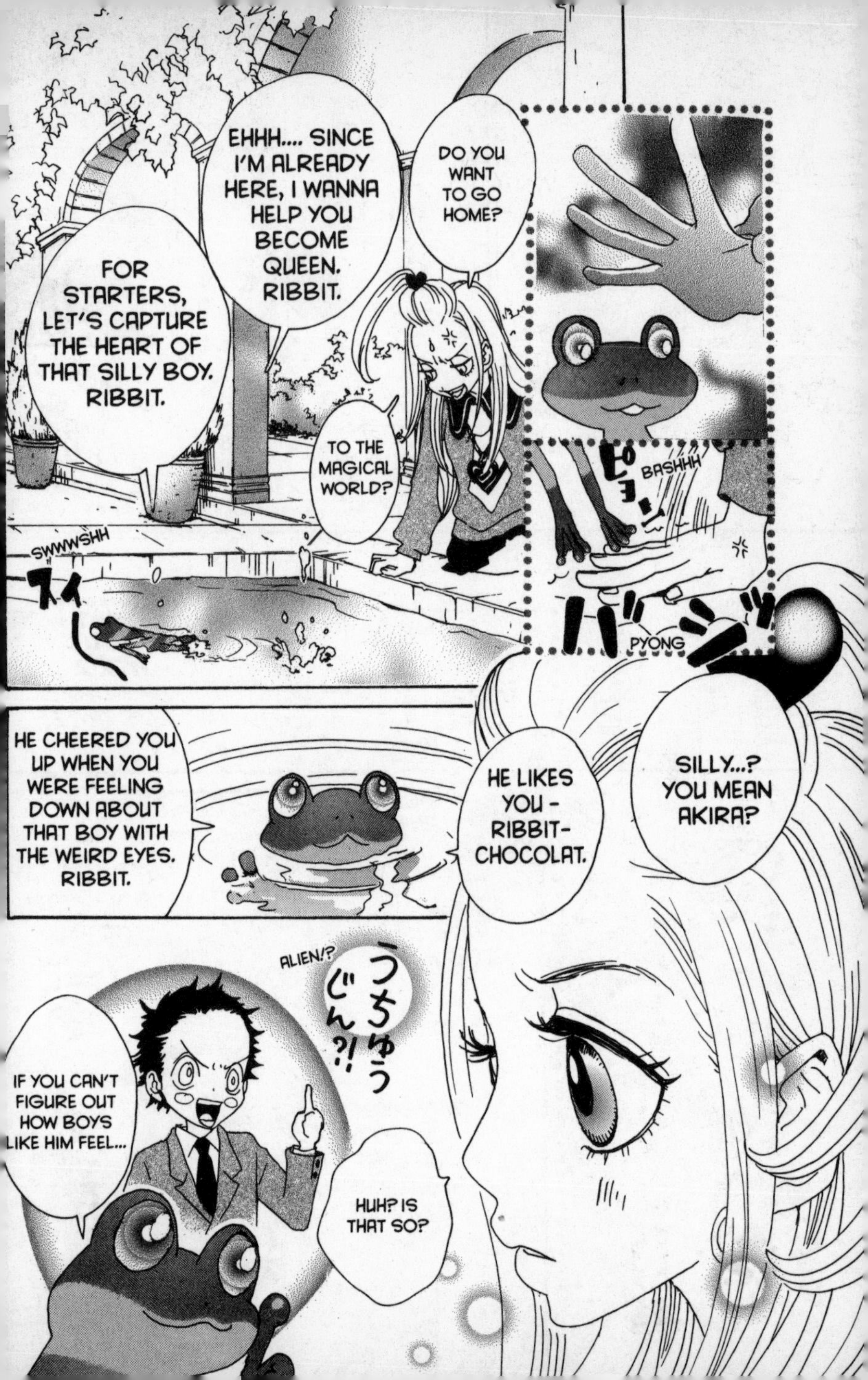
ピョン
PYONG
バシッ
BASHHH
DO YOU WANT TO GO HOME?
TO THE MAGICAL WORLD?
EHHH.... SINCE I'M ALREADY HERE, I WANNA HELP YOU BECOME QUEEN. RIBBIT.
FOR STARTERS, LET'S CAPTURE THE HEART OF THAT SILLY BOY. RIBBIT.
スイ
SWWWSHH
SILLY...? YOU MEAN AKIRA?
HE LIKES YOU -RIBBIT- CHOCOLAT.
HE CHEERED YOU UP WHEN YOU WERE FEELING DOWN ABOUT THAT BOY WITH THE WEIRD EYES. RIBBIT.
うちゅうじん?!
ALIEN!?
HUH? IS THAT SO?
IF YOU CAN'T FIGURE OUT HOW BOYS LIKE HIM FEEL...

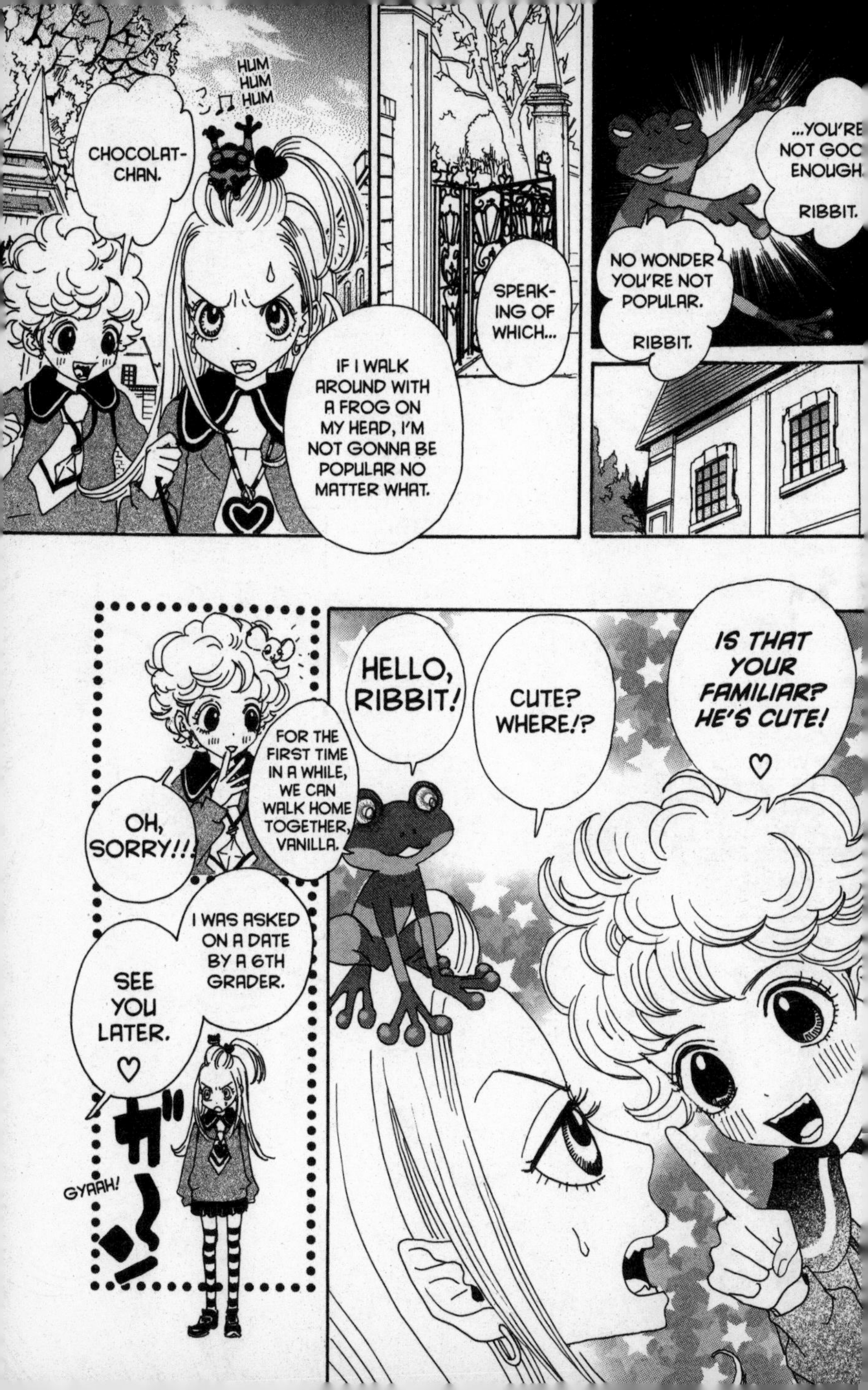
...YOU'RE NOT GOO ENOUGH. RIBBIT.
NO WONDER YOU'RE NOT POPULAR. RIBBIT.
SPEAK-ING OF WHICH...
HUM HUM HUM
CHOCOLAT-CHAN.
IF I WALK AROUND WITH A FROG ON MY HEAD, I'M NOT GONNA BE POPULAR NO MATTER WHAT.
IS THAT YOUR FAMILIAR? HE'S CUTE! ♡
CUTE? WHERE!?
HELLO, RIBBIT!
FOR THE FIRST TIME IN A WHILE, WE CAN WALK HOME TOGETHER, VANILLA.
OH, SORRY!!!
I WAS ASKED ON A DATE BY A 6TH GRADER.
SEE YOU LATER. ♡
GYAAH!

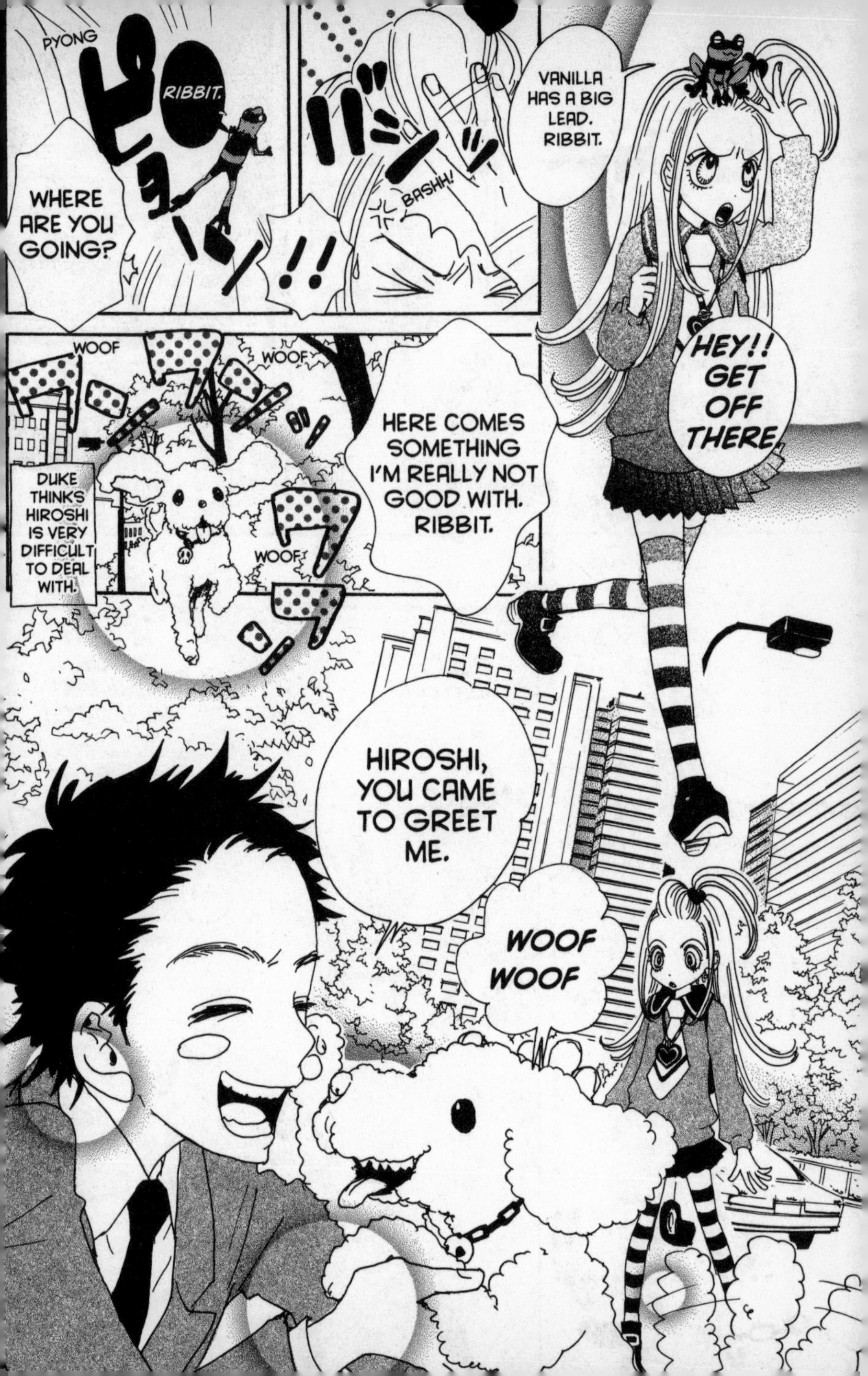
VANILLA HAS A BIG LEAD. RIBBIT.
HEY!! GET OFF THERE.
BASHH!
!!
RIBBIT.
PYONG
WHERE ARE YOU GOING?
HERE COMES SOMETHING I'M REALLY NOT GOOD WITH. RIBBIT.
WOOF
WOOF
WOOF
DUKE THINKS HIROSHI IS VERY DIFFICULT TO DEAL WITH.
HIROSHI, YOU CAME TO GREET ME.
WOOF WOOF

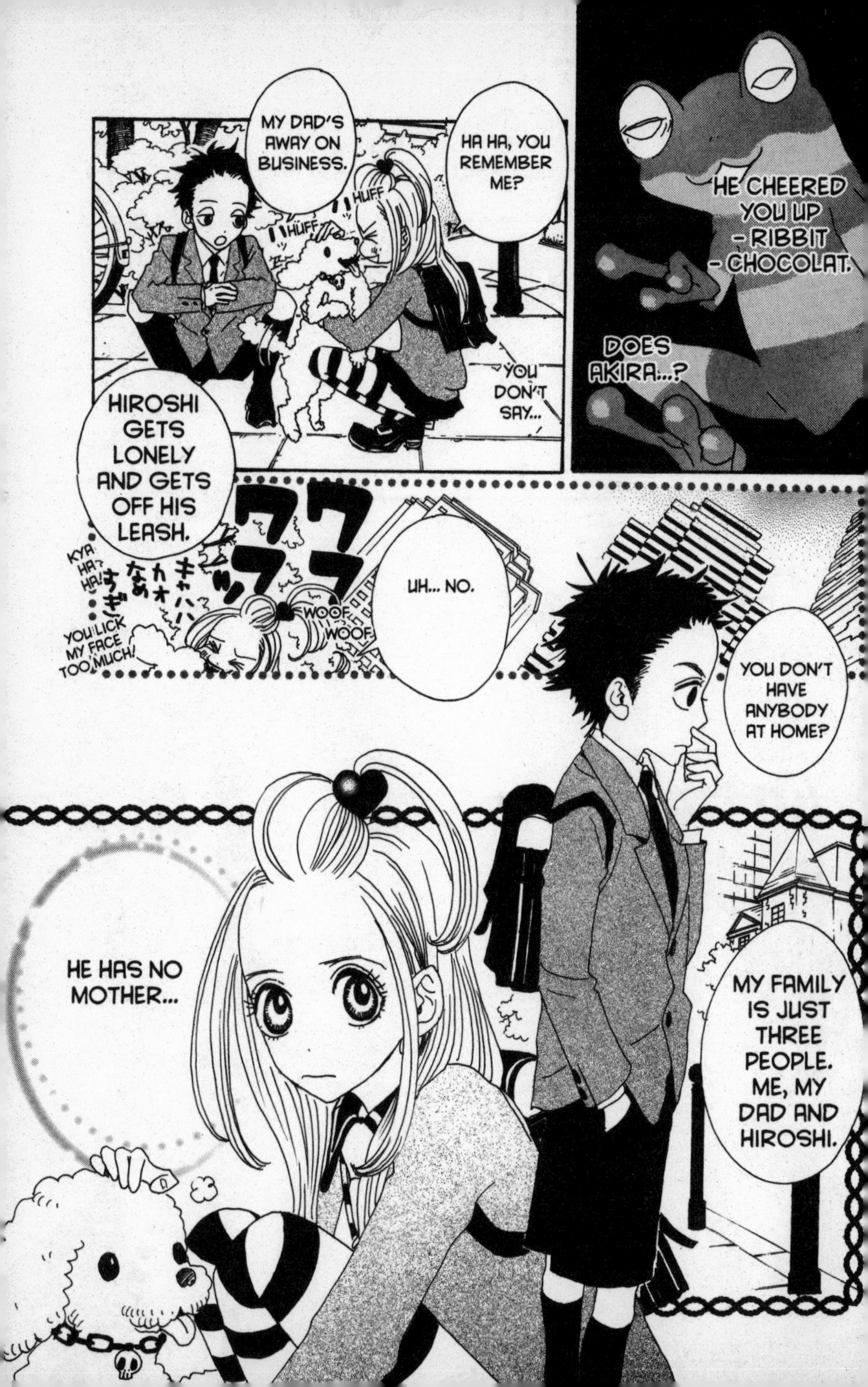
HE CHEERED YOU UP - RIBBIT - CHOCOLAT.
DOES AKIRA...?
HA HA, YOU REMEMBER ME?
MY DAD'S AWAY ON BUSINESS.
HUFF
HUFF
HUFF
YOU DON'T SAY...
HIROSHI GETS LONELY AND GETS OFF HIS LEASH.
YOU DON'T HAVE ANYBODY AT HOME?
UH... NO.
WOOF WOOF
KYA HA HA!
YOU LICK MY FACE TOO MUCH!
MY FAMILY IS JUST THREE PEOPLE. ME, MY DAD AND HIROSHI.
HE HAS NO MOTHER...

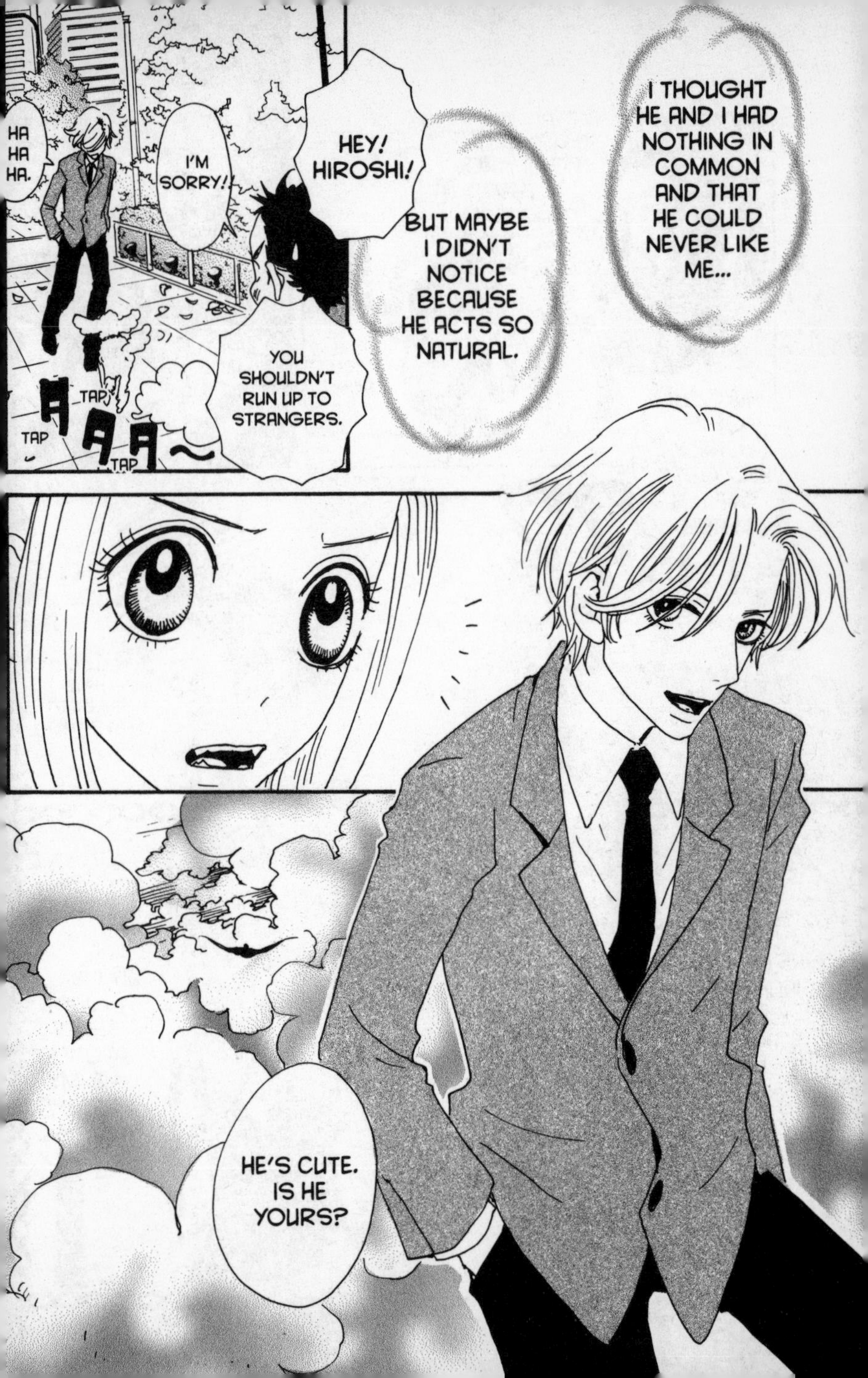
I THOUGHT HE AND I HAD NOTHING IN COMMON AND THAT HE COULD NEVER LIKE ME...
BUT MAYBE I DIDN'T NOTICE BECAUSE HE ACTS SO NATURAL.
HEY! HIROSHI!
I'M SORRY!!
YOU SHOULDN'T RUN UP TO STRANGERS.
HA HA HA.
TAP
TAP
TAP
TAP
HE'S CUTE. IS HE YOURS?

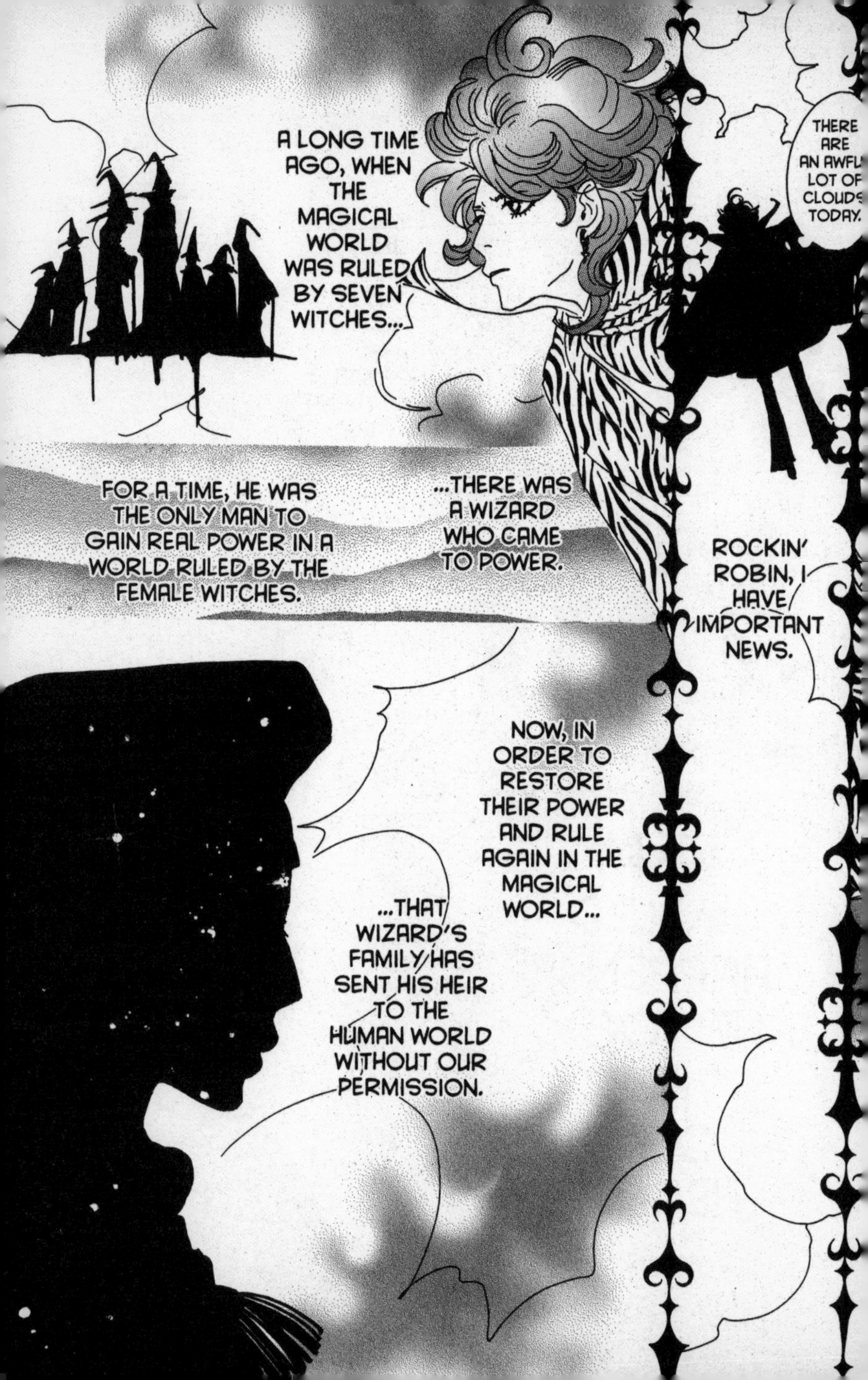
THERE ARE AN AWFUL LOT OF CLOUDS TODAY.
ROCKIN' ROBIN, I HAVE IMPORTANT NEWS.
A LONG TIME AGO, WHEN THE MAGICAL WORLD WAS RULED BY SEVEN WITCHES...
...THERE WAS A WIZARD WHO CAME TO POWER.
FOR A TIME, HE WAS THE ONLY MAN TO GAIN REAL POWER IN A WORLD RULED BY THE FEMALE WITCHES.
NOW, IN ORDER TO RESTORE THEIR POWER AND RULE AGAIN IN THE MAGICAL WORLD...
...THAT WIZARD'S FAMILY HAS SENT HIS HEIR TO THE HUMAN WORLD WITHOUT OUR PERMISSION.

THEY SENT HIM TO THE SAME SCHOOL AS OUR TWO POTENTIAL QUEENS!
NATURALLY, THESE TWO ARE HIS TARGETS.
IF THEIR HEARTS ARE TAKEN...
THE SITUATION WOULD BE A DISASTER.
WHAT WOULD HAPPEN IF HE TOOK THEIR ONLY HEART?

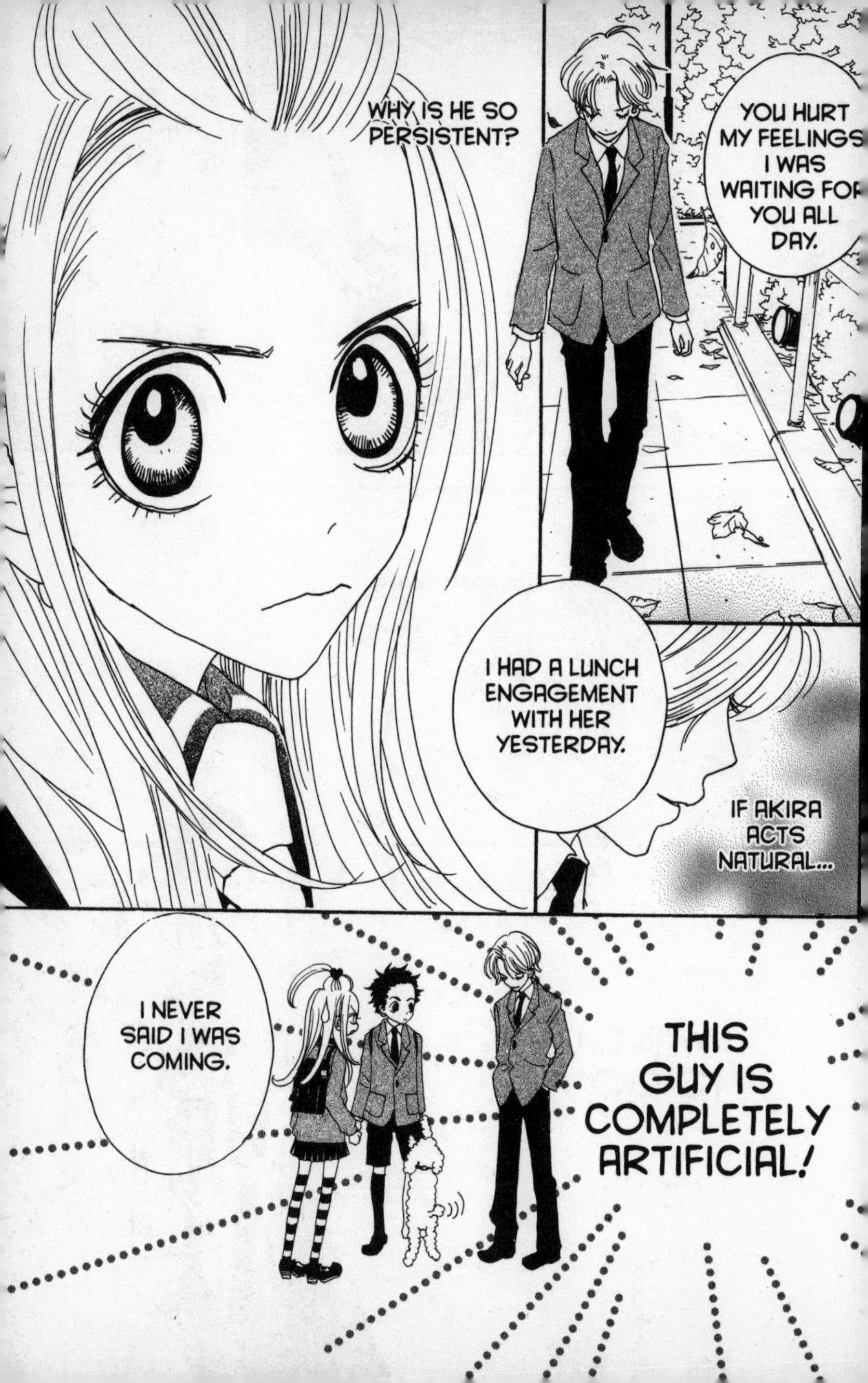
YOU HURT MY FEELINGS. I WAS WAITING FOR YOU ALL DAY.
I HAD A LUNCH ENGAGEMENT WITH HER YESTERDAY.
IF AKIRA ACTS NATURAL...
WHY IS HE SO PERSISTENT?
THIS GUY IS COMPLETELY ARTIFICIAL!
I NEVER SAID I WAS COMING.

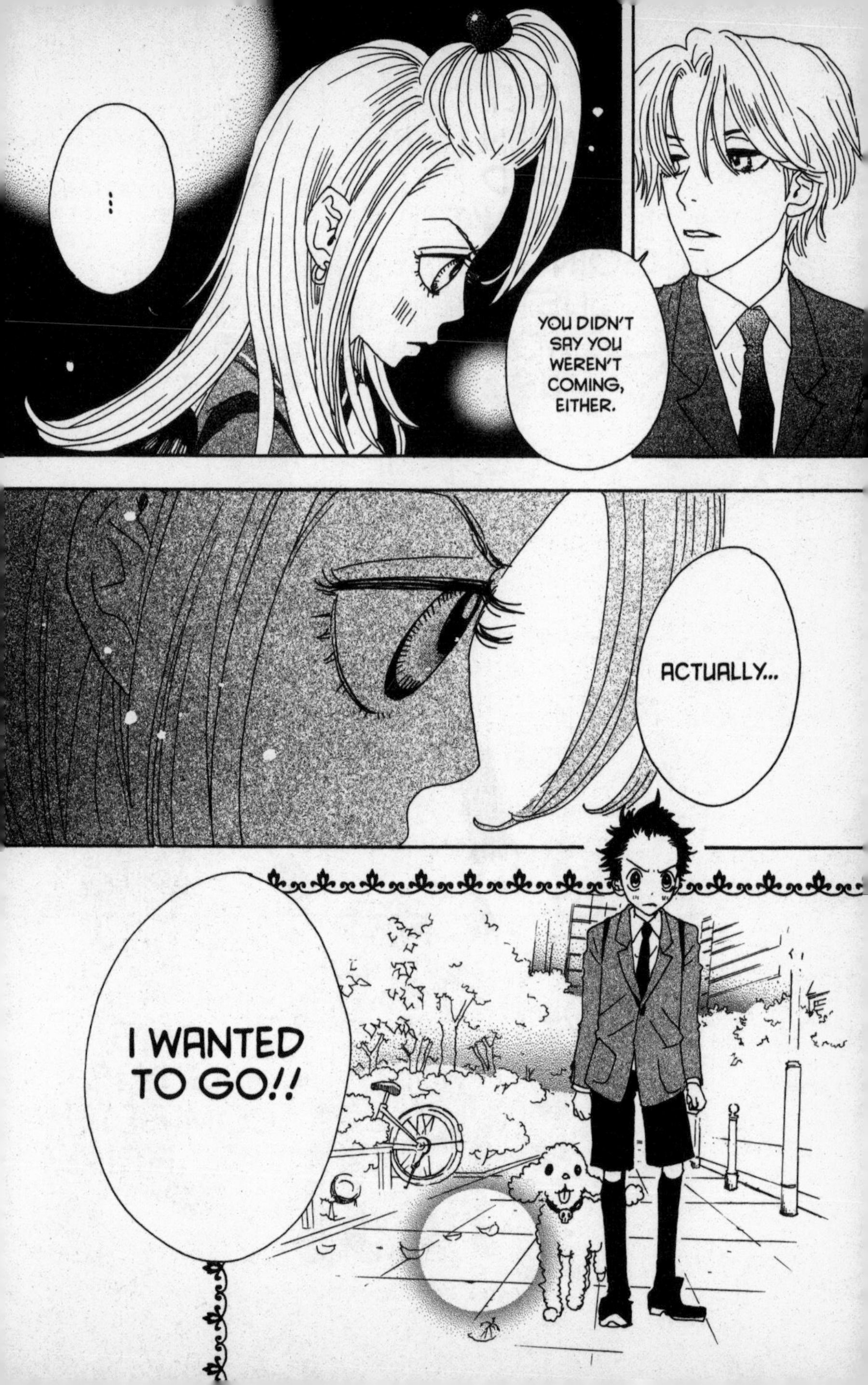
YOU DIDN'T SAY YOU WEREN'T COMING, EITHER.
...
ACTUALLY...
I WANTED TO GO!!

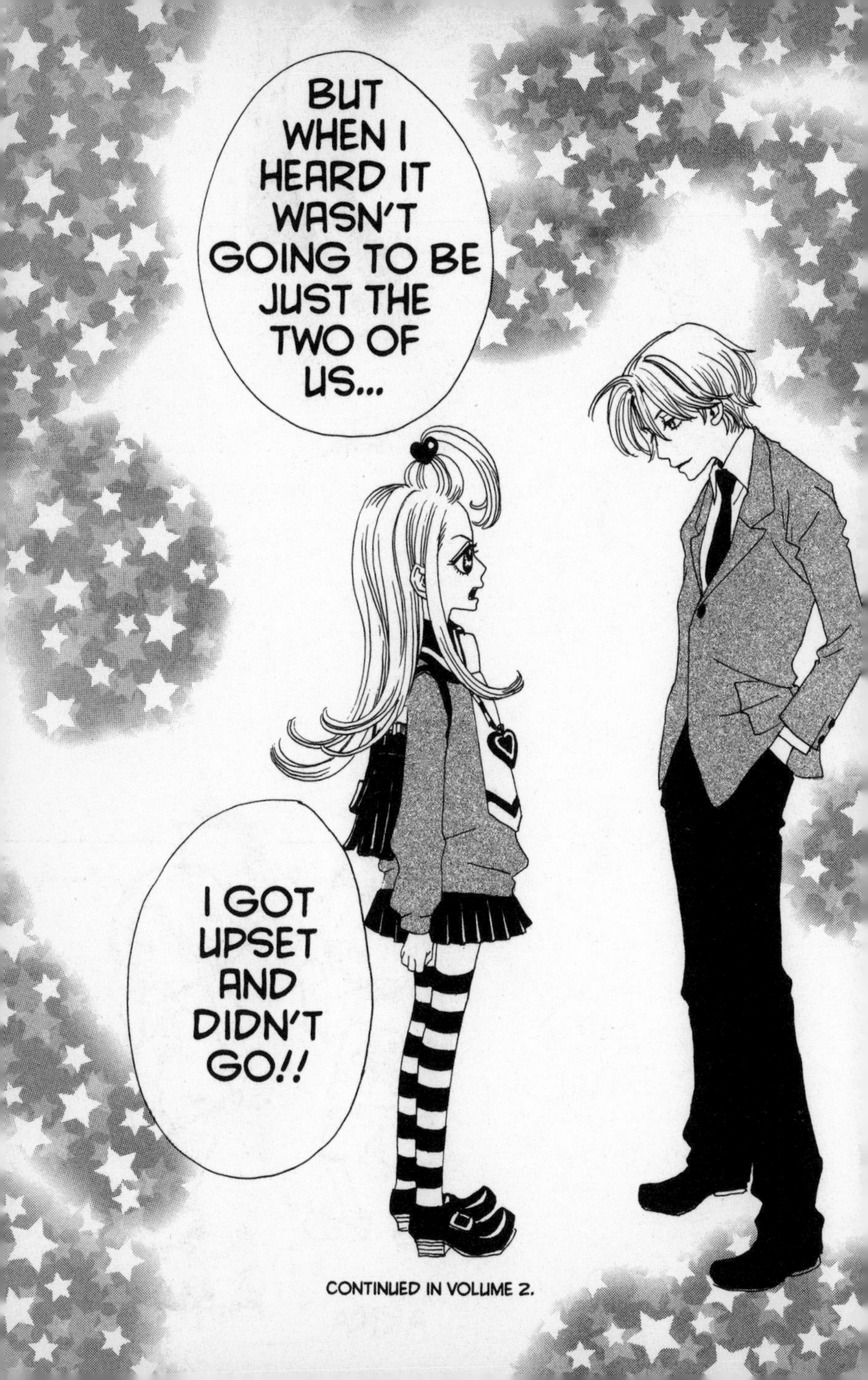
BUT WHEN I HEARD IT WASN'T GOING TO BE JUST THE TWO OF US...
I GOT UPSET AND DIDN'T GO!!

CONTINUED IN VOLUME 2.

AKIRA   PIERRE

About the Creator

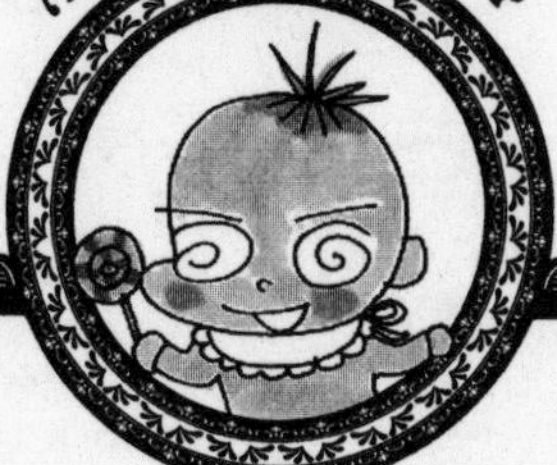

Moyoco Anno

Her birthday is March 26.

Her zodiac sign is Aries, her blood type is O, and she is from Tokyo.

She debuted in 1989 with the story "Mattaku ikashita yatsura daze" in the Bessatsu Shojo Friend special issue "Juliet." Other popular works include "Hana to Mitsubachi," "Sakuran," and "Bijin gaho" (an essay about beauty), among others.

She loves flowers and water, and enjoys hobbies such as walking in the mountains and hills, and dieting.

TRANSLATION NOTES

For your edification and reading pleasure, here are notes to help explain some of the cultural and story references from our translation of *Sugar Sugar Rune 1*.

MY NAME IS CHOCOLAT.

PAGE 5, THE SPELLING OF CHOCOLAT'S NAME

The French word for chocolate. Sometimes the Japanese prefer the French pronounciation, particularly if the person or thing has a more expensive or fragile connotation. In this case, chocolat infers prettier, probably expensive, gourmet chocolate.

VANILLA MIEUX.
Y... YES.

PAGE 12, VANILLA'S FULL NAME

Vanilla's full name is Vanilla Mieux. "Mieux" means "good" in French.

BAM!
AND THE DAUGHTER OF THE WITCH CIN-NAMON...
...CHOCOLAT MEILLEURE?
UH... SHE'S NOT HERE?

PAGE 13, CHOCOLAT'S FULL NAME

Chocolat's full name is Chocolat Meilleure. "Meilleure" means "better" in French.

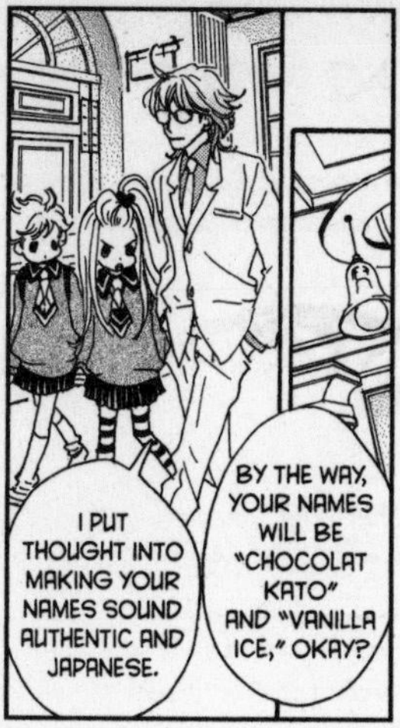
BY THE WAY, YOUR NAMES WILL BE "CHOCOLAT KATO" AND "VANILLA ICE," OKAY?
I PUT THOUGHT INTO MAKING YOUR NAMES SOUND AUTHENTIC AND JAPANESE.

PAGE 23, CHOCOLAT'S ASSUMED NAME, CHOCOLAT KATO

In Japanese the names are spoken surname first, and then given name. So Chocolat's full name used in the human would would be spoken in Japanese as Kato Chocolat. In the Japanese language, the usage of different Chinese characters ends up producing the same sound. In the case of the characters in the original Japanese manga, Kato shokora (Kato Chocolat) means "sugar added chocolate" with completely different Chinese characters.

PAGE 23, VANILLA'S ASSUMED NAME, VANILLA ICE

Vanilla's Japanese name while she is in the human world is Vanilla Ice. In Japan, there is an ice cream, which sometimes comes in a bar, called Vanilla Ice. It is popular among kids.

PAGE 26, WHAT DID HE MEAN BY GIANT?

When the boy says "Giant," he is referring to Doraemon's "Giant," or in other words, a bully.

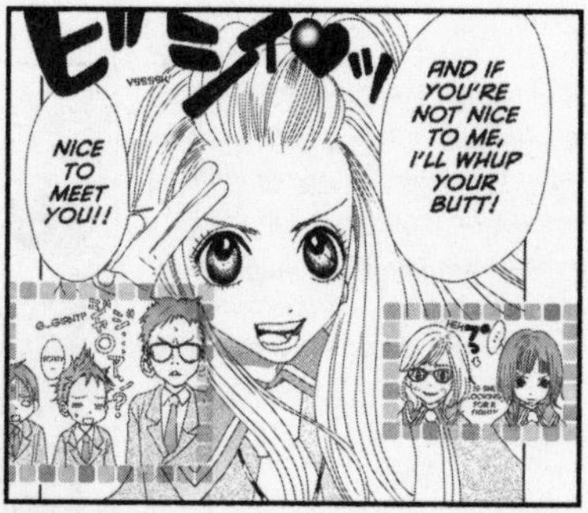
AND IF YOU'RE NOT NICE TO ME, I'LL WHUP YOUR BUTT!
NICE TO MEET YOU!!

PAGE 31, AGRANDISSMENT

This is a magical word Chocolat uses to signify enlargement. It is French for expansion

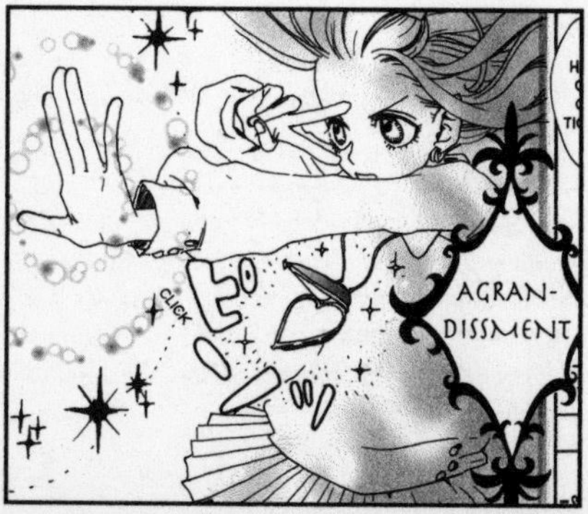
AGRAN-
DISSMENT
CLICK

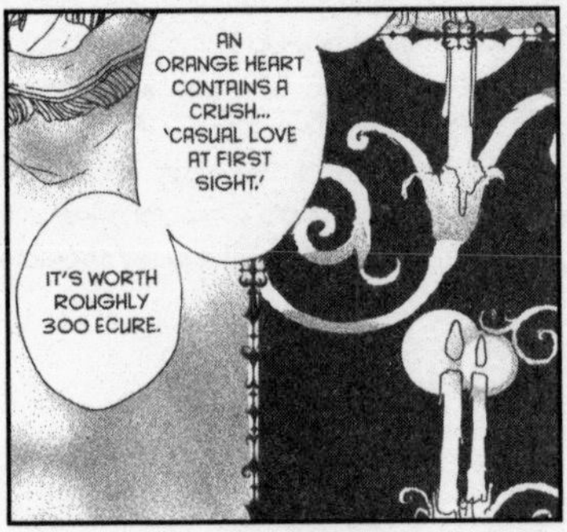
AN ORANGE HEART CONTAINS A CRUSH... 'CASUAL LOVE AT FIRST SIGHT.'
IT'S WORTH ROUGHLY 300 ECURE.

PAGE 62, WHAT ARE ECURE?

Ecure is the form of currency in the Magical World.

PAGE 69, WHAT'S A CAT TONGUE COURSE?

Cat tongue is a Japanese term used to describe people who can't eat hot stuff, such as hot soups or a hot meal, and prefers their food at cold temperatures. In Japanese culture, cats are thought to have a sensitive tongue and do not eat hot food. So a cat tongue course would consist of only cold foods.

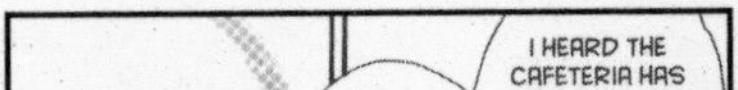
I HEARD THE CAFETERIA HAS A SPECIAL MENU CALLED THE 'CAT TONGUE COURSE' JUST FOR HIM.
AND IT'S ALL COLD FOOD.
I'VE DECIDED.
CELERY WITH SPECIAL SAUCE, JELLIED CAVIAR...
...AND COLD PASTA WITH SHRIMP AND TOMATOES!!

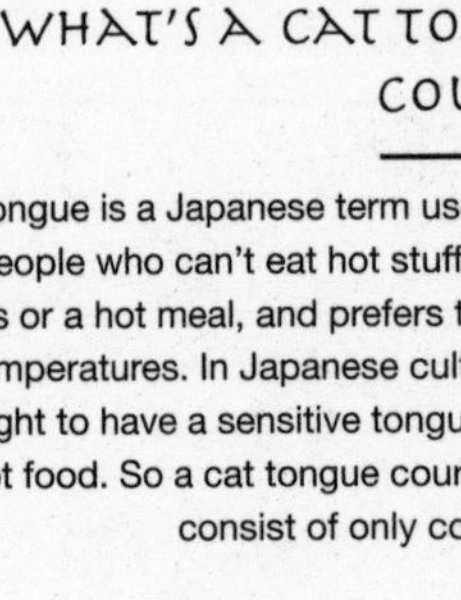

CHOCOLA

WHY IS HER NAME SPELLED AS "CHOCOLA" ON PAGE 140?

The artist spelled Chocolat's name as "Chocola" because in the French pronunciation of the word, the "t" is silent. The Japanese would pronounce it in the French fashion. So the artist wrote the name as a direct phonetic spelling of how the Japanese would say it.

Page 166, What's "Love Love"?

"Love love" is a casual Japanese term often used among young people and kids. "Love love" means you are in love with someone, and it suggests the mood and the act of being together with the loved one. It can be used as a verb, adverb, or noun.

THAT'S MIMURA-KUN, ISN'T IT? PEOPLE ARE TALKING ABOUT YOU!!
EVEN IN MY CLASS, THEY'RE SAYING YOU TWO ARE "LOVE LOVE"!!
YOU'RE *NOT* IN LOVE WITH HIM, ARE YOU?

ANYWAY, THANKS FOR YER BIZNESS!
LOOKIN' FORWARD TO YER NEXT ORDER.

Page 184, How Come the Magical World Mail Order Catalog Delivery Man Talks Funny?

This delivery man speaks with a Kansai accent. We have tried to capture the feel of this accent in English.

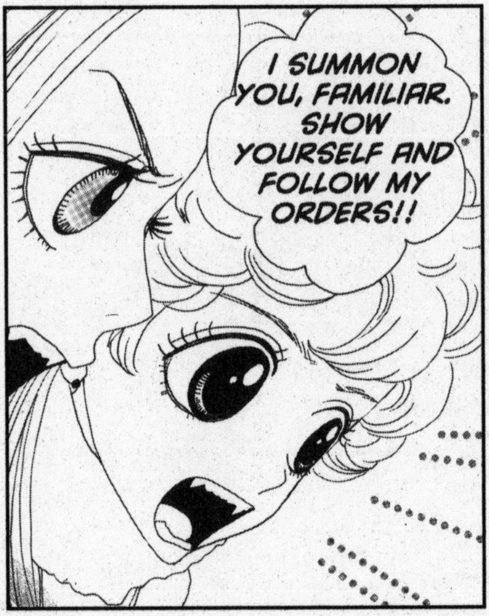
I SUMMON YOU, FAMILIAR. SHOW YOURSELF AND FOLLOW MY ORDERS!!

PAGE 186, WHAT'S A FAMILIAR?

A familiar is a magical creature who serves a witch or wizard.

PAGE 187, WHY DID BLANCA CALL HER VANILLA-CHAMA?

Since Blanca is a magical mouse, she can speak, but she still has a mouse accent. Normally she should say "sama" instead of "chama," but her accent makes her say "chama." It sounds a little like baby talk.

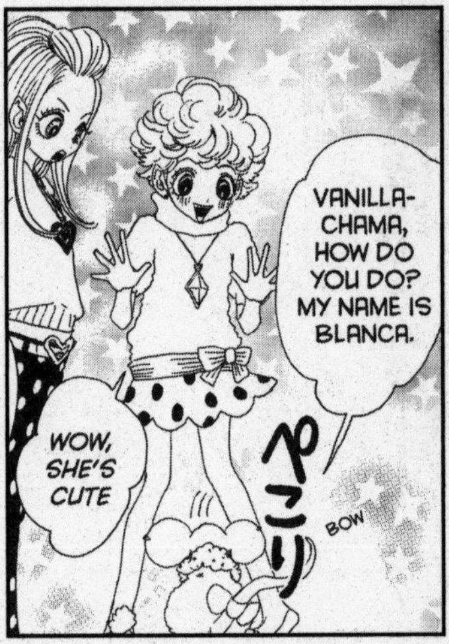
VANILLA-CHAMA, HOW DO YOU DO? MY NAME IS BLANCA.
WOW, SHE'S CUTE
ぺこり
BOW

PREVIEW OF VOLUME 2 OF
SUGAR SUGAR RUNE

We are pleased to present you with the opportunity to take
an early look at the second volume of *Sugar Sugar Rune*.
Volume 2 will be available in English in March 2006.
For now, you'll have to make do with the Japanese version.

Enjoy.

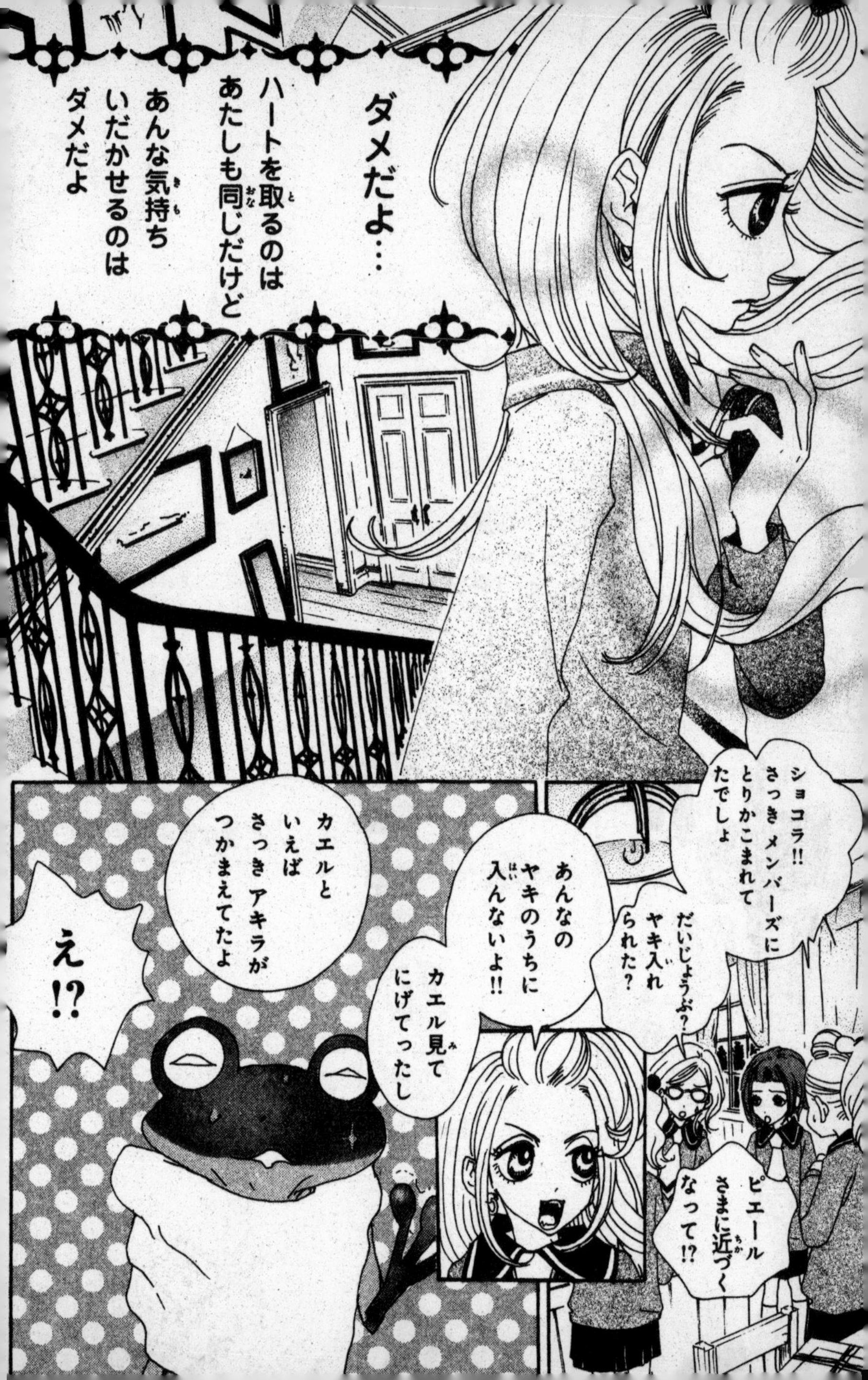
ダメだよ…
ハートを取るのはあたしも同じだけど
あんな気持ちいだかせるのはダメだよ
ショコラ!! さっき メンバーズにとりかこまれてたでしょ
だいじょうぶ? ヤキ入れられた?
ピエールさまに近づくなって!?
あんなのヤキのうちに入んないよ!!
カエル見てにげてったし
カエルといえばさっき アキラがつかまえてたよ
え!?

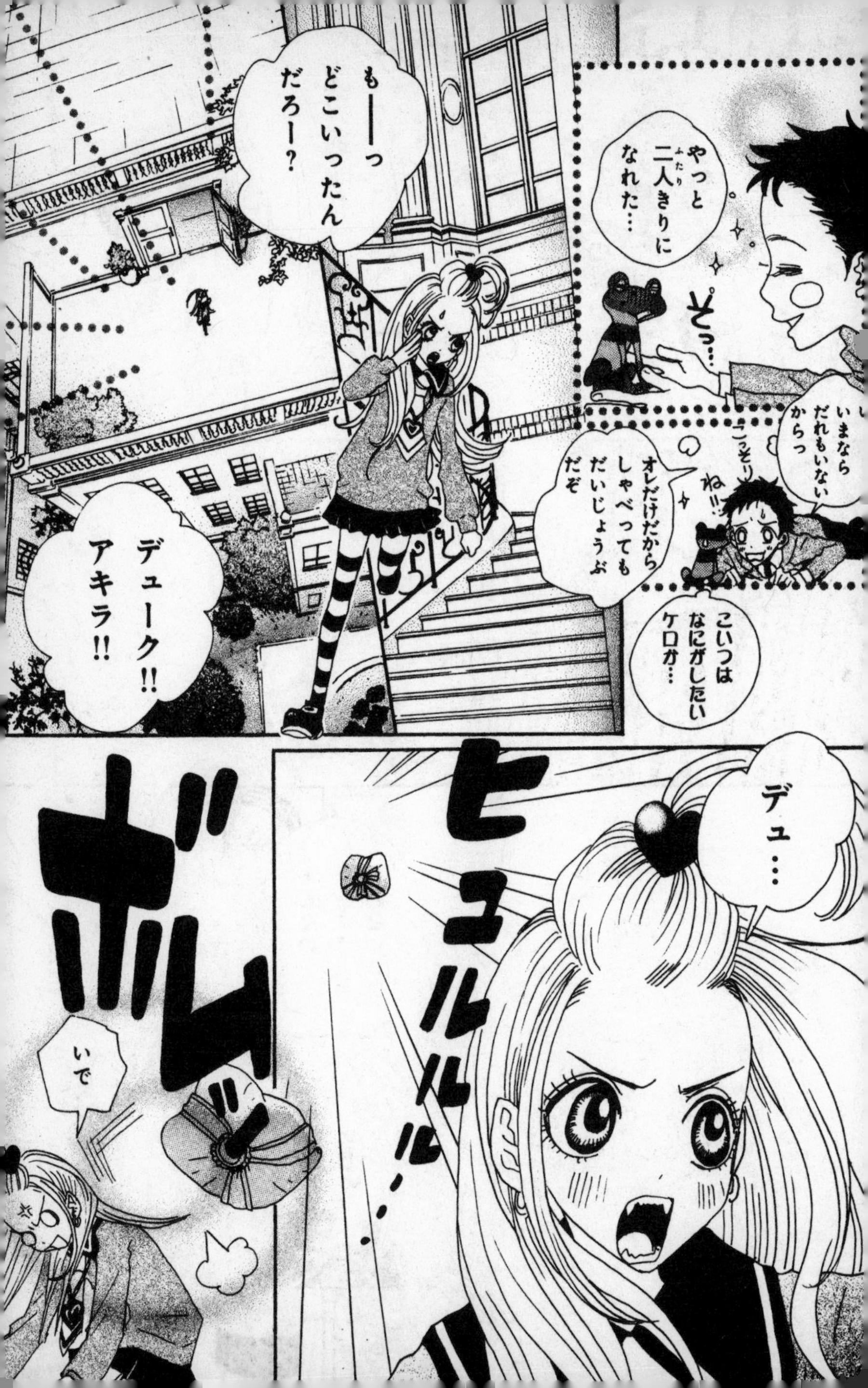
やっと二人きりになれた…
そぉっ…
いまならだれもいないからっ
こっそり
ね!!
オレだけだからしゃべってもだいじょうぶだぞ
こいつはなにがしたいケロか…
もーーっ どこいったんだろー?
デューク!! アキラ!!
デュ…
ヒュルルルル…
ボムッ
いで

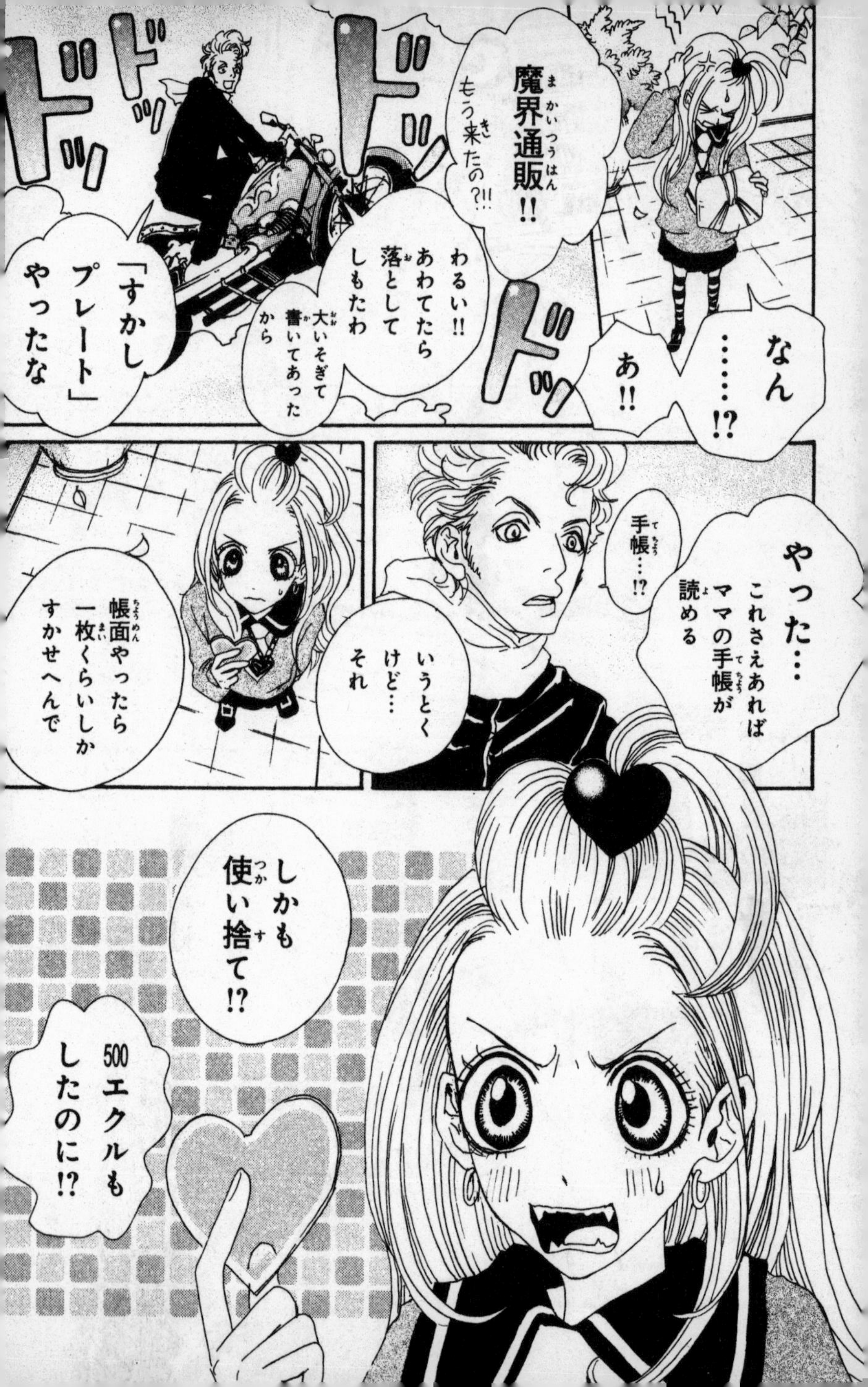
なん……!?
あ!!
ドッ
魔界通販!! もう来たの?!!
ドッ
ドッ
ドッ
わるい!! あわてたら落としてしもたわ
大いそぎて書いてあったから
「すかしプレート」やったな
やった… これさえあればママの手帳が読める
手帳…!?
いうとくけど… それ
帳面やったら一枚くらいしかすかせへんで
しかも使い捨て!?
500エクルもしたのに!?

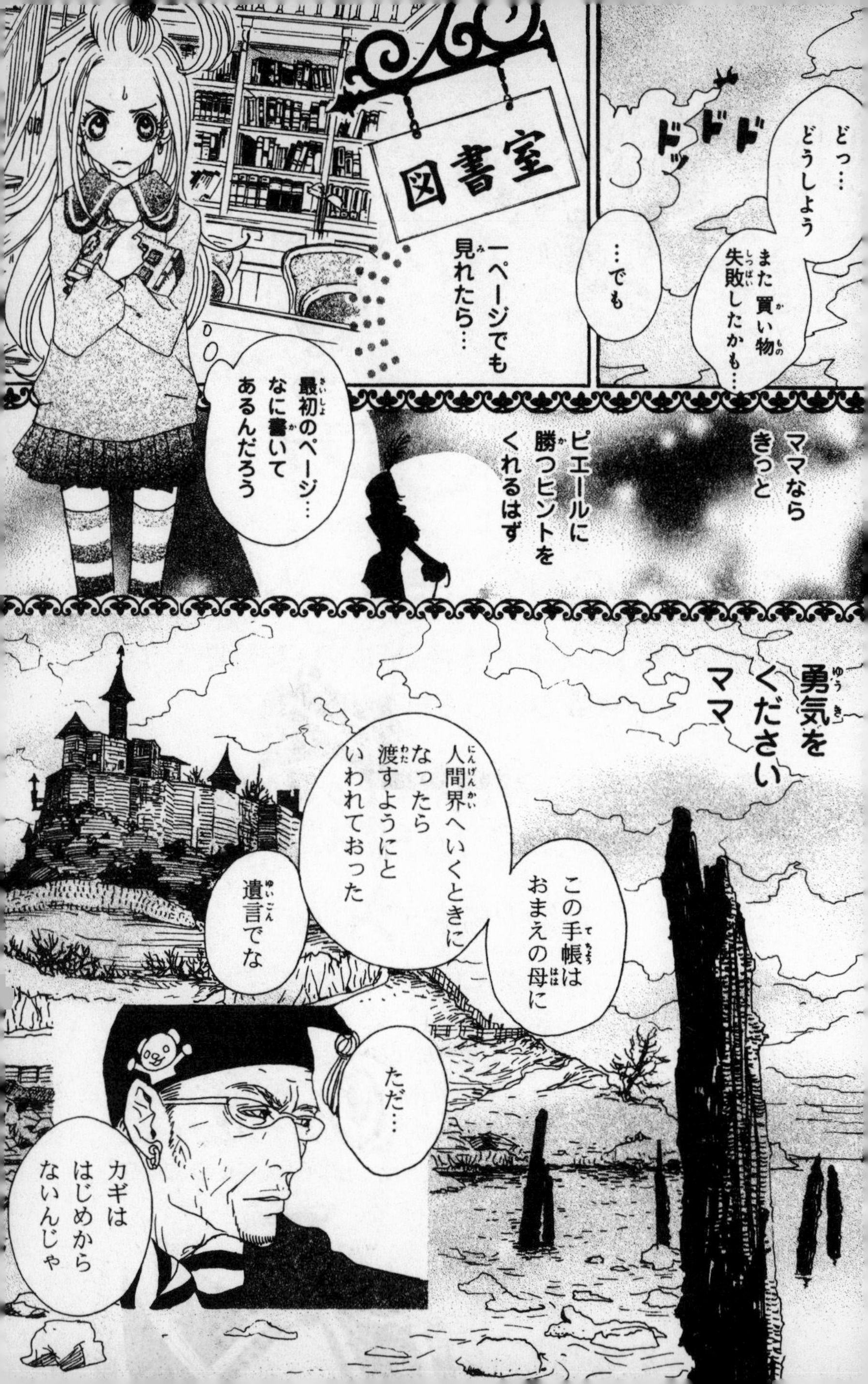
どっ…どうしよう
ドドドッ
また買い物失敗したかも…
…でも
図書室
一ページでも見れたら…
ママならきっと
ピエールに勝つヒントをくれるはず
最初のページ…なに書いてあるんだろう
勇気をくださいママ
この手帳はおまえの母に
人間界へいくときになったら渡すようにといわれておった
遺言でな
ただ…
カギははじめからないんじゃ

TOMARE!

STOP!

YOU'RE GOING THE WRONG WAY!

MANGA IS A COMPLETELY DIFFERENT TYPE OF READING EXPERIENCE.

TO START AT THE BEGINNING, GO TO THE END!

THAT'S RIGHT!

AUTHENTIC MANGA IS READ THE TRADITIONAL JAPANESE WAY—FROM RIGHT TO LEFT. EXACTLY THE OPPOSITE OF HOW AMERICAN BOOKS ARE READ. IT'S EASY TO FOLLOW: JUST GO TO THE OTHER END OF THE BOOK, AND READ EACH PAGE—AND EACH PANEL—FROM RIGHT SIDE TO LEFT SIDE, STARTING AT THE TOP RIGHT. NOW YOU'RE EXPERIENCING MANGA AS IT WAS MEANT TO BE.